Instructor's Resource Manual to accompany

LITERATURE

READING ✸ REACTING ✸ WRITING

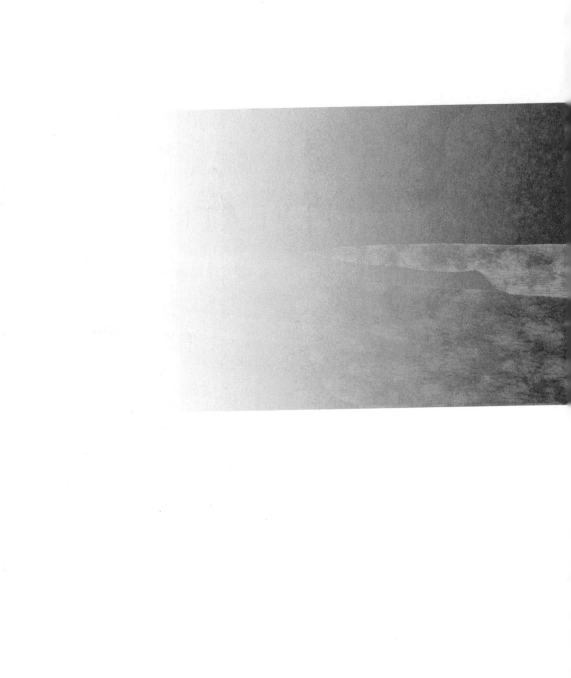

Laurie G. Kirszner
University of the Sciences in Philadelphia

Stephen R. Mandell
Drexel University

Instructor's Resource Manual to accompany

LITERATURE

READING ✸ REACTING ✸ WRITING

Fifth Edition
Compact Fifth Edition
Portable Fifth Edition

THOMSON
✸
HEINLE ™

United States • Australia • Canada • Mexico •
Singapore • Spain • United Kingdom

THOMSON

HEINLE

Instructor's Resource Manual to accompany
LITERATURE: READING, REACTING, WRITING
Fifth Edition
Laurie Kirszner and Stephen Mandell

Publisher: Michael Rosenberg

Senior Editor: Aron Keesbury

Editorial Assistant: Marita Sermolins

Production Editor: Michael Burggren

Marketing Manager: Katrina Byrd

Manufacturing Coordinator:
  Mary Beth Hennebury

Compositor: G & S Typesetters, Inc.

Project Manager: Matrix Productions, Inc.

Photography Manager: Sheri Blaney

Photo Researchers: Jill Engebretson,
  Sarah Evertson

Interior Designer: Garry Harman,
  The ArtWorks

Cover Designer: Brian Salisbury

Printer: Maple-Vail

ISBN 0-8384-5878-5

Printed in the United States of America.
1 2 3 4 5 6 7 8 9 10 08 07 06 05 04 03

For more information contact Heinle Publishers,
25 Thomson Place, Boston, Massachusetts 02210 USA,
or you can visit our Internet site at http://www.heinle.com

Contents

Introduction

The Writing Activities, Group Activities, and Discussions in this Instructor's Resource Manual are designed to reinforce the main themes of the selections. No fixed order governs the activities; for example, not all writing activities should be done before discussions. Assigning stories from the Further Readings section will enhance and reinforce understanding of each section's theme and provide resources for papers and further class discussions through contrast and comparison.

PLANNING YOUR SYLLABUS

Everyone has to begin his or her teaching career somewhere; the sample syllabi in this guide are designed to aid the new instructor who needs resource materials. If this is your first or second semester of teaching, you will find that you are entering a period of noble experimentation. The sample syllabi should be used as guides; include or exclude whatever would best suit your course. Keep in mind that the typical introductory literature course is likely to change during the semester or quarter as you learn more about your students' interests and needs; do not be afraid to title your syllabus "Tentative" and make changes during the term as necessary. Here are some things to consider as you construct your syllabus.

Time Factors

We assume that you will be teaching a one-semester or one-quarter course. If you are teaching a two-semester (or two-quarter) sequence, you have the advantage of covering much more material. Because of the limitations placed on a one-semester course, an instructor cannot cover everything. The syllabi on pages xxvii–xxxviii should be used as guides; don't be afraid to make changes, to add or subtract reading assignments based on the needs of the course. Beginning instructors often make the mistake of overloading students with reading because they are uncertain as to how else to use class time. Remember that this manual contains numerous in-class writing and/or collaborative exercises that promote critical thinking. You will find that students enjoy them and that shifting the focus from the text to their responses to the text engages students and often leads them to insights into the work at hand.

Departmental Requirements

In some departments, faculty are given *carte blanche* in designing their syllabi. However, most departments have a certain number of required written assignments, and your department may expect you to cover a certain amount of reading in the course. To save time, you might ask whether your department keeps sample syllabi on file so you may tap into what your colleagues are doing in the course.

Students' Needs and Interests

This literature text is designed to fill a wide variety of academic needs; it is up to you to determine as soon as possible what your students' specific needs are. It is always a good idea to assign a diagnostic in-class writing assignment that enables you to discern where your students are as writers. A good way of monitoring their analytical skills is to assign a short poem (for example, "Metaphors" by Sylvia Plath, which presents the reader with a riddle to be solved), divide the students into groups, and allow them to explore the poem's possible meanings. You may also wish to give students short questionnaires in which you ask them how much time they spend per week watching television, what books they have read recently for pleasure, and how many pages they read per hour. Once you have ascertained what your students' needs and interests are, you will find it easier to tailor your course to them.

Your Goals and Preferences

It is always a good idea to include a statement of course goals in your syllabus. One thing to decide is whether your course is primarily a literature survey or a writing course in which literature is the focus. (The departmental requirements should determine this.) If your goal is to cover a certain amount of material within a given time, you will probably want to give quizzes to make sure that students are doing the reading. If your course is primarily a writing course, you may want to lessen the reading workload somewhat so that students have time enough to focus on their writing assignments. One goal that we all agree on is our desire to help students to love literature as much as we do; the best ways to achieve this are to allow for free play of ideas in the classroom and to make sure that students are not so overwhelmed by their workload that they don't enjoy what they are reading.

Student Conferences

The best way to maintain contact with students and to help them through trouble spots is to hold student/teacher conferences regularly. Check with your department to find out what its policy is on office hours and conferences; some departments will encourage you to hold a week of conferences at midterm.

USING *LITERATURE: READING, REACTING, WRITING* IN YOUR CLASSROOM

Using Reader Response in Your Classroom

Reader-response theory, in direct opposition to formalism, suggests that the interaction between reader and text is central to interpretation and that it is the reader who in fact brings the text to life. Those opposed to reader-response theory tend to be uncomfortable with the inherently open-ended nature of interpretation that occurs with reader-response criticism. No interpretation is absolute or "correct," and the reader may even produce a new interpretation upon rereading and re-reacting to the text. Opponents of reader-response theory have questioned the "validity" of reader-response interpretation because of its fluid nature. Thus, one might ask, what determines a valid or correct reading of a text? Reader-response theory places the responsibility on the reader, whose interpretations are based on his or her personal experiences, background, social context, and how he or she uniquely responds to what is written.

The Reading and Reacting questions in *Literature: Reading, Reacting, Writing* encourage this sort of fluidity and wide possibility for interpretation. The questions do not have built-in "correct" answers; instead, the reader is encouraged to validate answers and responses through his or her reaction to the text. Although you still expect students to construct an argument based on evidence from the text, the reader-response approach provided by the Reading and Reacting questions will involve students in the reading and give them a personal stake in their interpretations. You may find that when you use these Reading and Reacting questions, class discussion may become more lively, even controversial, as students learn to trust their own responses to texts.

Similarly, the journal entries encourage a variety of responses from students. For example, for the story by Katherine Mansfield, "Miss Brill," the Journal Entry asks students to "Write a character sketch of Miss Brill, inventing a plausible family and personal history that might help to explain the character you see in the story." A journal entry such as this presents virtually endless possibilities, as students draw from their own experiences and backgrounds in extrapolating from what they have found in the text.

As the drafts of student papers illustrate, however, reader-response theory is not an "anything-goes" methodology; rather, it offers students an opportunity to interact with the text while at the same time grounding their responses in what is written in the text. In their writing, students will still have to build a case based on textual evidence, but the reader-response process enables them to come to their interpretations with a sense of personal engagement.

Using Research in Your Classroom

To help students begin to incorporate research into their writing about literature, *Literature: Reading, Reacting, Writing* contains two casebooks for each of the three genres. Each casebook contains, in addition to the work itself, source materials that introduce students to working with research as well as a variety of critical perspectives. Because one of the aims of most courses in writing about literature is to continue the process of teaching students how to use research effectively in their writing, it is important that students continue to work on how to use outside sources. Students need a great deal of practical experience in integrating sources into their writing and in documenting them effectively; the source materials in the casebooks will enable you to assign writing in which students may draw from and document sources but do not have to locate source materials themselves. You may find this particularly useful since it can be quite difficult to teach students how to discern which critical articles they might find in doing their own research are reliable; in using the casebooks, you circumvent this part of the process and prevent it from becoming a distraction from writing. (You may, of course, ask students to locate additional sources to use in conjunction with those printed in the casebooks.)

Whether students are using the critical articles in the casebooks (or articles they discover through their own research), they will need continuing practice in how to document sources correctly. You will find that even students who have recently had a course on the research paper may need a great deal of review. The Appendix, "Documenting Sources," contains a concise approach to MLA documentation that includes the documentation of online sources, as well as sample literature papers that use the latest MLA documentation format.

Using Literary History in Your Classroom

The author headnotes in *Literature: Reading, Reacting, Writing* are useful ways of grounding particular readings in time and place. Students will respond well to being reminded that these works, while part of what we consider the literary canon, are the products of individuals whose work comes from their own particular historical and personal circumstances. One way to illustrate this point to students is to ask them to speculate how a specific work would differ if its writer had been female instead of male or had lived in the twentieth instead of the nineteenth century. It is illuminating to take a story such as Kate Chopin's "The Story of an Hour," for example, and ask whether this story could have been written by a man, and if so, how it would differ.

Using Literary Criticism in Your Classroom

As your students grow more sophisticated in applying their analytical skills to the study of literature, you will be able to introduce them to the field of literary criticism. Most chapters open with a collection of critical views for discussion, and many selections are accompanied by a "Critical Perspective" question that gives students a focal point for discussion. An awareness of literary theory is important even for nonmajors (i.e., the vast majority of students) — not, as they will assume, because works of criticism introduce a "right answer" to their deliberations, but for precisely the opposite reason: they illustrate the point that our own critical perspectives determine our reading of a text. Therefore, there is no right answer; there is only the interpretive process itself. Students will want to turn to critical articles to find absolute truth; you will have to encourage them to view the opinions of critics as the basis for further discussion, emphasizing that in using and documenting critical sources, they are not citing the Voice of Authority.

Be sure to point out the Index of Key Terms, which students may miss if you do not show them where it is. These terms will be essential to students' understanding of critical materials.

Using Electronic Resources in Your Classroom

Students are likely to enjoy and benefit from the use of audio, video, and other electronic supplements to literary texts that they are reading. Many of these resources can be found on *Lit21: Literature in the 21st Century* CD-ROM, which will be discussed in detail later.

Original film adaptations of some of the fiction works in *Literature: Reading, Reacting, Writing* are available in VHS or DVD format from Heinle. In addition to the film adaptations of these stories, the films include exclusive interviews: *A Worn Path* by Eudora Welty has an interview with Welty following the film; *Cathedral* by Raymond Carver has an interview with Carver's widow, Tess Gallagher; *A & P* by John Updike has an interview with Updike. Another film available is *An Interview with Tillie Olsen*, a twenty-minute interview with Olsen where she discusses her story, "I Stand Here Ironing" and includes a reading from the story following the interview. Please contact your Heinle sales representative for more information about these films.

Using *Lit21: Literature in the 21st Century* CD-ROM in Your Classroom

Every copy of Laurie Kirszner and Stephen Mandell's *Literature: Reading, Reacting, Writing* comes with a free copy of *Lit21: Literature in the 21st Century* CD-ROM. Supplementary CD-ROMs often go unused because instructors assume, in some cases rightly, that they will prove confusing and/or disruptive. Some instructors are also understandably reluctant to incorporate new technology into a course that is already working well for them and their students. *Lit21* is designed to be as user friendly as possible and does not assume a particular level of proficiency on either the part of instructor or students. The following introduction gives instructors a brief walkthrough of the CD-ROM and ideas of how to incorporate its resources into the classroom. After examining the CD-ROM itself, instructors will clearly see how *Lit21* can enrich students' learning experience and allow instructors more flexibility.

As instructors begin working with students on the different elements of literature, interactive instructions available on *Lit21* can help prepare students for lectures and discussions. Each literary element has an accessible, one-paragraph explanation of the element, highlighted examples taken from the text, and two gradable quizzes. Because many students will be unfamiliar with literary terminology, these quizzes provide an ideal opportunity to stop and process what they have learned so far. Besides examining a particular element, the interactive instruction also serves as an example of how to annotate a text. Instructors can assign the element readings and quizzes prior to class, evaluate students' knowledge, and find what needs to be reinforced during class. On the other hand, instructors might ask students to use these activities as a way of reviewing after class.

Similar quizzes for all fiction and drama selections also exist on *Lit21*. These plot quizzes allow students to test themselves outside the classroom environment on the content of the literature selection. By having students quiz themselves in advance of a discussion, instructors can increase the chances that students will have thoroughly read the text and come to class prepared with comments and questions of their own. Having these quizzes available saves time both in and out of the classroom — not only will instructors not need to prepare quizzes, but also the grades can be submitted directly to instructors, leaving more class time for lecture and discussion.

Explicating works of literature are popular assignments, and one of the chief advantages of *Lit21* is the way it walks students step by step through the process of annotating a primary source and then, if instructors assign a research paper, finding secondary sources. The "Explicator" is a tool that allows students to open a text and be guided through the process of annotation for select literary elements. With many electronic texts from which to choose, students select an element highlighter where they mark up the text. Each highlighted segment then has a note attached to it that the student writes. The notes that the students make in this way can be graded as they are — if, for instance, instructors assign the annotation as a journal entry — or they can be made the basis of a paper. Flexibility also exists in the "Explicator"; students can cut and paste any text to annotate, as well as have a "free annotate" highlighter that is not associated to any preselected element. There are any number of variations on this basic approach. If instructors teach a section on a particular element — say, rhyme — they might ask students to annotate rhyme in several different pieces of literature. On the other hand, instructors could ask students to thoroughly annotate one work for all the elements possible, creating an outline or basis for an explication essay, a research paper, an analysis essay, or a reader-response essay.

If instructors assign a paper with a research component, *Lit21* can be an important supplement to the materials provided in the text. By providing access to background material and articles on nearly every author, *Lit21* makes the research process easier for students and gives instructors considerable flexibility in designing assignments. To begin preliminary research, students can explore the Web links for more than 250 authors that are provided on the CD-ROM to learn more about an author of interest. All Web sites listed in the Web links have been thoroughly checked to ensure that they are both reliable and engaging. These Web links are a logical first step in the research process, but they have other uses as well. Any time a short story is assigned by an author with a link, students can use the link to find background information on that author. These links have the potential of saving valuable class time in that they can supplement or even replace introductory lectures. They will also afford instructors an opportunity, if desired, to discuss the differences between reliable and unreliable Web sites. Finally, the links will provide students who do not have experience with the Internet a guided introduction to this important resource.

Once students have annotated a piece, decided on a tentative thesis, and have found information on the author, they can begin finding secondary sources. Each copy of *Lit21* allows students access to InfoTrac College Edition, an online database that gives students access to articles from thousands of scholarly journals and magazines. Since many of the articles are available in full text, ask students to find three sources using InfoTrac College Edition and then have them write a paragraph for each source, summarizing it and explaining why they think it is relevant to their thesis. Students would then be in a position to discuss the sources they have found in class, as well as have the beginnings of a research paper outline.

As more supplemental resources, *Lit21* includes audio and video files for a number of works from the text. The audio files in particular can be helpful when teaching poetry selections. Students who have not read much, or any, poetry may initially have difficulty identifying some of the sonic elements, such as alliteration and assonance that occur so frequently in verse. Such students may also have difficulty hearing the difference between blank verse and free verse. The readings allow students to listen to these elements repeatedly both before and after classroom lectures and discussion. If instructors teach in a classroom that has access to a computer (with speakers), a reading can be played for the class before beginning discussion. For example, instructors might ask students to reflect on Browning's, "My Last Duchess" both before and after hearing it read out loud as a reader-response essay or a journal entry, in order to see if their understanding of the piece changes or deepens after hearing the reading. If there is a change, why do students think this is the case? What do they see as the chief advantages of hearing a piece read out loud? Are there any potential drawbacks?

The readings and video clips also provide a painless way to introduce discussions of the different elements of literature discussed in the text. Students are often bored or intimidated (or both) when confronted with literary terminology. Rather than begin immediately with a discussion of tone or character, instructors might have students read a short story — "Bartleby the Scrivener," for example — and then ask them to jot down their reactions to the scene in the story included on *Lit21*. Instructors can ask students to watch the scene and write a journal entry or a reader-response essay. Do the characters look and behave the way the students imagined them? Why or why not? What might students have changed about the staging of that particular scene? What can they conclude about the importance of this scene to the story as a whole? Once students begin to see the impact that the different elements have on readers (and viewers or listeners), it may prove easier to engage them in a discussion of these elements.

The video interviews with authors are another helpful resource. When they think about authors at all, students often think of them as distant, otherworldly figures who throw words down on paper in a fit of inspiration. The author interviews on *Lit21* offer an ideal opportunity for students to gain insight into the creative process and to learn that the authors they are reading have to confront some of the same issues as writers that they themselves face. These interviews can also serve as a source of discussion questions. Preview an interview and select several questions the author addresses that students should consider. Then, after discussing these questions with the class, ask them to watch the interview at home and to write a short essay or journal entry on the ways in which the author's answers did or did not fulfill their expectations.

For an additional $5, students can also have access to the Literature Resource Center Database, where entries are available for more than 250 authors in the text. This database is exceedingly easy to use and provides researchers with bibliographies and overviews of the authors' careers, which can help provide a broader context for the information students would be likely to find through a search on InfoTrac College Edition. In some cases, the Literature Resource Center provides links from bibliographies to Web sites and full-text critical articles dealing with the author's work. For example, give students several research tasks and ask them to carry out each task on InfoTrac College Edition and the Literature Resource Center.

The preceding is only a few suggestions about how instructors can use *Lit21* to support the classroom, and there are undoubtedly an infinite amount of uses for instructors and students. The basic package (without the Literature Resource Center) is available free to instructors and each student who purchases *Literature: Reading, Reacting, Writing*. Whether instructors decide to make it an integral part of the course or simply use it now and again, *Lit21* supplements any class and makes any students' learning experience more rewarding.

Genre- and Theme-Based Approaches

Two of the most common approaches to Composition and Literature or Introduction to Literature courses are by genre and by theme. Following this brief introduction to genre- and theme-based approaches, you will find a thematic table of contents to give you some ideas for organizing your course around themes. We also include both genre- and theme-based course syllabi, as well as syllabi for semester and quarter systems. As you read the following discussion and look at the various syllabi, keep in mind that we are not suggesting that one approach to organizing a course is superior to another. All we mean to do is present two alternatives for organizing your course.

The strength of a genre-based approach is that instructors can delve deeply into what constitutes a particular genre and focus on its technical aspects. Because a genre-based approach to teaching an introductory course seems to be the most popular (and traditional) approach, this text is organized as such. More and more, though, some instructors are developing courses that are organized less around technical aspects of genres (seen by some as artificial constraints for a course in composition and literature typically taught to first-year students) and more around themes that students find interesting. Reader-response and other poststructuralist critical theories have contributed to this trend; it is certainly true that finding themes that engage students allows for a continuity of ideas, discussions, and paper topics. For students, connections are often easier to make between the works themselves and their own lives if interesting themes are developed for the course. Still, a technical discussion (of the sonnet, e.g.) is not out of place in such a thematic approach. When the three major genres (fiction, poetry, drama) are combined in a theme-based approach, students can begin to grasp the idea that literature is an avenue for understanding life; consequently, answering the questions "So what?" and "How do you *know?*" becomes less incumbent upon the instructor and more a role students can fulfill.

The best teaching is the result of a collaborative effort — most obviously between teacher and student in a literature course, but also among colleagues. Included in this resource manual are some suggested themes for your course, and sample syllabi to guide you as you develop your own. You can vary the "read-and-discuss" format of the traditional literature class with *Lit21*, films, conferences, group work, and so on. Also, if at all possible, try to devote at least one class during a quarter (and two during a semester) to a workshop class, during which students discuss and critique (in small groups or as a class) their own photocopied drafts.

Thematic Contents

PARENT/CHILD RELATIONSHIPS

Fiction

Andrea Barret, The Littoral Zone
Rick Bass, The Fireman
Amy Bloom, Hold Tight
Ethan Canin, The Carnival Dog, the Buyer of Diamonds
Junot Diaz, Aguantando
William Faulkner, A Rose for Emily
Mary Ladd Gavell, The Swing
Nadine Gordimer, Once upon a Time
Gish Jen, Chin
Raj Kamal Jha, Domestic Help
Lorrie Moore, How to Talk to Your Mother (Notes)
Tillie Olsen, I Stand Here Ironing
William Faulkner, Barn Burning
D.H. Lawrence, The Rocking-Horse Winner
Richard Russo, Dog
Flannery O'Connor, A Late Encounter with the Enemy
Jonathan Safran Foer, A Primer for the Punctuation of Heart Disease
Amy Tan, Two Kinds
Anne Tyler, Teenage Wasteland
Joyce Carol Oates, Where Are You Going, Where Have You Been?
Alice Walker, Everyday Use
Hisaye Yamamoto, Seventeen Syllables

Poetry

Adrienne Rich, A Woman Mourned by Daughters
Raymond Carver, Photograph of My Father in His Twenty-Second Year
Judith Ortiz Cofer, My Father in the Navy: A Childhood Memory
Theodore Roethke, My Papa's Waltz
Dylan Thomas, Do Not Go Gentle into That Good Night
Lucille Clifton, My Mama Moved among the Days
Robert Hayden, Those Winter Sundays
Seamus Heaney, Digging
Simon J. Ortiz, My Father's Song
Sylvia Plath, Morning Song
Sylvia Plath, Daddy
Donald Hall, My Son, My Executioner
Sharon Olds, Rite of Passage
Yehuda Amichai, My Father

Drama

GENDER CONFLICTS

Fiction

Drama

INITIATION/RITES OF PASSAGE

Fiction

Syllabi

These six syllabi are meant to be used as guidelines for an instructor designing his or her own syllabus. There are an infinite amount of ways *Literature: Reading, Reacting, Writing* can be used in the classroom, and these are merely suggestions. The first two syllabi are the class schedules that Laurie Kirszner and Stephen Mandell use for their classes. Both teach classes that meet twice a week, although all the syllabi can be altered to fit other timetables and teaching styles. Note the different approaches Kirszner and Mandell use — Kirszner uses a modification of a genre-based approach by weaving the genres together rather than concentrating on a single genre at once, whereas Mandell follows more of a thematic approach. The four remaining syllabi are examples of two genre-based approaches (one semester, one quarter) and two thematic approaches (one semester, one quarter). Be sure to establish clear guidelines (perhaps in a separate assignment sheet handout) for word length and suggested topics for all the papers.

INSTRUCTOR: LAURIE KIRSZNER

Texts: Kirszner, Laurie, and Stephen Mandell. *Literature: Reading, Reacting, Writing*, 5th ed. Boston: Heinle, 2004.
      Kirszner, Laurie, and Stephen Mandell. *The Pocket Handbook*, 2nd ed. Boston: Heinle, 2003.

Week 1   Introduction to Poetry and Fiction
1. Introduction to the course: assignments, text, and policies. Read Understanding Poetry and Reading and Writing about Poetry chapters. Read "Stopping by Woods on a Snowy Evening," "1(a," "Constantly Risking Absurdity" and "ABC."
2. Read Understanding Fiction and Reading and Writing about Fiction chapters. Read "Eveline," "Kansas," and "A Primer for the Punctuation of Heart Disease."

Week 2   Introduction to Drama; Plot
1. Read Understanding Drama and Reading and Writing about Drama chapters. Read "Trifles" and "Beauty."
2. Read Plot chapter in Fiction. Read "The Rocking-Horse Winner" and "Once upon a Time."

Week 3   Plot
1. Read "A Rose for Emily" and "Porphyria's Lover."
2. Read "The Lottery" and "Saboteur."

Week 4   Writing a Paper about Literature
1. Read "A&P." Film: Heinle Original Film Series in Literature, *A&P*.

2. Writing a paper about literature. Read model student papers in Reading and Writing about Literature chapter.

Week 5   Paper Conferences
1. Classes will not be held. Required paper conferences will be scheduled during class time and at other arranged times.

Week 6   Finding Parallels
1. Read "Where Are You Going, Where Have You Been?" and review casebook materials.
2. Read "The Story of an Hour" and "The Disappearance."

Week 7   Setting
1. Read Setting chapter in Fiction. Read "Battle Royal" and "Harlem." First paper due.
2. Read "Greasy Lake" and three poems about nature. Review for midterm exam.

Week 8   Character
1. Midterm exam
2. Read Character chapters in Fiction and Drama. Read "Gryphon" and "When I Heard the Learn'd Astronomer."

Week 9   Character: *Proof*
1. Read *Proof*, act 1.
2. Read *Proof*, act 2. Read "My Son, My Executioner."

Week 10   Point of View
1. Read Point of View chapter in Fiction. Read "Big Black Good Man" and "The Cask of Amontillado."
2. Review Selecting an Appropriate Point of View. Read "Doe Season."

Week 11   Theme
1. Read Theme chapter in Fiction. Read "The Things They Carried" and "The Soldier."
2. Read "Poems about War" in Discovering Themes in Poetry chapter. Read "Dulce et Decorum Est."

Week 12   Paper Conferences
1. Classes will not be held. Required paper conferences will be scheduled during class time and at other arranged times.

Week 13   Theme: *Marty*
1. Film: *Marty*
2. Read *Marty*.

Week 14   Review
1. Second paper due. Read "The Third and Final Continent." Review for final exam.
2. Final exam.

INSTRUCTOR: STEPHEN MANDELL

Texts: Kirszner, Laurie, and Stephen Mandell. *Literature: Reading, Reacting, Writing*, 5th ed. Boston: Heinle, 2004.
   Kirszner, Laurie, and Stephen Mandell. *The Brief Handbook*, 4th ed. Boston: Heinle, 2004.
   The theme of this course will be "Conformity and Rebellion." This large theme will be divided into two subordinate themes: "The Self and Society" and "Taking a Stand." The emphasis of the course will be on critical thinking and writing. Students will be expected to demonstrate their ability to read actively and to think critically about a text. To accomplish these goals, students will be given a series of assignments that require them to do research. These assignments get progressively more complex — moving from relatively simple essays that rely on a single source to more difficult essays that rely on multiple sources.

Conformity and Rebellion

Unit 1: The Self and Society
Instructors can assign any works from the list below.

Short Fiction

Chopin, "The Story of an Hour"
Gordimer, "Once upon a Time"
Faulkner, "A Rose for Emily"
Mansfield, "Miss Brill"
Baxter, "Gryphon"
Olsen, "I Stand Here Ironing"
Faulkner, "Barn Burning"
Wright, "Big Black Good Man"
Hawthorne, "Young Goodman Brown"

Poems (Instructor's Choice)

Plays

Sanchez-Scott, *The Cuban Swimmer*
Wilson, *Fences*

Unit 2: Taking a Stand
Instructors can assign any works from the list below.

Short Fiction

Updike, "A&P"
Chopin, "The Storm"
Faulkner, "Barn Burning"
Hawthorne, "Young Goodman Brown"
Jackson, "The Lottery"
Steinbeck, "The Chrysanthemums"
Kaplan, "Doe Season"
Welty, "A Worn Path"
Tyler, "Teenage Wasteland"

Poems (Instructor's Choice)

Plays

Glaspell, *Trifles*
Wasserstein, *Tender Offer*
Williams, *The Glass Menagerie*

Week 1   Unit I: The Self and Society
1. Read Understanding Literature and Reading and Writing about Literature chapters
2. Reading selections
3. Journal 1 due

Week 2
1. Read Reading and Writing about Fiction chapter
2. Reading selections: Fiction
3. Draft of essay 1 due
4. Journal 2 due

Week 3
1. Reading Selections: Fiction
2. Workshop: Discuss essay 1; review MLA documentation
3. Final draft of essay 1 due
4. Journal 3 due

Week 4
1. Read Understanding Drama chapter
2. Reading selections: Drama
3. Workshop: Discuss essay 2 and return essay 1
4. Introduce essay 2.
5. Journal 4 due

Week 5
1. Read Reading and Writing about Drama chapter

2. Reading selections: Drama
3. Workshop: draft of essay 2 Due
4. Journal 5 due

Week 6   Unit II: Taking a Stand
1. Reading selections: Drama
2. Essay 2 due
3. Workshop: Introduce essay 3
4. Journal 6: Midcourse assessment
5. Midterm exam

Week 7
1. Read Understanding Poetry chapter
2. Reading selections: Poetry
3. Return essay 2
4. Workshop: Discuss essay 3
5. Journal 7 due

Week 8
1. Reading selections: Poetry
2. Workshop: draft of essay 3 due
3. Journal 8 due

Week 9
1. Reading selections: Poetry
2. Essay 3 due
3. Journal 9 due

Week 10
1. Reading selections: Summarize course
2. Workshop: Return essay 3
3. Final exam

SEMESTER (GENRE)

Note: Establish clear guidelines (perhaps in a separate assignment sheet handout) for word length and suggested topics for all the papers.

Week 1   Introduction to Literature
1. Introduction, syllabus, in-class writing (diagnostic)
2. Review of in-class writing; overview of common writing problems
3. Understanding Literature

Week 2   Reading and Writing about Literature
1. Reading and Writing about Literature review of the writing process
2. Fiction —"The Secret Lion"
3. Discuss initiation theme and compare to "The Secret Lion."

Week 3   Writing Papers about Fiction
1. Updike, "A&P"
2. Mansfield, "Miss Brill," or Walker, "Everyday Use"
3. Faulkner, "A Rose for Emily"

Week 4   Plot
1. Jackson, "The Lottery"
2. Lawrence, "The Rocking-Horse Winner"
3. Workshop (Students work in groups to generate ideas for a comparison/contrast paper. Discuss concepts such as using quotations from stories, organizing a comparison/contrast paper, etc. For example, compare and contrast the role of tradition in two stories or the irony of winning but losing.)

Week 5   Character
1. O'Connor, "A Good Man Is Hard to Find"
2. Baxter, "Gryphon"
3. Erdrich, "Fleur"
   First Paper Due

Week 6   Point of View
1. Gildner, "Sleepy Time Gal"
2. Kaplan, "Doe Season"
3. Wright, "Big Black Good Man"

Week 7
   Fiction Casebook: Oates, "Where Are You Going, Where Have You Been?"
   Second Paper Due (source-based)

Week 8
1. Understanding Poetry
2. Reading and Writing about Poetry
3. Workshop (Students work in groups to generate responses to poems.)

Week 9
1. Voice — two or three selections
2. Word Choice, Word Order — two or three selections
3. Conferences (review response papers)
   Third Paper Due (response focusing on a single poem)

Week 10
1. Imagery — two or three selections
2. Figures of Speech — two or three selections
3. Form — two or three selections

Week 11
   Langston Hughes Poetry Casebook
   Fourth Paper Due (source-based)

Week 12   Introduction to Drama
1. Understanding Drama
2. Reading and Writing about Drama
3. Plot; Glaspell, *Trifles*

Week 13
  Ibsen, *A Doll House*
  Fifth Paper Due

Week 14
1. Character
2. Chekov, *The Brute*

Week 15
  Drama Casebook: Williams, *The Glass Menagerie*
  Sixth Paper Due (source-based)

QUARTER (GENRE)

Week 1
1. Introduction, syllabus, in-class writing (diagnostic)
2. Understanding Literature
3. Reading and Writing about Literature

Week 2
1. Reading and Writing about Fiction
2. Plot
  Gordimer, "Once upon a Time"
3. Faulkner, "A Rose for Emily"

Week 3
  Character Choose one or two:
    Updike, "A&P"
    Mansfield, "Miss Brill"
    O'Connor, "A Good Man Is Hard to Find"
    Baxter, "Gryphon"
  Point of View
    Gildner, "Sleepy Time Gal"
    Poe, "The Cask of Amontillado," or Wright, "Big Black Good Man"

Week 4
  Fiction Casebook: Gilman, "The Yellow Wallpaper"
  First Paper Due

Week 5
1. Understanding Poetry
2. Reading and Writing about Poetry

3. Voice — two or three selections
4. Word Choice, Word Order — two or three selections
5. Sound — two or three selections

Week 6
1. Imagery — two or three selections
2. Figures of Speech — two or three selections
3. Form — two or three selections

Week 7
1. Emily Dickinson Poetry Casebook
2. Conferences
   Second Paper Due

Week 8
1. Understanding Drama
2. Reading and Writing about Drama
3. Plot
   Glaspell, *Trifles*

Week 9
   Character
   Miller, *Death of a Salesman*

Week 10
   Drama Casebook: Shakespeare, *Hamlet, Prince of Denmark*
   Third Paper Due

SEMESTER (THEME)

Week 1
1. Introduction, syllabus, in-class writing (diagnostic)
2. Understanding Literature
3. Reading and Writing about Literature

Parent/Child Relationships

Week 2   Fiction
1. Reading and Writing about Fiction
   Tyler's "Teenage Wasteland"
2. Olsen, "I Stand Here Ironing," and Tan, "Two Kinds"

Week 3   Poetry
1. Understanding Poetry
2. Reading and Writing about Poetry
3. Plath, "Daddy" and "Morning Song"
   Hall, "My Son, My Executioner"
   Cofer, "My Father in the Navy: A Childhood Memory"

Hayden, "Those Winter Sundays"
or Group reports on Poems about Parents

Week 4 Drama
1. Understanding Drama
2. Reading and Writing about Drama
3. Williams, *The Glass Menagerie* or Wasserstein, *Tender Offer*
   First Paper Due

Initiation/Rites of Passage

Week 5
1. Updike, "A&P," and Kaplan, "Doe Season"
2. Frost, "Nothing Gold Can Stay," and Olds, "Rite of Passage"
3. Hawthorne, "Young Goodman Brown"

Week 6
1. Ríos, "The Secret Lion," and Glück, "Gretel in Darkness"
2. Carroll, "Jabberwocky," and Stevens, "Anecdote of the Jar"
3. Baxter, "Gryphon," and Whitman, "When I Heard the Learn'd Astronomer"
   Second Paper Due

Power/Powerlessness

Week 7
1. Gilman, "The Yellow Wallpaper"
2. Kincaid, "Girl"
3. Glaspell, *Trifles,* or Shakespeare, *Hamlet, Prince of Denmark*

Week 8
1. Lowell, "Patterns"
2. Faulkner, "Barn Burning"
3. Wilson, *Fences*
   Third Paper Due

American Dream/Nightmare

Week 9
1. Hughes, "Harlem"
   Cummings, "next to of course god america i"
   Whitman, from "Song of Myself"
   Updike, "Ex-Basketball Player"
2. Fiction Casebook: Oates, "Where Are You Going, Where Have You Been?"

Week 10
   Miller, *Death of a Salesman*
   Fourth Paper Due

Difference/Diversity

Week 11
1. Tan, "Two Kinds"
2. Wright, "Big Black Good Man"
3. Walker, "Everyday Use"

Week 12
1. Erdrich, "Windigo"; Silko, "Where Mountain Lion Lay Down with Deer"; Dunbar, "We Wear the Mask"; Emanuel, "Emmett Till"
   Fifth Paper Due

Love and Relationships

Week 13
1. Chekhov, *The Brute*
2. Faulkner, "A Rose for Emily," and Pothier and Gibbons, Jr., "A Woman's Wintry Death Leads to a Long-Dead Friend"
   or Group Reports on Poems for Further Reading: Poems about Love

Week 14
   Ibsen, *A Doll House*, or Strindberg, *The Stronger*

Week 15
1. Chopin, "The Storm" and "The Story of an Hour"
2. Atwood, "You Fit into Me"
   Greenberg, "The Faithful Wife"
   Swenson, "Women"
   Sexton, "Cinderella"
   Sixth Paper Due

QUARTER (THEME)

Week 1
1. Introduction, syllabus, in-class writing (diagnostic)
2. Understanding Literature
3. Reading and Writing about Literature

Parent/Child Relationships

1. Reading and Writing about Fiction
2. Olsen, "I Stand Here Ironing"
3. Faulkner, "Barn Burning"
4. Yamamoto, "Seventeen Syllables"

Week 2
1. Understanding Poetry
   Reading and Writing about Poetry

2. Plath, "Daddy" and "Morning Song"
   Hall, "My Son, My Executioner"
   Hayden, "Those Winter Sundays"
   Heaney, "Digging"

Initiation/Rites of Passage

Week 3
First Paper Due
1. Updike, "A&P"
   Faulkner, "Barn Burning"

Week 4
1. Hawthorne, "Young Goodman Brown"
2. Kaplan, "Doe Season"
3. Ríos, "The Secret Lion"

Week 5
1. Baxter, "Gryphon"
2. Joyce, "Araby"
3. Olds, "Rite of Passage"
   Whitman, "When I Heard the Learn'd Astronomer"
   Glück, "Gretel in Darkness"
   Second Paper Due

Power/Powerlessness

Week 6
1. Gilman, "The Yellow Wallpaper"
2. Faulkner, "Barn Burning," and Neruda, "The United Fruit Co."
3. Lowell, "Patterns"

Week 7
1. Understanding Drama; Reading and Writing about Drama
2. Glaspell, *Trifles,* or Strindberg, *The Stronger*
   Third Paper Due

American Dreams/Nightmares

Week 8
1. Miller, *Death of a Salesman*
2. Wilson, *Fences*

Week 9
1. O'Connor, "A Good Man Is Hard to Find"
2. Fiction Casebook: Oates, "Where Are You Going, Where Have You Been?"
   Fourth Paper Due

Violence and War

Week 10
1. Group reports on Poems for Further Reading: Poems about War
2. Gordimer, "Once upon a Time"
3. Randall, "The Ballad of Birmingham"; Brooks, "The *Chicago Defender* Sends a Man to Little Rock"; Hughes, "Harlem"; Emanuel, "Emmett Till"
   Fifth Paper Due

CHAPTER 1

UNDERSTANDING LITERATURE

WRITING ACTIVITIES

1. Ask students to write for a few minutes about their previous experiences with literature. What have they read because they were required to? What have they read because
   they chose to? How do the two experiences differ? Ask them to discuss what they have
   just written. Be prepared to discuss your own experiences, but let students begin the
   discussion.
2. Ask students to write about their best experience with reading literature and their
   worst experience with reading literature. Ask them to speculate about why they enjoyed a particular book, story, poem, or play, but did not enjoy another.
3. Ask students to write about why they prefer a particular kind of literature. For example,
   they may prefer to read prose rather than poetry; they may like to read about characters who resemble themselves or about characters who are unlike themselves; they may
   be interested in particular themes; or they may have favorite authors. Be prepared to
   discuss your own literary preferences.

GROUP ACTIVITIES

Divide students into groups and ask them to examine your syllabus and the book's
table of contents. You might ask each group to consider one theme or genre and
ask each group to come up with a list of selections they would choose to read for
the course. If possible, incorporate at least one suggestion from each group into
your syllabus. You might then assign each group's choice to the whole class, or you
might consider a free-reading assignment in which groups or individuals decide
which reading selection(s) they will consider.

CHAPTER 2

READING AND WRITING ABOUT LITERATURE

WRITING ACTIVITIES

1. Briefly discuss the way "My Arkansas" by Maya Angelou is highlighted and annotated in the text. Then, choose another poem — or a story or a dramatic excerpt — to highlight and annotate as a class.

2. Plan an essay that could be written about the second work that has been discussed above. You might want students to write the essay, to write just the introduction for the essay, or to focus on planning the essay at this point.

3. Ask students to write about their previous experiences with writing about literature. Did they enjoy it? What were their difficulties? Did they consult secondary sources or not? What is the one thing they most need to improve about their writing?

GROUP ACTIVITIES

You might ask students to highlight and annotate a text and plan an essay in groups (as in Activities 1 and 2 above) and then ask them to work individually to write that essay. Or, after the group-planning activity, you may want each student to plan and write his or her own essay on a topic that has not been discussed.

FICTION

CHAPTER 3

UNDERSTANDING FICTION

GARY GILDNER

Sleepy Time Gal

WRITING ACTIVITIES

1. Ask students to rewrite the ending of the story based on how they believe the narrator would like for the story to end.
2. Have students write a news article based solely on the story's presumed facts.
3. Students can research and write an essay on both the social and economic effects of the Depression on small towns such as the one mentioned in the story.

GROUP ACTIVITIES

Divide students into three groups. Ask one group of students to list the mother's contributions to the story (¶ 3, 4, 7, 8).

Another group of students should trace the narrator's contributions to the events of the story (¶ 3, 6, 8). Have them analyze these contributions, keeping in mind the narrator's comments in paragraphs 2 and 3.

A third group of students could find the lyrics to the 1924 song "Sleepy Time Gal" and examine what the words imply in terms of marriage for the young lady in the story. (Students can easily find these lyrics on the Internet.)

DO YOUR STUDENTS KNOW . . .

Even in the midst of the Depression, 60 to 80 million Americans found money to attend the movies. Most film historians agree that the movies of the era provided more than escapism, reflecting real social problems and issues of the time.

DISCUSSION

The use of a first-person narrator in a story often establishes a relationship that elicits either trust or distrust between the reader and the narrator. Note in paragraph 2, "I will try to tell it the way he did, if I can." The narrator's modest statement to the reader conveys a sense of a personal sharing of information. A third-person omniscient narrator would distance the reader from the story by completely deleting the present narrator's voice, and thereby this sense of sharing.

Based on the Group Activities, students might debate whether the narrator is male or female. Have them support their opinions with discussions of how the two perspectives differ. Let them answer this question: Which of these perspectives lends itself more toward fiction writing and which toward journalism? The author is a male, but the reader is not certain whether he intentionally gives an impression of a female narrator, whether he makes a point of showing a presupposed difference between the two perspectives, or whether he, in order to present a better "story," uses both perspectives.

MARGARET ATWOOD

Happy Endings

WRITING ACTIVITIES

1. Ask students to write an additional section for "Happy Endings." This section should fit into the story as it currently stands without disrupting it or undercutting Atwood's main point.
2. Ask students to take Section A and flesh it out into a three-page story of their own.
3. Ask students to write a paragraph-long plot outline (similar to Section A) that deals with an aspect of life other than romantic relationships.

GROUP ACTIVITIES

Divide the class into three groups. Ask one group to brainstorm reasons why relationships succeed. Ask another to discuss why they fail. Ask the third group to list clichés about relationships that they see around them.

DO YOUR STUDENTS KNOW . . .

Although the names John and Mary ranked as the most popular names for babies throughout the twentieth century, they no longer even make the top ten. According to Social Security card applications for births in 2000, the most popular names that year were Jacob and Emily.

DISCUSSION

The language in "Happy Endings" is deceptively, almost childishly simple, so it is unlikely you will have to spend much time reviewing vocabulary with your students. The real challenge, even for sophisticated readers, is deciding what to make of Atwood's innovative formal structure. The more diligent students may be frazzled by the thought of having to distinguish different plots, and it may be helpful for the class as a whole if you diagram the different story lines on the board.

"Happy Endings" is not so much a short story as a series of very short stories, or sections, some of which are interrelated. The stories resemble in many ways the simple tales children are taught when they are first learning to read. Atwood achieves this effect by using simple language, short declarative sentences, present tense, and the generic names — John and Mary — of the most frequently recurring characters. While the style of the stories may be naive and childish, their content is anything but. Several involve sex, one involves suicide, and one manages to squeeze in adultery, drugs, a love triangle, and a murder-suicide. Much of the pleasure of reading the story as a whole comes from this obvious disconnect between style and substance.

Given the fact that there are several different, mutually exclusive plot lines in "Happy Endings," it will be easy for students to become confused while trying to keep these plots straight and determine the connections between them. Begin by asking the students to consider the relationship between Section A and the rest of the sections. Section A represents a kind of idealized relationship, one in which things proceed happily and without incident. John and Mary meet, marry, live happily, and then die. Each of the other plot lines, even though they all eventually connect back to A, involves a series of complications that frustrate and in some cases destroy the characters.

It is important for the students to understand that Atwood is writing not just about literature but about life and real-life relationships. If the plots we encounter in much fiction are similar, this is because the basic outlines of so many real lives are similar. Even if two lives seem radically different, they will end in death, the great equalizer. As Atwood says, "The only authentic ending is the one provided here: *John and Mary die. John and Mary die. John and Mary die.*" Atwood is also, by implication, writing about the ways in which people unwittingly play their parts in the cliché-ridden scripts that life provides them. The characters in these different stories certainly do things, and fairly dramatic things in some cases. There is never a sense, though, that they are making active choices. None of the characters is a fully realized individual, and this is the real tragedy in even the happiest of the stories.

The obvious question, then, is whether Atwood's vision of life is hopeless. After all, every life, however happy or unhappy, fulfilling or unfulfilling, ends in death. It is important to note, however, that Atwood ends by saying that there is more to fiction — and, by implication, more to life — than plots, which she characterizes as "just one thing after another, a what and a what and a what." In the last sentence, she urges the reader, "Now try how and why." A worthwhile life is given its value not so much by what happens in it as by the motivations of the person living it and by the way he or she negotiates its ups and downs. Atwood's final statement, then, is surprisingly hopeful: Individuals may be doomed to die, but they have the power to make the lives they live between birth and death engaging and meaningful.

You might consider teaching this story with "A Primer for the Punctuation of Heart Disease," "Cowboys Are My Weakness," or "Kansas." The first of these selections is in its own way as formally inventive as Atwood's story, whereas the second examines male/female relationships. "Kansas" is about a crucial choice and its repercussions.

JONATHAN SAFRAN FOER

A Primer for the Punctuation of Heart Disease

WRITING ACTIVITIES

1. Ask students to write about a word, figure of speech, sound, gesture, or facial expression that they believe is unique to their family's "language."
2. Ask students to invent several of their own punctuation marks and to provide an explanation and in-context usage for each mark.
3. Ask students to write a short research essay on either the Holocaust or heart disease.

GROUP ACTIVITIES

Divide the class into groups of three to four students. Ask each group to write a three-minute dialogue consisting of approximately 50 percent spoken material and 50 percent silence. Each group will select two members to perform its dialogue. Before each dialogue is performed, the group will write it out on the board, using Foer's punctuation for the whispered, shouted, or unspoken portions.

DO YOUR STUDENTS KNOW . . .

In the next thirty years, the number of senior citizens will reach 80 million. One study shows that one out of four Americans over age forty-five would rather discuss sex with their children than discuss death with a parent.

DISCUSSION

The thing that makes this story so interesting to read — its formal inventiveness — is also what will make it challenging for many students. It might be best to begin a discussion by trying to look past the formal aspects and asking students what the story is really about and what the author's central point is. Then, when the class has reached some consensus, ask them how the innovative punctuation used throughout does or does not help convey that point. Of course, it is impossible to separate form and content, but breaking the story down in this way may make it more manageable for students.

It is commonplace that many of the most important things in our lives and relationships are not said, but understood. In this view, the silences in a conversation are as important, sometimes more important, than the words that are said. Foer's story is an ambitious attempt to give this silence a written form by punctuating it. It is clear that the narrator wants more direct communication with his family and that this new system of punctuation he has devised is a kind of substitute for it. With one exception, these examples are all taken from the narrator's family life, and one might say that his family has, as no doubt all families have, its own language.

There are two great silences in the narrator's life: one surrounding the heart disease that runs in his family and the other concerning his grandmother's experiences as a Jew in World War II Europe. The first topic is referred to most often, as the title of the story would suggest, but the second forms a kind of backdrop. There are certain parallels between the two concerns: One cannot help being born Jewish any more than one can help being born with a genetic predisposition to heart disease, yet millions of Jews were killed because of their ethnic background, and people die every day of heart disease. There is a sense, then, in which the narrator and his family feel doubly doomed. Their response is to be doubly cautious and to take refuge in silence.

As the story progresses, it becomes clear that the narrator's family communicates primarily in silence and that this is largely because they are afraid. They are afraid of mentioning the terrible events of the Holocaust, of discussing the heart disease that threatens most of them, of admitting to themselves and each other that they are in some ways unhappy. Although the narrator to some extent regrets these silences, he himself uses silence to keep his mother from discovering anything about his sex life. He does this because he does not want her to know how depressed he is by the fact that he only has "relations" with girls, rather than "relationships." Once the students have had a chance to discuss these issues, shift the focus of the discussion to the author's stylistic experiments. Look at any places in the text where students found the punctuation confusing. The most likely place for this to happen is in ¶ 80–112. Here Foer creates a dialogue between the narrator and his father in which all of the symbols that have been explained are used and in which several new ones are introduced without explanation. The portion of this dialogue beginning at ¶ 95 is particularly challenging, in that it consists almost entirely of punctuation. At this point, the question becomes whether Foer wants his readers to follow what is being said (or rather, not said) or whether one would have to be a participant in the dialogue in order to understand it fully.

Consider teaching this story with "How to Talk To Your Mother (Notes)," which is also a "how-to" story about family communication; "The Fireman," which examines a relationship in which much goes unsaid; and "My Father," which expresses the tender feelings a man has for his deceased father.

CHAPTER 4

READING AND WRITING ABOUT FICTION

WRITING ACTIVITIES

1. Briefly discuss the way "The Secret Lion" by Alberto Alvaro Ríos is highlighted and annotated in the text. Then, choose another work to highlight and annotate as a class.
2. Plan an essay that could be written about the second work that has been discussed. You might want students to write the essay, or you might want them to concentrate on planning at this point.
3. Ask students to write about what they have learned about reading and preparing to write about fiction.

GROUP ACTIVITIES

You might ask students to highlight and annotate a text and plan an essay in groups (as in Activities 1 and 2 above) and then ask them to work individually to write that essay. Or, after the group-planning activity, you may want each student to plan and write his or her own essay about a topic that has not been discussed.

CHAPTER 5

PLOT

KATE CHOPIN

The Story of an Hour

WRITING ACTIVITIES

1. Ask students to compare and/or contrast women's roles in love and marriage in the 1800s with those of the current day.
2. Ask students to write about a point in their lives when they too experienced "a brief moment of illumination."
3. Ask students to write an alternative ending for the story.

What did marriage mean to men? For men? For women?

GROUP ACTIVITIES

Divide students into groups and ask them to brainstorm to develop two lists: a list of ways in which marriage can change men and a list of ways in which it can change women.

DO YOUR STUDENTS KNOW . . .

During the period of 1871–1878, Great Britain recorded 30,641 cases of injury and 9,113 of death from railroad accidents. In 1833, in the United States, the first train wreck with passenger casualities was recorded. In the 1870s, the Bessemer steel-making process pioneered laying steel railways that helped decrease the amount of train accidents from the broken nails of earlier iron railways.

DISCUSSION

The basic exposition is wrapped up in the first two paragraphs, and initially, students may be quick to oversimplify this story. Students may wonder exactly where the story is set, and they may speculate about the outward details of the Mallards' marriage. How long have they been married? Do they have children? Are they happy? Encourage students to focus on what Chopin *does* present and develop here. Her emphasis is on the protagonist and her unexpected reaction to news of her husband's untimely death. Chopin is interested in the inner workings of the mind and what happens to the soul when someone loses a loved one, yet gains oneself (Q 1).

Chopin's development of the main character is presented subtly. Without the distraction of action and dialogue, the reader is able to concentrate on what Mrs. Mallard is thinking and feeling. Thus, Chopin allows the reader to enter the mind of her protagonist (Q 2).

When Mrs. Mallard hears the news of her husband's untimely death, she responds with genuine grief. She experiences all the emotions that generally accompany the death of a loved one and weeps "at once with sudden, wild abandonment, in her sister's arms." In fact, Mrs. Mallard "knew she would weep again when she saw the kind, tender hands folded in death, the face that had never looked save with love upon her." The Mallards clearly did not have a loveless marriage (Q 4). Students, however, may be quick to assume otherwise. They may accuse Mrs. Mallard of heartlessness, or they may believe Mr. Mallard was abusive; in either case, they may simply assume that she is happy to be rid of him. Encourage students to avoid oversimplification, however, and to look more closely at the character Chopin so carefully develops.

When Mrs. Mallard retreats to her room to be alone, she undergoes a catharsis and experiences an unexpected yet disturbing feeling of liberation. She realizes for the first time that "there would be no one to live for during those coming years; she would live for herself" (Q 6). At first, she cannot define the feeling, but she knows "that there [is] something coming to her and she [is] waiting for it, fearfully." It is "subtle" and "elusive," but when it comes and possesses her, she sees "beyond that bitter moment a long procession of years to come that would belong to her absolutely." Despite her love for her husband, she feels "there would be no powerful will bending her"; instead, she is "free, free, free." The central conflict comes here, and it is an inner conflict in the mind of the protagonist. Chopin's antagonist is in fact Mrs. Mallard. She has trouble accepting this dichotomy within her, and she struggles with two conflicting emotions. It is unthinkable to her that she might feel such a terrible "relief" when faced with her beloved husband's death, because to realize something like this at such a time is inappropriate (Q 5).

The title, too, sheds light on the central conflict. The title seems to suggest that in this short "hour," Mrs. Mallard experiences honest feelings and lets go of long-repressed emotions. Students might think that the title "The Joy That Kills"—the title of a film adaptation of this story — is more appropriate (and ironic) because it refers directly to the more socially acceptable reason for her death (Q 3).

Students may have a difficult time with the end of the story and may express varied reactions. Some might be surprised or even angry (Q 7). A closer look at the way the ending is foreshadowed might prove helpful at this point. The reader might be somewhat prepared for the doctor's final diagnosis of heart disease because the first line states, "Mrs. Mallard was afflicted with heart trouble." Indeed, Mrs. Mallard may have "died of heart disease" if we think of the heart in a metaphorical sense, referring to love and marriage. It might then be argued that Mrs. Mallard's heart attack is a result of her loss of a newfound freedom. Students might also pick up on the irony here. Mrs. Mallard's heart attack is not the result of her expected joy at seeing her husband alive but a response to her unbearable realization that he is indeed alive (Q 8). A conclusion in which the couple are happily reunited, or one in which Mrs. Mallard dies without seeing that her husband is alive, might have been less ambiguous and therefore less satisfying (Q 9–10).

You might consider teaching this story with "Miss Brill"— another story about a woman's epiphany — or "The Storm," another story by Chopin.

FURTHER READING

Bonner, Thomas Jr. *The Kate Chopin Companion. American Short-Story Writers. 1880–1910.* Ed. Bobby Ellen Kimbel. New York: Greenwood P, 1988. 245.

Inge, Tonette Bond. "Kate Chopin." *American Short-Story Writers, 1880–1910.* Ed. Bobby Ellen Kimbel. *Dictionary of Literary Biography.* Vol. 78. Detroit: Gale, 1988. 90–110.

NADINE GORDIMER

Once upon a Time

WRITING ACTIVITIES

1. Have students rewrite the story as if it were a newspaper article. Then, have them write an editorial commenting on the events the article describes.
2. Ask students to explore in writing the role of fear in this story. Is it a cause of violence or a result — or both?
3. Ask students to retell (in writing) a current news event as a fairy tale.
4. Ask one or more students to bring in articles (such as David Gonzalez's *New York Times* article cited in Further Reading below) that describe situations similar to that depicted in this story.

GROUP ACTIVITIES

To highlight the theme of fear, ask the students to trace the following developments through the story (they might also work through Q 2 of Reading and Reacting in the text):

Ask one group to look at references to "trust." They will note that in ¶ 1, the trustworthy characters are the servants. Paragraph 2 suggests that these servants are of "another race." In ¶ 3, the maid suggests that bars be installed, and the family follows her advice. In ¶ 5, unemployed members of the race are treated as "not trusted." The wife's desire to help these hungry people is squelched by the maid and the husband, who do not trust the unemployed. The reasons for a lack of trust are not given; however, we can infer that differences in race and economic status cause fear.

Ask another group to look at the physical changes that occur in the house throughout the story: ¶ 1, the neighborhood watch sign; ¶ 2, electronically controlled gates; ¶ 3, bars and alarm system; ¶ 6, higher walls; ¶ 9, metal coils. What was probably a very comfortable, attractive suburb has become ugly and closed because of fear. The effect of fear is apparent not only on the outside but also from within. "So from every window and door in the house where they were living happily ever after they now saw the trees and sky through bars . . ." (¶ 3).

Finally, ask a group to look at the way the little boy is affected by each change in the house. In his innocence, he plays with the electronic gates (¶ 2). His cat sets off the alarms (¶ 3), and his tricycle is locked up every night (¶ 5). Students will then see the irony of the climactic part of the story, when the boy is entangled in the razor coils around the house: he has been acting out a fairy tale, but the fairy tale created by Gordimer becomes a very real horror. The fear that traps the family causes its destruction.

DO YOUR STUDENTS KNOW . . .

High levels of violence remain an enduring legacy of apartheid in South Africa. According to a 2002 report, each day in South Africa, an average of 59 murders, 145 rapes, and 752 serious assaults occur.

DISCUSSION

This story, which has elements of both parable and fairy tale, has a deceptively simple structure and style, masking a very important message about fear, walls, and racism. As you begin your discussion of the story, you may need to provide some background information about the political situation that existed in South Africa, Gordimer's home country, when the story was written — particularly the concept of apartheid.

After providing this background, ask the students to think about the title of the story and its connotations. "Once upon a time" suggests a fairy tale, something far from the realities of a South African township. It also establishes expectations about what will come in the story, including a "happily ever after" ending (Q 2). Also, the story uses a flat tone, drawing readers into the world of the story without foreshadowing the horror that occurs at the end (Q 5).

Not only is the ending unlike that of a fairy tale, but also Gordimer dispels our standard notions of fairy tales by using the "happily ever after" phrase at the beginning of the story. The exposition describes, then, the sorts of things that normally occur at the end of the fairy tale: the happy family, the things they have, the security they feel. The exposition, however, leaves out a great many specific details, including the characters' names and the precise location of the story. Readers should realize that this "fairy tale," which goes beyond the point of happily ever after, could happen to anyone in any place (Q 6).

As students think about the organization of the plot, they will note that it presents events in strict chronologic order. However, many of the clues that normally indicate chronology are lacking from the story. Instead, the action moves along with a series of contrastive conjunctions, each suggesting that a current security measure is not enough and that more must be done. For example, in ¶ 6, the family extends the security wall that surrounds the house. Paragraph 7 begins with the word *but*: The wall is not enough to ease their fear, so they will add something else. Gordimer's decision to move the plot forward by contrasting increased security measures with escalating fears allows readers to feel the increasing sense of panic that brings the plot to its climax (Q 4).

Before discussing the climax, you might ask students when they think the conflict in the story is introduced and how Gordimer foreshadows the climax. Some students will note the extensive references to security measures in the first two paragraphs, suggesting from the start the sort of conflict that will bring the story to its climax. Others may believe that the conflict centers on race relations, pointing to the references to the servants in ¶ 1 and the last line of that paragraph (Q 1, Q 3, and also group activities above).

As students think about the nature of the conflict, they should note that the antagonist in the story is not a person; rather, the conflict lies within the characters, for the source of the problem is fear (Q 7, 8), which is based on isolation and ignorance (Q 10).

You might close your discussion of the story by asking students whether or not the conflicts in the story are resolved by the end. Although the physical representation of the fear is destroyed when the family cuts the coils to get to the little boy, the problems between the races and the fear are never fully confronted.

Class discussion could relate this story to students' own lives. For example, what security precautions/devices are they aware of? Many students are familiar with car alarms, home security systems, personal security devices, Mace, and so on — and perhaps even with weapons owned for self-defense. Ask students if they see such "defensive" measures as necessary, dangerous, or reassuring. Many students will find it difficult to see that events like those in the story could happen in the United States (Q 9); others may not find it at all difficult to imagine such events taking place here.

You might consider teaching this story with "I Stand Here Ironing" or *The Glass Menagerie* (parent/child relationships).

FURTHER READING

Gonzalez, David. "Seeking Security, Many Retreat Behind Bars and Razor Wire." *New York Times* 17 Jan. 1993: 1, 36.

Gordimer, Nadine. *Conversations with Nadine Gordimer.* Ed. Nancy T. Bazin and Marilyn D. Seymour. Jackson: U of Mississippi P, 1990.

———. *The Essential Gesture: Writing, Politics, and Places.* New York: Knopf, 1988.

STEPHEN DOBYNS

Kansas

WRITING ACTIVITIES

1. Ask students to write their own alternative version of the encounter between the boy and the farmer.
2. Ask students to write an alternative version of the boy's life after the farmer drops him off in Lawrence. What might he have done instead of becoming a professor and then a minister?

3. Ask students to take one of the alternative versions of the encounter between the boy and the farmer and expand it into a three-page story.

GROUP ACTIVITIES

Divide students into three groups. Assign each group one of the three alternative versions of the encounter between the boy and the farmer. Ask each group to come up with reasons why the dying man might prefer that version to what actually happened.

Divide students into three groups. Ask each group to reorder the three alternative versions and give reasons why Dobyns chose the original order. Ask them, too, to explain why they think their new order might work.

DO YOUR STUDENTS KNOW . . .

Carnegie Hall, built in 1891 through the funding of businessman and philanthropist Andrew Carnegie whose charitable donations throughout his life total near $350 million, remains one of the world's most important stages for the musical arts. To play this stage is to be recognized as a success.

DISCUSSION

You may want to begin the class by having the students review what happens in the first twenty-five paragraphs of the story. Important details can be put on the board, and students can refer to these while working in groups or when the class as a whole reconvenes. This activity helps keep students from getting lost as they examine the alternative versions of the story. Although there are points in the story where students may become confused, the plot as it is initially given is relatively simple: A young hitchhiker accepts a ride with a farmer who is pursuing his wife and her lover with the intent of killing them. The boy never sees the end result of this chase, but the fact that he did nothing to intervene haunts him for the rest of his life. Even on his deathbed, he dreams alternative versions of the event (Q 2). Most of the important details are provided in the opening paragraph of the story. We know the age of the boy, the geographic setting, the era, and the fact that the farmer is armed. We can also guess, though we are not yet told this, that the farmer is in pursuit of the couple in the blue coupe. We have not yet been told the farmer's motivation (though it isn't hard to guess), and we haven't yet been given any background information on the boy (Q 1). More details emerge in the paragraphs that follow. What we are not told, and what the boy himself never finds out, is what actually happened (Q 5).

It is difficult to say from the story itself whether or not the boy's life is changed by the encounter, and this may be something to focus on in class discussion. We know that he didn't become a professional pianist as he had planned, but it is hard to know if this is due to lack of talent or to a shifting sense of priorities. It is interesting to note, however, that he eventually becomes a minister. In this profession, he would be regarded as something of an expert on matters of right and wrong, and he would be required to intervene in the lives of his congregation. It may be that this choice of career was motivated in part by a desire to make amends for his inaction at a crucial moment in his life (Q 3). Part of the reason for his failure to act is that he does not want to jeopardize his plans for his future. The fact that he may have sacrificed three lives in order to safeguard plans that never come to pass is what troubles him for the rest of his life.

As the main character is dying, the reader is given three alternative versions of the event that took place years earlier. In the first, the farmer catches up with his wife and her lover and kills them and himself. In the second, the boy talks the farmer into going to the police. In the third, the boy tries to prevent the farmer from killing his wife and her lover and ends up being shot himself. A number of phrases and details from the first twenty-five paragraphs are repeated in each of these alternative versions, and the essential setting is the same. The couple is driving a coupe, the farmer is driving a pickup, and the farmer is armed. Other details — the boil on the farmer's neck, for example — also help connect these alternatives to what actually happened (Q 9).

The first of these three scenarios is what might well have happened had the farmer caught up with the blue coupe. The other two show the boy intervening in the situation more directly and are the kind of revisionist thinking we engage in when we wish we had acted more nobly or courageously than we did in a given situation. The first version, though least flattering to the main character, is the most believable, since it does not portray him as acting in a more courageous way than he actually did (Q 7). By inserting these alternative histories at a point in the story when the main character is on his deathbed, Dobyns shows us how the incident has preyed on the man's mind (Q 6).

We are not told what the dying man is listening for in the distance, but the most likely answer is that he is listening for gunshots. Because he has no idea how the farmer's pursuit ended, there is a real sense in which it never has ended for him. The sound of gunshots, though terrible, would bring him some closure (Q 8). He only achieves closure —both figuratively and literally — when the men from the funeral home zip him up in his body bag. This image haunts the son who witnesses it because it teaches a sobering lesson: His father, at a crucial point in his life, risked the lives of others in order to guarantee a life that he did not in fact live and to forestall a death that was in any case inevitable (Q 10).

You might want to ask the class what the boy's responsibility was in this situation. Ask them, too, to consider whether he would have had more of a responsibility to act if the farmer hadn't been armed and whether he would in fact have acted. Students may assume that the boy would have been more likely to act. Point out, though, that the boy was at least as afraid of the farmer's determination as he was of his weapon (Q 4). Finally, ask students to consider the ultimate significance of this event for the boy (Q 11).

You might consider teaching this story with "Sleepy Time Gal," "A Good Man Is Hard to Find," and "Do Not Go Gentle into That Good Night." The first two selections deal in various ways with turning points in individual's lives, and "Do Not Go Gentle into That Good Night" deals with the issue of dying. Because of its violent nature, "A Good Man Is Hard to Find" may provide particularly interesting parallels with "Kansas."

A Rose for Emily

WRITING ACTIVITIES

1. Have students read the story, stopping after each of the numbered sections to record their thoughts about the developing plot of the story, their opinions about Emily, and their expectations about the ending.
2. Have students write a series of newspaper articles about the discovery of Homer's body and/or have them write Emily's obituary.
3. Have students write entries from Emily's diary at different times during her life. (They can begin with her childhood or young adulthood.)

DO YOUR STUDENTS KNOW . . .

Arsenic, a naturally occurring metal compound, causes muscle spasms, nausea, vomiting, abdominal pain, cardiovascular failure, and, finally, death — depending on the amount ingested. It is fatal to ingest more than 60 parts per million of arsenic in water. However, arsenic in low levels has been known to cure syphilis and some forms of leukemia.

DISCUSSION

Since the story appears in the section on plot, the focus of the discussion should center on Faulkner's use of nonchronologic narrative. Before analyzing the effects of this arrangement of events, students must have a clear sense of the chronology (for example, over forty years have passed between the death of Emily's father and Emily's own death). If students do the newspaper assignment suggested above, they will have ordered the events of the story chronologically (Q 1). As students describe the events in the story, discuss which events are part of the exposition (that is, the background in Section I, and the events in Sections II and III); which event serves as a climax (Homer's refusal to marry Emily in Section IV); and how all the facts are finally brought together in the last two paragraphs, forming the denouement (Q 3). The following chronology may be helpful:

> Emily's father dies (when she is thirty).
> Homer comes to town.
> Emily's relatives visit.
> Emily buys arsenic.
> Emily's relatives are called.
> Homer disappears.
> The relatives leave.
> Homer returns.

Murder occurs.
The house develops an odor.
Emily refuses to pay taxes.
Colonel Sartoris remits taxes from date of Emily's father's death.
Emily shuts herself in the house.
Aldermen visit.
Emily dies at age seventy-four.

Once the actual chronology of events has been established, ask students to compare the actual events with the order in which they are presented. This comparison can lead to a discussion of foreshadowing in the plot of the story: purchasing the poison (¶ 34), detecting the offensive smell (¶ 15), shutting off the top floor of the house (¶ 51), and so on (Q 2). In addition, the students should note that the unconventional order of events in the exposition of the story creates suspense (in contrast to the straightforward accounts in the newspaper articles students wrote).

If students have done Writing Activity 1 as they read the story, then they may discuss their reaction to the jumbled order. For example, the presentation of events lets students move from the very negative images of Emily in the first sections (¶ 6) to the more sympathetic view of later sections (¶ 25). Encourage students to look for the explicit descriptions of her in the story — when she is fat, when she is thin, what colors she wears. In addition, students should note how Emily's voice (appearing in Sections I and III) adds to her eccentricity and to the way readers view her (Q 9). The plot of the story is thus tied to Emily's characterization, and the narrator's obvious sympathy for her, which may be viewed as sentimentality (Q 10), makes the discovery of murder and necrophilia at the end even more disturbing.

The students may also comment on the fluidity of the plot. Even though the events are not in order, Faulkner keeps the story moving by using short transitions containing time references (see the phrases in Q 5). These phrases not only advance the action but also discourage undue attention on any single event. Thus, the suspicions aroused in readers when the smell occurs diminish when the narrator tells us that it went away "after a week or two" (¶ 15).

One way to structure the discussion from this point forward would be to list several of the following elements that affect (and are affected by) the ordering of events. Students can tackle each small part in turn, or they might work on them in groups.

Conflict: The plot is also driven by the development of different conflicts (Emily and Homer, Emily and her father, Emily and the town). Perhaps the most interesting of the several are those between Emily and herself, especially in view of the fact that Faulkner felt that the only thing worth writing about is "the human heart in conflict with itself" (Nobel Prize acceptance speech, 1950). Students may need some background about the Civil War and the values that stereotypically characterize the Old South to understand the conflicts here. Emily's desire both to maintain family status and to marry, her decision to take a lover (and a Yankee, at that) despite tradition and religion, her decision to murder her lover when he refuses to marry her, and her decision to atone for the murder by "loving" the man after his death — these are all tensions developing below the surface in her character (Q 4).

Narrative Voice: Students should also look at the role of the storyteller here. The use of the first person plural narrator helps to explain Emily's need to conform to certain social and moral standards. This narrator, representing the views of the town, is like many voices in small Southern towns, rife with gossip and the latest tidbits about a community's more colorful members. The narrator is not impersonal; the selection and presentation of the primary events reflect subjective decisions on the part of the town to emphasize or ignore potential problems in Emily's life. The town chooses to focus on Emily's romantic life and family status (¶ 25, 32–33, 44, 45), taking the responsibility to call in a minister when visible propriety is violated, but ignoring and shunning responsibility for her purchase of poison shortly before Homer's disappearance (Q 6).

Setting: Students can look at the role of setting (both time and place) as it relates to the plot, the voice of the narrator, and the conflicts in the story. Students should look for elements of the story that make it Southern — the influence of traditions, the keeping of a typically black family servant, the role of the clergy and relatives, and class considerations. As a final note on setting, you might want to discuss the gothic elements in the story — the old house, the mysterious comings and goings, the smell, the strange servant, the closed rooms.

To conclude, you might encourage students to speculate about why Faulkner might have deleted the deathbed scene (Q 7). Finally, return to the question of the title (Q 9). The rose may be seen as a memory, a tribute, a graveyard memento for Emily. In this sense, the story itself is the rose. With this in mind, students should consider the well-known interpretation that Emily represents the South and its dying customs during the period of Reconstruction. Although Faulkner himself refused to give credence to a North versus South interpretation, students may see in Emily the struggles of change and compromise that marked the South during its transition from an aristocratic, agricultural society to a more industrialized region (Q 8). However, the conflicts in Emily are only part of this interpretation: The voice of the town reveals how the South sees itself and its past. At times, its ugliness is obvious, but time and circumstance may encourage a romanticized view of what the South represents (a "moonlight and magnolia" idea), just as the townspeople develop a nostalgic memory of Emily when she dies. The rose, then, might also be a tribute for a dying culture or for the death of a certain vision of that culture. In fact, some students may see Homer himself, preserved for eternity, as the title's rose.

You might teach this story with "Once upon a Time," "You Fit into Me," or "Daddy" (love/hate relationships).

FURTHER READING

Allen, Dennis W. "Horror and Perverse Delight: Faulkner's 'A Rose for Emily.'" *Modern Fiction Studies* 30 (Winter 1984): 685–96.

Winchell, Mark R. "For All the Heart's Endeavor: Romantic Pathology in Browning and Faulkner." *Notes on Mississippi Writers* 15.2 (1983) 57–63.

LORRIE MOORE

How to Talk to Your Mother (Notes)

WRITING ACTIVITIES

1. Ask students to pick a section of the story and write another diary entry, this time using the mother's point of view.
2. Ask the students to look at the music presented throughout the story and write a paper on the role of music in developing the theme. (Or they can consider the function of music here and in "Teenage Wasteland" and/or "Where Are You Going, Where Have You Been?")
3. Compare the story with another work that deals with parents and children: "Two Kinds" or "I Stand Here Ironing."

GROUP ACTIVITIES

The divisions of the story may be confusing to some students, who will see the segmentation and chronology as indicative of a lack of plot. For them to see exposition, climax, foreshadowing, and so on within the plot, ask them to work in groups to trace the use of certain repeated ideas or motifs in the story, and to determine how these repetitions help shape the plot (Q 4, 5, 6, 7).

The first group should trace the use of *heart* imagery. Moore recounts various important dates in the development of artificial hearts, something nonhuman. Students should recognize that the permanent artificial heart of 1982 foreshadows the closing of the narrator's heart toward her mother. The next mention of the heart is the transplant in 1967, at the same time the mother comes to live with Ginny. The "emptinesses" (¶ 42) she mentions at this point reminds the reader that the rift in communication has not been mended; there has been no successful sharing of hearts in her own world. In 1963, the temporary artificial heart parallels Ginny's own awareness of temporary relationships and the lack of solidity and reality in her own emotions. And her father dies of a heart attack.

A second group can trace the images of *babies* and *pregnancy*. This theme, underscoring the differences between mother and daughter (the daughter is not a mother), begins in the first section. In 1981, the narrator recounts meeting mothers on the bus. Note that the communication problem that she has with her own mother is extended to these mothers as well. In 1975 she begins references to her own pregnancies. Another aspect of this theme involves the development of Ginny's attitude toward abortion: "decide what you must do" (¶ 26, 1975), "try to decide what you should do" (¶ 36, 1970), "you have an abortion" (¶ 54, 1961). In 1943, she asks her mother about babies and the baby who died.

A third group could trace the ideas of *containers* and *things contained*. (This may be too difficult for some students — use your own judgment.) This theme begins with the refrigerator image in the first section, which foreshadows the birth paragraph at the end. Paragraph 9 (1979), which discusses the house, is interesting in this respect. The house had contained her; now she has it within herself.

The house had a room that you could see from the outside, but there was no door to reach it from the inside. This image relates to the choice of narrative voice for the piece: There is a problem in communication for Ginny concerning her mother, but she cannot get at it from the inside, so she addresses herself from without, as "you" (Q 8). Other reflections of this theme are the trash bags (1968), the Dead Sea Scrolls (1947), and her own birth (1939). This whole theme suggests a sense of disconnectedness that Ginny is trying to overcome — both with her mother and with herself. Each image seems to build up to the final scene, her own birth, in which the original separation occurred. This scene is a climax, in a sense, because it suggests that the problems Ginny is facing are inherent — the origin of the problem came with entrance into life itself.

A fourth group could trace the references to *talk between mother and daughter*: ¶ 19, 1977 (reference to *chrissakes*); ¶ 28, 1974 (mother's senility); ¶ 32, 1972 (mother's use of the wrong name); ¶ 47, 1964 (daughter's refusal to come to a Thanksgiving dinner); ¶ 55, 1960 (mother's suggestion of things for the daughter to write about); ¶ 62, 1956 (daughter's note to tell mother about books she is reading); ¶ 68, 1951 (reference to menstruation); ¶ 70, 1947 (daughter's singing to her mother); ¶ 73, 1946 (request to go to Ellen's); ¶ 81, 1939 (mother's understanding when daughter tries to talk to her). These references again emphasize the distance between mother and daughter, which has widened consistently since birth. At no point in the story is there valid and real communication; the historical references allow the extent of the inescapable generation gap to be fully realized.

Students might also enjoy working in groups to write evaluations of this story's unusual style and structure (Q 10).

DO YOUR STUDENTS KNOW . . .

As improved health care increases our life spans, middle-aged children (primarily daughters) with jobs and families of their own often become the primary caretakers for aging parents. Nursing home costs run from $40,000 to $60,000 annually.

DISCUSSION

Students may begin their study of this work by thinking about what elements characterize "how-to" or "self-help" books. (You might bring a few of these to class.) Their ideas may lead to a discussion of what normally is the subject of such books: losing weight, succeeding in business, fixing up the house. What is not expected is a simple formula for something as complex as communicating with a parent — a topic with which many students will be familiar.

As students go over the elements of a how-to book, they will probably note that chronology is important, because there is normally a set of instructions that lead to a desired outcome. Moore plays to this fact and purposely inverts the chronology in the style of a journal written in reverse from 1982 to 1939. Ask students why Moore does this. To get students to focus on the effect of this strategy, you might ask them whether or not Ginny really knows how to talk to her mother. As they begin to understand that the story is as much about *not* communicating as it is about successfully talking, they may begin to sense that the backwards chronology is a tool for highlighting key points in a breakdown in communication (Q 1, 4, 9). The chronology and style of the story reinforce the theme of broken communication. By eliminating the clues and frames readers expect to use in understanding a story, Moore challenges the flow of communication between her text and the reader, just as this flow is blocked between the daughter and her mother.

Finally, students will note that there is more than one conflict in the story. The primary conflict, however, seems to be between Ginny and herself, a part of her which will never relate to her mother. It is this portion of Ginny's life that causes her a great deal of discomfort and pain, and that acts as antagonist (Q 2).

Moore has stated that she wrote *Self-Help* (the collection where this story appears) to explore different styles of narration. She often dangles phrases in midthought, omits subjects from sentences, and jumps from memory to memory, mimicking human thought patterns, much like the way one jots down notes (Q 1).

In reverse order, and almost like a game of word association, she weaves the plot using the three abortions as anticlimactic points of reference to the "Three Little Fishies" (¶ 84) (Q 5). The use of second-person narration effectively distances the narrator from the pain of remembering her relationship with her mother, her father, and her lovers. Yet it neither disguises nor lessens the tension of the battle between the narrator and herself, her regrets, and her sins of commission and omission (Q 2). This in turn drives the plot, much as in a process essay: a series of steps, start to finish (or as here, finish to start), beginning and ending with her aloneness.

You might want to teach this story with "I Stand Here Ironing," "Once upon a Time," "Barn Burning," "Daddy," "My Son, My Executioner," or *Oedipus the King* (parent/child relationships).

FURTHER READING

McInerney, Jay. "New and Improved Lives." *New York Times Book Review* 24 Mar. 1985: 32.

Towers, Robert. "Moveable Types." *New York Review of Books* 32 (15 Aug. 1985): 26–29.

CHAPTER 6

CHARACTER

JOHN UPDIKE

A&P

WRITING ACTIVITIES

1. Have students retell in writing the story's events from Lengel's point of view — or from Queenie's.
2. Sammy begins the final section of the story with this line: "Now here comes the sad part of the story, at least my family says it's sad but I don't think it's sad myself." Ask students to write one or two paragraphs explaining why this story is or is not "sad."
3. Ask students to write a few sentences to explain what exactly it is about the three girls that appeals to Sammy.

GROUP ACTIVITIES

Divide students into two groups. Ask one group to imagine Sammy's life after he leaves the A&P. For example: What kind of job does he find? Does he marry and have children?

The other group of students should imagine Sammy's life based on the assumption that he marries Queenie. What is his profession? Is he happy? Is Queenie really different from the "sheep"?

DO YOUR STUDENTS KNOW . . .

In 1883, Charles Stillwell of Philadelphia, Pennsylvania, invented the machine that makes brown paper bags. Merchants began using the bags as an advertising tool, like printed logos on bags today. Twenty million brown paper bags are used annually in supermarkets.

DISCUSSION

This initiation story is a good one to begin the course with because Sammy's decision making can lay the foundation for discussing any number of works that you might read during the course, for example, Faulkner's "Barn Burning" or Baxter's "Gryphon." Because the story is placed in the chapter on character, you might begin by discussing students' responses to Sammy. Do they like him? Do they trust his account? Do they know people like him? Students should help you define what kind of person Sammy is and what his attitudes toward the town, the A&P, and his "world" are. Ask students for specific support for their opinions. For example, it is easy to see that Sammy is bored with his job by the ways in which he responds to and describes the people around him: Shoppers are "sheep" who wear hair curlers and baggy pants (Q 2). Sammy shows he recognizes the direction in which he is headed when he mentions Stoksie's situation: "Stoksie's married, with two babies chalked up on his fuselage already, but as far as I can tell that's the only difference. He's twenty-two, and I was nineteen this April" (Q 1, 2). Such details prepare readers for Sammy's decision to quit.

Queenie and her friends appear to be exceptions to the sheep. Sammy begins by stereotyping them (¶ 1–5), but he soon recognizes their individuality — especially Queenie's. She is more than a simple stock character (Q 4). The supermarket is a very structured place, with many rules (keep right, bring a list, wait in line, wear a shirt and shoes, select an item from the top of a display, and so on [Q 5]), but Queenie violates some of these rules, so Sammy admires her. On the one hand, he wants Queenie (he's attracted to her); on the other hand, he wants to *be* her (Q 3).

Answering what Sammy gains from quitting may be the most crucial part of discussion; let students talk this out and direct them as necessary. Is he trying to impress the girls? Trying to do the right thing? Looking for a way out of his job? Some students will think that he makes a good decision and that he is beginning to mature; others will argue that he quits just to impress the girls, and when that fails, he is sorry that he has acted so rashly (Q 8).

Ask the class if they think that it is true that "once you begin a gesture it's fatal not to go through with it" (¶ 31). What does this idea mean to Sammy? How does such an idea justify his quitting, even though Sammy seems to have second thoughts about it at the time? Sammy begins the second part of the story with: "Now here comes the sad part of the story . . ." (¶ 12). Point out the somber tone of the final three paragraphs and the narrator's dramatic (perhaps melodramatic) last line. What, if anything, is "sad" about this episode in the A&P?

Ask students if this story would have the same impact if it were set somewhere other than the A&P (a carwash or fast-food restaurant, for example). They may come up with locations that they think would substitute for the A&P, but many students will argue that the store takes on a "personality"—becomes a character in the story — that is difficult to duplicate in an environment that is less structured for the customers than a grocery store is. But it is Sammy's strong reaction to the store and to his job that gives the A&P its significance (Q 6).

Sammy's imagination creates his unhappiness with the A&P. For example, from a quick study of Queenie and her friends and what they buy (herring snacks), he concludes that their socioeconomic class is higher than his own. Ask students if they trust Sammy's judgments. Is he right about the girls (and the others in the store — customers and employees alike)? Or, does Sammy do a disservice to Queenie, Lengel, and the others (Q 7)?

Ask students to speculate about where Sammy will be in ten years (Q 9). Will he still judge women according to their appearance? How will he feel in thirty years about "sheep"? Will he react any differently to "witch[es] about fifty"? Will he have discovered whether women have minds or not (Q 10)?

You may want to compare this story to "Barn Burning" or "Gryphon" (initiation stories).

FURTHER READING

Klinkowitz, Jerome. "John Updike." *American Novelists Since World War II*. Ed. Jeffrey Helterman and Richard Layman. *Dictionary of Literary Biography*. Vol. 2 . Detroit: Gale, 1978. 484–92.

McFarland, Ronald E. "Updike and the Critics: Reflections on 'A&P.'" *Studies in Short Fiction* 20 (Spring/Summer 1983): 95–100.

Shaw, Patrick W. "Checking Out Faith and Lust: Hawthorne's 'Young Goodman Brown' and Updike's 'A&P.'" *Studies in Short Fiction* 23 (Summer 1986): 321–23.

KATHERINE MANSFIELD

Miss Brill

WRITING ACTIVITIES

1. Have students write a continuation of Miss Brill's life after the story ends. How has her experience in the park changed her life? Is she still an actress performing in a play?
2. Have students write a physical description of Miss Brill based on details from the story and on what they can infer from what they learn about the character.
3. Have students write a letter from Miss Brill to a beloved niece or nephew in which she tries to put a positive, "stiff-upper-lip" spin on her daily activities.

GROUP ACTIVITIES

Divide students into groups and have each group write a scene from a play in which Miss Brill interacts with other characters in the story.

Divide students into two groups. Have the first group describe Miss Brill as the old couple might perceive her. Ask the second group to describe what the young couple might think of her. Then ask each group to contrast these views of Miss Brill with her view of herself.

DO YOUR STUDENTS KNOW . . .

The word *eavesdropping* originated in the seventeenth century, when one might stand beneath a house's eaves to hear private conversations.

DISCUSSION

Students generally grasp the fact that Miss Brill is an onlooker in life, a spectator who does not actually participate in what goes on around her. Because of the use of a limited omniscient point of view, the readers sit at the elbow of the main character and observe the events through the eyes of that character. In "Miss Brill," we see her perception of herself as she has charitably constructed it; however, her assertion that she is "expert" at "sitting in other people's lives" is usually read by students as nosiness (Q 1).

A striking example of Miss Brill's inadvertent characterization of herself through her observations of the people around her is her description of the woman in the ermine toque (a small, round close-fitting hat): "Everything, her hair, her face, even her eyes, was the same color as the shabby ermine, and her hand, in its cleaned glove, lifted to dab her lips, was a tiny yellowish paw." Miss Brill is able to see the stranger's shabbiness but not her own. This description suggests that Miss Brill has no objective awareness of herself and the way she appears to other people, a suggestion borne out by her illusion that she is an actress with a part in the "play" around her. To her, involvement in this play constitutes interaction, and her role is essential: "No doubt somebody would have noticed if she hadn't been there; she was part of the performance after all" (Q 2). Although she thinks her part is important, readers know that in fact she is just a spectator (Q 3).

Miss Brill's conception of herself as an actress is part of her attempt to glamorize her life and her own importance. Ask students to think about Miss Brill's past (Q 9). Has she been an actress or a businesswoman? Is she a widow? Does she have a daughter or son, a brother or sister? She has at some point been affluent enough to afford ermine. Or was the ermine given to her by friend or relative or lover — or purchased in a secondhand store? Would the story be more or less effective if the author had furnished these details (Q 10)?

There is a marked discrepancy between Miss Brill's self-perception and the way others perceive her. This disjunction is dramatically illustrated by the conversation between the boy and girl. The girl describes her as a "stupid old thing" who is not wanted, who is, indeed, in the way. "'Why does she come here at all — who wants her? Why doesn't she keep her silly old mug at home?'" the boy asks (Q 4). When Miss Brill overhears this conversation, it shatters her illusions about herself (Q 6).

It is clear that this experience has dramatically changed Miss Brill. On her way home from the park, instead of buying honeycake, her favorite Sunday treat, she goes directly home "to her little dark room — her room like a cupboard" (Q 7). This passage refers us back to ¶ 5 where she characterizes the other people in the park on Sunday as "odd, silent, nearly all old, and from the way they stared, they looked as though they'd just come from dark little rooms or even — even cupboards!" Ironically, as in her description of the shabby ermine toque, she fails to perceive herself in the same harsh light in which she casts other people (Q 8).

If we follow the course of the fur piece, we see that its story parallels that of Miss Brill. In the beginning, her description of it brings it to life. Calling it a "dear little thing," she removes it from its box, brushes it, and "rub[s] the life back into the dim little eyes." The fur as she personifies it is an important character in the story, the only character with whom she has any genuine emotional contact. In addition, when the girl compares the fur to a "fried whiting" in ¶ 14, it is worth pointing out that brill is also a type of fish (an edible European flatfish), implying that the fur functions as a kind of alter ego for Miss Brill. In the end, when she returns the fur to its box "quickly, without looking" and thinks she hears something crying, it is really her own cry that she hears (Q 5).

You may want to have students read this story along with "Rooming Houses Are Old Women," a poem about loneliness and isolation, or "A Worn Path," a story about an elderly woman who, unlike Miss Brill, has a strong sense of purpose and a focus in life.

FURTHER READING

Nathan, Rhoda. *Critical Essays on Katherine Mansfield*. New York: Hall, 1993.
Tomalin, Claire. *Katherine Mansfield: A Secret Life*. New York: Knopf, 1988.

CHARLES BAXTER

Gryphon

WRITING ACTIVITIES

1. Before students read this story, ask them to write one or two paragraphs about a substitute teacher they have had.
2. Have students characterize the types of classmates they have had and write a descriptive sentence or two about each — for example, the teacher's pet, the class clown, the bully.
3. Have students write a story in which the children are ten years older. They should focus on whether or not Miss Ferenczi's predictions come true.

GROUP ACTIVITIES

Divide the students into four groups. Assign each group one of the stock characters: the troublemaker — Carol Peterson; the bus buddy — Carl Whiteside; the brown-noser — Bobby Kryzanowicz; and the whiner — Jeannie Vermeesch. Ask the students to develop these characters more fully in a scene with Tommy.

DO YOUR STUDENTS KNOW . . .

The gryphon, with origins in the Near or Middle East, appears in Indian, Greek, and Roman cultures as a symbol of strength and vigilance. Greeks recognize the gryphon as the "Hound of Zeus" for its ability to dominate both earth and sky, whereas the gryphon symbolizes Jesus Christ's duality as both human and divine, according to Christian legend.

DISCUSSION

"Gryphon" is useful for teaching character description (Miss Ferenczi), character development (Tommy), and stereotype (stock characters — the students in Tommy's class). Your students may mention Miss Ferenczi's physical description and how it changes as the story progresses (¶ 6, 10, 11, 89, 115), her history (¶ 14), her approach to teaching and school (¶ 9, 16, 28, 48), her magic (¶ 64, 90, 116), and even her lunch (¶ 43, 51) (Q 2, 3, 5). Ask them to discuss the way she treats the students and whether her character is sympathetic. Tommy develops as he learns the importance of the imagination (¶ 40–42, 75, 89), and he is probably the student most impressed by the substitute (Q 7). Perhaps because Tommy is a budding writer, he pays great attention to detail (¶ 18, 95, 114). Tommy's classmates should be familiar to your students: the troublemaker — Carol Peterson (¶ 1–2); the bus buddy — Carl Whiteside (¶ 68–78, 96–104); the brown-noser — Bobby Kryzanowicz (¶ 5, 60); and the whiner — Jeannie Vermeesch (¶ 15–16); among others. Tommy's mother may be discussed as a foil to Miss Ferenczi (¶ 83, 111) (Q 6).

Charles Baxter's belief in "memory's unsettling power" is evident in Tommy's adult memory of a substitute teacher he had in fourth grade who was unlike the "town's unemployed community college graduates" (¶ 6), a woman who taught him how to make the most of his imagination (Q 7). Although parts of the story suggest an adult perspective with the narrator's mild indictment of the American educational system, others are clearly from a child's view — for example, the explanation of what makes Carol "bad." Have your students compare the first and last paragraphs of the story with Miss Ferenczi's lessons. Also ask them to discuss whether or not they think she is a good teacher (Q 9). This discussion can serve as the basis for discussing the traditional educational processes of memorization in contrast to more imaginative, less traditional approaches. Indeed, the last sentence of the story captures the essence of why so many American students find education boring.

The title "Gryphon" and the reference to Pinocchio, whose nose grows whenever he tells a lie, underscore the significance of imagination, fantasy, and mysticism in the story (Q 1, 4). Whether Wayne "the dead fool" Razmer's drawing the Death card means a literal death or a figurative death (is his fortune, then, very different from Carol's?), it brings an end to Miss Ferenczi's substituting at this school (Q 8). You may need to introduce (or have students research and report on) the significance of Tarot cards, particularly the Death card, and mythological concepts of metamorphosis and reincarnation.

Your students may also be interested in discussing lies, white lies, and the interpretation of facts for one's own benefit (Q 8). Mark Twain once said, "When I was younger, I could remember anything, whether it had happened or not." Your students can certainly appreciate the importance of changing a few details or exaggerating some facts to "improve" a story.

You may want to have students write about Miss Ferenczi's past — or, they might write a response to Q 10, taking a position on whether "Gryphon" is ultimately a disillusioning or a reassuring story. You may also be interested in showing the *Wonderworks* television series film of "Gryphon," which sets the story in the inner city. In addition, the poem "When I Heard the Learn'd Astronomer" can work with this story.

FURTHER READING

Hansen, Ron. "Web-footed Babies and People in Extremis." *New York Times Book Review* 25 Aug. 1985: 18.
Kakutani, Michiko. Rev. of *Through the Safety Net*, by Charles Baxter. *New York Times* 26 June 1985, sec. 2: 23.

JHUMPA LAHIRI

The Third and Final Continent

WRITING ACTIVITIES

1. Ask students to write about a time when they have felt ill at ease in a new place or situation.
2. Ask students to write a short research paper on the custom of arranged marriages in Indian families.
3. Ask students to write a short research paper on the public reaction in America to the first Moon landing.

GROUP ACTIVITIES

Divide the class in half. Ask one group to brainstorm reasons why the narrator and his wife should return to India when they retire. Ask the other group to list reasons why they should stay in America.

Divide the class into three groups. Assign each group one of the following characters: the narrator, Mala, or Mrs. Croft. Then ask each group to find the section of the text that they think says the most about their character.

DO YOUR STUDENTS KNOW . . .

Some people still believe that the 1969 *Apollo 11* lunar landing was a government hoax. They claim that government officials were so afraid that America was losing the "space race" that they hired movie producers to fictionalize the Moon landing with lights, camera, and action.

DISCUSSION

Though Mrs. Croft begins as a comic stock figure, a slightly senile old woman out of step with the modern world, this picture changes as the story progresses (Q 1, 5). It is not so much that Mrs. Croft herself reveals great depths. Rather, we learn from her daughter, Helen, how she was widowed and had to support her family by giving piano lessons (Q 7). We also learn that this woman, who is still relatively independent, is 103 years old. The narrator is impressed by Mrs. Croft's perseverance and independence. He is especially impressed by the fact that she did not experience her widowhood as something disabling. The narrator's own mother went insane when her husband died, and the narrator spent much of his childhood taking care of her. There is an implication that at least part of his mother's reaction to widowhood was culturally determined and that Mrs. Croft's approach strikes him as preferable (Q 8). Mrs. Croft becomes an important figure in his life, especially when he learns how old she is. Suddenly, these two very different people have something in common: each is from a world — in her case, the late 1800s; in his, Calcutta — that is very different from Cambridge, Massachusetts, in 1969. By the end of the story, he is able to say, "hers was the first life I had admired."

Mala, the narrator's wife, is not introduced until relatively late in the story. Her arranged marriage to the narrator may seem shocking or incomprehensible to many students, though it is certainly possible that some students in your class will come from cultures where arranged marriages are still practiced (Q 9). Isolated from her family and in a new country, Mala is at first homesick and withdrawn. The timing of her arrival is fortuitous, though, since the narrator has had a chance to acclimate somewhat to life in the United States. It is important, too, that he has had the chance to get to know and admire Mrs. Croft. This personal connection to his new country allows him, in his own halting way, to assist Mala in her adjustment. Finally, it is during a conversation with Mrs. Croft that the couple first begin to develop a relationship.

India is obviously crucial for the narrator. He spent his formative years there, and although he has adjusted to life in America, he still retains many aspects of his native culture, even after almost thirty years (Q 4). England was a relatively brief yet nonetheless important interlude. There are long-standing ties between Indian and English culture, and the narrator lives with other Bengalis while in London. No matter how acclimated he becomes to the United States, England will always be the first new country he experienced (Q 3). He arrives in the United States on the day of the first Moon landing, and Mrs. Croft makes repeated references to this event. It doesn't seem, though, that the narrator is ever as impressed by it as she is. It may be that he feels his own journey is every bit as remarkable as that undertaken by the astronauts (Q 10). North America is the narrator's "final continent" in that he and his wife have decided to retire and presumably die here (Q 3).

Be sure to ask the students how they feel and how they think the narrator feels, at the end of the story. In many ways, his is a successful life, and it would be wrong to say he is unhappy. At the same time, the ending is faintly melancholy. There is a gap between the narrator and his son, a gap caused by differing experiences and upbringing. The narrator is glad that his son finds American culture familiar and comfortable, yet he knows that he and his son are less close because of it (Q 6, 11).

You might want to teach this story with "Dead Man's Path," "Chin," or "The Swing." The first two selections deal in different ways with cultural strains and adjustments, and the third relates the experience of a woman who feels she and her son have grown apart.

MARY LADD GAVELL

The Swing

WRITING ACTIVITIES

1. Ask students to write about a time in their lives that they wish they could revisit.
2. Have students interview someone whose children have grown up and moved away and write up their notes.
3. Ask students to write an alternative version of this story in which the narrator has access to the adult James's thoughts.

GROUP ACTIVITIES

Divide the class into three groups. Ask each group to come up with a symbol that the author could have used in place of the swing.

Divide the class into two debating teams. One team will argue that the main character was dreaming or hallucinating, whereas the other will attempt to show that the boy was really there.

DO YOUR STUDENTS KNOW . . .

Phenology is the branch of science that studies the response of living organisms to the seasonal, cyclical patterns in the environment in which they live, including birth and death.

DISCUSSION

Fantasy and reality are difficult to tell apart in this story — at some points, they are even indistinguishable — and this may be challenging for some of your students. You may find it useful to begin by asking them if they feel the boy is actually there or if the main character is simply imagining him (Q 10). Some students may just have left home for the first time, and their parents may be going through the same difficult process as the mother in "The Swing." Older students may have experienced the process from the point of view of the mother.

The main character is past middle age, perhaps in her seventies. She and her husband are retired, and her only son, James, is grown and has a family (Q 2). Her current relationship with James is unsatisfactory. She tries to talk with him, but he has little interest in engaging in a real conversation with her. This is a source of frustration for her; she wants the kind of intimacy they had when he was a child. Because her husband was not in good health, she and James did even more together than they might otherwise have. As an adult, he shares information with her, but she is more interested in his feelings. It would be an unfair generalization to suggest that mathematicians are cold, distant people, but the fact that James is engaged in work that demands strict logic and a knack for abstraction does seem relevant (Q 5).

Adding to the main character's dissatisfaction is the fact that she has become cut off from the other people in her life. Her husband, Julius, pays little attention to her and needs to be taken care of and humored. While it seems unlikely that he was ever very attentive, we are told that the situation has grown worse in recent years (Q 3). Julius has always needed her help, and it may be that he has gradually withdrawn from her because he resents his own dependence (Q 4). She tries to keep in touch with several old friends, but they are so self-involved and obsessed with their own aging that they are of little help.

Her situation changes for the better when she begins having dreams or visions — it is difficult to say which — of James as a child. We are told that she has only recently begun to dream again as she has grown old, and it may be that her dreams are a compensation for a daily life that is no longer as fulfilling as it once was. The young James appears to her every few nights on the swing in the yard, and they become reacquainted. The swing is an important symbol in the story, a fact signaled by its being used as the title. Though any symbol can have multiple meanings, this swing primarily symbolizes the freedom and playfulness of youth (Q 9).

For a while, her meetings with the younger James at the swing give the main character back some of this spirit of playfulness, along with the intimacy they once shared. She has the added joy of seeing her son not as a polite but shallow man, but as vibrant and full of curiosity about life (Q 6). These conversations, as simple and childish as they are, are transformative for her. She feels, ironically enough, more intellectually stimulated by this child than by her adult son, a mathematician, or by her husband, an engineer (Q 8).

As important as these visits are to her, they eventually end when the younger James announces he can no longer meet with her. She is able to retain her composure while he is there but begins to cry as soon as he is gone. She realizes that she no longer has his support and companionship, and she perhaps wonders whether she will be able to maintain her new attitude without him (Q 7). Despite the grief she is clearly feeling, the story ends on a hopeful, if melancholy, note. Julius has seen the boy too, and this shared experience may help to reconnect husband and wife.

You might consider teaching this story with "Hold Tight," "Domestic Help," and "Group Photo with Winter Trees." All three selections deal with the desire to hold on to those who are taken from us by time or death.

CHAPTER 7

SETTING

KATE CHOPIN

The Storm

WRITING ACTIVITIES

1. Ask students to write a prequel to the story, describing Calixta's relationship with Alcée.
2. Compare Calixta with Emily (Faulkner's "A Rose for Emily"). Both are Southern women who become involved with men outside of marriage. Why is Emily's relationship destructive, but Calixta's is not?
3. Students who are uncomfortable with the "immorality" of the ending might want to write a new ending that they consider more appropriate.

GROUP ACTIVITIES

Before assigning the story, have students brainstorm on ways in which authors and filmmakers have used the weather to underscore a theme or to set a certain mood. Have them give plenty of examples — you might write these on the board. Select the answers that reveal the associations that students make between weather patterns and emotional states. From this set of relationships, students should focus on the expectations created by the title "The Storm." Ask them to examine the relationship between the storm and the plot, as well as their own expectations of what the storm setting should mean (Q 8). They should take special notice of any times when the plot deviates from what is expected.

DO YOUR STUDENTS KNOW . . .

Because people lie even in anonymous polls on adultery, infidelity rates range from 25 to 75 percent of men and 15 to 16 percent of women. Psychologists surmise that as many as half of all men and women engage in extramarital affairs.

DISCUSSION

If the students work through the Group Activity, they should be prepared for the discussion of the storm's development throughout the story (Q 1). The storm begins in Part I with characteristic stillness, and it "bursts" at the end of this section.

In Part II, we again see the warning signs for the storm — the heat, darkness, and finally sporadic rain. By the middle of Part II (¶ 13), the rain has come full force, in a deluge that threatens to come into the house. Following the downpour, the lightning and thunder begin (¶ 19). By the end of Part II, the storm subsides into quiet rain (¶ 28), and in ¶ 30, it stops. The storm is not mentioned again until the last line of Part V, which simply mentions its passing (Q 7).

Discussing how the progress of the storm parallels the lovemaking of Calixta and Alcée might be useful. As students point out the details mentioned above, list these in a column on one part of the board. Then, in a separate column, have students list the stages of the plot. They should pay special attention to the causal relations between weather and plot as well as between plot and character development (Q 1).

In Part I, Bibi and Bobinôt decide to remain at Friedheimer's store for the duration of the coming storm, leaving Calixta alone. Some students may mention that they foresee tension because of the description of the weather in ¶ 1 — the "sinister intention from the west, accompanied by a sullen, threatening roar." This expectation is false because what happens later in the story is not presented as evil (Q 3). Students may also notice two other details related to plot. First, Bobinôt buys Calixta a can of shrimp. Ask the students what they think this detail suggests about the relationship between Calixta and her husband. Some may feel that this action suggests insecurity in their relationship; others may feel that it reflects a strength in the marriage. Either way, ask students to watch for further clues about the relationship. Second, the last sentence of the paragraph suggests a calmness that contrasts with the opening paragraph. Students should see that beyond being afraid of the storm, Bibi is not afraid for his family (Q 2, 3). Thus, in Part I, readers may develop a variety of expectations about the characters and the plot.

In Part II, the relationship between plot and storm is most evident. Students should note that the first sentence of the paragraph is related in mood to the last sentence of Part I. Calixta is also not worried; she is secure in her family relationships. So secure is she that initially she does not even notice the coming storm. However, students should see that the storm begins to have visible effects on her physically before she begins to do something about it. In particular, the weather before the storm causes her to "undo her white sacque at the throat." Have students look for other elements of sensuality that prepare the reader for Alcée's arrival.

The next causal relation between storm and plot is established when the rain falls in such torrents that Alcée has to come into the house to avoid being drenched (Q 4, 5). When Alcée enters the house, we begin to see Calixta and her home from his perspective: She has a fuller figure, vivacity, melting blue eyes, disheveled yellow hair. These details increase the story's level of sensuality. In ¶ 13, growing sexual arousal is mirrored by the growing storm with "a force and clatter that threatened to break the entrance and deluge them there."

The parallel between the storm and sexual arousal continues in Part II. The storm casts a mist around the cabin, making the two characters seem all the more alone. And again, a specific weather pattern causes the next step in the plot

(Q 4, 5). The lightning strikes a chinaberry tree with such force that Calixta is frightened into Alcée's arms. The next logical step is a kiss.

The paragraphs that follow describe the passion of the two lovers. Students should notice at this point that the relationship between the storm and the lovers begins to change. They now ignore the crashing torrents. The lovemaking becomes a "mysterious ritual," "a birthright," "the undying life of the world." The act is described here in very positive terms; it is not the sombre and threatening act suggested in Part I. Although not directly stated, it seems that nature follows the lead of the lovers, not the other way around. Eventually, the storm stops, and the Sun comes out. The section ends with Calixta's laughter.

In Part III, we see the aftermath of the storm. Here again, contrary to our expectations, the aftermath is quite positive, suggesting that people, not weather, set the tone. Bobinôt fears his overscrupulous wife, a note implying something about their relationship before the storm, and perhaps his reason for buying the shrimp. However, Calixta does not respond to him in anger as he has expected, and the section closes with a picture of great family contentment. Sections IV and V repeat the theme that the lovemaking is good for both partners. Clarisse is much happier after Alcée suggests in his letter that she and the babies stay a month longer.

Some students may be disturbed by the closing comments and the lack of condemnation for the adultery. Ask students why they think Chopin ends the story the way she does. Also ask them why they think she chose not to publish it in her lifetime (Q 9, 10). Students might also reflect on how the setting — in 1890s, Louisiana — affects the actions of the characters (Q 6).

You may want to teach this story with "To His Coy Mistress," "Living in Sin," or "My Last Duchess" (love/sex relationships) or with the poems about love in the Discovering Themes in Poetry chapter.

FURTHER READING

Aaron, Daniel. "Review." *New York Times Book Review* 8 Feb. 1970: 5, 30.
Inge, Tonette Bond. "Kate Chopin." *American Short-Story Writers, 1880–1910.* Ed. Bobby Ellen Kimbel. *Dictionary of Literary Biography.* Vol. 78. Detroit: Gale, 1988. 90–110.

SHERMAN ALEXIE

This Is What It Means to Say Phoenix, Arizona

WRITING ACTIVITIES

1. Ask students to try to remember some family stories. Have them choose one and retell it in a paragraph. How "true" do they believe this story is? Do they see the story as history or as myth?
2. Ask students to write about the possible effects of modern technology on the Native American storytelling tradition.

3. Ask students to write about how the relationship between Thomas and Victor is like and unlike a relationship they have with a friend or relative.

GROUP ACTIVITIES

Divide students into groups and ask each group to brainstorm about the plot and characters of the "new story" Thomas hears at the end of "This Is What It Means to Say Phoenix, Arizona" (Q 9).

DO YOUR STUDENTS KNOW . . .

Technology meets the tradition of storytelling and song at the American Indian Radio Satellite (AIROS). A service of Native American Public Telecommunications, this international system transmits issues-based and cultural programming to native peoples worldwide.

DISCUSSION

It might be useful to begin discussion by talking about stereotypes associated with Native American culture. Encourage students to discuss what comes to mind when they think of an Indian reservation. In this story, life on the reservation is characterized by poverty and alcoholism. No one on the reservation has any money "except the cigarette and fireworks salespeople," and even the tribal council can't provide more than $100 for the proper burial of a tribal member. This modern-day reservation has no warriors and sacred tribal rituals. Instead, Alexie portrays a collapse of culture and a loss in tribal continuity. His brave young warriors are morally bankrupt teens who get drunk and beat another member of the tribe for no reason, and then quickly scatter for fear of being dragged "to some teepee" and made to listen "to some elder tell a dusty old story" (Q 1).

Alexie creates additional settings here as well to further highlight the decay of the Native American culture and its incongruity in modern-day American society. On the plane, Thomas stands out as a "crazy Indian storyteller with ratty old braids and broken teeth" who inappropriately attempts to flirt with "a beautiful Olympic gymnast." He is clearly out of his element, and Victor is "ready to jump out of the plane" from embarrassment. He knows that "nobody back home on the reservation would have believed it" (Q 3). The trailer in Phoenix where Victor's father died, another setting presented in this story, is a place of death and decay. We learn that Victor's father died of a heart attack and that he "[lay] in that trailer for a week in hundred-degree temperatures before anyone had found him." Everything in the trailer "had that smell stuck in it or was useless anyway." Even the road through Nevada is barren of life save for a jackrabbit that falls victim to the road and is crushed beneath the pick-up's tires. Victor says that the jackrabbit is "'the only thing alive in the whole state and we just killed it'" (Q 2).

Although the story's mood is humorous at times, it is haunted by the harsh realities of modern-day life on the reservation. Thomas's stories serve as a reminder of the loss of the tribal community ties and the break-down of the culture (Q 4).

The stories, mythical and sometimes prophetic, serve as a means of understanding "that can change or not change the world." The oral tradition in Native American culture is also a means of cultural preservation. Nevertheless, Thomas's stories are ridiculed and ignored by tribe members, and he is regarded as a crazy storyteller "whom nobody [wants] to listen to." His stories, however, reveal truths, both real and mythic, and are a remnant of a culture rich in tradition and spirituality (Q 7).

Throughout the story, Alexie flashes back to Victor's and Thomas's childhood, blending past and present history and myth (Q 10). These glimpses into the past enable the reader to see the history of the two men's friendship and to better understand why both men are the way they are today. We learn that Victor and Thomas played together as boys and that at the age of seven, Thomas warned Victor of Victor's father's weak heart. We are told that at the age of twelve, Thomas saved Victor from a wasps' nest, and that had Thomas not come by, "he might have died there, stung a thousand times." At the age of thirteen, Thomas has a dream that sends him to Spokane "to wait for a sign." His vision is of Victor's father, and Thomas realizes that his dreams have been saying, "Take care of each other." By the age of fifteen, however, Thomas is still telling his stories, and now "nobody [wants] to be anywhere near him because of all those stories." When Victor gets drunk and beats Thomas, it is "for no reason at all" (Q 6).

Thomas is ridiculed and shunned because of his stories, and for this reason, Victor chooses to forsake his friend. Victor seems to know in his heart, however, that Thomas's stories have real meaning and serve an important purpose within the tribe. Regardless, Victor and Thomas cannot remain friends when they return to the reservation because there, "Thomas would remain the crazy storyteller who talked to dogs and cars, who listened to the wind and pine trees." Thomas understands and says, "I know how it is. . . ." He realizes that if Victor were to remain his friend, Victor would have to endure ridicule from his friends as well (Q 5). Victor, perhaps, speaks for the tribal community when he admits his shame and asks, "Whatever happened to the tribal ties, the sense of community?" He is ashamed because he realizes that "the only real thing he [shares] with anybody [is] a bottle and broken dreams" (Q 8).

This story's title is perhaps most simply interpreted as an explicit reference to the trip to Phoenix — in other words, as the "real story" of the trip and of the meaning behind it. Perhaps too it identifies the story as a tale with both literal and figurative meanings, one which contains within it the history of two men and, perhaps, of a people (Q 8).

You might teach this story alongside "Once upon a Time," which also interweaves truth and myth, or with a selection of poems by Native American poets (such as N. Scott Momaday, Louise Erdrich, and James Welch) represented in the text.

FURTHER READING

Busch, Frederick. "Longing for Magic." *New York Times Book Review* 16 July 1995: 9.

Price, Reynolds. "One Indian Doesn't Tell the Other." *New York Times Book Review* 17 Oct. 1993: 15.

RALPH ELLISON

Battle Royal

WRITING ACTIVITIES

1. Ask students to write a brief definition of racism and to give an example of racism they or someone they know has encountered.
2. Ask students to write a paragraph on why they think the young black men in the story were subjected to the humiliation of the battle royal.
3. Ask students to explain why they think Ellison introduces the naked woman into the story.

GROUP ACTIVITIES

Divide the class into two groups. Ask one group to formulate a definition of *healthy humility* and the other to define *unhealthy humility*.

Divide the class into two debating teams. One will argue that the narrator did the right thing by accepting the scholarship. The other will argue that he should have refused it.

DO YOUR STUDENTS KNOW . . .

Helen Bannerman, a British woman living in India in 1899, wrote *Sambo*, a book about an Indian boy to amuse her children. Over the years, the story, without her permission, was revised by others, who added racist stereotypes of African-Americans.

DISCUSSION

There are a number of aspects of "Battle Royal" that will be troubling for some students. One of the most obvious is the blatant racism of the onlookers, in particular their frequent use of racial slurs such as "nigger" and "coon." It is important to raise this issue with the class early on so that students feel comfortable enough to participate freely in the discussion. Find out what the students know about segregation in the South and fill in any important gaps in their knowledge. It is the ubiquity and acceptability of racism in that time and place that allow this battle royal, with all of its racist elements, to occur (Q 1).

The narrator is reluctant to participate in the battle but does so without protest. He is caught in a double bind here. He has come to deliver a speech on the importance of humility. Open defiance, then, would be at odds with the content of the speech, and he would lose the approval of the men who invited him there (Q 3). On the other hand, he does not want to detract from his speech's "dignity." Ask students whether they think the humility the narrator advocates in his speech is compatible with dignity. The statement that the narrator's grandfather makes on his deathbed also puts the narrator in what he feels to be an impossible situation. Although he is sincerely humble, his consciousness of the way his grandfather viewed humility makes him feel that he is deceitful. It is fitting, then, that his graduation speech, in which he stresses the importance of humility for his people, should be connected with both his greatest success and his greatest humiliation. His grandfather would no doubt agree that humility is important, but he would view it as a weapon rather than a token of respect or friendship (Q 2, 4).

When he and the other fighters are led into the ballroom, the narrator is shocked to see how the prominent whites of the town behave when they shed the inhibitions of polite society. A naked white woman performs a provocative dance for the spectators, is assaulted by some of them, and only narrowly escapes with the help of others. The whites take a perverse pleasure in forcing the young black men to be in her presence while preventing them from giving any expression to the feelings her presence arouses. When the woman is gone, the sexual energy she calls up in the spectators is channeled into bloodlust (Q 6). This may be a difficult passage for some of the students to discuss, but it is important to a full understanding of the story.

The fight itself is a chaotic spectacle. The ballroom, filled with smoke and the smell of alcohol and sweat, is described in such a way that the reader has a sense of pent-up violence even before the fight starts (Q 5). When it does start the participants have all been blindfolded to ensure that the fight is not only violent but also comical. The spectators are in fact afraid of the young men in the ring, and the use of blindfolds is a way to ensure that they appear foolish and clumsy (Q 7).

The narrator's speech remains important to him even after it is clear that he is in part being humiliated because of it. Even when he is at his lowest, he still wants the approval of the white spectators (Q 8). When the superintendent states that the narrator will "lead his people in the proper paths," he means that he will encourage his people to be humble and obedient and to be content with their position in a segregated society (Q 9). The whites of the town approve of the ideas the narrator expresses in his speech, but they are afraid of the intelligence he displays in articulating those ideas. Indeed, the only time they really pay attention to his speech is when he slips up and says "equality" instead of "responsibility."

After the narrator has finished his speech, the school superintendent presents him with a gift, a scholarship to a Negro college. Have the class discuss what the narrator means when he says, "I was so moved that I could hardly express my thanks." It is obviously ironic that he should feel grateful after the humiliation he has suffered. Ellison is making an important point, though, about the ways in which racism affects self-image and how people are taught to be grateful even to their oppressors (Q 10). Something good may in fact come out of this situation: The narrator now has an educational opportunity he might not otherwise have had. The price of that opportunity, though, is an almost total loss of dignity (Q 12).

Early in the story, the narrator talked about his grandfather's deathbed advice, and he ends by relating a dream he has the night after the battle royal. In his dream, his grandfather instructs him to open a series of envelopes, in the last of which is a document with the message, "To Whom It May Concern, Keep This Nigger Boy Running." The dream is an indication that not only will his grandfather's curse not let him have peace, but also white society will continue to harass him.

You might consider teaching this story with "The Carnival Dog, the Buyer of Diamonds," "Big Black Good Man," and "We Wear the Mask." The first selection deals with issues of self-respect and perseverance, and the other two address issues related to racial prejudice.

FURTHER READING

Busby, Mark. "Ralph Ellison." *American Novelists since World War II, Sixth Series*. Ed. James R. Giles and Wanda H. Giles. *Dictionary of Literary Biography*, Vol. 227. Detroit: Gale, 2000. 128–140.

Dickstein, Morris. "Ralph Ellison, Race and American Culture." *Raritan* 18 (Spring 1999): 30–51.

TILLIE OLSEN

I Stand Here Ironing

WRITING ACTIVITIES

1. Have students write a letter from the narrator to Emily or have them write a letter from Emily to her missing father.
2. Students may be interested in writing a scene of dialogue between Emily and her mother.
3. A student could write a report on the social welfare programs available to families during the Depression and read the report to the class.

GROUP ACTIVITIES

Divide students into three groups. Each group should devise four or five questions about the Depression to ask a grandparent or someone who lived through that era as a working mother or as the child of a working mother (Q 3, 9). After the interviews, have groups meet again to consolidate their findings and discuss with the class whether or not their research substantiates the events and emotions in the story.

DO YOUR STUDENTS KNOW . . .

Dr. Benjamin Spock became the foremost expert on child rearing with his 1946 book, *Common Sense Book of Baby and Child Care*. His simple, encouraging approach and use of plain talk appealed to parents, who made his book the biggest seller after the Bible.

DISCUSSION

The title suggests both point of view and setting. Point out to students that Depression-era irons were heavy, not like the lightweight, technologically advanced irons we have now. Women used to refer to ironing as "pressing" clothes because it took a certain amount of pressure to get wrinkles out. Although the story is set in the 1950s when irons were lighter, *everything* had to be ironed; there were no wrinkle-free fabrics. Because ironing used to be such a time-consuming chore, it's no wonder the narrator seems to be always ironing.

Ask students if they believe the events in this story could occur today. Despite recent social, political, and economic changes, especially regarding opportunities for women, most students will agree that these events can and do occur today (Q 1).

The title provides the beginning and ending images of the story, and the narrator refers to it twice in her memories. Ironing is mindless work, but it actually provides a good time to think. Thus, in ¶ 4, the narrator suggests a certain irony when she says, "When is there time to remember . . . ?" Much of the narrator's life has been defined by drudgery and poverty (Q 2). She is also trying, in a sense, to "press"—with "iron will"—her life into an understandable order that will help her explain (to herself) what she has done, the choices she has made. The narrator implies that she would do things differently a second time, but given the circumstances, *could* she? The last image (¶ 56) suggests that she desperately hopes her daughter's life will be better than hers (Q 5, 6).

The narrative point of view of the story is first-person, with Emily's mother as the narrator. This narrative form is called interior monologue; it is more controlled than stream of consciousness, allowing us to see the mother's guilt about the fact that Emily's life has been so different from the younger children's. Some of your students may think that the narrator is a bad mother, pointing out that she does not want to talk with the teacher and that she implies that it is too late to do anything for Emily (Q 4).

Some students will assume that the narrator is addressing her comments to a school counselor; others will believe that the monologue is aimed at authority figures in general — at all the institutions that have failed her (Q 8). Ask students whom they blame for the narrator's problems. Most will argue that the "times" are at fault. Point out that the author makes the narrator a sympathetic character. Young and abandoned, the narrator was forced to work in a Depression-ridden country (¶ 11, 12). Moreover, she had the new parent's fear of breaking the baby (¶ 6) (Q 5). The narrator's life was not by any means easy while Emily was a child (Q 7), but students will not find any evidence of self-pity, even when she talks about her husband (¶ 8).

Some students may find this a painful story to discuss. The narrator's feelings of guilt contribute to the painful nature of the story. Ask students what she feels she has done wrong and if she has been the best mother she could be under the circumstances (Q 3). Be sure to point out the paradox: The parent must be separate from the child in order to "care" for the child. Talk about the acts of love the mother observes. (You might even discuss Robert Hayden's "Those Winter Sundays" for comparison.) When her husband leaves her, the mother is forced to make choices for Emily that she does not have to make for the later children: She leaves her with the downstairs neighbor (¶ 8); she sends her to the father's family (¶ 10); she has to leave her in a day-care center that is like a "parking place" (¶ 12). When Susan is born, Emily has to remain isolated for two weeks because of the contagious nature of her illness, and later she is sent away to a convalescent home (¶ 26–33). The mother works hard to provide, but she never hugs, touches, or holds Emily. Even the old man, a neighbor, gently reprimands her for not smiling (¶ 17). She saves her affection for the younger children. It is interesting to note that Tillie Olsen gave up writing to care for her four children during the Depression.

Students may be puzzled by Emily's becoming a comedian, a "clown." This irony is often seen in life, as well, as people attempt to replace what is missing from their lives. You may want to point out to students that many clowns traditionally paint a tear on their cheeks over their makeup. That fits in with the mother's comment that "she tells me everything and nothing." Clowns can make us laugh, but we know little of them as individuals, nor do we know why so many are alcoholics. The clowning façade juxtaposed with the comment about being dead soon from an atom bomb explosion may initially confuse some students or seem oxymoronic. See how other students respond to that: Teenagers understand about not revealing what is really going on with them (Q 10).

See what your students make of ¶ 55. They may comment that it is cold and indifferent, not a memory but an itemization, as if the mother is rehearsing to give a bureaucratic presentation or to fill out an official form.

Ask students how well the narrator knows her own daughter. Have them search for ways the narrator and her daughter resemble each other. Still, they are different, apart, as seen when the narrator is surprised when she sees Emily perform; mother hardly recognizes daughter (¶ 48). And one of her first comments refers to "all that life that has happened outside of me, beyond me" (¶ 3). Have students speculate about the identity of the caller. It is probably a teacher because school is mentioned several times; even though Emily is nineteen, she is behind others her age (Q 8).

You may want to teach this story with "Teenage Wasteland," "Those Winter Sundays," or "My Son, My Executioner" (parent/child relationships).

FURTHER READING

Barr, Marleen. "Tillie Olsen." *Twentieth-Century American-Jewish Fiction Writers.* Ed. Daniel Walden. *Dictionary of Literary Biography.* Vol. 28. Detroit: Gale, 1984. 196–203.

Elman, R. M. "The Many Forms Which Loss Can Take." *Commonweal* 75 (8 Dec. 1961): 295–96.

PAM HOUSTON

Cowboys Are My Weakness

WRITING ACTIVITIES

1. Ask students to describe their ideal landscapes.
2. Ask students to write about any myths they have learned from movies.
3. Ask students to imagine how the narrator's life changes after her realization that she has been living a fiction that doesn't suit her.

GROUP ACTIVITIES

Divide the class into three groups. The first will brainstorm reasons why the narrator should begin a relationship with David. The second will make the case for Monte. The third will explain why neither man represents a desirable alternative to Homer.

Divide the class into two groups. One will argue that the narrator should return to the East Coast and begin her life over. The other will give reasons why she should remain in the West.

DO YOUR STUDENTS KNOW . . .

The heroic figure of the cowboy has been popularized by Hollywood and literature as a metaphor for American independence and strength, but this image sharply contrasts with cowboys' real lives of tedious, difficult work, poor living conditions, and economic hardship.

DISCUSSION

The most challenging aspect of this story for students will be the fact that the narrator becomes increasingly suspicious of her own motivations as things progress. Students who have no firsthand knowledge of the West may have some of the same difficulty that the narrator does in distinguishing between myth and reality. She moved west with an idealized vision of the West and the people who inhabit it. In particular, she was looking for a cowboy, a man who would be rugged and individualistic, yet sensitive and honorable (Q 2). Her view of the West itself is just as idealized. Aside from the description she gives in the first paragraph of her perfect home, there are relatively few descriptions of the western landscape. The most detailed are those that appear toward the end of the story, when it briefly seems that myth and reality could coincide (Q 3, 4).

The narrator grew up in a family that never stayed home during the holidays, and as a result, she feels rootless and cut off from tradition. A cowboy, at least in Hollywood films, is both traditional and utterly dependable. Her "weakness" for cowboys, then, may reflect a need for the kind of stability her parents didn't give her (Q 7). The fact that she hasn't managed to find a cowboy after living in the

West for ten years, and after moving from the cities into rural areas, is an indication that the kind of man she is looking for may not exist (Q 1). By the end of the story, the narrator suspects that this may be the case, yet she is still out West and still looking for her perfect man and home (Q 5).

The story focuses on the narrator's relationships with three men: Homer, David, and Monte. Homer is a wildlife specialist with whom she is romantically involved. She initially thought that Homer was the cowboy she was looking for, but she has become increasingly disillusioned with him. Aside from the fact that he is chronically unfaithful, Homer is emotionally distant and seems uninterested in her and her concerns. David is the owner of a ranch where Homer and the narrator are staying while Homer researches a local deer herd. David is kind, sensitive, artistically inclined — everything that Homer is not. It is David's presence, more than anything, that makes the narrator aware of the fact that there is something unhealthy about her taste in men. Monte is a cowboy working on David's ranch (Q 8). Although Monte is not quite the archetypal Hollywood cowboy, he nevertheless exudes the rugged sensitivity the narrator has been seeking (Q 8, 11).

Despite the fact that Monte is seemingly her perfect man, the narrator leaves him behind. This marks the beginning of her realization that she has lived her life according to a fiction she no longer believes. The title, then, is ironic; the narrator's real weakness is not cowboys but a tendency to confuse myth and reality (Q 9). By the time the story concludes, she has come to see that this kind of fiction making is a common human characteristic and ultimately limiting. It has taken her years to come to this realization; you might want to ask your students why they think it has taken her so long (Q 6, 10).

You might consider teaching this story with "Happy Endings," "General Review of the Sex Situation," and "The Littoral Zone." All three selections deal with difficult relationships between men and women.

FURTHER READING

West, Kathryn. "Pam Houston" *American Short-Story Writers since World War II, Fourth Series*. Eds. Patrick Meanor and Joseph McNicholas. *Dictionary of Literary Biography*, Vol. 244. Detroit: Gale, 2001. 170–80.

CHAPTER 8

POINT OF VIEW

RICHARD WRIGHT

Big Black Good Man

WRITING ACTIVITIES

1. Ask students to write a paragraph in which they discuss the reasons, other than racial prejudice, why Olaf is afraid of the sailor.
2. Students can write a paragraph in which they compare modern-day racial stereotypes with those expressed by Olaf. In what ways are these stereotypes alike? In what ways are they different?
3. Ask students to write about a time when they made faulty assumptions about someone.

GROUP ACTIVITIES

Is Olaf a racist? Divide students into groups and have them examine the story carefully to compile evidence of Olaf's racism.

Divide the students into two groups. The first group should rewrite the ending of the story so that Olaf's racist fears are realized. The second group of students should briefly retell the story with Olaf as an African-American and the sailor as a white man. Then ask both groups what conclusions they can draw about racial prejudice.

DO YOUR STUDENTS KNOW . . .

Following World War I and well into the 1960s, African-Americans, particularly writers and artists — for example, James Baldwin and Wright himself — left America for Europe. Black intellectuals both from America and Africa found a sense of artistic freedom and social acceptance in France that America lacked.

DISCUSSION

You may want to begin by discussing point of view and by defining the various types of irony. In "Big Black Good Man," the third-person limited omniscient point of view enables the reader to enter Olaf's mind and see things that Olaf himself can't see. Clearly, Wright uses this narrative technique to establish dramatic irony. Because the story is told from Olaf's point of view, there is no overt acknowledgment of racial prejudice. The story would be entirely different if the sailor narrated it. From the sailor's point of view, Olaf's prejudice, which he would find obvious, would be in the foreground (Q 1). Similarly, in the United States in the 1950s, racism would have been more blatant, whereas in Copenhagen, traditionally a more homogeneous society as well as a more racially tolerant one, racism takes place on a more subtle level (Q 8).

It appears that Olaf is overwhelmed by the sailor, even afraid of him, not only because of his "intense blackness" but also because of his "ungainly bigness": Olaf "felt as though this man had come here expressly to remind him how puny, how tiny, and how weak and how white he was." To Olaf, the man's presence is an affront, designed to reveal to him his own inadequacies. Although Olaf denies that his reactions to the man are motivated by racial prejudice, the reader is aware that Olaf's repeated references to the man's color belie this (Q 3). At first, Olaf's fears may seem reasonable, since the sailor addresses him "in a resounding voice" that "filled the small office." He speaks in a commanding voice "in a manner that indicated that it was taking it for granted that Olaf would obey." However, as the story progresses, we realize that Olaf's perceptions may be affected by his racial assumptions: "God oughtn't make men as big and black as that . . ." (Q 4). It is not until Lena is introduced that we have independent testimony that the sailor is, in her words, "'just a man'" and not a sinister "black giant." Lena's nonchalant response to the sailor shows us that Olaf has in fact been overreacting. Clearly, her perceptions are not burdened by the racial prejudice that we now see underlies Olaf's reactions (Q 5).

The fact that Richard Wright is a well-known African-American author ensures that we read this story ironically, without undue sympathy for its protagonist. If its author were white, we might mistakenly assume that we were meant to share Olaf's perceptions of the sailor. Indeed, irony operates on many levels in the story. For instance, the title itself is ironic: "big" and "black" are used by Olaf repeatedly throughout the story to suggest the man's supposed malevolence, and their juxtaposition with the word *good* has an effect that would be comical if they did not so dramatically underscore Olaf's prejudice. Dramatic irony enables us to understand Olaf's racism in a way he himself cannot. His individual utterances are verbally ironic in that we understand them in a way that is different from how he means them (Q 6). When Olaf uses figures of speech such as "the black giant" and "hunk of blackness" to describe the sailor, we are aware, as he is not, that these are racist tropes. Finally, the story hinges on situational irony, where Wright turns our expectations upside down. In the end, we are led by Olaf, the unreliable narrator, to expect murder and mayhem; however, the sailor's generous act forces us to confront not only Olaf's racist assumptions but also our own (Q 6). The sailor's bafflement and benevolence when he learns of Olaf's expectations confirm that he is indeed good as well as big and black (Q 9).

One interesting characteristic of "Big Black Good Man" is that not much really happens. The tension in the story comes from the juxtaposition of Olaf's prejudiced view of the sailor with the view of the sailor as he actually is. The addition of other narrative elements — external action, violence, a change of scene, for example — would detract from the point Wright is trying to make (Q 11).

You might want to teach this story with "The White City" or *Fences*.

FURTHER READING

Gates, Henry Louis Jr., and K.A. Appiah, eds. *Richard Wright: Critical Perspectives Past and Present*. New York: Amistad, 1993.

Macksey, Richard, and Frank E. Moorer, eds. *Richard Wright: A Collection of Critical Essays*. Englewood Cliffs: Prentice Hall, 1984.

EDGAR ALLAN POE

The Cask of Amontillado

WRITING ACTIVITIES

1. Ask students to write a paragraph in which they speculate about why Montresor hates Fortunato.
2. Ask students to compare Montresor with other characters who seek revenge because of their notion of honor — for example, Emily Grierson ("A Rose for Emily") or Abner Snopes ("Barn Burning").
3. Divide students into four groups. Ask each group to rewrite the first three paragraphs of the story or a portion of the dialogue from a different point of view: first-person (Fortunato), first-person (the person who hears Montresor's account and then retells it), third-person limited omniscient, and third-person omniscient. Then ask students to compare their different responses to Montresor and Fortunato in each account.

GROUP ACTIVITIES

Divide the students into two groups. Have each group look for examples of irony in Montresor's speech and action (¶ 5, 20, 35, 36, 42, 52, 55).

Assign the story as a class play. Individual groups should be assigned the following tasks: Prepare the script; cast classmates for the roles and direct the production; research and create costumes; furnish props, sound effects, and backdrops.

DO YOUR STUDENTS KNOW . . .

Carnival season in Italy begins in January and continues through Mardi Gras, the day before Ash Wednesday. Masked balls, parties, and gaiety mark the period before the beginning of Lent, a forty-day period in the Christian tradition marked by reflection and repentance.

DISCUSSION

Students beginning a study of point of view in literature will have no trouble identifying Montresor as a first-person narrator. What may cause trouble for them is seeing how point of view shapes their responses to the characters and to the action of the story.

Although students will most likely condemn the actions of Montresor, only the first-person narrative gives the slightest cause for sympathy: Montresor says that he has suffered much and has been insulted (Q 1, 9). Besides giving Montresor a chance to rationalize the crime, the first-person narrative voice makes the whole piece read as a confessional, a catharsis for a heart that has "grown sick" (¶ 89) (Q 8). With this reading in mind, you might ask the students what role the listener plays in the narrative, noting that a listener is explicitly addressed in ¶ 1. The narrator apparently assumes that his audience will be sympathetic to his tale (Q 7). Perhaps, then, the listener might be a member of the clergy to whom he is confessing. Students will disagree about whether Montresor enjoys the act of confession more than he enjoyed committing the crime (Q 10). With this in mind, ask students if they think Montresor is a reliable narrator (Q 2).

One reason Montresor seems to expect his audience to understand his crime is that he believes his sense of honor justifies his actions. Although honor may be important to students, honor as a basis for murder is inconsistent with the laws of a democratic society, where justice is not determined by a single individual; thus, students may find it hard to assume the role of sympathetic listener (Q 2). Point out to the students that revenge and honor are general themes, and Poe relies on them to spark a measure of sympathy for the narrator. You might also ask the students if their response to Montresor would be different if they knew the nature of Fortunato's offense.

Having seen how the point of view affects the reader's view of Montresor, the students can then consider Fortunato. Although pitied as a victim, Fortunato is not portrayed favorably by Montresor. First of all, Fortunato is dehumanized by being presented to the reader in a clown costume. Second, the narrator accomplishes his scheme by playing on Fortunato's pride (students can see this by looking at the repeated references to Luchresi) (Q 6). Finally, the last sound we hear coming from Fortunato is the ringing of the bells on his hat, not his voice. Students might consider here what implications this last sound has. Is Fortunato's shaking his head a gesture of defiance or of helplessness? Is Fortunato dying honorably by refusing to beg? Or is he just drunk? (Q 4, 5).

Once students see how point of view affects characterization, they can move to irony. Assign the first group activity to enhance this discussion. Students will also find irony in the coat of arms and motto of the Montresor family. As Montresor presents it, the coat of arms represents a righteous figure (a man's heel) crushing an evil figure (the snake). The motto, *nemo me impune lacessit*, stands in contrast to the Christian concept of forgiveness that many students will associate with righteousness (Q 5). You might also point out that the very fact that Fortunato forgets the family motto and emblems adds to the insult that Montresor feels he has received. Ironically, Fortunato admires the coat of arms, suggesting that he is unaware of Montresor's purposes (Q 3, 4).

Finally, you should ask students to consider setting (Q 7). Montresor is able to plan his revenge so that Fortunato dies in the midst of the great Montresor family. We know that it is carnival time, so the servants will be out of the house, and the principal characters will be masked. Fortunato is likely to be drunk, and Montresor has a ready alibi for his own actions. Finally, the story's action and setting suggest a descent into hell, farther and farther away from the known world and the laws that govern it. The bones and nitre complete the hellish scene, making the story even more horrible.

To conclude, ask the students to consider why Montresor has finally decided to reveal his secret after fifty years of silence.

You might want to teach this story with "The Yellow Wallpaper," "The United Fruit Co.," or *The Glass Menagerie* (power/powerlessness).

FURTHER READING

Carlson, Eric W. "Edgar Allan Poe." *American Short-Story Writers Before 1880*. Ed. Bobby Ellen Kimbel. *Dictionary of Literary Biography*. Vol. 74. Detroit: Gale, 1988. 303–22.

Gargano, James W. "The Question of Poe's Narrators." *College English* 25 (Dec. 1963): 177–81.

WILLIAM FAULKNER

Barn Burning

Before assigning this story, note the caveat on page 52 at the end of this discussion about preparing students for the racist language in Faulkner's story.

WRITING ACTIVITIES

1. Have students write a five-minute response to Abner's line: "'You got to learn to stick to your own blood or you ain't going to have any blood to stick to you'" (¶ 28).
2. Have students write a paragraph explaining why Abner tracks manure into Major DeSpain's house and onto his rug.

GROUP ACTIVITIES

Have one group of students research life in the South during the Reconstruction era and present this information to the class.

Another group of students should address Abner's behavior during the Civil War and his lack of loyalty to his fellow soldiers or their cause in lieu of his lesson to Sarty: above all else, remain loyal to your family (¶ 28) (Q 7).

DO YOUR STUDENTS KNOW . . .

Sharecropping is a system in which a farmer too poor to own land farmed another person's land in return for a small portion of the crop. This system was instituted in the South following the Civil War as a way to oppress freed slaves and maintain ownership of property. This caste system, based on land ownership rather than race, came to include poor whites without land and lasted until after World War II.

DISCUSSION

You may want to begin by discussing Faulkner's Yoknapatawpha County and the class structure embodied by the individuals who inhabit it. Faulkner begins "Barn Burning" by introducing the conflict Sarty sees between the world and his father. In the store, hungry and afraid because his father is not "providing" for his family, Sarty feels mostly "despair and grief, the old fierce pull of blood" (¶ 1). This conflict, between what is right or just for those outside the family and the pull of blood, drives the narrative and provides the conflict that will destroy the family (Q 4). Ask students what other conflicts are apparent here. They will probably mention North versus South, wealthy versus poor, and aristocratic versus "white trash," among others. In Abner's mind, and probably in the minds of DeSpain and the others who inhabit the story, the rigid class structure provides a kind of order — a code for living — that makes such conflicts unavoidable (Q 4).

Still, if Abner did not go out of his way to antagonize his employers, these conflicts would probably lie dormant, at least until another person with a sense of unfairness — which Abner seems to possess — came along and rebelled in some way. In this respect, one conflict in the story is the loss of an old order to a new, "progressive" (or New South) order. You may want to discuss the Group Activity on the Reconstruction era in the South at this time. Also, you can discuss Abner's lack of loyalty to his fellow soldiers or their cause during the Civil War.

To demonstrate the effect of these conflicts on Sarty, Faulkner uses the italicized passages, expressing the first-person point of view of Sarty himself. "Barn Burning" is, in this respect, Sarty's story. The third-person limited omniscient point of view, along with the first-person passages, reveals that Sarty is the one character who struggles with choices; he is the dynamic character who ultimately chooses justice over blood (Q 1, 2). Faulkner could have told the story from another point of view — Ab's or his wife's. But the adults have already made their choices; Sarty is in the process of choosing (Q 9).

Ask students what they think of Abner. His lack of loyalty and his entrepreneurship in horse-thieving are in some ways reminiscent of the opportunists who exploited the country during and after the Civil War. Does this make Abner "bad"? You might ask students *why* Abner feels that people owe him something

(Q 6). Some will suggest that he abuses Sarty by beating him. While this is true, Abner's "responses" to Sarty are always without "heat," as he hits the mules that pull the wagon. Abner's indignation is a carefully channeled rage that manifests itself in barn burning — a calculated and malicious act intended to make a clear statement about the inequities of class that were part of life in the post–Civil War South. Certainly the story has to do with Sarty's realization of his own moral vision. But over and above this is the social setting of the story, one in which men like Ab Snopes are never admitted into the houses of their social betters, except to do some menial task (Q 10). It is the disparity between what the "haves" own and what Abner cannot achieve that burns in him. The jealousy and rage — the results of what he perceives to be the unfairness of life — drive Abner to burn barns, an act that results in his death — if indeed the shot Sarty hears at story's end marks the death of Abner (Q 5, 7).

Sarty's faith in Abner, though shaken at the end of the story, indicates the child's need to believe in his father. Life is difficult enough for Sarty without the knowledge of what the story's third-person narrator reveals about Abner's character. Sarty's ignorance and innocence, the fact that he does not know the "truth" about his father, make him even more sympathetic (and pathetic) (Q 8).

This story works well when taught with "A&P," "Gryphon," and other initiation stories, and it also works well with "Daddy" or *Death of a Salesman* to examine difficult family relationships. A short video starring Tommy Lee Jones as Abner Snopes is part of PBS's American Short Story series. About thirty minutes long, it can generate good discussion of point of view, casting, arrangement of plot, and other topics. (If students are not sure whether Abner dies at the end of the video, have them count the number of people Sarty sees on the wagon as he watches his family leave town.)

The use of the word *nigger* in the story and the film is apt to make students (and instructors) uncomfortable. Note that the word appears in dialogue and that the word *Negro* is used in exposition. Ask students to discuss the connotations of these terms. Encourage them to think about how dialogue is used in this story to achieve realism as well as drama (Q 3). You should address this use of language before assigning the story.

FURTHER READING

Hiles, Jane. "Kinship and Heredity in Faulkner's 'Barn Burning.'" *Mississippi Quarterly* (Summer 1985): 329–37.

Skaggs, Merrill Maguire. "Story and Film in 'Barn Burning': The Difference a Camera Can Make." *Mississippi Quarterly* (Winter 1983): 5–15.

Skei, Hans H. "William Faulkner." *American Short-Story Writers, 1910–1945, Second Series.* Ed. Bobby Ellen Kimbel. *Dictionary of Literary Biography.* Vol. 102. Detroit: Gale, 1991. 75–102.

GISH JEN

Chin

WRITING ACTIVITIES

1. Ask students to rewrite a portion of the story from the point of view of Chin's father.
2. Ask students to write about an aspect of their culture that might be difficult for someone else to understand.
3. Ask students to write a short research essay on the difficulties faced by a particular group of immigrants to the United States.

GROUP ACTIVITIES

Divide the class into three groups. Ask the first group to discuss the narrator, the second group the narrator's father, and the third group Chin's mother. Pose the following question to each group: Is there anything your character could have done to keep Chin from being beaten? If so, why didn't he or she do it? If not, why not?

DO YOUR STUDENTS KNOW . . .

Methods of discipline by immigrants are often seen as abusive by American child protection services. According to Harvard psychologist Mary Waters, parents who come to America find a clash between accepted punishments in their native culture and those in their adopted home.

DISCUSSION

The boys at school torment Chin by throwing rocks at him because he is different and seems almost subhuman to them. The narrator feels compelled to join in so as not to become a target himself. He sympathizes with Chin, though, having seen how the other boy is beaten at home, and he tries to miss when he tosses his rocks (Q 4).

Most of what the narrator knows about the Chin family comes from living directly across from them. From this vantage point, he and his family are able to see and hear what happens in the Chins' kitchen — almost as if they were watching a television. Since most of the Chins' arguments are conducted in Chinese, the narrator and his family are restricted to making educated guesses about the violence occurring next door. If Chin himself were narrating the story or if he were able to confide in the narrator, we would have a clearer sense of the inner workings of his family, but we would lose the additional perspective that the narrator brings to the story (Q 2).

As the story progresses, it becomes clear how the cultural differences between the two families and the failure of the narrator's family to understand its neighbors preclude any chance of real communication. The narrator's family makes a number of unjustifiable assumptions about both Chinese and American culture.

His mother assumes that the Chins keep their windows closed because they are used to warmer weather in China, and the narrator believes that there is nothing culturally distinctive about his own family, which he refers to as "vanilla" (Q 6).

Chin's mother and sister return to their home because they have nowhere else to go. It is clear that the narrator's father is conflicted. On the one hand, he is upset by what he has seen and wants to help the two women. On the other hand, he is reluctant to become involved in what he considers to be another family's private affairs (Q 8).

Looking back, the narrator can view the differences between his family and Chin's with an appreciative eye. This is not to say the narrator enjoys a perfect family life. The relationship between his parents is not, to judge from the limited information we are given, a happy one. Still, the narrator can appreciate that he was subjected to corporal punishment only once and that he had a far easier life than someone like Chin. He can also see that his father, despite his indecisiveness, was a fundamentally decent man.

The narrator tells the reader early on that he has an exceptionally high IQ. This information is important for a number of reasons. It helps explain to some extent his feelings of sympathy for Chin, who he admits was smarter than he was. It may also help explain why Chin's predicament made such an impression on him (Q 3). The narrator is still, years later, an "underachiever." Chin, although he does quite well in English and history, receives only a C in math, and it appears that the beatings his father administers are intended to motivate him to do better (Q 7). It may be that, grateful as he is for his own relatively mild upbringing, the narrator wishes he, like Chin, had been pushed to apply himself more (Q 1).

You might consider teaching this story with "The Carnival Dog, The Buyer of Diamonds," "The Third and Final Continent," "What We Heard about the Japanese," and "What the Japanese Perhaps Heard."

BESSIE HEAD

Looking for a Rain God

WRITING ACTIVITIES

1. Ask students to propose ways that could have prevented the tragedy occurring in this story.
2. Ask students to rewrite the story from Ramadi's point of view.
3. Ask students to write a short research essay on famine in the southern part of Africa.

GROUP ACTIVITIES

Stage a trial for Mokgobja and Ramadi. Begin by dividing the class into two groups. One will brainstorm evidence for the prosecution, and the other for the defense. Assume that the two men have been charged with first-degree murder. Once the evidence has been gathered, let each of the opposing teams pick one member to represent it. Then pick a jury composed of an equal number of students from each of the opposing teams. Any students who have not yet been assigned a role can play the part of journalists covering the trail. Once the case is decided by the jury, all the students can discuss their experience.

DO YOUR STUDENTS KNOW . . .

Blood holds great significance in African traditional religions because blood is thought to cleanse individuals and society, as well as to pacify the spirits. Blood rituals, especially in sacrifices, are seen as a link between the physical and spiritual world.

DISCUSSION

The language of "Looking for a Rain God" is simple and clear, and the plot is uncomplicated, so students are unlikely to have significant difficulties with the stylistic aspects of the story. The chief challenge in teaching the story is that some students will be so horrified by the murder of the two girls that they will be unable to muster any sympathy for Mokgobja and Ramadi. Since the narrator is third-person and objective, we are given only slightly more access to the minds of the killers than to the minds of their victims. While this style of narration does allow the narrator to maintain a restrained tone throughout, it may also prevent some readers from identifying more closely with the two men (Q 1). If this issue comes up, be sure to emphasize the fact that it is possible to understand and even sympathize with a person without necessarily approving of his or her actions.

Remind students of the conditions the villagers enjoyed before the drought came. Although the landscape was hardly lush, water and food were relatively easy to find. As the drought progresses, the villagers' situation grows more and more desperate. When Mokgobja's family reaches their lands, the situation only grows worse. The entire family is under tremendous strain, and although the women do not really cause the deaths of the girls, their loss of self-control puts an additional mental stress on the men (Q 9). It is only the children who, because they do not realize the seriousness of the situation, carry on as before (Q 3). By the time Mokgobja and Ramadi sacrifice the two girls, they have been pushed to the breaking point by deprivation and the threat of starvation (Q 5). The family is ostensibly Christian and have been attending a Christian church for years, but as the situation worsens, they turn instead to the traditional religion of their people for a solution. This suggests that their belief in Christianity, however sincere it may be, is not as deeply rooted as their belief in the practices of their ancestors (Q 4).

It is clear that the narrator, although not condoning what the men have done, is sympathetic. The ending of the story is particularly bleak because, even though the killers are punished, there is no real sense that justice has been done (Q 6). The court that passes the sentence does not take into account — partly, no doubt, because they are so difficult to quantify — the tremendous stresses the men were under. Yet it is these stresses, aside from the details of the crime itself, that are the most pertinent facts in the case (Q 7). If there is a moral to the story, it is that human beings are capable of terrible things when placed under extreme stress.

It may be difficult for students in the present-day United States to imagine a natural catastrophe this prolonged (Q 2). In discussing the story with your students, you might stress the ways in which the African landscape itself is an antagonist and in which the story exemplifies the classic theme of humankind versus nature. Don't neglect, though, to touch on the other themes present in the story. Look in particular at the conflict between tradition and modernity and between the differing worldviews of native peoples and colonists (Q 8).

You might want to teach this story with "The Fireman," "The Lottery," "The Second Coming," and *Antigone*.

FURTHER READING

Beard, Linda Susan. "Bessie Head's Syncretic Fictions: The Reconceptualization of Power and the Recovery of the Ordinary." *Modern Fiction Studies* 37 (Fall 1991): 575–90.

MacKenzie, Craig. "Bessie Head." *South African Writers*. Ed. Paul A. Scanlon. *Dictionary of Literary Biography*. Vol. 225. Detroit: Gale. 205–12.

CHAPTER 9

STYLE, TONE, AND LANGUAGE

JAMES JOYCE

Araby

WRITING ACTIVITIES

1. Ask students to retell the story from the young woman's point of view.
2. Have students choose some of the imagery or details in the story — when Joyce describes the garden in back of the priest's house, for instance — and write about why these details are significant.
3. Ask students to write a one- or two-paragraph comparison of this story and "The Secret Lion," another story about innocence and disillusionment.

GROUP ACTIVITIES

Ask one group of students to record the religious allusions in the story and discuss how these serve to develop the central theme of lost innocence.

Another group of students should compare and contrast "Araby" with "A&P," which also describes a boy's hopeless infatuation with an unattainable woman and a richly detailed setting (the supermarket) that is central to the story (as the bazaar is in "Araby").

DO YOUR STUDENTS KNOW . . .

After centuries of colonization, the Act of Union of 1800 absorbed Ireland as a part of Great Britain. Ireland gained partial independence in 1916 when twenty-six of its thirty-two counties were named a free state. Ireland remains a nation split between independent republic and colonized land.

DISCUSSION

Begin by defining *epiphany* (a moment of illumination in which something hidden or not understood becomes immediately clear) and explaining its importance in modern fiction. Give examples from other stories. The epiphany in "Araby," according to Joyce, takes place during the discussion the boy overhears in the bazaar between the young girl and the two young gentlemen. It is at this moment that the boy sees Mangan's sister as a normal girl and not a holy icon, when he sees how vain and pretentious he has been — how average, normal, even vulgar the whole situation is. At this moment he decides to give up his quest. As defined by Joyce, *epiphany* means "a sudden spiritual manifestation, whether in the vulgarity of speech or of gesture in a memorable phrase of the mind itself" (Q 10). For the adult narrator, this epiphany is memorable because of the crushing disillusionment he feels and the lesson learned about life (Q 7).

This is a story of incongruities, of dramatic contrasts. Many of these contrasts are so subtle that most of your students will fail to see them or even believe they are there after you point them out. Every element of the piece — from diction to imagery — contributes to this effect. For instance, as the boy describes his deep love for the girl, his diction is quite formal, elevated, inflated, pompous, and overly romantic (¶ 5, 6, 24) (Q 1). This elevated speech is fueled not by a young boy's raging hormones, but by his naively romantic conceptions of love (Q 3). Juxtaposed against the young boy's formal diction is the common speech of his aunt and uncle and the banal conversation heard in the bazaar. The more emotional the boy is, the more figurative his language becomes (Q 2). This subtle parody of young love (and romance literature) lays the foundation for what occurs at the end of the story. The boy's language — syntax as well as diction — lends an almost religious significance to the girl and the bazaar ("I recognized a silence like that which pervades a church after a service," ¶ 25) while ignoring the banality of his day-to-day life in Dublin (Q 5). Between the two extremes of the girl and the exotic bazaar, Joyce describes the mundane existence of the boy in heroic terms, and the ironic situation becomes evident when the boy encounters reality at the end of the story (Q 4).

Words like *flaring, impinged, chafed,* and *girdled* show the heightened emotional state of a boy who is projecting his strong feelings outward. Joyce uses unusual words to do more than reflect the boy's emotional state; however, Joyce often deliberately chooses a word because it has ironic overtones and symbolic import (Q 6). For instance, the statement that North Richmond Street is "blind" suggests more than the fact that the street is a dead end: blindness — the inability to see clearly — is an important theme in the story. Another example of irony comes in ¶ 15, when the boy says "my heart 'misgave' me," for although his heart has doubts, it is his heart that has caused him to go on a false quest. And there are many other puns, such as when the boy's schoolmaster says in ¶ 12 that he hopes the boy is not "beginning to idle" (idol).

Like most of Joyce's details, the priest's choice of reading materials shows more than his literary taste; these books give the reader insight into both the priest and the boy, and they heighten the discrepancy between what the boy perceives and what the reader understands. All three of the books have central figures whose strange incongruities mirror the boy's mistaken beliefs. A queen regarded as a whore and murderess, a dead priest's Protestant manual, and a hero who escapes prison disguised as a nun — these deceptions reflect the boy's own falseness.

The story is filled with religious allusions, and these references serve to develop the theme of lost innocence central to the story. Early on, the boy is unable to clearly judge the priest, who is not nearly so "charitable" as the boy believes.

Linked with this description of the priest is an obvious description of a "wild garden" containing an apple tree in its center; this image suggests the forbidden fruit for which the boy searches so passionately throughout the story (Q 8). For more extensive information regarding literary and religious allusions in "Araby," refer to Harry Stone's excellent article listed below.

You may want to teach this story with "A&P," "Young Goodman Brown," "Doe Season," or *Oedipus the King* (innocence/experience).

FURTHER READING

Stone, Harry. "'Araby' and the Writings of James Joyce." *Antioch Review* 25 (1965): 375–410.
Wills, Walter. "John Updike's 'A&P': A Return Visit to Araby." *Studies in Short Fiction* 30.2 (1993): 127–33.

ANDREA BARRETT

The Littoral Zone

WRITING ACTIVITIES

1. Ask students to write about another setting in which Jonathan and Ruby could have met and fallen in love.
2. Ask students to suggest an alternative profession for Jonathan and Ruby and explain how this alternative might change the story.
3. Ask students to write a short research paper on the effects of divorce on children.

GROUP ACTIVITIES

Divide the class into groups and ask each group to prepare a scientific presentation on the relationship between Jonathan and Ruby. Encourage the students to use the board to diagram the various relationships and factors involved.

Divide the class into groups and ask each group to decide whether Jonathan and Ruby, having gotten divorced from their previous spouses, should have married each other.

DO YOUR STUDENTS KNOW . . .

While nearly half of first marriages will end in divorce, New York University's Child Center reports that 55 percent of second marriages will meet the same fate.

DISCUSSION

Students may initially be put off by the relative abundance of scientific terminology in this story. After all, words like *Fucus*, *Hildenbrandtia*, *hydrozoans*, *icthyologist*, and *ornithologist* do not often come up in the speech (or writing) of nonspecialists.

Although consulting the footnotes may be helpful, it is not necessary that readers have a full understanding of all the terms. The important thing to note, in most cases, is how the clinical nature of the language provides an ironic contrast to the passionate sexual attraction that develops between Jonathan and Ruby (Q 2).

The chief exception to the above rule is the term *littoral zone*, which as the title is central to the story. The littoral zone is defined in the story as "that space between high and low watermarks when organisms struggled to adapt to the daily rhythm of immersion and exposure." This definition applies not only to the physical landscape with which the two scientists are engaged when they first meet, but to their emotional life together. The narrator tells us that the two, once they began talking to each other, "swam in that odd, indefinite zone where they were more than friends, not yet lovers." There is also a parallel with their current life together, which seems to be constantly shifting, as does the story itself, between present and past. It is significant that Jonathan and Ruby, though they are scientists and therefore observers of natural processes, are not exempt from these processes themselves, even in their personal lives (Q 1, 8).

Tone is another, subtler issue of language. Although this is the story of a tumultuous, passionate relationship, the narrator's tone remains restrained throughout. Along with this restraint comes the omission of certain scenes that would have called for a more emotional tone. We are not privy, for example, to any of the fights the two must have had with their respective spouses. Nor do we see them trying to explain their actions to their young children. This restraint is entirely appropriate because the story is not so much about passion as about the ebbing of passion (Q 9, 10).

You might also want to discuss the different settings in the story. If the students do not notice it, point out the importance of the fact that Jonathan and Ruby meet on an island. Isolated from their families, tired and overworked, they are lonely and turn to each other (Q 5). Their isolation also makes it temporarily possible for them to forget that other people's lives will be affected by their affair. Without their families there, the two paint pictures of their home lives that are unrealistically gloomy (Q 3, 4). It is only when they return to the mainland and see their families waiting for them that they begin to understand the inevitable pain that they will cause their spouses and children (Q 11).

Ask the class whether Jonathan and Ruby, given the choice, would do it all again. When they first began their relationship, they were acting out of passion, and it is doubtful that kind of passion could coexist with the knowledge they now have of the consequences — bad and good — of their actions (Q 7). They are painfully aware of what they have lost — their original families, their jobs, their homes — and they are increasingly aware that what they gained — momentary satisfaction — does not seem adequate in retrospect (Q 6). All that they really have to talk about now is the past (Q 4).

Consider teaching this story with "A Primer for the Punctuation of Heart Disease," which discusses the ways in which the most important things are often unspoken, "Dog," which examines the damage done to a child as a marriage falls apart, and "Living in Sin," a portrait of a once passionate relationship that has become suffocating.

FURTHER READING

Cole, Diane. "From Andrea Barrett, Another Kind of Science Fiction." *Chicago Tribune Books* 4 Feb. 1996: 7.

Rauch, Molly E. "Review of Ship Fever and Other Stories, by Andrea Barrett." *Nation* 262 (1996): 32–33.

ERNEST HEMINGWAY

A Clean, Well-Lighted Place

WRITING ACTIVITIES

1. After a brief discussion of codes and how they operate in this story, ask students to write one or two paragraphs about codes of behavior they have had to follow, such as those found in the Boy Scouts, the military service, college, dorms, fraternities or sororities, or even their families. What are the positive and negative aspects of these codes? Are rules for sports any different? You may want to mention the 1992 movie *A Few Good Men*, which explores both the need for and the danger of behavior codes.
2. Have students write about a place in which they have taken refuge and what kind of comfort the place provided.

GROUP ACTIVITIES

Have groups of students copy down sentences from the story that seem awkward or at least unusual, such as sentence two in the story's first paragraph. Ask them to describe the kind of sentence structure most commonly used. In addition, ask them to determine if the diction is formal or informal and to support their conclusion by pointing to certain words. Finally, see if they can identify any figures of speech. How does the absence of these figures influence the style and tone of the story (Q 8)?

DO YOUR STUDENTS KNOW . . .

A strong correlation exists between alcohol use and suicide. In fact, many suicide victims have high levels of alcohol in their blood at the time of death.

DISCUSSION

You may want to begin your discussion by describing the Hemingway "code" to students. Explain how his heroes are frequently numb, emotionally wounded people who have had their values destroyed. Their only solace lies in a stoic acceptance of their fates. Frequently, their only escape from the cynicism and brutality of society is in simple, repetitive tasks. In these small arenas, it is still possible for them to face life with grace, dignity, and style.

Even though there is no "hero" in this story, the setting itself is a metaphor for Hemingway's code. Gradually, through the repetition of the words *clean* and *light,* and of the images associated with the café, the reader begins to realize that the bar is the stage on which the older waiter lives out his code of life. (Physical elements — the placement of light, the polished bar — compensate for the underlying sense of terrifying "nada," which, like the shadows themselves, surrounds this one clean oasis of light (Q 1). In living this way, the older waiter salvages something. He understands the difference between coming to a clean, well-lighted place like this and drinking at home: "It's not the same," he says (¶ 58). He understands the old man because both are aware of the nothingness surrounding them, and both are committed to the significance of the bar, the physical thing compensating for the loss of faith and hope — for Hemingway, abstract values.

The two waiters have entirely different concepts of "nada" (Q 10). As a result, when they repeat this word, the reader gradually becomes aware of its full significance and meaning, something that escapes the younger man, who lacks the experience, insight, and need (loneliness) old age brings. The clipped exchanges — especially in the opening dialogue — help highlight the differences between the two waiters and their ability to sympathize with the old, deaf customer (Q 2). The dark, somber tone of this story may not be oppressive to most readers because Hemingway's style — his use of short, declarative sentences and his omission of qualifying words and figures of speech — reflects the sparseness of the setting and the mood of a bar's closing time (Q 3). With what at first seems an objective, detached presentation, this style allows him to construct, slowly, image by image, a somber, haunting portrait of the older waiter. Only at the end of the story does the reader see fully the darkness within his soul. In this way, Hemingway's style and tone are superbly suited to the central point of his story: that we can salvage something from the "nada" if we do our work well and, above all else, retain our dignity (Q 4).

Hemingway uses Spanish in the story to indicate that the two waiters are actually speaking in that language. You might want to point out to students that, by using Spanish, Hemingway indicates that these men are speaking Spanish without distorting their words to approximate dialect (Q 5).

It is ironic that the café is described as "clean" and "pleasant" because late-night bars are usually anything but clean, and their inhabitants and mood anything but pleasant (Q 6). Gradually, as it does every night, darkness creeps into the bar and into the older waiter's consciousness. Toward the end of the story, Hemingway tries to convey this darkness to us by employing a limited omniscient point of view and taking us inside the thoughts of this character (¶ 76, 85, for example).

FURTHER READING

Beegel, Susan F. "Ernest Hemingway." *American Short-Story Writers, 1910–1945. Second Series.* Ed. Bobby Ellen Kimbel. *Dictionary of Literary Biography.* Vol. 102. Detroit: Gale, 1991. 127–65.

Johnston, Kenneth G. *The Tip of the Iceberg: Hemingway and the Short Story.* Greenwood, FL: Penkevill, 1987.

Smith, Paul. *A Reader's Guide to the Short Stories of Ernest Hemingway*. Boston: Hall, 1989.

FLANNERY O'CONNOR

A Good Man Is Hard to Find

WRITING ACTIVITIES

1. Some people consider the term *lady* to be politically incorrect. Ask students to try to define *lady*. What does it mean to be a "lady" today? What did it mean in 1955 when this story was first published? Is its connotation positive or negative? Why do students think some women object to the word's use?
2. Compare the values that O'Connor sees as representative of the Old South with those in Faulkner's "A Rose for Emily" that motivate Emily's actions and that determine how she is treated by others.
3. Write a monologue from The Misfit's point of view. What are his emotions and thoughts about the future after killing the family? This could be written in the form of a confession to a member of the clergy or to police.

GROUP ACTIVITIES

Many critics support the theory that O'Connor's writing possesses a "preoccupation with the demonic" and that she balances this preoccupation with a moment in which the character meets a God of grace. Preston M. Browning, Jr., describes these as "those moments when her characters undergo a traumatic collapse of their illusions of righteousness and self-sufficiency" (Petry). Divide students into three groups. Have one identify The Misfit's chances of grace and have another group identify the grandmother's moment of grace. The third group should look for any passages that might hint at a "preoccupation with the demonic."

BACKGROUND INFORMATION

O'Connor is a Catholic writer, and although not all critics choose to analyze her work in this religious context, at the heart of her characters' words and actions are theological concepts — faith, sin, free will, judgment, redemption, and grace. These ideas cannot be defined in general enough terms to satisfy all readers' religious faiths and experiences. Indeed, for O'Connor, such concerns are complex and reflect the mystery of existence. However, the following excerpts from her essays in *Mystery and Manners: Occasional Prose*, as well as commentary, should clarify O'Connor's authorial intentions in "A Good Man Is Hard to Find."

- On Catholic faith and artistic vision: "When people have told me that because I am a Catholic, I cannot be an artist, I have had to reply, ruefully, that because I am a Catholic, I cannot afford to be less than an artist. . . . Part of the complexity of the problem for the Catholic fiction writer will be the presence of grace as it appears in nature, and what matters for him is that his faith not become detached from his dramatic sense and from his vision of what-is" ("The Church and the Fiction Writer" 146–47). In another context, O'Connor details the basic beliefs of her faith: "The universe of the Catholic fiction writer is one that is founded on the theological truths of the Faith, but particularly on three of them which are basic — the Fall, the Redemption, and the Judgment" ("Catholic Novelists and Their Readers," 185).

To briefly explain these three concepts—

- The Fall is the original sin that came with Adam and Eve's disobeying God's will.
- The Redemption, made possible by Christ's crucifixion and resurrection, occurs with baptism's erasing of original sin.
- The Judgment comes after death, with God judging a person's life to determine whether the destination is heaven, purgatory, or hell.

- On sin, the devil, and salvation: "The serious writer has always taken the flaw in human nature for his starting point, usually the flaw in an otherwise admirable character. Drama usually bases itself on the bedrock of original sin. . . . For this reason the greatest dramas naturally involve the salvation or loss of the soul. . . . Our salvation is a drama played out with the devil, a devil who is not simply generalized evil, but an evil intelligence determined on its own supremacy" ("The Church and the Fiction Writer" 167–68). Whereas sin is the rejection of God's will (known through the Bible and the Church's doctrines and traditions), grace comes with the acceptance of God's will.
- On free will: "Does one's integrity ever lie in what he is not able to do? I think that usually it does, for free will does not mean one will, but many wills conflicting in one man. Freedom cannot be conceived simply" ("On Her Own Work" 115). Free will, then, involves conflicting choices of either accepting or rejecting God. This theological concept led to the Protestant Reformation in the sixteenth century, when John Calvin argued that salvation came from faith alone, as opposed to the Catholic Church's doctrine of a combination of faith and good works.
- On grace: O'Connor explains that in "A Good Man Is Hard to Find" the moment of grace offered and accepted is when the grandmother realizes that The Misfit "is one of her children" and thus recognizes "the mystery of God's will" ("On Her Own Work" 116). This necessary condition for salvation is God's gesture towards humans, and the person's heart must be open to receiving this moment of grace. One cannot realize salvation or redemption without being in a state of grace.

Thus, O'Connor believes that the grandmother's gesture — reaching out to The Misfit — makes this story work, because it signifies "the Divine life and our participation" in this sense of mystery. As O'Connor explains, "Her head clears for an instant and she realizes, even in her limited way, that she is responsible for the man before her and joined to him by ties of kinship which have their roots deep in the mystery she has been merely prattling about so far. And at this point, she does the right thing; she makes the right gesture" ("On Her Own Work" 111–12).

In fact, to underscore the grandmother's journey from sin to grace, O'Connor revised this story to make her more directly responsible for the family's fate. In an earlier published version (1953), road construction causes the detour. Ironically, grace comes as a result of The Misfit's violence. O'Connor has explained that "violence is strangely capable of returning my characters to reality and preparing them to accept their moment of grace. . . . I don't want to equate The Misfit with the devil. I prefer to think that, however unlikely this may seem, the old lady's gesture, like the mustard-seed, will grow to be a great crow-filled tree in The Misfit's heart, and will be enough of a pain to him there to turn him into the prophet he was meant to become" ("On Her Own Work" 112–13).

DO YOUR STUDENTS KNOW . . .

John Wesley, the founder of the Methodist Church, believed in salvation through obedience to God. His belief in the providence of God and his sense of mission may be related to his salvation from a burning building at age six.

DISCUSSION

Many students will find this story unnerving and may be unwilling to see beyond the violence. Some will see the violence as gratuitous; others will consider it appropriate, even necessary (Q 10). To help students move past their discomfort, you might begin by discussing the story's conclusion, looking at the circumstances surrounding The Misfit's shooting of the grandmother. Students may need some help understanding the concept of grace in order to see what effect O'Connor is creating here. If you explain this concept, they should be able to see that the grandmother's moment of identification with The Misfit (signaled by physical contact) helps her achieve a state of grace just before she is killed. Despite differences in upbringing, status, and "good works," the grandmother is, in essence, the same as The Misfit before God. Thus, although the grandmother has tried to play confessor to The Misfit, she learns that she too needs absolution. The closeness she feels to The Misfit is indeed a gift of grace (Q 9).

To further understand the impact of the grandmother's last gesture, students should discuss her development as a character up to that point in the story. Ask students to describe aspects of the grandmother that "fit" their understanding of what being a lady is. You should also ask them which of those aspects they find particularly troublesome. For example, students may point to her speech, as well as her concern for clothes, as reflecting her standing and her upbringing. Also, they may note that she is concerned about what kind of "people" one comes from, a typical interest for Southern gentility or those who, like the grandmother, aspire to gentility. On the negative side, they may note her habitual interfering (¶ 1, 2, 13) and her infatuation with the past (¶ 18, 22, 26, 45), seen in her reference to *Gone with the Wind* (¶ 24) (Q 6). She is attached to the life of the plantation, to a time in which class lines were clearly drawn (note her reaction to the "Negro" boy in ¶ 20). The quality of being a "lady" is certainly not presented positively here — it is ironic — and O'Connor uses the negative qualities to emphasize a connection between The Misfit and the grandmother. The grandmother's name is therefore not given, because she represents a type — a type of needy humanity, neither all good nor all bad.

In the same way, The Misfit is not given a name, only his criminal title. He, too, represents a type of humanity. Just as good and bad both reside in the grandmother, he too exhibits both qualities: His criminal nature demonstrates an expected negative trait, and his identification with Christ reveals an unexpected positive trait (¶ 129). In the end, he is transformed by the touch of the woman. Even though he recoils from her touch as if bitten by a snake, suggesting the "fallen" quality in both himself and the grandmother, he realizes that there is nothing in earthly life that could be pleasurable, not even the violence that marks his own life (¶ 142). This conclusion underscores O'Connor's theme: All humans need grace to find meaning in life.

The characters are portrayed negatively through figures of speech, selected dialogue, and narrator's comments. For example, Red Sam has a "stomach hung over [his trousers] like a sack of meal swaying under his shirt" (¶ 34). The words of June Star contribute to readers' poor opinions of her (¶ 4, 7, 31) (Q 2). Finally, the narrator's sarcastic tone adds to our dislike for both the grandmother and the father: "he didn't have a naturally sweet disposition like she did" (¶ 29) (Q 1). One interesting point about these characters is that, despite their own good opinions of themselves, they fail to exhibit the virtues of truly good people. Indeed, a good man *is* hard to find. See ¶ 37–43.

This story also builds characterization through the use of language. The grandmother tends to use fairly standard speech; however, she also makes use of Southern colloquialisms — vulgar language, really — such as *pickaninny* and *nigger*, which give away pretention to gentility (Q 3). The Misfit, on the other hand, uses a dialect that suggests his uneducated status, yet it is rhythmic, poetic — even biblical (compare ¶ 109, 112) (Q 5). The monotonous pattern of his speeches suggests that the events of his life have become blurred and that he has fallen into cycles of violence. Sometimes he seems to be in a trance — or possessed — or on automatic pilot. The repetitions and rotations reflect his inability to connect the crimes with the punishments as well as his feeling of being trapped by a system from which he cannot escape, a condition many people experience today. Here again the universality of his type is clear: a misfit, trapped by the absurdity of life (Q 8).

The obvious class connotations of The Misfit's speech highlight another feature of the story that students need to see: irony. One example of irony is that the lower-class criminal, The Misfit, attempts to be polite (¶ 109) (Q 4). Another is that the "lady" uses words like *nigger*. The irony again underscores the ambivalence that O'Connor portrays in determining who is good and who is bad — some of the very characteristics that should define a "lady" are found in a brutal criminal, and vice versa. Absolute good or evil is not to be found in people. Another instance of irony is the narrator's comment about the reason the grandmother dresses up for the trip: If she were found dead on the road, she would still be seen as a lady. Iron-ically, she not only dies but also does so in a most unladylike circumstance (Q 4). In addition, her comment is one of many subtle foreshadowings that occur in the story: for example, the earlier references to The Misfit (¶ 1, 40) and the descrip-tion of the car carrying the three men as "hearse-like" (¶ 70) (Q 7).

To close your discussion, you might ask students to consider the implications of the title, in light of both the story and what they have learned about O'Connor's views about faith and grace. The title reflects the biblical principle of Romans 3:23: All people are fallen, and all are in need of grace. Reading I Timothy will provide additional insights into the story's theme about family values and explain why Timothy is the story's only place name not on the map of Georgia. Also con-sider the story of Diogenes, who went around with a lantern looking for an hon-est man but never found one.

You might want to teach this story with "Where Are You Going, Where Have You Been?," "Harlem," or *Death of a Salesman* (American dream/nightmare). Also consider comparisons with "A&P," "Once upon a Time," or *Oedipus the King* (innocence/experience).

FURTHER READING

Asais, Frederick, ed. "*A Good Man Is Hard to Find*." New Brunswick, NJ: Rutgers UP, 1993.

May, John R. "Flannery O'Connor." *American Novelists Since World War II*. Ed. Jef-frey Helterman and Richard Layman. *Dictionary of Literary Biography*. Vol. 2. Detroit: Gale, 1978. 382–87.

O'Connor, Flannery. *Mystery and Manners: Occasional Prose*. Ed. Sally and Rob-ert Fitzgerald. New York: Farrar, 1969.

Petry, Alice Hall. "Miss O'Connor and Mrs. Mitchell: The Example of 'Every-thing That Rises.'" *The Southern Quarterly* 27.4 (summer 1989): 5–15.

Zaidman, Laura Mandell, ed. *A Good Man Is Hard to Find*. The Heinle Casebook Series in Reading, Research, and Writing. Laurie G. Kirszner and Stephen Mandell, ser. eds. Boston: Heinle, 1999.

TIM O'BRIEN

The Things They Carried

WRITING ACTIVITIES

1. Ask students to write a creative paper describing a group therapy session for surviving members of the company who are trying to adjust after the war.
2. Have students write a letter from Lieutenant Cross to Martha, describing any of the events or characters from the story.
3. Let students compare the story to any of the war poems in the book.
4. Ask students to write a letter requesting a disability pension on grounds of post-traumatic stress disorder from the point of view of Jimmy or another man in his outfit.

GROUP ACTIVITIES

Ask students to look up the word *carry* in the dictionary (or you may bring in an enlarged photocopy of an entry) listing all the definitions and senses of the word that they can find. Then, ask them to see how many uses of the word they can discover in the story. As they explore these various meanings, they will begin to see that "carrying" plays multiple roles in the story: It is a descriptive term for the monotony and senselessness of the war, but it is also an active part of the soldiers' coping (Q 2, 3).

DO YOUR STUDENTS KNOW . . .

One lingering legacy of Vietnam is the fate of the nearly 2,000 men listed as Missing in Action (MIA). Both the U.S. and Vietnamese governments claim no servicemen remain alive, but some families of MIAs believe their loved ones may still be alive. Efforts continue to find and return bodies of those unaccounted for.

DISCUSSION

There are several ways of approaching a discussion of this story. First, since the story appears under the heading of style, tone, and language, you might begin by asking how each of these elements relates to the story's theme. For example, the strong language ("fuck off," "What the hell," and so on) lends realism to the story. Also, there are no quotation marks in the story, so that narrative and dialogue are interwoven, adding to the sense of ambiguity and blurring alluded to in ¶ 39. The story's flat tone reinforces these themes as well, creating a sense of emotional detachment for men whose "principles were in their feet" (¶ 39) (Q 1). Finally, the use of "hard vocabulary to contain the terrible softness" (¶ 67) emphasizes a dichotomy between the reality of the war and the mechanisms the characters use to shield themselves from the pain and horror they experience every day. The language may seem cruel and inhumane to students, but O'Brien shows how it necessarily distances a soldier from the facts of the war. This distancing, like the things soldiers carry, is a coping device (Q 7).

Students should also notice the length of paragraphs throughout the story. The general pattern begins with one or two long paragraphs, followed by one or more very short paragraphs. Then there are more long paragraphs consisting of detailed lists. This pattern reflects the paths that the men follow: Long boring stretches interrupted by sudden short episodes of violence, such as the death of Lavender and the burning of Than Khe (Q 5).

Another stylistic device used to highlight ambiguity and senselessness is repetition. For example, the repetition of the fact of Lavender's death (every reference to him mentions that he was shot) underscores the theme of monotony; facts and places run together for the soldiers. The repeated references to Martha also add to this effect, serving as a constant reminder of a world outside the craziness of the war (Q 6). Finally, the repeated long lists give the reader the feeling of plodding and restlessness that the soldiers feel (Q 4). This combination of brutality and monotony is also reflected in "Dulce et Decorum Est."

The constant repetition may make it difficult for students to see elements of a plot; however, they should be able to identify a traditional exposition, climax, and denouement. The exposition introduces the main characters and the basic device of listing, which will hold the entire story together. The climax begins in ¶ 19, with the full details of the episode surrounding Lavender's death. Notice that this is the only event in the story that has a date — April 16. All the other facts of the story are presented in relation to Lavender's death. Thus, the development of the plot is determined by the various characters' reactions to Lavender's death.

The denouement is interesting in that it shows how the men deal with the absurdity of the war. For example, they joke about finding a moral for Lavender's senseless, random death. Students should look at how different characters respond to the situation: Cross feels guilt; Kiowa is just glad to be alive and wants to talk; Sanders and Dobbins try to be funny. Consequently, the entire company burns the village, trashing everything. Each man is trying, in his own way, to carry (and deal with) the senselessness of Lavender's death (Q 3), and together they engage in an equally senseless act of "retaliation."

Students may need some background on the Vietnam War and the political environment that surrounded it in the late sixties and early seventies. Since "carrying" things parallels the soldiers' attempts to find a purpose for their stay in Vietnam, students need to understand the differences between this war and previous wars in which the United States has been involved. Ask the students if they know why the United States was in Vietnam. (Some of them may have parents who served there.) Then ask them if they can find a statement of the U.S. mission anywhere in the story. As the students begin to see that there is nothing certain about what the men are doing in Vietnam, nothing to tie together all the things that they carry, they will begin to understand how detached the men and their actions are from the causes of the war. Those tangible things that they carry become the reference points for their lives: "for all the ambiguities of Vietnam, all the mysteries and the unknowns, there was at least the single abiding certainty that they would never be at a loss for things to carry" (¶ 39).

Students should also note that the craziness of the war was not just a result of the American presence. O'Brien draws a forceful parallel between the two adversaries in the war by describing the dead Viet Cong soldier whose thumb becomes a souvenir and good luck charm for Bowker (¶ 28). Although the VC soldier does not get the same treatment that Lavender does, some students will say that a certain amount of respect is shown for him — "he patted the stomach, almost affectionately" (¶ 30) — and others will suggest that the VC is dehumanized while Lavender is very human. In both deaths, the soldiers look for a moral. Ask students to compare the morals of the Vietnamese soldier's death and Lavender's death: without a larger framework, the ending of both lives is crazy and pointless (Q 9).

To close the discussion of the story, you might ask students to think about a possible sequel to the story. Will Cross really be able to change, to let go of the images that he carried as an escape tool and give himself fully to the war? Students should note that Cross's burning of Martha's pictures is a symbolic gesture of his complete removal from the world outside the war (Q 6). Finally, ask students to consider what will happen to the soldiers in their attempt to "carry on" (¶ 100) (Q 8).

This story is "metafiction," defined by critic David Lodge as "fiction about fiction: novels and stories that call attention to their fictional status and their own compositional procedures" (*The Art of Fiction*, Penguin). Some readers find this sort of fiction overly self-conscious, even distracting — and, therefore, not "real." Do your students find the stylistic devices intrusive, or does the complex language add something vital to the story (Q 10)?

You might want to teach this story with poems about war, such as "Dulce et Decorum Est," "For the Union Dead," or "Death of the Ball Turret Gunner."

FURTHER READING

Baughman, Ronald, ed. *Dictionary of Literary Biography Documentary Series*. Vol. 9. Detroit: Gale, 1991. 137–214.

Harris, Robert R. "Too Embarrassed to Kill." *New York Times Book Review* 11 Mar. 1990: 8.

CHAPTER 10

SYMBOL AND ALLEGORY

NATHANIEL HAWTHORNE

Young Goodman Brown

WRITING ACTIVITIES

1. Write a series of diary entries describing the changes in Brown from Faith's point of view. How does she expect to deal with him in the future?
2. Ask students to write about two or three characters who are isolated from society, comparing both the causes and results of their isolation — for example, Goodman Brown, Emily ("A Rose for Emily"), Abner Snopes ("Barn Burning"), the narrator of "The Yellow Wallpaper," Krogstad in *A Doll House*, and so on.

GROUP ACTIVITIES

Assign three groups of students one of the following critical perspectives — psychoanalytic, biographical, and feminist — and have them interpret "Young Goodman Brown" from that viewpoint.

Using the twelve interpretations of "Young Goodman Brown" found in *Nathaniel Hawthorne: Young Goodman Brown*, edited by Thomas E. Connolly, choose six students to lead discussions on how each critic views the story.

Ask another group of students to compose Brown's obituary as it might appear in a church bulletin.

DO YOUR STUDENTS KNOW . . .

Although many theories explain the reasons behind persecution of innocents as witches, money may have been the root of evil in Salem. Disputes based on economics and social lines split Salem literally in two: Salem village and the town. These conflicts may have fueled the hysteria.

DISCUSSION

Many students who are encountering literature for the first time will find this story a challenge because they are used to a single "right" interpretation of a work. As students begin the story, they will soon make the obvious allegorical connections, and they may think that the entire story has a neat, fixed interpretation. For example, they will recognize that Young Goodman Brown represents the common or nondescript (Brown), inexperienced (Young), and upstanding (Goodman) citizen who has not yet had his faith tested. Faith, the wife, represents the faith that connects him to that which is good. In the same way, the forest represents the dark side, the evil that is part of human nature, whereas the town of Salem is the seat of light and goodness (Q 5, 6).

However, the allegory is not so clear-cut. First of all, Hawthorne carefully weaves expressions of uncertainty throughout Brown's forest experience, so the reader is never sure whether the events are real or imagined (¶ 13, 36, 42, 56, 71). Do citizens of Salem gather in the wood for a Satanic ceremony? Are they just going about their daily business? Has Brown dreamed it all (Q 7)? Thus, the story has more than a single literal meaning and a single allegorical meaning. The introductory material in the chapter suggests, for example, that the staff the old man carries is a symbol with multiple referents, creating a complex vision of sin in the story. In the same way, the pink ribbons that Faith wears may suggest innocence, the presence of good on Earth, a simple reminder of faith, or simply femininity. They are pink, reflecting the ambiguous mix of both innocence (white) and experience (red). The presence of the ribbons, like the staff, suggests more than a one-to-one correspondence of the literal and the figurative (Q 6).

As students struggle to sort out the differences between symbol and allegory, between a single meaning and many, they will begin to understand the role of ambiguity in the story. Hawthorne's stories, and this one in particular, emphasize the natural depravity in all people, even the most pious saints. However, people are not wholly evil, as is suggested by the devil in the story: "evil is the nature of mankind" (¶ 65). Human beings must live with a certain degree of ambiguity because evil and good coexist, as do the reason of the intellect and the passion of the heart (cf. Romans 7:21: "So I find this law at work: When I want to do good, evil is right there with me"). This ambiguity makes it impossible to find a coherent theological message in this story (Q 10).

The creation of ambiguity is important to Hawthorne as a writer; most of his fiction centers on such ambiguities as are found in this story. It is Brown's inability to tolerate this coexistence of good and evil that leads to his misery and unhappy death at the end of the story (Q 8, 9). You might ask students why Hawthorne extends the story to Brown's death, rather than ending it after the vision. The effects of Brown's "absolutism" lead to isolation and misery.

The third-person narrative point of view, which is limited to the thoughts of Brown, also adds to the story's ambiguity. With a first-person narrator, one expects to have some unanswered questions because the view of one person is likely to be incomplete. This third-person narrator, however, does not supply answers to Brown's questions or clarifications for his misunderstandings. Rather, he addresses readers directly (¶ 72), telling them to decide for themselves about the veracity of the story. Thus, the narrator's ambiguity —his playful obfuscation — underscores the ambiguity in the whole work (Q 1).

Brown's journey is necessary because all humans are tempted to taste what is evil, "to penetrate, in every bosom, the deep mystery of sin" (¶ 63). Furthermore, initiation is also required of people. If they are to truly live, they must test their souls — wrestle with the moral choices available to them. In a sense, then, Brown's journey is a journey into his own soul — to see what is there and how he can deal with it (Q 3). For this reason, Brown's companion on the road is not unexpected (¶ 12) because he is ready to taste the other side. However, Faith, in both the literal and allegorical senses, causes him to hesitate a bit and be late (Q 2).

What Brown finds is that he shares with everyone a common desire to sin — and in this case, almost all the sins attributed to the community around him are sexual (aborted babies, elders who desire young girls, and so on) (Q 4). Whether hidden or flaunted, sexual desires are common to all people — especially to a newlywed such as Brown who, presumably, has experienced sex for the first time. By refusing the sinful part of himself, he rejects the community of the fallen and, by implication, all of humanity.

This rejection accompanies him back into the light of Salem. Since he will not participate in the community of the fallen, he cannot participate in the community of the saints. Thus, in two senses, he rejects community. For Hawthorne, isolation is damnation. While avoiding the moral sins toward which the darkness of his heart yearns, Brown commits a more grievous error: developing a sense of pride. He becomes psychologically twisted, unable to recognize his kinship with the other members of the community. He chooses to fight the evil of the world alone, much as he is alone in his rejection of evil in the forest. Some critics have also suggested that he intellectualizes his struggle, separating the head from the heart, thereby creating a lack of balance in his life (Q 8).

Because this story is rich in symbolism and suggests several interpretations, you might wish to use the work as an exercise in the practice of literary criticism.

You may want to teach this story with "A Rose for Emily," "Barn Burning," "The Yellow Wall-Paper," or *A Doll House*.

FURTHER READING

Connolly, Thomas E., ed. *Nathaniel Hawthorne: Young Goodman Brown.* Columbus, OH: Merrill, 1968.

Shaw, Patrick W. "Checking Out Faith and Lust: Hawthorne's 'Young Goodman Brown' and Updike's 'A&P.'" *Studies in Short Fiction* 23 (Summer 1986): 321–23.

SHIRLEY JACKSON

The Lottery

WRITING ACTIVITIES

1. Have students write about a situation in which a change was overdue, but any proposal to improve it was met with "but that's the way we've always done it."
2. Have students choose one of the characters in the story and write a page of stream-of-consciousness showing what that person is thinking during the ritual.
3. Have students report on Jackson's responses to the letters she received concerning "The Lottery." You will find these in *Come Along with Me* (New York: Viking, 1968).

GROUP ACTIVITIES

Divide the students into two groups. One group should explore possible interpretations of the following symbols in the story: the village square, Mrs. Hutchinson's apron, Old Man Warner, slips of paper, the black spot, summertime, the block box itself, and the names Adams, Summers, Graves, Warner, and Delacroix (Q 1, 2, 3, 4, 5). The second group should research familiar rituals, such as weddings and funerals, and address the symbols that are closely linked to them.

DO YOUR STUDENTS KNOW . . .

According to a study conducted in the 1970s by psychologist Stanley Milgram, people remained obedient to authority even when ordered to inflict pain upon another person. "Teachers" (study participants) were instructed to punish "students" (actors for the study) by inflicting electric shocks for incorrect responses to questions. Sixty percent of the participants sent out the maximum 450 volts of electricity when encouraged to do so by study administrators.

DISCUSSION

After students have prepared the group activities above, have them present this information to the class. The many possible answers they suggest will demonstrate that symbols, unlike allegorical elements, have a range of meaning. Base your discussion on the explanation at the beginning of Chapter 10, which also addresses the black box.

In discussing the ritual findings from the group activities, have students describe personal rituals such as the way their families celebrate holidays or birthdays, the way they prepare for a big test, or the process they go through to get ready for a date. Be sure to talk about the power of ritual and its importance in communities and to individuals.

Students may wonder how a ritual can continue even after those who participate in it have forgotten its significance. Ask them to try to explain why married couples wear rings or why brides throw their bouquets after the wedding (Q 9).

First-time readers may be shocked at developments in the story. They will be interested to learn that when the story first appeared in *The New Yorker* in 1948, it evoked a considerable response. Ask students why they think people would have been upset, even angry (Q 10).

"The Lottery" creates conflict within readers, as we grow more and more uncomfortable with what is happening in the story. Some students may suggest that the conflict emerges when Tessie Hutchinson starts to resist complying with the ritual. Ask them to discuss *why* the lottery has continued for generations. (Their answers can only be speculative, as the story does not offer explanations.) Expect students to be uncomfortable with the ritual. They will also see that, except for Mrs. Hutchinson, no one seriously questions the ritual. Someone might recognize that the conflict in the story is between the reader's skepticism and the characters' blind acceptance of a violent tradition. You may find it interesting to talk about the harmful power of superstitions and mindless conformity, as well as the effectiveness of the element of surprise that Jackson achieves. You may want to suggest another conflict in the story: between the characters' dark actions and the picture-perfect setting. On the simplest level, conflict occurs at the end between Tessie and the others, but the story's conflicts run deeper than this. The key to the story lies in understanding that the lottery is a sacrificial fertility ritual held each June to insure bountiful crops. Old Man Warner says, "Lottery in June, corn be heavy soon" (¶ 32).

Have students find foreshadowing, which becomes more pronounced as the story unfolds. They may comment on the facts that the children are nervous — boys talk quietly initially, and girls talk among themselves (¶ 2); the men's jokes are quiet — they smile, but do not laugh (¶ 3); villagers keep a distance from the box and hesitate when asked to help (¶ 4). There is also Jack Watson's response (¶ 16) and the men's behavior (¶ 20) (Q 7, 8). Students should also mention the boys' piling stones, the setting in the village square, and Mrs. Hutchinson's growing uneasiness.

Students are usually more comfortable discussing irony than other conventions. This story offers them many opportunities to do so, beginning with the title and its connotations, especially in this day when state lotteries promise people a lifetime income (Q 6). Students will recognize irony in the villagers' hurry to get home for lunch (¶ 1), in Mrs. Hutchinson's concern about leaving dishes in the sink (¶ 9), in her friendliness with Mrs. Delacroix, who then chooses a stone so large she can hardly carry it (¶ 8, 74), and in her willingness to participate until Bill draws the black mark (¶ 45 marks the beginning of her change).

The mob violence that occurs in "The Lottery" is ritualistic; whereas in "The Ballad of Rudolph Reed," it comes from fear and prejudice. In each case, it is a dehumanized ganging up on an innocent person.

FURTHER READING

Jackson, Shirley. *Come Along with Me: Part of a Novel, Sixteen Stories, and Three Lectures*. Ed. Stanley E. Hyman. New York: Penguin, 1995.

Janeway, Elizabeth. "The Grotesque around Us." *New York Times Book Review* 9 Oct. 1966: 58.

Nebeker, Helen E. "'The Lottery': Symbolic Tour de Force." *American Literature* 46 (Mar. 1974): 100–07.

ALICE WALKER

Everyday Use

WRITING ACTIVITIES

1. Ask students to write one paragraph on what quilts mean to Maggie and one paragraph on what they mean to Dee/Wangero.
2. Have students write about the title's significance.

GROUP ACTIVITIES

Divide the students into two groups. Ask the first group to select specific passages from the text that foreshadow the outcome of the story. Have the second group of students research the story of the Prodigal Son and compare it to "Everyday Use."

DO YOUR STUDENTS KNOW . . .

Quilts, long recognized as a part of Americana, were used by slaves heading North as maps to freedom. Specific quilt patterns contained covert signals. The quilt itself was hung on a fence or clothesline so runaway slaves could see it as they passed.

DISCUSSION

You could begin by having students who have family-made quilts at home ask their parents or grandparents where they came from, or have them identify any other heirlooms they or their parents may have. Quilts have received a great deal of attention recently. Alice Walker's essay "In Search of Our Mothers' Gardens" would be worth sharing with your class. In this work, Walker celebrates both gardens and quilts as ancestral forms of creativity. Your students have probably heard of the AIDS quilt and will appreciate what it stands for. Also ask them to look at the quilt on the cover of their text and at the inside front cover that explains the significance of the quilt's patterns. Patchwork quilts were traditionally made from old clothes or leftover fabric. It took a community effort to piece the top and to complete the quilting process. Some traditional quilt names, in addition to the ones in the text, are Wedding Ring, Double Wedding Ring, Log Cabin, Trip Around the World, Ohio Star, Churn Dash, Rail Fence, and Court House Steps (Q 1).

Unlike the symbols in "The Lottery," which are closely allied with ritual, those in "Everyday Use" have different meanings for the three women. For Maggie, quilts symbolize her everyday life, her devotion to her family, and her fond memories. For Dee/Wangero, they, like her new name, represent a heritage that is for show, not for use. She wants to hang the quilts on her wall — perhaps to impress her politically correct friends, but not to shelter the intimacy of marriage, childbirth, and growing old with someone (Q 2, 3). In the dasher, the mother sees the handprints from hours of churning; Dee/Wangero sees an artistic arrangement. "Dee" is a family name; she changes that to one more culturally correct (Q 4). To the narrator, heritage means people — Aunt Dee, Stash, her husband, her church, her community. To Dee/Wangero, heritage is in the abstract and is capitalized. The one place Dee/Wangero seems genuinely at home is at the dinner table, which provides basic nourishment. Ironically, she could find the emotional and psychic nourishment she seeks if she embraced her upbringing as enthusiastically as she has her "roots" (Q 6, 7, 9).

In addition to the quilts, other things have symbolic significance in the story. For example, the family yard suggests safety and warmth — although the family must work hard to keep it clean. Dee's Polaroid camera suggests her superficiality and modernity. It also stands as a reminder of the bankruptcy of a society that values instant gratification more than it does the work and craft that go into making a quilt (Q 8).

Because this story contains many details, students should look closely at the descriptions of the mother (¶ 5, 13), Maggie (¶ 7, 9), the arrival of Dee/Wangero (¶ 19, 20, 21), and the home (¶ 1, 14). You may need to explain the processes of churning butter, decorating the yard with designs as it was swept every morning, and the mother's request to "ream it out," meaning to pronounce slowly, syllable by syllable.

Some students will not understand why the mother gives the quilts to Maggie instead of to Dee/Wangero; they will think that displaying them is more important than using them. You could stage an interesting debate among your students about this issue. Which sister do they think should get the quilts? Maggie willingly relinquishes the quilts because she has gotten used to second-best, and no one has ever said "no" to Dee. Also, Maggie knows she has the memories to cherish (Q 5).

Some of your students will consider Dee greedy and egocentric, interested only in what she can get. Has her education helped her or alienated her from the family? What function does the television show serve? Ask students which of the two daughters is more contented with her life. Maggie accepts her past as a part of herself; Dee sees the past as something separate from herself (Q 3).

If you are teaching this story to students who live at school and have been at college for longer than one semester, ask them to write about how home is now "different" from what they remember before going to school. You may also have them write about how education can divide families.

You may want to teach this story as a companion to "Two Kinds." Quilts also play an important part in *Trifles*. Some students have said that this story reminds them of the New Testament story of the Prodigal Son. Summarize the Prodigal Son story and encourage a discussion about it. Like many other southerners of her generation, Walker (b. 1944) was raised on Bible stories (Q 10).

FURTHER READING

Christian, Barbara T. "Alice Walker." *Afro-American Fiction Writers after 1955*. Ed. Thadious M. Davis and Trudier Harris. *Dictionary of Literary Biography*. Vol. 33. Detroit: Gale, 1984. 258–71.

Walker, Alice. *In Search of Our Mothers' Gardens*. San Diego: HBJ, 1983.

———. *The Writer on Her Work*. London: Virago P, 1992.

RAYMOND CARVER

Cathedral

WRITING ACTIVITIES

1. Ask students to rewrite the story from the blind man's perspective.
2. Ask students to write a short research essay on the ways in which the blind perceive reality.

3. Ask students to write about a time when they found they had misjudged or underestimated someone.

GROUP ACTIVITIES

Break the class into three groups. Ask each group to decide on a symbol that could have been used in place of the cathedral.

DO YOUR STUDENTS KNOW . . .

The Federal Communications Commission licenses ham, or amateur, radio operators who create an on-air community across the globe for pleasure and are called on in times of natural disasters when other communication modes fail. The ARRL, the national association for amateur radio, is the largest organization of ham radio operators in the country; they currently have 163,000 members.

DISCUSSION

Much depends on how students view the narrator. There a number of points, especially early in the story, where he says and does things that may make them cringe. On the one hand, if they initially view him as wholly unsympathetic, they may not care about the breakthrough he achieves by story's end. On the other hand, if they are oblivious to his shortcomings, they may not see that he has made a breakthrough at all.

The narrator never tells us his name, but we learn a good deal about him. He has difficulty communicating with his wife; he is insecure about their relationship; he drinks too much, and he smokes marijuana; he is unhappy with his job; he has an irrational prejudice against the blind, and he may be a racist. Even before the blind man arrives, the narrator is bothered by the visit. Not only does the blind man have a relationship with his wife that predates his own, but also his wife is able to share things with the blind man that she never could share with her own husband. The relationship is intimate in another, more tangible way: The last time his wife and the blind man saw each other, the blind man touched her face. She remembers this so clearly because it was the only time anyone had tried to "see" her face with his hands. Even on a physical level, then, the blind man knows the narrator's wife in a way that he cannot.

The cathedral is obviously the central symbol of the story. To the blind man, it represents the human endeavor, a task no one of us will ever see completed. The symbol has other meanings as well. Cathedrals are meeting places between Earth and heaven, places of transcendence. For the narrator, his participation in the drawing of a cathedral is a moment in which he rises above his narrow individualism. By drawing a cathedral with the blind man, the narrator is able to "see" a new way of experiencing the world, a way that involves sharing with another person. If he and his guest were both able to watch the television, they would each see the cathedral without needing to communicate with each other. Each would be left with his own vision of the world. The narrator is initially unable to describe the cathedral because he is not used to communicating what he knows to another person. One of the questions the story raises is whether one can fully know or experience something in isolation from others. There are other, less striking symbols throughout the story that touch on the same basic theme. The three characters share drinks and a meal. The narrator's wife and the blind man share thoughts and experiences via cassette tapes. The narrator and the blind man share a joint. It could also be said that the narrator and the blind man share different but complementary knowledge of the narrator's wife.

In the end, the narrator experiences the same kind of learning that his wife does via her recorded correspondence and will perhaps be more emotionally open to her himself. (Q 10) She had presumably left her previous husband because she was unable to get close to him (or to anyone else, because of their frequent moves). When she married the narrator, then, she must have hoped he would be someone with whom she could communicate. We know from his narration that he is both perceptive and capable of growth. The blind man, who helped her through the dissolution of her first marriage, may have saved her second.

You might consider teaching this story with "Battle Royal," "On First Looking into Chapman's Homer," and "God's Grandeur." Each selection involves a moment of discovery.

FURTHER READING

Nesset, Kirk. "Insularity and Self-Enlargement in Raymond Carver's 'Cathedral.'" *Essays in Literature* 21 (Spring 1994): 116–29.

Trussler, Michael. "The Narrowed Voice: Minimalism and Raymond Carver." *Studies in Short Fiction* 31 (Winter 1994): 23–38.

RICHARD RUSSO

Dog

WRITING ACTIVITIES

1. Ask students to write a paragraph about why the narrator chose to name the dog after it had already died.
2. Ask students to write the scene in which the father tells his wife and son he is leaving them.
3. Ask the students to retell the story in the father's words.

GROUP ACTIVITIES

Have groups of students brainstorm an alternative title for the story. Each group should be prepared to explain why its title works as well as, or better than, Russo's.

DO YOUR STUDENTS KNOW . . .

More than half of American dog owners say that they are more attached to their pet than to another person, reports the American Pet Association. Nearly 7 million compare their feelings for a pet to those for their children.

DISCUSSION

Most students, even those who do not like dogs, will be able to relate to and sympathize with the narrator's predicament. Difficulties will most likely arise not with what the story says directly, but with what it leaves unsaid. It will be important to spend a fair amount of discussion time on why the father gets his son such a decrepit dog and on the ways in which the son will be different from his father.

Although the narrator begins "Dog" by saying that it is his parents' story, it is really the story of the dissolution of a family, of a child starved for understanding, a mother left alone to cope with a situation she is incapable of handling, and a father who is so uninterested that his eventual abandonment of his family must seem almost redundant (Q 1). The fact that both of the narrator's parents tell the story in almost the same way serves to give it an added sense of objectivity (Q 2).

On the one hand, the narrator wants a dog because he is a lonely child. His parents, on the other hand, do not want a dog for the same reasons that they really do not want a child. His parents, especially his father, do not want to deal with a being that is willful, energetic, and mischievous; they do not want to deal with any being that will not listen to what adults term "reason" (Q 4). This is why his father gets his son a dog that is so old: it will be less trouble (Q 5). The dog is a concession, something to keep his son quiet and under control; for the son, it is a symbol of his parents' refusal to give him the understanding he needs (Q 8).

The first time in the story that the father shows any real interest in his son is when the boy names the dead dog "Red." It is admittedly a strange time to name a dog, but the narrator feels the need to personalize his connection to the dog he got and then lost within the space of a half hour. To do otherwise would have been to show the same insensitivity that characterizes his father (Q 6). Strangely enough, the narrator becomes, through this act of quiet defiance, more interesting to his father. The father, who has always been more interested in books than in his child, suddenly hears that child say something that is as odd yet seemingly right as a line from a piece of good fiction. It is ironic but fitting that the father later becomes known as "the father of American Literary Theory." He is undoubtedly a better father to abstract ideas than he is to a flesh-and-blood person (Q 7).

The story ends with the father's realization that his son will never see things the way he does. The father views people in strictly utilitarian terms: His wife is useful because she cooks and takes care of their son; his son, on the other hand is a distraction and of no immediate use (Q 3). The narrator will never view other persons — or dogs, for that matter — in this way (Q 10).

Consider teaching this story with "The Littoral Zone," "Aguantado," "Oedipus," or "My Papa's Waltz," all of which examine conflicted relationships between parents and children.

FURTHER READING

Ingalls, Zoe. "A Novelist Finds Humor in Academic Woes." *Chronicle of Higher Education* 43 (48): B8–B9.

CHAPTER 11

THEME

DAVID MICHAEL KAPLAN

Doe Season

WRITING ACTIVITIES

1. Ask students who are hunters to describe their first experience with hunting. Has hunting changed them in any way?
2. The story's final line seems to bring together most of the elements that contribute to the theme of the story. Ask students to write one or two paragraphs about the last line — what do they make of it?
3. Ask students to write a paragraph on what they think Kaplan's attitude is toward hunting. What makes them think so?

GROUP ACTIVITIES

Ask one group of students to identify the conflicts in the story and to note any similarities between them.

Have another group of students substantiate which role, male or female, Kaplan seems to favor in this story.

A third group could reference parallels between "Doe Season" and "Boys and Girls."

DO YOUR STUDENTS KNOW . . .

The Americas' deer population prior to European arrival is estimated at 50 million. By 1900, that figure had dropped to half a million across Canada, the United States, and northern Mexico, mostly due to deer hunting.

DISCUSSION

In hunting, all the elements of an initiation plot are present (innocence versus experience, life versus death, realization of the *fact* of death), making it a common coming-of-age ritual in literature (Q 1). Here, though, the initiation also marks Andy's loss of androgyny. The innocence lost is more than an innocence of childhood, for Andy becomes Andrea and learns that she must join her mother in the metaphorical ocean of womanhood, complete with the "terrible" yet "inevitable" gulf that separates that world from the world of men. Ask students to think about how the story might be different if Andy were a boy (Q 9).

Kaplan sets up several conflicts in the story, women versus men, for example. Ask students to identify conflicts between people in the story. They will probably identify several, including Andy versus Mac, Andy versus Charlie, Andy versus her mother, Andy versus her father, and Charlie versus her father. Additionally, conflicts exist between nature and human beings, the woods and the ocean. These conflicts help communicate the theme of loss of innocence and Andy's consequent loss of ties to the woods that she once enjoyed (Q 2). Ask students if they think that Andy's ability to inspire the trust of animals costs the doe its life. Some will argue that it does, that this ability in fact destroys both the doe and Andy herself. Some students will see Andy's experience as an "extraordinary" moment of recognition, one that is as inevitable as the ocean's call to her in the story's final line (Q 10).

You should also relate this idea to the comments Andy's father makes that animals "come right up to her." Her father's comments ironically foreshadow Andy's dream (Q 5). With the dream — her hand buried in the doe's chest, cupping the living heart — Andy begins to realize the true "nature" of what she has done. The dream also makes clear the role blood plays regarding theme in the story. Blood is the life force, and Andy's recognition of what she has done — spilling blood — gives her the experience that moves her to womanhood. Along these lines, when the "steaming rush of blood" flows onto Andy from the doe's chest, the doe looks at her "gently," suggesting a bond. It is, after all, the menstrual flow of blood that connects all female animals, Andy included. Thus, the references to blood, especially in the dream, accentuate the experiences that will lead Andy to her inevitable future (Q 4). You might tell students that in some cultures it is tradition for a young boy to drink the blood of his first kill.

The contrast between the woods and the ocean suggests the story's theme, first because the woods are identified as the male domain and the ocean as the female domain. This sets up the conflict between father and mother, male and female. Andy *attempts* to choose the former, but the latter calls to her, and Andy's immersion into the world of her mother is unalterable. Additionally, the woods are not "always the same," as Andy learns. At story's end they become for her like the ocean, empty and moving. Andy's experience with the doe "lies hidden" in the woods but alters the woods forever. The contrast, then, marks Andy's loss of innocence and the introduction to her future (Q 3).

Andy gains her knowledge only reluctantly. She feels the tug of the male world and wants to fit in, while the pull of the female world is terrible to her. She prays that the hunting party will get a deer because she wants to fit into the male adult world, but she does not like the realities of that world once she shoots the doe. She attempts to hold onto her innocence — and the comforting idea of unchanging woods — but she cannot (Q 5, 6). The penis discussion with Mac reinforces this theme, demonstrating Andy's reluctance to "grow up."

Although Andy's mother is not an active participant in the story's events, her presence is important because she represents womanhood. Andy does not want to face the reality that she, too, will become a woman, and ¶ 45 suggests this attitude (Q 7).

Ask students what they think Andy has learned and what remains for her to learn. Many will agree that hunting, as presented in the story, is at least not an innocent activity; some will suggest that it is an evil practice (Q 8). Avid hunters will defend it.

You could compare this story to other initiation stories, such as "A&P," "Barn Burning," and "The Secret Lion." The most obvious parallels may be found in "Boys and Girls."

FURTHER READING

Gold, Sarah. "Cold Comfort." *Village Voice* 32 (2 June 1987): 50.
Wood, Susan. "Children without Parents." *New York Times Book Review* 14 June 1987: 41.

D. H. LAWRENCE

The Rocking-Horse Winner

WRITING ACTIVITIES

1. Ask students to rewrite paragraphs 1, 2, and 3 in a first-person narrative as told by Paul.
2. Have students write the story as a newspaper article reporting the facts, then write a feature article highlighting the human interest angle.
3. Ask students to write a eulogy for Paul, focusing on his age, his differences from and similarities to other children, and his relationship with his parents and his uncle (Q 7).

GROUP ACTIVITIES

To understand the story's complex characterization, have three groups of students focus on the following aspects:

- One group should characterize Paul's mother and analyze her motivations by using specific details from the text (Q 5).
- Another group should characterize and analyze Bassett and Uncle Oscar, finding specific passages to support each observation (Q 5).
- A third group should locate specific references about the various secrets that the characters keep from one another and should expand on how these secrets relate to the main ideas of the story. Some themes to explore are the isolation of the human spirit, the inward journey each person must undertake for self-understanding, the desire and need for approval, greed as a motivator, and the effect of misplaced priorities on people's lives.

DO YOUR STUDENTS KNOW . . .

Horse racing became a professional sport in England in the eighteenth century with the formation of the Jockey Club in 1750 to promote camaraderie between breeders and racers. This organization is still the governing body of the sport and in peak training season possesses over 50 miles of turf and track, with nearly two thousand horses.

DISCUSSION

By using a third-person omniscient point of view, Lawrence distances the reader emotionally from the events in the story. Thus, several critics contend that the theme is one of "the destruction of a family that chooses money above affection" (Murray 196) (Q 1).

Lawrence begins the story like a fairy tale: "There was a woman who was beautiful, who started with all the advantages, yet she had no luck." Yet the ending, contrary to that of most fairy tales, is not happy because Paul, the protagonist, dies (Q 2).

Paul seeks the approval and love of his mother by attempting to gain the luck required to have more money; however, he dies because of "the misdirected spiritual emptiness of his quest" (Murray 196). Even on his deathbed, Paul cries out, "Do you think I'm lucky, mother? . . . Mother, did I ever tell you? I *am* lucky!" His shocked and emotionally distant mother replies, "No, you never did" (Q 3).

If we consider the rhythm of the story's words (Q 4), we hear the squeaking of the springs of Paul's rocking-horse, which he rides incessantly: "There must be more money! There must be more money!" The need for more money, as well as the anxiety this need produces, is evident in the mother's attitude toward her children: "She married for love, and the love turned to dust. She had bonny children, yet she felt they had been thrust upon her, and she could not love them. They looked at her coldly . . ." (¶ 1). Everyone thought she was "such a good mother" but "only she herself, and her children themselves, knew it was not so. They read it in each other's eyes" (¶ 1).

We find further evidence of tension and anxiety in the house (Q 4) in this passage: "The mother had a small income, and the father had a small income, but not nearly enough for the social position which they had to keep up." This supports some critics' descriptions of the story as a "satire on a society governed by a money ethic," and the belief that Lawrence's stories often portray an "upper-class financial anxiety and social pretension," and "modern man's mad mechanical gallop for wealth and material goods" (Murray 196).

In addition, the mother's failure to be financially successful "made deep lines come into her face" (¶ 4). Even in the midst of apparent wealth, the children sense the tension over money. "The children could hear it all the time, though nobody said it aloud. They heard it at Christmas, when the expensive and splendid toys filled the nursery. . . . And the children would stop playing, to listen for a moment. They would look into each other's eyes, to see if they had all heard. And each one saw in the eyes of the other two that they too had heard" (¶ 2).

When Paul questions his mother about their financial situation, he is told that they are poor because they are unlucky, which makes his mother very unhappy and thereby distant (¶ 8, 19, 20).

And so Paul begins his journey to find the luck that will bring the money that he believes will make his mother happy and that will bring her close to him.

When he tries to convince his mother that he is lucky (¶ 33), his mother only laughs bitterly at his insistence (¶ 37) (Q 6).

You might ask students what the rocking-horse symbolizes in relation to the theme of the story (Q 8). In one respect, it serves as Paul's desperate means of escape from an unhappy family situation: "He *knew* the horse could take him to where there was luck, if only he forced it. So he would mount again and start on his furious ride, hoping at last to get there. He knew he could get there" (¶ 44).

You may or may not want to explore a relationship some critics find between the "trance-like actions" of Paul's furious horse-riding and the state achieved through "masturbation, physical and psychic" (Murray 196). The sexual overtones tend to support this interpretation as it describes the rocking-horse "staring fixedly. . . . Its red mouth was slightly open, its big eye was wide and glassy-bright" (¶ 42). In addition, the reader is told that Paul "would speak to nobody when he was in full tilt" (¶ 51), and when he finishes his ride, Paul announces fiercely, "Well, I got there! . . . his blue eyes still flaring, his sturdy long legs straddling apart" (¶ 53). The sexual nature of the riding can also be inferred when Paul's mother discovers him in the darkened room and "heard something plunging to and fro. . . ." When she turns on the light, she finds Paul "madly surging on the rocking-horse." And as "his eyes blazed at her for one strange and senseless second . . . he fell with a crash to the ground" (¶ 219–26).

If the eyes are the windows to the soul, ask students to consider the repetitive references to Paul's "blazing blue" eyes.

Question 10 provides an opportunity for students to research the practices of meditation and self-hypnosis. Various theories about a collective consciousness and states of increased awareness and heightened knowing might be explored to answer this question.

You might consider teaching this story with Shirley Jackson's "The Lottery" in which "winning" a lottery leads to a sacrificial death.

FURTHER READING

Murray, Brian. "D. H. Lawrence." *British Short Fiction Writers, 1915–1945*. Ed. John H. Rogers. *Dictionary of Literary Biography*. Vol. 162. Detroit: Gale, 1996. 182–99.

HISAYE YAMAMOTO

Seventeen Syllables

WRITING ACTIVITIES

1. Ask students to freewrite a paragraph describing a setting in nature. When they have finished, ask them to turn the paragraph into a haiku and to consider the difficulty of expressing their ideas in only seventeen syllables.

2. Ask students to write about a friend or relative (the person may be imaginary) who came to America from another country. What problems did the person have in adjusting to American life? What aspects of his or her own culture did this person maintain?
3. Have students compare and contrast any two of the characters in the story and explain the differences between them.

GROUP ACTIVITIES

Have students pair off and ask them to tell their partners the story of a significant event in their lives. Then have each student write down the story his or her partner has told, using only seventeen syllables to tell the entire story. Each pair can then join another pair to discuss the difficulties they had in telling their stories in such a restricted form. Have the whole class discuss how the restrictions of haiku parallel the other restrictions placed on characters in "Seventeen Syllables."

DO YOUR STUDENTS KNOW . . .

Shinju, which translates as "inside the heart," was a form of suicide used by Japanese couples when their love faced obstacles. Their deaths were symbolic of their undying love, and they believed that in the afterlife they would be reunited.

DISCUSSION

You may want to begin with a discussion of haiku. Then ask why someone might like to write haiku — what is its attraction? What happens to communication when all meaning is packed into such a circumscribed form? The title "Seventeen Syllables" steers us to haiku itself as a central metaphor for (1) the difficulty of communicating in two different languages and (2) the consideration of women's roles in a traditional society such as that of Japan (Q 1).

Although the story never really explains why Rosie's mother begins writing haiku, an appreciation of the elegance and delicacy of the form itself helps us contrast it with the rigors of the tomato farm and its utilitarian conception of nature. Certainly, we can surmise from Rosie's father's behavior (e.g., grunting, cheating at solitaire, speaking with excessive loudness to Mrs. Hayano) that a soul as delicate and poetic as Mrs. Hayashi's would welcome a creative outlet (Q 1). The conflict between the two of them and their priorities — farm work versus poetry — is what fuels the action of the story (Q 5). Mrs. Hayashi stops writing haiku because Rosie's father has successfully defeated her attempts to be an autonomous, creative self (Q 1). In smashing the *Hiroshoge*, Mr. Hayashi has put an end to her poetic persona, "Ume Hanazono" (Japanese for "plum flower-garden"), who is so much less compliant, and more intense, than her everyday self (Q 3). Ume Hanazono is an "earnest, muttering stranger who often neglected speaking when spoken to and stayed busy at the parlor table as late as midnight scribbling with pencil on scratch paper or carefully copying characters on good paper with her fat, pale-green Parker" (Q 2). As Rosie and her mother sit watching the dying fire, it is the death of Ume Hanazono they are watching; in the battle between farm work and poetry, farm work has won.

Rosie's mother's writing of haiku brings the conflict between her and her husband, which is both personal and sociological, to a climax. The smashing of the *Hiroshoge* causes Rosie's mother to confess to the real reasons behind their arranged marriage, and in so doing, she describes Rosie's father as "a young man of simple mind [. . .] but of kindly heart." The kindly heart is not much in evidence in "Seventeen Syllables," but this description illuminates the reasons behind his obvious restlessness and even jealousy in the face of haiku: He is too simple, and perhaps too uncultured, to appreciate the simple elegance of his wife's art (Q 10). A class difference is implied between them as well, as Rosie's mother responds to the elegant Mr. Kuroda's formal Japanese by easily imitating his style, whereas Rosie's father responds to it by destroying a print by a Japanese master, a picture that in its refined natural beauty resembles a haiku. Obviously, Mr. Hayashi's impatience can be explained by his needing his wife's help on the tomato farm, but it is ironic that in his destruction of "Ume Hanazono," he is destroying the artifacts of his own culture (Q 3).

This destruction is mirrored in Mrs. Hayano, who acts as a foil for Rosie's mother. Childbirth has left Mrs. Hayano, reputedly "the belle of her native village," a shuffling, trembling wreck who, despite her condition, has gone on to have three more children (Q 4). When Rosie's mother begs her at the end not to marry, perhaps it is a vision not only of her own fate but also of Mrs. Hayano's — of someone destroyed by her circumscribed social role as surely as Ume Hanazono has been (Q 4). Tradition and gender roles have removed both women's options (Q 7).

You may want to have students debate whether the main character of the story is Rosie or her mother and to compare this story to Tillie Olsen's "I Stand Here Ironing" in which it is also hard to say whether the emphasis lies on the mother or the daughter (Q 6). Ask them to examine the problems Rosie and her mother have in communicating: The mother knows little English; the daughter's Japanese is not as good as she pretends it is. Ultimately, difficulty of communication — a major theme of "Seventeen Syllables" — exists on every level: between husband and wife, mother and daughter, and nearly everyone in the story (Q 8). This difficulty arises from the intrinsic difficulty of language itself, of putting meaning into words, which is as hard as writing haiku (Q 8, 9, 10).

You may want to teach this story with "The Yellow Wallpaper," "The Faithful Wife," or *The Cuban Swimmer*.

FURTHER READING

Mistri, Zenobia Baxter. "Seventeen Syllables: A Symbolic Haiku." *Studies in Short Fiction* 27 (Spring 1990): 197–202.

Osborn, William P., and Sylvia A. Watanabe. "A Conversation with Hisaye Yamamoto." *Chicago Review* 39 (1993): 34–43.

EUDORA WELTY

A Worn Path

WRITING ACTIVITIES

1. Ask students to write a paragraph characterizing Phoenix Jackson. How do the reader's perceptions of her differ from the way the other characters perceive her?
2. Ask students to write about the significance of the title "A Worn Path." What does the title suggest? How is it connected to the theme of sacrifice?
3. Have students write about personal experiences of self-sacrifice. Are they conscious acts of kindness, or do they occur on a more subtle level?

GROUP ACTIVITIES

Have students work in groups to brainstorm possible interpretations of the day-dreams Phoenix experiences.

Ask students to form groups and consider all the possible symbols in the story. How is the setting symbolic? The many references to birds? The obstacles Phoenix must overcome? The white man who helps her?

DO YOUR STUDENTS KNOW . . .

The phoenix, the mythical bird said to rise again out of its own ashes, is found in mythology across many cultures. Generally considered a symbol of the Sun and life after death, the phoenix appears on the crest of the post-apartheid South African government.

DISCUSSION

The first paragraph of the story sets the scene for a journey of hardship and sacrifice as we are introduced to the protagonist, an old woman making her way along the path. She uses a "small cane made from an umbrella" as her guide, "tapping the frozen earth in front of her" (Q 1). Although Phoenix Jackson is old and has trouble seeing, she is not blind and helpless. In fact, she knows not to trust her eyesight and instead relies upon alternate senses, depending "on her feet to know where to take her." She has made this trip before, and it is a familiar "worn path." Although her skirts snag in the brush and she mistakes a scarecrow for a ghost, her senses are strong, and she is a wise and tenacious old woman who commands respect (Q 3).

When she encounters the black dog that comes at her and sends her into a ditch, a white man comes along and helps her. Initially, he assumes that she is one of those "old colored people" who simply "wouldn't miss going to town to see Santa Claus." But when he points his gun at her face, she bravely stands and faces him. Surprised at her fearlessness, he marvels, "you must be a hundred years old, and scared of nothing." She again demonstrates strength and nobility when the attendant at the pharmacy rudely questions her: She "looked above her head" and "gave a twitch to her face as if a fly were bothering her." Although she commands respect, she is not above stealing a nickel or accepting charity for her grandson. She is forced to resort to trickery to get what she needs in order to overcome her poverty and a life governed by the constraints of racism (Q 6, 7).

Much like a knight on a quest for the Holy Grail, Phoenix encounters a series of obstacles that she must overcome before she can obtain the precious elixir of life for her grandson. She faces obstinate hills that seem to shackle her feet, thorny bushes that tear at her skirts, and a mad dog that knocks her into a ditch. She performs miraculous feats, such as crossing a log in a creek bed and crawling through a barbed-wire fence, "spreading her knees and stretching her fingers like a baby trying to climb the steps" (Q 2). Her quest, however, is not motivated by selfishness. Instead, as readers learn at the end of the story, her journey is one of self-sacrifice for her sick grandson. This theme of sacrifice and humility pervades the entire story, and students may marvel at the selfless and humble manner with which Phoenix goes about her journey. You might want to point out the irony in the attendant's assumption that she is a "charity case." In fact, her acts are charitable, and she has learned clever ways to overcome obstacles of poverty and racism, which are the other themes that lurk beneath the surface of this story (Q 4). Another interpretation is that this quest is in fact a futile ritual because the grandson is dead. And his death is the only obstacle in Phoenix's journey that she cannot overcome.

You might want to provide some background about the mythical phoenix, an immortal bird that regenerates itself. Clearly, the old woman's name is symbolic as she, too, regenerates her grandson's life with her repeated pilgrimages along the worn path for the lifesaving potion (Q 5). Students might see Phoenix as heroic, but it is important to point out that part of what makes her actions so noble is the deeply ingrained habitual nature of her selfless act. She even forgets why she has made the long, arduous journey, and she is humble and apologetic in her forgetfulness, "like an old woman begging a dignified forgiveness for waking up frightened in the night." She explains, "I'm an old woman without an education. It was my memory fail me." Although she lacks a formal education, she is wise in her capacity for human grace, and it is in her simple and humble ways that she reveals this life-giving sagacity (Q 8).

You can teach this story with "Miss Brill," "Rooming Houses Are Old Women," or *The Cuban Swimmer*.

FURTHER READING

Appel, Alfred. *A Season of Dreams: The Fiction of Eudora Welty*. Baton Rouge: Louisiana State UP, 1965.

Welty, Eudora. *The Eye of the Story: Selected Essays and Reviews*. New York: Vintage, 1979.

RICK BASS

The Fireman

WRITING ACTIVITIES

1. Ask students to write a paragraph about Kirby from the point of view of his first wife.
2. Have students write about another type of work that might have brought Kirby the same fulfillment.
3. Ask students to write about the type of work they consider most meaningful and why.

GROUP ACTIVITIES

Divide the class into two groups. Ask one group to research the reasons firefighters give for doing the work they do. Ask the other group to research the most common reasons for the success or failure of marriages.

Divide the class into two groups. Ask one group to come up with reasons the story would have worked better with a first-person narrator. Ask the other group to come up with reasons why the third-person limited omniscient narrator was the best choice.

DO YOUR STUDENTS KNOW . . .

According to the National Volunteer Fire Council, in 2002 volunteer firefighters comprised 73 percent of the total estimated 1,064,150 volunteer and paid firefighters across the country. In 2000, sixty-four volunteer firefighters died in the line of duty, with the leading cause of death being heart attacks.

DISCUSSION

At least some of the students will be engaged by the sense of danger and excitement in the fire-fighting scenes. The greatest confusion for the class will likely come in those parts of the story where Bass develops an extended metaphor (Q 10) or where he explains the ways in which Kirby's work as a fireman affects his personal relationships.

Although the connection between Kirby's work and his family life may not be immediately apparent to students, it is central to the story. It is important that students understand that, strange though it may seem, Kirby is intensely grateful for fires. One of the ironies of the story, then, is that Kirby, who saves others from fires, has in fact been rescued by these same fires (Q 5). The fact that he might die on any call makes him and his wife more appreciative of each other than they would otherwise be, thus saving their marriage. Fire fighting has given him a sense of how vulnerable the physical structures of homes are, and it has also helped him appreciate how emotionally fragile the bonds of the family unit are (Q 3). "The Fireman" is an especially apt title for the story because there is really no separation between Kirby's roles as husband and father and his work as a fireman (Q 7).

There is an implication that Kirby's first marriage failed because he and his first wife were unable to bring a similar sense of urgency and gratitude to their relationship (Q 1). In a way, the divorce from his first wife has strengthened his relationship with their daughter, Jenna. Because they only have a limited amount of time to spend together, Kirby is determined to make the most of that time (Q 2, 6).

Although the story is not moralistic, a number of lessons can be drawn from it. Families are delicate constructions that need to be carefully watched and that need, on occasion, to be rescued. In a larger sense, life itself is a fragile thing (Q 8). Truly important work, work that satisfies both the worker and those he or she serves, takes this fragility into account and is closely connected to the rest of the worker's life (Q 7, 8). Kirby's full-time job gives him no sense of accomplishment and leaves no lasting impression on him because he feels no connection to the end result of his work. As a firefighter, on the other hand, Kirby can immediately see the difference his work makes. He also knows that his immediate community values this work (Q 4). Although the story is not explicitly religious, Kirby's fire fighting can certainly be seen as a calling, and it provides him with a view of the world and a way of finding his place within it (Q 8).

One of the central paradoxes of "The Fireman" is that Kirby needs to attain a certain distance from his own life in order to see it objectively and be grateful for it. His relationships remain vital to the extent that he can step back from them from time to time (Q 10). If the class doesn't pick up on this, you can point out how the third-person limited omniscient narrator lends a sense of detachment and objectivity to the story that would have been more difficult to maintain with a first-person narrator. Fire fighting may be able to save Kirby's relationships for now, but it is doubtful whether it can do so indefinitely. Kirby will eventually, provided he survives, grow too old to fight fires. Then, he will either have to find some other way of appreciating and relating to his family or watch those relationships collapse (Q 9).

You might want to teach this story with "Happy Endings," "A Primer for the Punctuation of Heart Disease," and "Pitcher." The first two selections deal with the difficulties of maintaining authentic relationships, and the third explores the metaphorical possibilities of a profession.

FURTHER READING

Coates, Joseph. "A 'Natural' Writer Who Won't Grow Up." *Chicago Tribune Books* 11 Dec. 1988: 1, 12.

Coleman, Ancilla F. "Rick Bass: Contemporary Romantic." *Publications of the Mississippi Philological* (1990): 53–58.

CHAPTER 12

CHARLOTTE PERKINS GILMAN'S "THE YELLOW WALLPAPER": A CASEBOOK FOR READING, RESEARCH, AND WRITING

USING THE CASEBOOK

This fiction casebook has been assembled with the intent of providing students with the material they require to write a research-based critical essay on "The Yellow Wallpaper." The casebook includes the story itself, critical commentaries on it, and a variety of materials included to give a sense of the story's biographical and societal context. You could choose to have the students write such a paper based solely on the resources provided, or you could ask them to do further research. Some of the criticism included (the brief essay by Marty Roth, for example) will provide leads for students seeking further sources.

You may also want to look at the sample student essay provided. Discussing the strengths and weaknesses of an actual paper will help give students a concrete sense of your criteria and may answer a number of their questions before they even arise. This will also give you an opportunity to illustrate your requirements regarding issues such as formatting. "The Yellow Wallpaper" can be effectively analyzed using the methods of a number of critical schools, feminist criticism being perhaps the most obvious. The selection from *The Madwoman in the Attic* by Gilbert and Gubar will provide students with an example of this approach. If students choose to work with feminist criticism, they could also refer to historical texts such as "Petition to the New Jersey Legislature," which will give them a sense of the difficulties faced by women in the 1800s who attempted to secure equality. Since the story is about a woman's descent into madness, it could also be profitably analyzed using psychological criticism. "Gilman's Arabesque Wallpaper," by Marty Roth, provides an overview of the opinions in Gilman's day regarding the harmful effects of wallpaper on mental health.

Other ways of using the casebook may better fit your plans at a given point in the semester. Even before you reach the stage of assigning a critical essay, you might use the materials as the basis for discussion. After discussing "The Yellow Wallpaper," you could assign one of the critical pieces and then discuss it as well. You might, for example, assign Gilbert and Gubar's piece, which gives a reading of the story itself and also provides students with a sense of the literary climate in which it appeared. You could also make use of Gilman's own writings that are included ("Why I Wrote the Yellow Wallpaper" and "From The Diaries of Charlotte Perkins Gilman").

READING AND REACTING

1. Ask students what evidence they find in the story that would support the thesis that Gilman is making a feminist statement.
2. Ask the students what they think the wallpaper symbolizes. Who is the woman under the wallpaper, the woman the narrator sees creeping around at night?
3. Ask students why they think Gilman chose a first-person narrator.
4. Ask students why John's sister is introduced into the story. Is she an essential character?
5. Ask students to find evidence that the narrator's situation is being made worse by the attitudes of her society toward women.
6. Ask students to explain the importance of the narrator's writing. What statement, if any, is Gilman trying to make about women writers?
7. Ask students to characterize John's attitude toward his wife.

WRITING ACTIVITIES

1. Have students rewrite the story from John's point of view. Ask them to write this new story as if it were a journal John is keeping.
2. Ask students to write an essay arguing that a certain moment in the story marks a point of no return for the narrator. What is the last point at which someone could intervene and prevent her complete breakdown?
3. Have students write several journal entries made by the narrator immediately before her marriage to John.

GROUP ACTIVITIES

Divide the class into small groups and ask each group to elect one member as note taker. Have the groups brainstorm lists of the qualities that they think — based on the story itself — would have characterized the "ideal" woman of 1899. When the groups are finished, ask the note takers to write these lists on the board. Then the class as a whole can discuss the similarities and differences between the two lists.

DISCUSSION

If you have already spoken with the class about untrustworthy narrators, they may at first be uncertain whether or not they can believe the narrator's version of events. This will be an important issue to discuss with them at the outset. Certain things that the narrator says are obviously untrue and meant to be understood as such. (There is no woman under the wallpaper, for example.) Just as obviously, however, there are statements by the narrator that are intended to be accurate. Even at the end of the story, when she has completely lost her sanity, she is able to describe John's actions relatively dispassionately and in some detail. It is important that readers place *some* trust in the narrator. After all, if her husband, brother, and sister-in-law are not treating her more or less as she says they are, then Gilman's story loses much of its polemical power. (Q 1)

On one level, any student who enjoys a good horror story can derive pleasure from "The Yellow Wallpaper." It will be difficult for students to fully appreciate the story, however, without a sense of the conditions experienced by women in the late 1800s and early 1900s. Besides discussing the above materials, consider having students look through the story for statements that give a sense of the status of women. Evidence for the negative impact of society on women can be seen throughout the story. John makes a diagnosis, and the narrator's brother supports it. John's sister, who as a woman might be expected to have some sympathy for the narrator, participates in what is quite literally a conspiracy to keep her calm, mindless, and inexpressive. (Q 5) There can be little doubt that Gilman is making a point about the ways in which women participate in the oppression of their own gender. (Q 1, 4)

The story is told in first person, in the form of occasional jottings by the narrator. There are a number of advantages to this approach. One is technical: By casting her story in the form of a journal, Gilman gives us an intimate look at the narrator's worsening state and allows us to follow the path of her madness. Another advantage is that, since she is herself a female writer, Gilman has a vested interest in making her profession appear not only respectable but beneficial. (Q 3, 6) The benefit of writing in particular and of self-expression in general is in fact one of the story's important themes. Early on, the narrator suspects that her husband's mistaken diagnosis is the reason she is not getting better. This intimation (which she couches in parentheses) is not something that she feels comfortable admitting out loud; it is, however, something she is able to *write:* "I would not say it to a living soul of course, but this is dead paper and a great relief to my mind." Throughout the story, the narrator attempts to come to terms with herself and her situation through the act of writing. If she were able to do this — or, more correctly, if she were allowed the freedom to do this more completely — she might be able to halt her decline. (Q 6)

As it is, the thoughts and feelings she is unable to express on writing paper find their expression in an unhealthy way in her obsession with the patterns in the wallpaper. A critic applying the principles of Freudian psychoanalysis to this story might see this as a classic example of the ways in which repressed thoughts find other means of expression. It is important to note that these repressed thoughts and emotions, when they finally break through, turn out to be quite powerful. Not only do they destroy the sanity of the narrator herself, but they also render her husband powerless. One of the great ironies of the story is that John, who imagines he is completely in control of the situation, turns out to be nearly as helpless as his unfortunate wife. He tries to calm her and ends by making her more agitated; he tries to mock her into sharing his rationalism, and she loses her grip on reality. (Q 7) At the story's end, John faints and lies helpless on the floor as his wife literally crawls over him. While it is true that she is reduced almost to the status of an animal, John himself is unconscious and therefore both literally and figuratively lower than she is. This reversal of power roles might be seen as a feminist triumph if it were not for the fact that the narrator could not effect it without losing her own sanity.

The wallpaper is obviously a symbol, but a symbol of what? In part, at least, it symbolizes the disorderly thoughts and emotions the narrator is experiencing. One of her earliest descriptions of the paper gives us a sense of this: "It is dull enough to confuse the eye in following, pronounced enough to constantly irritate and provoke study, and when you follow the lame uncertain curves for a little distance they suddenly commit suicide, plunge off at outrageous angles, destroy themselves in unheard of contradictions." In part, then, the narrator resents the paper because it represents the unruliness and tendency toward self-destruction she fears in herself. (Q 2)

Although Gilman makes a number of polemical points about gender and writing, this does not mean that she neglects characterization. The narrator is a convincing, flesh-and-blood person experiencing conflicting impulses that, combined with her postpartum depression, drive her to a nervous breakdown. On the one hand, she is obligated to obey her husband; if he says she is to rest, then she has to rest. On the other hand, she is supposed to be taking care of her husband. As she puts it, "I meant to be such a help to John, such a real rest and comfort, and here I am a comparative burden already." In addition, her desire to care for her newborn child conflicts with the irrational fear that the child causes in her.

You might want to teach this story with "The Story of an Hour," *A Doll House*, and "Daddy." All three selections deal with women trying to establish their identifies.

FURTHER READING

Dock, Julie Bates, and Daphne Ryan Allen. "'But One Expects That': Charlotte Perkins Gilman's 'The Yellow Wallpaper and the Shifting Light.'" *PMLA: Publications of the Modern Language Association of America*. 111 (Issue 1): 52–66.

Hume, Beverly A. "Managing Madness in Gilman's 'The Yellow Wallpaper.'" *Studies in American Fiction* 30 (Spring 2002): 3–21.

Johnson, Greg. "Gilman's Gothic Allegory: Rage and Redemption in 'The Yellow Wallpaper.'" *Studies in Short Fiction* 26 (Fall 1989): 521–30.

Miskolcze, Robin, "Charlotte Perkins Gilman." *American Women Prose Writers*. Ed. Sharon M. Harris. *Dictionary of Literary Biography*. Vol. 221. Detroit: Gale, 2000: 148–58.

St. Jean, Shawn. "Hanging 'The Yellow Wallpaper': Feminism and Textual Studies." *Feminist Studies* 28 (Summer 2002): 397–416.

CHAPTER 13

JOYCE CAROL OATES'S "WHERE ARE YOU GOING, WHERE HAVE YOU BEEN?" A CASEBOOK FOR READING, RESEARCH, AND WRITING

USING THE CASEBOOK

The fiction casebook provides materials for a variety of potential assignments — for example, incorporating research material into criticism, examining professional critical style, seeing multiple critical perspectives on a single work.

One possible use of the casebook is as an introduction to the process of writing a source-based paper about literature. The casebook provides a convenient collection of source material that can be incorporated into student writing as practice before students do library research on their own. Students might begin by doing a preliminary study of the story without any reference to the additional materials. You might, for example, assign a character sketch, a thematic study of a symbol in "Where Are You Going, Where Have You Been?" such as Arnold Friend's gold car, or a study of the opposition between home and not-home in Connie's life. Once students have completed a first draft containing their own ideas, they can then move on to incorporate the ideas of the writers whose essays are included in the text. This sort of assignment allows the instructor to ensure that the primary analysis comes from students themselves and alerts the instructor to problems arising from students' early confusion between paraphrase and plagiarism.

A second use of the casebook approach is as a technique for modeling professional writing. Students might, for example, analyze the types of evidence used in the Schulz and Rockwood article to support an argument for a psychological interpretation of the story. Alternatively, you can use the Tierce and Crafton piece to introduce a study of critical refutation. They challenge the assumption that the character of Arnold Friend necessarily represents Satan.

Finally, you might use the casebook to illustrate and compare various critical approaches. A reader-response approach might be a good starting point, allowing students to think about how their own perceptions of the story are shaped by their ages and backgrounds. The Schulz and Rockwood article provides a detailed psychological criticism using several terms employed by psychological critics. Tierce and Crafton's article points out ambiguities that are problematic for the reader's interpretation and thus allows for an introduction to deconstruction as a literary technique. The numerous oppositions in the story (see discussion below) invite a structuralist approach. Finally, Connie's seduction might suggest a feminist perspective. Such a comparison and contrast of approaches would be appropriate as an introduction to criticism or as a summary at the end of a study of critical stances.

READING AND REACTING

1. Structuralist critics often look for oppositions that provide for tension within a story. Ask students to identify oppositions that structure this story.
2. Oates may be compared to Hawthorne because of the allegorical nature of her stories and because of the blending of dream and reality in her work. Ask students which elements of the story may be considered allegorical and why. How does Oates blur the distinction between what is real and what is dream in the story?
3. Ask students to identify the point of view in this story. How would the story be different if Oates employed a first-person point of view, telling the story from either Connie's or Arnold's perspective?
4. Ask students to explain the significance of the title.
5. Ask students if they expected the ending. Have them cite examples of foreshadowing in the story.
6. Ask students to respond to Connie's decision to go with Arnold at the end of the story. Why does she go? To what extent is she in control of this decision?
7. Ask students if they think Connie will die. Why or why not?

WRITING ACTIVITIES

1. Have students write on one of the minor characters (June, the mother, the father, Arnold's friend Ellie), arguing that he or she is an essential character in the story.
2. Ask students to compare this story to Hawthorne's "Young Goodman Brown." In both stories, the main characters meet with a Satan figure who seems to be expecting them. How are the stories alike? Different? Does either of them offer any sort of hope in the end?
3. The film version of the story, *Smooth Talk* (1985), stars Laura Dern and Treat Williams. Ask students to cast the leading roles of another version of the film. What qualities of the actors would contribute to character development for these two parts? Perhaps students could view the film and write about the differences between the story and the film.

GROUP ACTIVITIES

Oates claimed that the story "came to her" after she heard Bob Dylan's song "It's All Over Now, Baby Blue." Critics Tierce and Crafton ("Connie's Tambourine Man: A New Reading of Arnold Friend," reprinted in the casebook) mention other songs related to the story: "Mister Tambourine Man," "The Pied Piper," "Like a Rolling Stone." Divide the class into four groups and give each a copy of the lyrics to one of the songs. ("It's All Over Now, Baby Blue" appears in the casebook.) Have them discuss how each parallels the story.

DISCUSSION

If you begin your class discussion of this story with the Group Activities mentioned above, the song lyrics may provide a natural springboard for looking at this story in terms of the cultural movement of the 1960s. Students might then compare elements of the story that seem to be specific to the 1960s in general (James Dean–style dress, language, and music) and parts that seem to be more universal in terms of growing up and moving through adolescence. If you are incorporating your discussion of the story into a comparative look at critical methods, this initial discussion might involve reader response and historical criticism.

For a psychological approach, you might begin with the question of why Connie goes with Arnold at the end (Q 7 in Reading and Reacting above). The story itself suggests that Connie goes because of the threat to her family. Schulz and Rockwood argue that Connie gives in to her id because she does not have a map for negotiating the conflicting desires that confront her in the process of growing up ("In Fairyland without a Map: Connie's Exploration Inward in Joyce Carol Oates's 'Where Are You Going, Where Have You Been?'" reprinted in the text). Her obedience to the id is accompanied by a fragmentation of her self: Connie seems to be watching herself as she leaves the house. Connie's lack of conscious control over her actions suggests that she is mesmerized to some extent by Arnold; the lilting quality of his voice (¶ 59) and its similarity to chanting (¶ 62) explain how this hypnotism occurs. In addition, the music throughout the story provides a psychological background for Connie's submission to Arnold; having been obsessed with music from the beginning, Connie is very susceptible to Arnold's rhythmic seduction (Q 5 in Reading and Reacting above).

The narrator (third-person limited omniscient) frames the development of the story through Connie's eyes, further showing the reader how Connie's perspective shapes the narrative's depiction of her family and the character of Arnold Friend (Q 3 in Reading and Reacting above). His changes throughout the end of the story reveal the changes in Connie's own perception: at first she is pleased and excited that he has come to her (¶ 35, 46); then she begins to fear him as she sees more of what he is (his age in ¶ 79, the change in his voice in ¶ 88). Finally, she loses touch with her objective world and sees Arnold only in a blur (¶ 94, 105, 110).

From a feminist perspective, the story might be read as an illustration of the oppression of the female in a world where men seduce and destroy the female personality. In addition, Connie's world provides her with expectations about romance, but her experience provides no clear ideas about how to find a real love (¶ 10, 12). Instead, she is waiting for the hero of a song to come and make her feel good; her significance depends on the feelings that a fictional man can bring her. When discussing this feminist perspective, you might have students compare it to Sexton's "Cinderella."

The feminist approach might be supplemented by a structuralist discussion of some of the oppositions that shape the story, particularly in terms of characterization: innocence and experience, Connie and June, Connie and her mother, Connie at home and Connie away from home (Q 1 in Reading and Reacting above). Connie is beauty without experience, whereas her mother represents beauty tarnished by experience. Connie's beauty is a point of contention between mother and daughter, and it seems as if the mother cannot help her daughter deal with her good looks; she can only resent Connie (¶ 11).

Students may also wish to view the story as an allegory. For example, Arnold Friend represents a Satan figure. He comes in disguise, he presents himself as friend (fiend?), and he tempts the young girl. The apple he offers her is strikingly similar to the original tempter's plan: lust of the eyes (admiring the car, ¶ 24; Arnold's body, ¶ 46), lust of the flesh (his talk of being her lover in ¶ 75, 104), and the pride of life (Arnold's knowledge, ¶ 58; his statement that no one will come for her, ¶ 124, 153; and his calling her good, ¶ 168). Connie falls from innocence into experience. This fall seems to occur literally when she falls to the floor before her last attempt to get help on the phone (¶ 144); at this point, a "psychological rape" occurs, as the tempter stabs her again and again, and her will is lost (¶ 151). Once the fall occurs, Connie finds that what once seemed real and solid has taken on a new appearance (¶ 154), and her perception of the world changes, just as Eve's does after the fall in the Garden of Eden (Q 2 in Reading and Reacting above).

Finally, you might wish to interpret the story as cultural criticism, looking specifically at the title. Whereas these two questions are typically asked by parents of their children, the title is ironic because these parents have trapped Connie by not asking her the sorts of questions that would help her express her own feelings. If her parents did ask her such questions, they might be able to ease Connie's transition into adulthood. The questions in the title could also be seen as directed to different people — the first (where are you going?) to Connie, who will be "going" into adulthood in the arms of Arnold Friend, and the second (where have you been?) to the parents, who have not been able to nurture their daughter more successfully (Q 4 in Reading and Reacting above).

Having looked at the story from a variety of perspectives, you might ask the students to predict what happens next in Connie's life, basing their predictions on the different sorts of readings they have done.

- Feminist: Arnold has already seduced Connie and, in terms of her personality, she is already dead. Having stripped her of her self, he will follow by stripping her of her virginity and possibly even her life.
- Psychological: Arnold does not realize at the end of the story what color Connie's eyes are, suggesting that he is not really interested in her beyond sex. Given this indifference to her as a person and given his threats of violence to her family, we might expect that he will also kill her.
- Structural: Given the opposition between what is dream and what is objective reality as well as the contrast between innocence and experience, the parallelism suggests two possible predictions for Connie's future. On the

one hand, Connie may leave the romantic world of dreams and continue to live in the realistic world of experience. The transition between the worlds is violent (because Arnold will rape her), but there is no implication that Connie will die. Only her dreams will have died. On the other hand, one might conclude that the death of Connie's romantic view of the world and of men suggests that there will be a parallel physical death.

You might conclude your discussion of the story by looking at what sorts of criticisms the story implies about society — for example, its treatment of women, the problems with parent/child relationships, the relationship between fantasy and reality, the role of music and fantasy in the process of growing up.

FURTHER READING

Coulthard, A. L. "Joyce Carol Oates's 'Where Are You Going, Where Have You Been?' as Pure Realism." *Studies in Short Fiction* 26 (Fall 1989): 505–10.

Easterly, J. "The Shadow of a Satyr in Oates's 'Where Are You Going, Where Have You Been?'" *Studies in Short Fiction* 27 (Fall 1990): 537–43.

Hurley, D. F. "Impure Realism: Joyce Carol Oates's 'Where Are You Going, Where Have You Been?'" *Studies in Short Fiction* 28 (Summer 1991): 371–75.

Joslin, Michael. "Joyce Carol Oates." *American Novelists Since World War II*. Ed. Jeffrey Helterman and Richard Layman. *Dictionary of Literary Biography*. Vol. 2. Detroit: Gale, 1978. 371–81.

Pickering, S. F. "The Short Stories of Joyce Carol Oates." *Georgia Review* 28 (Summer 1978): 218–26.

Piwinski, D. J. "Oates's 'Where Are You Going, Where Have You Been?'" *Explicator* 49 (Spring 1991): 195–96.

CHAPTER 14

FICTION FOR FURTHER READING

The explications for the following stories suggest entry points for class discussion and/or Writing Activities and Group Activities not detailed in this portion of the text. They may also facilitate independent exploration of the reading selections and provide overviews for brief in-class discussions and writing activities comparing or contrasting these entries with stories in previous Fiction Chapters.

CHINUA ACHEBE

Dead Man's Path

DO YOUR STUDENTS KNOW . . .

Of the 120 million people living in Nigeria, 30 million are students. Primary education, which begins at age six, usually includes mathematics, English language, Bible knowledge, science, and one of the three main native languages (Hausa, Yoruba, and Ibo). Because the government oversees secondary schools, students graduate with a certificate only after passing a Common Entrance Exam for admission into a state government or federal school.

Despite its brevity, "Dead Man's Path" deals with a number of complex issues, most notably the clash between modernity and tradition and between Western and native cultures. Michael Obi prides himself on being progressive, but for him progress necessarily entails disregard and disdain for the things of the past. He makes headway, but only until there is a direct conflict with the villagers who use the pathway across school property for ceremonial purposes. When he closes the path and then refuses to reopen it, Obi provokes a violent reaction and deals a potentially fatal blow to his own career.

The ending is especially ironic, since Obi closed the path off specifically to avoid getting a bad evaluation from the white supervisor. As it is, his actions have alienated both whites and blacks, moderns and traditionalists. He would have been better off had he taken the village priest's advice: "let the hawk perch and the eagle perch." Although tolerance is often thought of as a modern virtue, it is clear that the traditional village priest is far more tolerant than the new headmaster, who tells the priest that the purpose of the school "is to teach your children to laugh" at the idea of a path for the dead.

For discussion, consider asking the students what they feel Obi's attitudes toward progress and tradition are. How do they define these terms? What positive and negative connotations does each term have?

TONI CADE BAMBARA

The Lesson

DO YOUR STUDENTS KNOW . . .

The F.A.O. in F.A.O. Schwarz stands for the founder's name, Frederick August Otto Schwarz, who opened his first toy store in 1862 in Baltimore, Maryland. He moved the company to New York in 1870 and moved to its acclaimed Fifth Avenue location in 1986. F.A.O. Schwarz now has twenty-two stores nationally.

Although most pieces of literature can be examined through a political lens, some lend themselves to this approach better than others. It is clear that Bambara's intent in "The Lesson" is to comment on economic inequalities and on the importance of making children politically aware. Consider having students research income disparities in the United States and look at different proposals for addressing these disparities.

Mrs. Moore is in a sense a social activist. Although she is not a teacher or relative of any of the neighborhood children, she feels that is "only right that she should take responsibility for the young one's education." Having a college education herself, she feels that she has a duty to further their education and make them aware of issues in the society. In this case, she does it by taking them to F.A.O. Schwarz, an expensive toy store. The students have some idea, based on the things they purchase or see their parents purchase, of what the necessities of life cost. They are amazed, however, at how much the toys in the store cost. A sailboat, for example, costs over $1,000.

By the end of the story, the narrator's friend Sugar has been led by this experience to question the structure of American society. Based on the obvious differences in income between the people who shop in the store and the people with whom she lives and goes to school, she concludes that the American system is unjust and "that this is not much of a democracy." The narrator has not come to this conclusion herself, but she does resolve to think further about the issue.

DONALD BARTHELME

A City of Churches

DO YOUR STUDENTS KNOW . . .

In *The Lonely Crowd*, sociologist David Reisman labeled America in the 1950s as "other directed," valuing stability and conformity rather than individuality. This tendency was reinforced by the then new medium of television, which conveyed a homogenous view of life.

Students who have seen reruns of the *Twilight Zone* may feel that this story has something of the same atmosphere. It is worth asking the students why they think Barthelme chose this method to convey his point. First, however, they will need to get a sense of what that point is. First and foremost, the story is about the dangers of conformity. Granted, there is a wide range of denominations to choose from in Prester, but they are all Christian denominations, and the people of the town all conform to the social expectations of their neighbors. One of these expectations is that no one live alone. Mr. Phillips considers the desire to do so "very unusual."

Under the guise of community and solidarity, the town of Prester is depriving its citizens of their individuality. The citizens of the town demand that Cecilia stay not because they find her an appealing person, but because she would fill a predefined slot. They want her to be their "car-rental girl." "Someone," Mr. Phillips says, "must stand behind that counter."

There are any number of institutions in society that encourage or enforce conformity. In this story, however, Barthelme is clearly concerned with the oppressive aspects of religious institutions. The inhabitants of Prester (the word means "priest" or "minister") not only work in churches but live there as well. There is no area of life, then, that is separated from church life.

AMY BLOOM

Hold Tight

DO YOUR STUDENTS KNOW . . .

According to the National Cancer Institute, because the median age of cancer diagnosis is sixty-eight, as Americans live longer, the rates of cancer will double by 2050. One out of eight American women will develop breast cancer.

As the narrator's mother slowly dies of cancer, the narrator behaves recklessly, and her father slips into alcohol abuse. It is both sad and fitting that the mother should die on her daughter's graduation from high school, since the death of a parent and graduation are both important times of transition.

This story provides an excellent example of the ways in which a carefully chosen allusion can enhance a work of literature. The last painting the narrator's mother completed was entitled "Lot's Wife." Although the narrator sees the painting only as "sad," her mother sees more in it. "Look again," she says. "The sky is so full and there is so much happening." In the biblical story, Lot's wife is turned into a pillar of salt because she looked back at her native city of Sodom as it was being destroyed by God. There is a parallel here between the mother's painting and her own situation. In creating it, she was warning herself that to remain too attached to the life she was leaving would kill her prematurely. To continue living until she actually died, she would have to let go of life.

This is not an easy lesson for her to put into practice, of course, nor is it easy for her husband and daughter to learn. They cannot help looking back at the past and regretting their loss. Having reviewed the story of Lot's wife, you might ask the class what they think this allusion adds to the story. You might also ask them whether they think it is desirable, or even humanly possible, to avoid looking back in a situation like this.

T. CORAGHESSAN BOYLE

Greasy Lake

DO YOUR STUDENTS KNOW . . .

Although Greasy Lake is a stand-in for an actual lake in New Jersey that inspired Bruce Springsteen, Route 88 is a major roadway in central New Jersey. It borders Asbury Park, immortalized in the album title, "Greetings from Asbury Park." Boyle claims the story itself was inspired by another Springsteen tune, "Spirit in the Night."

Suffering under the illusion of being "dangerous characters" (¶ 1), three friends, driving a Bel Air station wagon, crash headlong into a nightmare. Another illusion — mistaken identity (¶ 6) — spirals them through an assumed murder (¶ 13–14), an attempted rape (¶ 15–16), and their threatened discovery (¶ 17). Finally, the boys take a nose-dive into the black waters of Greasy Lake, crashing full force into a dead body, which is decidedly not an illusion (¶ 19–20) and which careens them head-on into what should be a moment of epiphany. However, while Boyle's characteristic blending of absurd and mundane relieves the violent tension, it also serves to stall, then halt, this moment of enlightenment.

At Boyle's trademark plot twist, the narrator repeatedly whines about losing the car keys (¶ 21) and then reflects, "I thought of the dead man. He was probably the only person on the planet worse off than I was. [. . .] My car was wrecked; he was dead. [. . .] There was no use getting philosophical about it. [. . . so] I put the car in gear. [. . .] shaking off pellets of glass like an old dog shedding water after a bath" (¶ 31, 34, 45).

ETHAN CANIN

The Carnival Dog, The Buyer of Diamonds

DO YOUR STUDENTS KNOW . . .

Within Orthodox Judaism, the human body is considered the physical part of a complex, spiritual being. After death, the body can be neither cremated nor embalmed. Autopsies and organ donation are generally discouraged because they are viewed as a desecration of the body.

Abe is obsessed with two things, perseverance and physical health, and he passes these obsessions on to his son. Although one might think that this would make Myron the perfect medical student, it has just the opposite effect. No matter how successful a doctor is, every patient is eventually going to die. Myron, who has been raised to regard physical heath with something approaching religious reverence, finds it impossible to deal with the gradual collapse and decay of healthy bodies.

The fight that concludes the story is a fight between two extremely stubborn men. It is important to note that when Myron says "I give," he is not simply surrendering. Rather, he is giving his father a gift by allowing him to win, just as he does earlier in the story, when he lets his father beat him in a race. You might have the class discuss Myron's surrender/gift. In particular, you might ask them what it means when Myron thinks, "This is my life." Is he simply passively accepting the conditions of his life, or is he actively embracing them?

STEPHEN CRANE

The Open Boat

DO YOUR STUDENTS KNOW . . .

Death due to hypothermia occurs at sea within twelve hours in water that is 70 – 60° Fahrenheit. Severe hypothermia occurs when the body's temperature is less than 90° Fahrenheit, resulting in heart failure, the most common cause of death.

Crane relates the story of four men shipwrecked in a small boat who attempt to reach land. As the story progresses, the reader gets a clear sense of the indifference of the natural world to human problems and of the relative powerlessness of human beings. The men are able to work together for the common good, but their desperation increases as they get closer to rescue. The more hopeful their situation becomes, the more they realize that every move they and their prospective rescuers make counts. When their first attempt to reach land fails, tempers begin to fray. Adding to this irony is the fact that the ocean, which had been relatively cooperative, becomes more of a danger as the boat approaches the shore. By the story's end, one of the men has drowned, and the survivors feel that they understand something about they sea and the natural world that those living entirely on land do not.

JUNOT DIAZ

Aguantado

DO YOUR STUDENTS KNOW . . .

According to sociologist David Popenoe, fatherless children are more likely to live in poverty, more likely to drop out of school, and more prone to delinquency, violence, and drug abuse.

Some students may be frustrated by the fact that the narrator's father never materializes. This is entirely appropriate, however, since the story is not about the man but about his absence. Consider asking the class how the story would have been different if we had actually met Papi. Would it have been better, worse, or simply different?

Papi's absence has a profound effect on his family. They are living in great poverty, and the education of the two sons is suffering because of it. When Papi first promises to return and then does not, the effect on the narrator is devastating. He goes berserk and alienates his already distraught mother in the process. The narrator, however, gradually adjusts to his father's absence and comes to view it as a given. At one point, he even says that he didn't realize "[t]hat this waiting was all a sham." The situation is far worse for his mother, who has lived five years in a kind of limbo and who has a clearer sense of what has happened than her youngest son.

As we learn in Section 6, there are almost religious aspects to Papi's absence. When Rafa imagines that their father will "come in the night, like Jesus," he is making reference to one of the apocalyptic passages in the New Testament. Indeed, there is a sense in which the father has become godlike. When he comes, he will change everything; it will be the end of one world and the beginning of another.

CHITRA BANERJEE DIVAKARUNI

The Disappearance

DO YOUR STUDENTS KNOW . . .

According to the FBI, 41,000 adults are listed as missing. Unless clear evidence shows that the person was taken against his or her will, these cases are not aggressively investigated.

He and she marry, but do not live happily ever after — in fact, she disappears.

Divakaruni objectifies the characters by not naming them — a technique that usually creates distance between reader and character. Here, however, the opposite occurs: The calculated attack on arranged marriages serves to humanize the couple.

He considers himself a "good husband" (¶ 10), yet insists that she not work and not wear Western clothes. He expects sex even when she passively resists, rationalizing that he would stop "if she really begged him, if she cried" (¶ 11). But she does neither. She takes her jewels and quietly leaves for her evening walk — never to return.

He reports that she is *missing* because to acknowledge that she *left* would shame him. So, eventually he packs away her belongings, holds a prayer service, and — thinking the matter is ended — he remarries. But her leaving continues to haunt him, and despite one moment of insight (¶ 29), he eventually retreats to his more comfortable "deep, dreamless sleep" (¶ 30).

LOUISE ERDRICH

Fleur

DO YOUR STUDENTS KNOW . . .

Boarding schools were an effective method for "Americanizing" the native populations, and children were forcibly removed from family, homelands, and culture. Separation from one's culture and assimilation proved as effective as the Indian Wars waged by the U.S. Army.

Like Misshepeshu, the water monster, Fleur represents a beautiful, seductive danger. People fear her power because she twice survives her encounters with Misshepeshu and destroys women. Pauline, the narrator, is a foil for Fleur in that she is not beautiful, seductive, or strong. She has no power. And although the story is about Fleur, it also reveals Pauline's own transformation from bystander to activist. Pauline derives strength by taking action against the men who rape Fleur. Furthermore, Fleur's baby, born strong and aware of her own power, carries out the theme of women empowering women.

GABRIEL GARCÍA MÁRQUEZ

A Very Old Man with Enormous Wings
A Tale for Children

DO YOUR STUDENTS KNOW . . .

In 1979, thirteen teens, who worked at McDonald's and lived in New York City's ravaged South Bronx, formed the Guardian Angels. This was a voluntary and weapon-free group, devoted to keeping the streets and subways safe from violent crime. Known for wearing red berets as a symbol of courage, the group now has worldwide chapters with twenty-five in the United States alone.

García Márquez's stories are empowered by his ability to combine legend, myth, and superstition with realism. The townspeople in this story fear and marvel at the old man with wings and treat him according to their own superstitions, religion, and fickleness. The church, seeking to determine the man's status by its established standards, bogs down in its own methodology and detail. The old man is an anomaly, but he keeps his counsel, responding only with patience and acceptance. The townspeople doubt him more when he fails to work "miracles" (¶ 10), but perhaps that is the point of the story: "According to your faith will it be done to you" (Matthew 9:29).

TIM GAUTREAUX

Same Place, Same Things

DO YOUR STUDENTS KNOW . . .

Although women who kill their husbands often recount lives of abuse, according to a 1990 study, these women tend to be violent, impulsive, and have past criminal records.

"Same Place, Same Things" provides an opportunity to discuss the ways in which setting influences the actions of characters. The time period of the story is particularly important, and you might consider having students research the Great Depression. Not only does the story take place in the Depression, but also in a rural area of Louisiana during a prolonged drought. None of the people Harry Lintel encounters is happy, and most are under a terrific strain. The pervasive sense of despair in the story is one of its most notable qualities.

Ada is particularly desperate, however. Not only is she ready to run off somewhere — anywhere — with the first man who comes along, but she has murdered her husband. She cannot endure "staying in the same place, doing the same things, day in, day out." Although it is certainly not true that she was forced to commit murder by her circumstances, it is important that students try to imagine themselves in her situation. There are obvious parallels between this story and "Looking for a Rain God" by Bessie Head. In each case the strains being felt by an entire community during a drought lead to violence.

The interesting irony of Harry Lintel's character is that, although he is a decent man, he depends on the misfortunes of others for his livelihood. As soon as a drought passes and pumps are no longer needed, he moves on to the next area. Ada is wrong, then, in thinking that Harry could provide her with real hope. Although he certainly sees different things in different places, he is really only moving from one desolation to another.

NATHANIEL HAWTHORNE

The Birthmark

DO YOUR STUDENTS KNOW . . .

Although plastic surgery exists in many cultures, its first recorded use was in India in 800 B.C. Written evidence shows that during this time in India, skin grafts were used for reconstructive work rather than beauty enhancement.

Hawthorne's emphasis on emotional ambiguity is clearly evident when Aylmer kills his wife. Aylmer's search for perfection and Georgiana's love for him drive her to participate in his obsession and ultimately lead to her death. The conflict between man and nature is also prominent in the story. Aylmer's assistant, Aminadab, represents nature in its darker, more physical form and contrasts with

Aylmer's vision of human perfection (¶ 25). His "gross, hoarse chuckle" might well be interpreted not as Aylmer thought, as an "expression of delight," but instead as nature's triumphant glee over human failure (¶ 90). Aylmer's obsession with perfection does not negate his love for Georgiana, but it does express Hawthorne's fascination with the darker side of human nature and the ambiguity of his sense of moral responsibility.

RAJ KAMAL JHA

Domestic Help

DO YOUR STUDENTS KNOW . . .

Domestic help is still employed in a majority of Indian homes in almost all social classes. A recent ad in a Calcutta paper offered $15–20 (U.S. dollars) per month for a domestic worker. Traditionally, workers are also given an annual gift of clothing.

Although the prose style of this story is clear and unadorned, students may be puzzled by the work as a whole. It is probably best, then, to walk through it with them step-by-step, making sure that they understand the major details of the plot. A maid, Bhabani, is about to leave the house where she has worked for twenty years. The family, we learn, has not been a happy one. The father, who is now dead, was an alcoholic who may well have been abusive. Bhabani was a source of comfort to the children during their difficult childhoods.

While waiting for her son to arrive with the car, Bhabani asks the narrator, a grown child of the family for which she has worked, to tell her a story. The narrator proceeds to tell the story of Bhabani's journey to the city after her marriage. Much of this secondary narrative is clear and a story that Bhabani herself characterizes as "not entirely wrong." The one puzzling element is the inclusion of a man referred to by the narrator as "the Stranger," a man traveling on the same train as the fictional Bhabani and her husband.

Students will likely be puzzled about the identity of the Stranger, and you may want to address this issue in group work. You might, for example, consider breaking the class into groups and asking each group to invent a believable identity for him. Also ask the class as a whole why Jha would introduce this element of uncertainty into the story. The narrator maintains that "[t]his is a story, the Stranger was a stranger." There is more to the matter than that, however.

HA JIN

Saboteur

DO YOUR STUDENTS KNOW . . .

Ha Jin, a pen name for Xuefei (pronounced shu-FAY) Jin, came to the United States from Beijing, China, in 1986 as a student of American Literature.

Jin taught himself English while working as a railroad telegrapher after serving the Chinese People's Liberation Army in 1976. When he applied to college after the Cultural Revolution, Jin was assigned his last choice as a major — English.

This story traces one man's transformation from a loyal citizen to a saboteur. When Mr. Chui is first accused of sabotage, he is confident that he will be vindicated by the system. In fact, it is unlikely that he would have yelled at the police if he hadn't thought their behavior would be frowned upon by their superiors. As the story progresses, however, it becomes clear that the police have no respect for the law and will stop at nothing to force him to confess to a crime he did not commit. Mr. Chui stubbornly refuses, until the police begin to torture his former student, Fenjin. The treatment Mr. Chui receives is ironic, given that he is, as he puts it, "a scholar, a philosopher, and an expert in dialectical Materialism." Dialectical materialism is the basic foundation of Marxist thought, but it is clear that the police are far less interested in upholding the ideals extolled by the communist government than in maintaining their own power.

Upon being released from prison, Mr. Chui sets out to deliberately infect the bowls used by the food vendors around the police station. Jin is making important points not only about the injustices of Chinese communism, but also about the ways in which these injustices corrupt and transform victims into the same kind of people as their oppressors. If Mr. Chui had simply struck back at his tormenters, there would have been a kind of crude justice to his actions. In fact, though, he is responsible for the deaths of two children who could not possibly have been involved in his ordeal. He has become, as Fenjin notes, "an ugly man."

JAMES JOYCE

Eveline

DO YOUR STUDENTS KNOW . . .

Ireland was one of the few European countries that experienced the emigration of a large number of single, unaccompanied females. By the beginning of the twentieth century, 700,00 women had left Ireland for domestic or factory work in the United States.

A creature of habit, Eveline at nineteen is old beyond her years: Physically and mentally, she is worn out, yet emotionally, she is inexperienced. Trapped in a life of drudgery and poverty, she still cannot risk the loss of what is familiar for the unknown, and so she refuses to go away with her lover. Her mother's dying words (¶ 17) serve as a warning to Eveline to heed her mind, not her heart, and they become, tragically, a portrait of what Eveline's life may become. Eveline longs to escape her life (¶ 5–9), and Frank offers escape, adventure, and respectability, but in the end, she is powerless to free herself.

JAMAICA KINCAID

Girl

DO YOUR STUDENTS KNOW . . .

In Antigua, abortion is illegal unless necessary to save the life of the mother. Despite government support for family planning and contraception, high numbers of unwanted births and illegal abortion occur. Fifteen percent of births occur to mothers under age twenty.

The mother's litany to her daughter both teaches and taunts. So expertly are these two entwined that the girl's sensibilities are lulled — something the reader also experiences through the story's rhythm and repetition. The advice and admonitions prepare the girl for an unsafe world, yet at the same time, the mother's advice borders on attempts to manipulate the child. For example, in the closing lines, the mother uses even her answer to the child's innocent question about feeling the bread to emphasize her own view of sexually acceptable behavior.

BERNARD MALAMUD

The German Refugee

DO YOUR STUDENTS KNOW . . .

In 1943, the Rosenstrasse Protest rescued 1,700 – 2,000 Jewish men married to non-Jewish German women who, with their German relatives, protested outside the Berlin welfare office where the men awaited transport. Rather than risk more outcry, Nazi officials released them, as well as twenty-five already sent to Auschwitz were returned.

Gassner's conflicts are centered on his statement "it is so ardouz [sic] to come back to life," which aptly describes his assimilation into a new culture and his separation from his Gentile wife (¶ 41). Gassner's depression is obvious to his English tutor, Martin Goldberg, when in a moment of intimacy, Gassner reveals his hatred of the German nation, his sense of betrayal both by Germany and by his wife, and his suicide attempt (¶ 37). The young tutor, fearful that Gassner might attempt another suicide, maintains a close watch on his friend.

Gassner eventually writes his speech, inspired by Goldberg's inaccurate suggestion about Walt Whitman's influence on German poets — and perhaps by the tutor's compassion (¶ 71). His physical and emotional conditions begin to improve, but two days after the successful lecture, Goldberg finds Gassner dead — gassed by the kitchen stove — a weapon overlooked in Goldberg's prior vigil (¶ 79, 82) and an irony that should be noted (a Jew gassing *himself*).

The events occurring in Germany affect and parallel Gassner's life and death, but his conversations about his wife and a letter from Gassner's anti-

Semitic mother-in-law (¶ 63–70, 87) offer readers the best way to understand his actions.

HERMAN MELVILLE

Bartleby the Scrivener

DO YOUR STUDENTS KNOW . . .

The Guild of Scriveners of York, England, was first established in the fifteenth century as a group of men and women allowed to conduct professional business who practiced the trade of writing, working with manuscripts, preparing legal documents, and light bookkeeping. Local guilds declined in the early nineteenth century when national guilds were established. The Guild of Scriveners of York was revived in 1991 as an association for accountants and lawyers.

Bartleby is difficult to interpret because he is "one of those beings of whom nothing is ascertainable" (¶ 1). However, the narrator, a Wall Street lawyer, describes himself as "an eminently *safe* man" and openly holds firm to his philosophy that "the easiest way of life is the best" (¶ 2). Throughout his dealings with Bartleby, the lawyer chooses the path of least resistance to avoid conflict and rationalizes his choices in every situation (¶ 51, 55, 84, 86, 89, 134, 165, 169).

The repeated "I would prefer not to" directly opposes the narrator's preferences and creates a wall, much like the literal walls that surround Bartleby, against which the narrator "begins to stagger in his own plainest faith" (¶ 42). The lawyer's fear of being affected by Bartleby pushes him to finally make a decision. But even after distancing himself physically, the lawyer cannot ease his way around Bartleby; indeed, he must directly confront Bartleby's emptiness and sorrow, pitting it against his own previously naive and optimistic view of the world.

Bartleby's life and death offer the narrator an opportunity to examine the issue of whether any one life holds meaning, or whether, like the dead letters Bartleby once handled, some people just fail to find their appropriate destinies (¶ 252).

ALICE MUNRO

Boys and Girls

DO YOUR STUDENTS KNOW . . .

According to a survey by the National Institute of Mental Health, nearly 7 million children are beaten up by a sibling at least once in a lifetime. Forty-two percent of children admitted to kicking, biting, or punching a sibling. As many as 109,000 had a knife or gun used against them by a sibling.

Two of Munro's favorite themes are the difficulties of being female and the desire for freedom, but this story moves beyond mere gender-role stereotyping to convey an overwhelming sense of the narrator's struggle to understand and accept the limitations imposed by her gender (¶ 11, 14, 64). The story's central conflict involves the daughter's struggle against society's determined role for females and her need to be free of these constraints. When she rebels, she does so because she decides that she is of "no use to anybody" (¶ 50). On first reading, this may seem to indicate submission to prevailing gender views, but Munro may be suggesting that the daughter has reached a level of maturity beyond that of the men in the story when she does without regret the only thing left to do.

V. S. NAIPAUL

B. Wordsworth

DO YOUR STUDENTS KNOW . . .

From 1845–1917, East Indians arrived in Trinidad and other islands of the Caribbean, primarily as indentured servants for plantations and large estates. Currently, 40 percent of the Trinidadian population is of East Indian descent.

In "B. Wordsworth," Naipaul combines a coming-of-age story with a complex meditation on postcolonial literature. When, at the end of the narrator says, "It was as though B. Wordsworth had never existed," he is making a comment about his old friend, but Naipaul also wants us to see larger implications in the statement. In literary/historical terms, there was not, in the Western world, a black equivalent to the English Romantic poet William Wordsworth. Naipaul is making two points here. First, he is noting the injustice committed by the Western world in failing to educate and treat as equal members of society those Africans it had forcibly located. Second, Naipaul, as a West Indian writer, is pointing out the folly of trying to imitate too slavishly the past writers of the colonial powers. There was only one Wordsworth, and B. Wordsworth, in trying to take on his identity, is really not a poet at all. Still, he does give the narrator a magical sense of the world, a sense that "when you're a poet, you can cry for everything." The boy sees possibilities in life that he never saw before, but he also realizes that such insight can bring with it tragedy.

JOYCE CAROL OATES

Shopping

DO YOUR STUDENTS KNOW . . .

The first shopping center in America, Country Club Plaza, opened in 1922 near Kansas City, Missouri and was modeled after Kansas City's sister city, Seville, Spain. In the mid-1980s, the first megamall was opened in Albert, Canada, complete with stores, a water park, and amusement rides.

Mrs. Dietrich and her teenage daughter Nola both seek and avoid their true selves amidst the crowds of mall shoppers and in the symbolic dressing and undressing associated with shopping. Both search for something different, but not on the racks of clothes.

Mrs. Dietrich shops carefully, holding on emotionally to Nola, yet seeking to maintain the delicate balance of "stiffness between" them (¶ 6). "Covertly" she watches Nola (¶ 18), hoping to see "herself again, reborn. . . . this time perfect" (¶ 28). Nola, on the other hand, "is a shrewd and discerning shopper," constantly pushing away from her mother, and thus, unclothing the realities of their lives (¶ 19, 22–26, 39, 63).

Sprawled on her seat in the mall, a disheveled woman sits covered by a "shape-less" coat, exposing her "inner thighs" (¶ 70). Nola is drawn to her, while Mrs. Dietrich is intent upon avoiding a confrontation. She believes the woman is too exposed, too open with her feelings, too obviously annoyed — exactly what Mrs. Dietrich struggles *not* to be, and exactly what Nola wishes her mother *would* be (¶ 10).

But only in one naked moment does Mrs. Dietrich's real anger and resentment show beneath the fraying seams of her usual calm. Then, she quickly repairs the hurt with closed lips and averted eyes (¶ 68, 72). In contrast, Nola attempts to strip away the false garments of their lives (¶ 47–53). Exhausted by the end of the shopping excursion, she dissolves in frustrated tears which she, like her mother, "frantically" tries to hide (¶ 72). And a frightened Mrs. Dietrich "wishes [that like the old woman] she had a cloak to draw over her daughter and herself, so that no one else would see" their nakedness (¶ 72).

FLANNERY O'CONNOR

Good Country People

DO YOUR STUDENTS KNOW . . .

Malebranche believed that since God contains all things, humans must experience all things through God. He theorized the idea of occasionalism, the concept that since all things come from God, even the most casual events in life are God's doing.

Manley Pointer, the con-man who comes to the house, is able to take advantage of both Mr. Hopewell and Joy/Hulga because they are too blinded by class prejudices to see him as he really is. Mrs. Hopewell idealizes the poorer country people around her, while her daughter disdains them. This story may be challenging for some students because of the way that O'Connor constantly upsets the reader's expectations. It is doubtful that she wants the reader to sympathize with Manley Pointer, but Joy/Hulga is far from being an admirable character.

In reading any of O'Connor's fiction, it is important to take into account her view of herself as a Catholic writer. While O'Connor is pointing out the ways in which people, in this case Manley Pointer, can misuse religion, she is equally critical of those who assume that faith is a childish quality they have outgrown. Joy/Hulga may be reading philosophical tracts on nothingness, but the uneducated Manley Pointer declares, "I been believing in nothing ever since I was born!"

Ask students what they think of Joy switching her name to Hulga. This is not simply a switch from a pretty name to an ugly one, but a deliberate renunciation of happiness, even if she does see it as "her greatest creative act." You might consider teaching this story with Ernest Hemingway's "A Clean, Well-Lighted Place," which includes a meditation on nothingness.

KATHERINE ANNE PORTER

The Jilting of Granny Weatherall

DO YOUR STUDENTS KNOW . . .

Well into the 1930s in the United States, a woman could sue for breach of promise following a broken engagement under what were called "heartbalm laws." She could sue for financial compensation to cover emotional wounds, benefits lost that she would have received by her future husband, and the time lost with her fiancé to find another man to marry. Now, most states have laws that allow a man to sue to ensure the "conditional gift" of an engagement ring is returned following a broken engagement. Despite the laws (while etiquette debates the return of the ring), courts are reluctant to intercede on affairs of the heart.

Although the time sequencing is disconcerting at times, the stream-of-consciousness narration creates a realistic impression of a dying woman's thoughts. It also allows for connections to be made between disjointed ideas that illuminate Granny's life. Granny emerges as a strong and courageous woman, capable of weathering all, including her own death. Although the priest is in the house, the anticipated sign from God does not arrive. Consequently, Granny resigns herself to being jilted once again — this time by Christ the bridegroom who does not appear (Matthew 9:15; 25:1–10).

CAROL SHIELDS

Fifteen Minutes in the Life of Larry Weller

DO YOUR STUDENTS KNOW . . .

Twenty-five thousand species of orchids exist in the world, with 110,000 hybrids. The flower has been recognized for its healing, antidepressant, and aphrodisiac qualities as far back as the ancient Greeks and Aztecs.

Before Larry Weller can take his first tentative steps toward taking charge of his life, he has to try on someone else's life (jacket) so that he can feel "something alive. Inside him, and outside him, too" (¶ 56). Larry's destiny has been determined by a series of mistakes (¶ 12, 24, 31, 42, 61), each "moving [him . . .] along." His struggle with his identity buffets him about until he understands three truths: No one at work will likely know the difference between the old and new Larry; he won't be able to enjoy his present activities; and if he becomes the new person who fits the jacket, he'll lose his girlfriend (¶ 28, 57, 59).

Remembering that the patient with no arms and legs remains a "real" person, Larry realizes he does not have to be someone else to be "somebody." No longer identifying with the "sheep" (¶ 15), Larry gets rid of the jacket and walks "straight toward the next thing that was going to happen to him" (¶ 66).

JOHN STEINBECK

The Chrysanthemums

DO YOUR STUDENTS KNOW . . .

Chrysanthemums, primarily identified with Japan, have been grown in China for over 2,500 years. This plant is considered a noble plant with properties that ensure longevity if eaten.

Initially, students may have a difficult time with this story because much in it is not explicitly stated but is instead implied through metaphors and symbols. For example, the setting in the first two paragraphs establishes the story's main theme of stunted growth and repressed desires. Steinbeck emphasizes the presence of fog that "closed off the Salinas Valley from the sky and from all the rest of the world," and "sat like a lid on the mountains and made of the great valley a closed pot." The fog acts as a lid that seals off the valley from the rest of the world and blocks out any sunshine in the winter.

"The Chrysanthemums" creates a metaphor for life and growth, and similarly, the pot, possibly symbolic of the home, is the place for planting and nourishing. But the valley where Elisa and Henry Allen live is described as a "closed pot," in keeping with the story's main idea. Likewise, Elisa and Henry's marriage lacks life and other elements necessary for nourishing a strong and healthy relationship. Students might consider similar relationships/marriages where growth is stunted and a spouse's needs are "pruned" or "clipped" instead of nourished. Interestingly, Henry is as frustrated as Elisa is. Both are victims — she of a society that does not take women's work seriously; he of an economic system that uses up men and then throws them away. Unfortunately, neither Henry nor Elisa can express this dissatisfaction, and as a result, it eats away at them and eventually estranges them from each other. Some students will consider this arrangement disturbing and unfair; others will see it as normal.

AMY TAN

Two Kinds

DO YOUR STUDENTS KNOW . . .

The Ed Sullivan Show, which began as a radio show called *The Toast of the Town*, became the longest-running variety show on television. On the air from 1955 to 1971, the show featured Elvis Presley in 1956 and introduced America to the Beatles in 1964.

Jing-mei's mother's expectations for her are motivated by her own losses as well as by a strong belief in the transforming power of America. Jing-mei thinks her mother seeks genius, but her mother wants only the best from her daughter. Jing-mei feels frustrated and unwanted because of this misconception and seeks acceptance for who she is. Determined to be independent and different from her mother, she still desperately needs her approval. Jing-mei eventually realizes that it takes both her mother's traditional Chinese values and her own Chinese-American experiences to make her whole, much as it takes the two separate musical compositions to create the completed song.

ANNE TYLER

Teenage Wasteland

DO YOUR STUDENTS KNOW . . .

Psychologists confirm that spanking children may get a quick response but may lead to long-term psychological problems including aggression, antisocial behavior, and future abuse of children or a spouse.

The major conflicts in Tyler's story center on the inability of Donnie to accept responsibility for his actions and his mother's reluctance to insist he do so. Initially, Donnie is a sympathetic character. Readers want to see Donnie's life turn around, but their sympathies are soon transferred to the parents, particularly to the mother. Although all parents make mistakes raising children, the Cobles fail to deal firmly with Donnie and lack confidence in themselves. If Donnie told the story from his point of view, however, the Cobles would surely appear inflexible and controlling. As in most of Tyler's works, at least one character attempts to solve problems by running from them.

POETRY

CHAPTER 15

UNDERSTANDING POETRY

This section supplements the text's coverage and offers some suggestions for class discussion or writing. Even when one explication is given for a poem, many others may of course be equally valid.

MARIANNE MOORE

Poetry

NIKKI GIOVANNI

Poetry

ARCHIBALD MACLEISH

Ars Poetica

DO YOUR STUDENTS KNOW . . .

At the height of the Depression in 1937, the Library of Congress created the position of Poet Laureate Consultant in Poetry to rejuvenate poetry in America. Each year, a poet is selected by the Librarian of Congress to represent the "poetic impulse" of the American public. During his term, Joseph Brodsky worked to add poetry to airports, supermarkets, and hotel rooms. Billy Collins, 2001–02 Poet Laureate, has created Poetry 180, a Web site to encourage daily readings of poems in America's high schools.

Students may enjoy beginning their study of poetry by discussing how poetry differs from prose. How do we know we are in the presence of a poem? Especially when we read narrative poetry, how can we tell a poem from a short story? Focusing on the way the poem looks and sounds is helpful. Students might compare these poems as poetry: All three include figurative language, especially metaphors and similes. MacLeish uses rhyme (mute/fruit, dumb/thumb) and alliteration ("silent as the sleeve-worn stone"). Giovanni says, "poetry is song," while Moore demands "imaginary gardens with real toads in them." What might they mean?

WRITING ACTIVITIES

1. What does Giovanni believe poets are trying to say? According to her definition, what is the role of the poet?

2. Giovanni says that "poems seek not acceptance but controversy." What does she mean? Do you agree?
3. Examine MacLeish's metaphors and discuss how they apply to poetry.
4. Do you think Moore really dislikes poetry? Support your answer with evidence from the poem.

WILLIAM SHAKESPEARE

That time of year thou mayst in me behold

To discuss this **sonnet** in relation to Shakespearean and Petrarchan form and to compare it with other sonnets, see the chapter on Form. Some of the figurative language in the poem is conventional — for example, associating autumn, sunset, and dying embers with aging; but the phrase "bare ruined choirs" seems more unusual. This image suggests both branches as well as an aging body. Why the religious association? Are we to imagine an empty church, a funeral? Note that each quatrain has a central metaphor that contributes to the sense of imminent loss addressed in the final couplet.

LOUIS ZUKOFSKY

I Walk in the old street

Like Shakespeare in "That time of year . . . ," Zukofsky speaks of songs and leaves, but in his poem it is spring, the season of hope, love, youth, rebirth. Still, the speaker does not seem young, and his elegiac tone resembles Shakespeare's. It is worth looking at words and images (old street, beloved songs, ripped doorbell) that suggest the speaker has been here before, years ago, and is returning to hear the songs "afresh." But he knows that time has passed, and he and the place have changed; he does not expect everything to be "the same."

E. E. CUMMINGS

l(a

You might begin by asking students what the poem looks like. Some students will probably notice that the symbol for the number one (1) and the letter "l" are very similar, and that the shape of the poem itself resembles them both; other students may feel that the poem looks like a falling leaf, an image that suggests autumn. Here, the concrete form clearly dominates and reinforces the meaning — the loneliness and isolation of the individual leaf (person) set against the passage of time. Read this poem with "in Just-" and "anyone lived in a pretty how town." In all three, Cummings plays with language and form, but the latter two poems are slightly more conventional; the poem "anyone . . ." even has stanzas and rhyme.

CHAPTER 16

DISCOVERING THEMES IN POETRY

ADRIENNE RICH

A Woman Mourned by Daughters

Despite the negative image of the mother in death ("swollen," "like a corpse pulled in from the sea") and in life ("crisp as a dead insect"), she seems in the last four lines to be united with the universe, at least to her daughter (the speaker), who feels compelled to do exactly as her mother would have wanted. The mother seems powerful in death. We often idealize people after they die and sometimes feel guilty about the way we treated them; whether the speaker in this poem does either is arguable. Ask the class to consider how different this poem might be if the speaker were a son.

RAYMOND CARVER

Photograph of My Father in His Twenty-Second Year

DO YOUR STUDENTS KNOW . . .

The idea of a doppelganger theorizes that each person is accompanied by a spiritual or ghostly counterpart. Reflected in the work of Immanuel Kant, this "shadow self" is thought to give a person ideas and advice through a process of mental osmosis. Kant postulated that there are two selves in each person and much of life is spent balancing the two selves.

The speaker is looking at a photograph of his father apparently taken before he knew him (possibly before he was born). Yet he reads into the photograph the characteristics of the man he knew. In the photograph, for example, the father holds a bottle of beer in his hand — but the son comments (in a pun on the word *holds*) that he, like his father, cannot hold his liquor. Students might find it interesting that the poet himself fought alcoholism. Some questions to discuss: Does the speaker also wish that he could be bolder? Why does it matter that he doesn't "even know the places to fish"? Does the son want to thank his father, or is he being ironic? You could compare this father/son relationship with those in Hayden's "Those Winter Sundays," Roethke's "My Papa's Waltz," Heaney's "Digging," Faulkner's "Barn Burning," Wilson's *Fences*, and Miller's *Death of a Salesman*.

JUDITH ORTIZ COFER

My Father in the Navy: A Childhood Memory

In 1994, Judith Ortiz Cofer told a class at Coker College in South Carolina that this is one of the few poems for which she consciously sought images to contribute to a picture of her father as a supernatural or heroic figure. She has him wearing his Navy dress whites, for example, rather than a regular uniform to reinforce holy and heroic associations. When asked, some students will be able to identify the religious allusions and images ("immaculate," "halo," "apparition," "rose from below," "parted the waters," "vigil," "angel heralding a new day," "evening prayer," Jonah and the whale). Some will also recognize heroic references to Odysseus, who visits the underworld (of shadows) and faces the sirens. Others will understand the Navy allusions: quasar, iron bellies of submarines, engines, dials. You will probably want to encourage discussion of how these seemingly disparate images work together, and what the child is feeling—love? Awe? Fear?

Poems about Parents

THEODORE ROETHKE

My Papa's Waltz

This poem may lead to spirited debate. Some students will be convinced the speaker was an abused child; others will insist such loving, joyful rough-housing is typical of fathers and sons. Students should find words or phrases to support their views. Often, students miss the sense of dancing around the kitchen and think "You beat time on my head" implies the father is angrily hitting his child. You may want to suggest another reading: the adult speaker's ambivalence as he recalls such childhood scenes. In support, you might contrast negative images (the alcohol making the boy dizzy, the mother's disapproving countenance, the boy hanging on "like death," the ear getting scraped) with positive ones (waltzing, romping, the boy "clinging" to his father's shirt as he is waltzed off to bed). The alcohol on the breath and the scraped knuckle suggest to some students a barroom brawl on the way home. Or, the knuckle and the "palm caked hard with dirt" may suggest manual labor. (Roethke's father owned a greenhouse.) A comparison with Hayden's "Those Winter Sundays" and Heaney's "Digging" works well.

DYLAN THOMAS

Do not go gentle into that good night

DO YOUR STUDENTS KNOW . . .

Improved medical technology in the twentieth century increased the average life span by thirty years, and recent human genome discoveries are leading toward new life-extension treatments. Life extension in yeast, worms, flies, and mice has been a success due to the manipulation of a genetic trigger that determines life span. Studies suggest such a genetic mutation also exists in humans, leading scientists to offer trials of life-extension treatments for humans by 2010.

To discuss this poem as a **villanelle,** see the chapter on Form. Some critics believe Thomas (the presumed speaker) chose this highly regulated form to treat his intense emotions in a controlled manner. Unlike other poets in this section, Thomas offers no details of either his father's life or his relationship with his father. His tone —half-begging, half-ordering his father not to give in, not to submit to the soothing temptation of death —makes clear he is not ready for his father to die. You might ask students to discuss why. Is Thomas angry with his father for dying before they have resolved conflicts? Does he feel his father is failing him, and if so, how? Is this poem about love, anger, disappointment, or some other emotion? Thomas describes the reactions to death of wise, good, wild, and grave men, suggesting his father is none of these.

LUCILLE CLIFTON

My Mama moved among the days

Many readers puzzle over what the "high grass" symbolizes and why the mother "seemed" to run back into it. You might start with questions about these. Some students will think the mother irresponsible, abandoning her children to lead her own life just as she has them almost grown. Others will see her as a timid soul, afraid to venture out into the world for which she has prepared her children — or as an earth mother, who goes back to the high grass to lead more children out. In a personal interview, poet Joan Murray offered another reading: Lucille Clifton raised six children of her own and has been dedicated to improving their lives. The mother in this poem also works for her children and can get them through the high grass to a better life, but cannot go herself, for she is defined by her own experience, which separates her from that next generation. Like Moses, she cannot cross into the promised land. Murray noted the importance of the word *seemed* in suggesting that the mother is not as free as her children think, not as untouched by life's troubles as her children believe. The speaker's use of the word *seemed* suggests that she now sees her mother more realistically.

ROBERT HAYDEN

Those Winter Sundays

A good way to begin is by asking about the speaker's tone: how does he seem to feel? Answers may include sad, sorry, guilty, remorseful, enlightened, regretful. Students might discuss what the adult speaker has realized about his father as years passed, how his feelings have changed, and what the "chronic angers" suggest. Some students may be confused by the word *offices*, which commonly means "places where one goes to work." They will need to know that the phrase "austere and lonely offices" refers to duties performed alone and may allude to religion (as the "good shoes" and the poem's title may suggest preparation for church). You may also point out the use of imagery and alliteration and the presence of exactly fourteen lines. Could it be called a modern sonnet? Note that in Reading and Writing about Poetry, this poem and "Digging" are compared in a student paper.

SEAMUS HEANEY

Digging

DO YOUR STUDENTS KNOW . . .

Irish homes have long depended on the cutting of turf from Ireland's bogs to supply heat and energy for homes. A slean is used to cut blocks of decaying peat and moss from the wetlands covering Ireland. The blocks are piled to dry for several months and then used for fuel. Dating back centuries in central Ireland, the Right of Turbary gave private individuals the right to cut from a bog. This permission was necessary due to the resettlement of confiscated lands during English rule.

The speaker "digs" with a pen; his father (a potato farmer) and grandfather (a turf cutter) dug with a spade. The speaker says he has no spade and compares his pen to a gun. Students should be encouraged to explain the comparison and also to discuss how his digging as a writer differs from his ancestors' work — and how he uses his pen to "dig" into his past and theirs. This poem is compared with "Those Winter Sundays" in a student paper in Reading and Writing about Poetry. You might also want to compare it with Carver's "Photograph of My Father in His Twenty-Second Year."

SIMON J. ORTIZ

My Father's Song

A member of the Acoma Pueblo community in New Mexico, Ortiz writes here about what he learned from his father, whom he now "misses." As he struggles for words to "say things," he remembers his father's voice and actions teaching him about life. He recalls planting corn with his father, an event associated with the tactile memory of "soft damp sand," and the discovery of a nest filled with "tiny pink" baby mice. His father's gentleness and the "catch" in his voice as he scoops up the babies and moves them to shade and safety create a link between father and son as two who revere life and "sing" of it. A comparison with "Digging" should lead to good discussion.

YEHUDA AMICHAI

My Father

This is a brief poem, and its central point — that the speaker's father was a kind, loving man — is an uncomplicated one. If students have difficulty with the poem, it will be with the images, which are surrealistic in a low-key way. The least transparent of these images occurs where the speaker says, "The memory of my father is wrapped up in/white paper, like sandwiches taken up for a day at work." It is probably best if students don't initially spend too much time puzzling over these lines. Encourage them instead to read through the entire poem in order to get a sense of the father's character. Once they have a sense of the kind of man he was, they can return to the first two lines and try to parse their meanings more closely. The image of sandwiches in paper, for example, is a homely one. Like the sandwiches, the memory of the speaker's father can be unwrapped or unfolded when he needs nourishment.

JILL BIALOSKY

The Boy Beheld His Mother's Past

This poem is a variation on a French form called the pantoum. A strict pantoum is written entirely in quatrains, and the second and fourth lines of each stanza become the first and third lines of each succeeding stanza. Bialosky no doubt chose the pantoum form because it so clearly establishes a link between past and future, which is after all one of the poem's main themes. She chooses to disrupt the form in the third stanza because it is at this point that the boy begins to realize that his mother's life might have gone very differently in the past and that it might take a different turn in the future. The inevitable progression of repeated lines is disrupted as the boy ponders the questions of fate and free will. The poem ends by repeating its first line, thereby signaling that the problem is insoluble.

Poems about Love

CHRISTOPHER MARLOWE

The Passionate Shepherd to His Love

SIR WALTER RALEIGH

The Nymph's Reply to the Shepherd

Written in the pastoral tradition of idyllic country life (groves, fields, lambs, birds, flowers), Marlowe's poem is also an elaborate seduction. A good way to begin is by asking students how successful they think the shepherd will be. Some will complain about his extravagant exaggerating or question his sincerity; others will note that he is not offering love or marriage — just material gifts. A comparison with

Robert Burns's "Oh, My Love Is like a Red, Red Rose" might be useful. Burns also exaggerates, but he promises love with his similes and hyperboles and does not seem to be asking for favors. A comparison with Marvell's "To His Coy Mistress" also allows students to see a seduction in the *carpe diem* tradition, with its implicit threat to the young woman: Time is passing, so if you do not give yourself to me now, you may end up dying a virgin. But the best companion to Marlowe's poem is Raleigh's "The Nymph's Reply to the Shepherd." Asking students why the nymph says no, or how the shepherd and nymph differ in their views of love, generates a good discussion or writing exercise.

THOMAS CAMPION

There is a garden in her face

Campion's typical lyric in the Elizabethan and Jacobean tradition includes several conventions: roses and lilies in the lady's complexion, her cherry-red lips, her pearl-white (or snow-white) teeth, her beautiful but killing eyes. Protective of her lips and her "wares" ("cherry-ripe" was a cry of fruit-sellers), this woman is independent, insisting upon deciding for herself when she will be kissed. It might be fun to compare her to Raleigh's nymph in "The Nymph's Reply to the Shepherd."

WILLIAM SHAKESPEARE

My Mistress' Eyes Are Nothing like the Sun

Students usually enjoy this antisonnet for its parody of the conventional hyperbole in love poems, such as Campion's "There Is a Garden in Her Face," or even the much later Burns poem, "Oh, My Love Is like a Red, Red Rose". This speaker is a realist — the kind of man Raleigh's nymph seeks — who loves his mistress as she is and wastes no time on excessive flattery or promises.

ROBERT BROWNING

Meeting at Night

Parting at Morning

Browning's rush of words and omission of complete sentences in "Meeting at Night" convey the intensity of his speaker's eagerness and anticipation as he hurries over sea and land to a reunion with his beloved. The speed of his boat causes the "startled little waves" to leap, and as he reaches the farmhouse, few readers are surprised to hear of "two hearts beating each to each." "Parting at Morning," however, offers a total reversal in mood and tone. As the Sun appears over the mountain following his straight golden path toward the speaker, the speaker seems ready to get back into his boat and depart — with no mention of the second beating heart of the night before. Browning indicated years after writing these poems that the second was the man's "confession of how fleeting is the belief" that the "raptures" of the first poem "are self-sufficient and enduring" as they seem at first. A comparison with Dorothy Parker's poem seems inevitable.

ELIZABETH BARRETT BROWNING

How Do I Love Thee?

In this popular sonnet from *Sonnets from the Portuguese* written to Robert Browning, Barrett Browning (re)counts the "ways" of her love, using the Petrarchan form. You might ask students to supply adverbs (and alternatives to adverbs already supplied) to describe how the speaker loves. For example, lines 2–4 might be called loving "infinitely" or "boundlessly" or "absolutely"; line 8 might be "modestly" or "straightforwardly."

EDNA ST. VINCENT MILLAY

What Lips My Lips Have Kissed

DO YOUR STUDENTS KNOW. . .

When this sonnet was written in the 1920s, the word *flapper* was coined to describe a young woman who rebelled against convention. Most American women were not flappers, but the flapper's shocking behavior allowed other women to explore Jazz Age freedoms without fear.

Although Millay herself was in her early thirties when she wrote this poem, she created a speaker who (like Eliot's "The Love Song of J. Alfred Prufrock") sees herself growing older. Unlike Prufrock, this woman has enjoyed romantic, sexual relationships. Still, the "unremembered lads" of those relationships are now "ghosts" or "birds" who have vanished from the "lonely tree" she has become. Her reference to men as birds is an interesting variation on the slang term for women (chiefly British). Comparisons not only with Prufrock but also with the speaker in Shakespeare's "That Time of Year . . ." will provide fruitful discussion of imagery and tone, and of differences in attitude toward love. See also Dorothy Parker's depiction of sex roles.

W. H. AUDEN

Stop all the clocks, cut off the telephone

The extravagance of the speaker's grief at the death of a lover balances between pain ("I thought that love would last forever. I was wrong.") and humor ("Prevent the dog from barking with a juicy bone"). The speaker seems to be directing a play — or directing traffic — spitting out orders to an unknown cast or crew to dismantle the universe now that the beloved is dead. However ambiguous the tone, the reader feels the enormity of the love and the grief.

DOROTHY PARKER

General Review of the Sex Situation

In her usual witty way, but perhaps without the bite one expects of her, Parker summarizes the stereotypical view of men's and women's attitudes toward love (what women want) and sex (what men want). Some popular controversial books, such as John Gray's *Men Are from Mars, Women Are from Venus* (HarperCollins, 1992) support the view that men and women are planets apart. A class could well debate the validity of Parker's apparent assertions. Is her conclusion ironic, undercutting all she has said and suggesting that the differences really do not matter? Or is she merely alluding to the eternal battle between the sexes?

SYLVIA PLATH   TED HUGHES

Wreath for a Bridal   A Pink Wool Knitted Dress

American poet Sylvia Plath was on a Fulbright fellowship in Cambridge, England, when she and Hughes (who would much later become Poet Laureate of England) were married in June 1956. Clearly, his poem recounts the actual wedding more realistically and with hindsight; her poem portrays their sexual and spiritual union more symbolically and with a passionate immediacy. Note Plath's use of almost pastoral nature imagery: the lovers lie in sense-assaulting cut-grass; the owl and cows approve their union. An interesting exercise would involve comparing the Hughes poem with Plath's description of the marriage in a June 18, 1956, letter to her brother Warren. See *Letters Home by Sylvia Plath*, selected and edited by her mother, Aurelia Schober Plath (Harper, 1972). Hughes alludes to their later marital problems when he says, "Before anything had smudged anything / You stood at the altar. Bloomsday." The wedding took place on June 16, Bloomsday in James Joyce's *Ulysses*; Plath's senior thesis was on Joyce; and Molly Bloom's "yes" parallels the traditional "I do."

Poems about War

RUPERT BROOKE

The Soldier

WILFRED OWEN

Anthem for Doomed Youth

Brooke's poem captures the British patriotism of the early years of World War I; Owen's, the disillusionment that followed. The titles highlight their differences in tone and outlook. Both died in the war. Brooke imagines himself a hero dying for the land he loves; should he die, his sacrifice will be a fair return for all he has received. Owen, angry and distressed at the loss of young lives around him, mourns the youths dying "as cattle," with traditional funeral prayers, bells, and choirs replaced by the sounds of rifle, shell, and bugle. This sonnet begins with a shocking image but ends quietly with the image of blinds being lowered at the end of the day, shutting out the world, as these young men have been shut out of it. A contrast between these poems should lead to discussions of contemporary views of war, especially with today's instant media coverage.

WILLIAM BUTLER YEATS

An Irish Airman Foresees His Death

Yeats called Owen's poetry morbid and sentimental. Students may enjoy contrasting the more matter-of-fact tone of this poem and its message about war with both Brooke's and Owen's. The speaker's attitudes toward his country, his enemies, his job, his life all suggest that Yeats sees those who die in wars not as heroes or martyrs but as ordinary men.

ROBERT LOWELL

For the Union Dead

DO YOUR STUDENTS KNOW . . .

A *trope,* from the Greek word for "turn," is the deviation of a word from its traditional or conventional use to a new, unique usage. This literary device depends on the use of metaphor and metonymy. Metaphors imply concrete and sensory comparisons; metonymy uses an object's attribute as a stand-in for that object.

Lowell begins with a symbol of decay — the abandoned aquarium with broken, boarded windows. Other images of loss accompanying "progress" appear as barbed fence and steamshovels that mar Boston Common to dig an "underworld" (hellish?) garage. Opposite, the monument to Robert Shaw (the poem's unnamed

Colonel, the hero who trained and led a black regiment during the Civil War, dying with half his men) "sticks like a fishbone / in the city's throat." Why? Because such heroism, like the aquarium, is gone? Because modernity has lost a respect for both nature and history? In place of the aquarium's fish are "giant finned cars," and Lowell notes that "there are no monuments for the last war here," just a commercial photo of a Mosler safe surviving Hiroshima. Note: Students who have seen the film *Glory* will recall Shaw's story.

DENISE LEVERTOV

What Were They Like?

DO YOUR STUDENTS KNOW . . .

Three forms of the written Vietnamese language have developed over many centuries, each adapted to the respective colonizing country. *Chu han,* developed in the years of Chinese domination, used Chinese characters to transcribe spoken Vietnamese and was used into the early twentieth century for official business and traditional literature. *Chu nom* was a vernacular script created by Portuguese missionaries attempting to master the Vietnamese language. Under French rule, the publishing industry and newspapers used *chu quoc ngu,* as both a unifying, modern writing system and a method for disseminating French culture.

Levertov participated in the March on the Pentagon during the Vietnam War and, with Norman Mailer, Robert Lowell, and many others, argued that artists needed to use their talents for political purposes. Students may disagree about the political purpose of this poem: Is it merely anti-Vietnam War or antiwar in general? Is it bemoaning the loss of a culture or berating those who may have unwittingly destroyed it? It may also be worth discussing who asks the questions and who answers them — a naive American and a wise Vietnamese? A college student and a professor?

CARL PHILLIPS

On the Notion of Tenderness in Wartime

This poem may prove difficult for students to interpret since the war referred to in the title is never mentioned directly in the poem itself. Instead, it forms a backdrop for the real subject, the separation of the speaker from his lover. Together with the ongoing drought where the speaker lives, it serves to convey a sense of the world as an inhospitable, hostile place. In the last two stanzas, the speaker talks in more detail about the relationship, in particular about the first time he and his lover made love. The lover's statement — "now we're alone in the world"— operates on at least two levels. In one sense, it means that the two lovers were set apart from the rest of the world by their new intimacy. In hindsight, though, the statement also seems prophetic, since each of the lovers is now "alone in the world" in the sense that the two are separated from each other. When the speaker says, "Sometimes, even here, it can still get that quiet," the quiet he is referring to is that which followed his lover's statement.

BORIS SLUTSKY

How Did They Kill My Grandmother?

In this painful, ironic poem, Slutsky's speaker answers a question from an unidentified questioner: "How did they kill my grandmother? / I'll tell you how they killed her." The opening immediately prepares the reader to identify whoever "they" are as murderers. Slutsky then presents the almost predictable but no less horrifying tale of Nazi atrocity, this time in a Russian town. He sets off particularly chilling lines on the right sides of the stanzas. The final line, "That is how she died there," almost sounds like a rebuke of the questioner — and perhaps the reader — as if the speaker means, "You wanted to know. Now you know. Are you satisfied?" Students might discuss how the speaker, identified as a soldier, arouses sympathy, horror, and anger.

BILLY JOEL

Goodnight Saigon

The obvious comparison to Denise Levertov's "What Were They Like?" could lead to some discussion of the way we view "the enemy" in any war and the way Americans viewed the Vietnam War. Levertov takes a more idealistic view, while Joel uses pop culture references to increase realism. But his song lyrics also emphasize the horrors and ironies of war through rhyme ("We came in spastic / Like tameless horses / We left in plastic / As numbered corpses") and repetition ("And we would all go down together"; "And we were sharp / As sharp as knives"; "And they were sharp / As sharp as knives").

YUSEF KOMUNYAKAA

Facing It

Anyone who has seen the Vietnam Veterans Memorial will recognize the poet's description before he identifies it. Most visitors, like the poem's speaker, say they were moved — often to tears — whether or not they knew anyone who fought in the war. Some readers may find the poem equally moving. The speaker moves in and out of the wall, becoming part of the names on the wall and merging with the other visitors. Students might look for optical illusions the speaker identifies (names shimmering on a blouse, an arm lost inside the stone) and discuss their effect and significance. The multiple meanings of the title include looking at the monument, facing its meaning, and facing the war experience.

WISLAWA SZYMBORSKA

The End and the Beginning

This poem is at once depressing and hopeful. It is depressing in that war appears to be an inevitability, almost a fact of nature. It is hopeful in that it celebrates the ability of human beings to do the hard work of rebuilding a society after a war. This is not exciting work, nor is it glamorous, which is why it receives little attention. Nor is it work that needs the support of grand ideas or schemes. Things are rebuilt and restored because they are needed, not because they fit into a political program. At this stage, ideology is unimportant, even undesirable. It was ideology, after all, that led to the war in the first place. Now the arguments for those systems of thought are thrown away in "the garbage pile." Forgetfulness of the ideologies and the war itself is a necessary part of the healing process. At the same time, however, the absence of memory obviously makes it easier for the events of the war to be repeated.

CHAPTER 17

READING AND WRITING ABOUT POETRY

WRITING ACTIVITIES

1. Briefly discuss the way "Those Winter Sundays" by Robert Hayden and "Digging" by Seamus Heaney are highlighted and annotated in the text. Choose another pair of poems for students to highlight and annotate in pairs or as a class.
2. Ask students to plan an essay that could be written about the second pair of poems you have chosen in Activity 1. You might want students to write the essay, or you might want them to concentrate on planning at this point.
3. Ask students to write about what they have learned about reading and preparing to write about poetry. How does writing about poetry differ from writing about fiction?

GROUP ACTIVITIES

You might ask students to highlight and annotate a text and plan an essay in groups (as in Activity 2 above) and then ask them to work individually to write that essay. Or after the group-planning activity, you may want each student to plan and write his or her own essay about a topic that has not been discussed.

CHAPTER 18

VOICE

You will notice that this guide approaches the poetry chapters according to two basic formats. The more common format includes suggested questions for discussion, group activities, and discussion; occasionally, suggestions for further critical reading are included. The second format applies to poems that are discussed in detail in the text. To avoid repetition, these poems are explicated and sometimes given additional suggestions for classroom discussion. When given only one interpretation of a poem, other readings may certainly be equally valid.

EMILY DICKINSON

I'm nobody! Who are you?

The speaker's voice is gently whimsical as she states her preference for anonymity and insists that the listener not reveal that there are two of them choosing to be nobodies, lest someone advertise the fact. For contemporary readers in this era of tabloid and exposé journalism, the unpleasant side of celebrity may seem even more apparent than in Dickinson's day. The line "How public — like a Frog —" clearly mocks those who seek fame, while the words "admiring Bog" may well mock fans and followers of celebrities.

LOUISE GLÜCK

Gretel in Darkness

DO YOUR STUDENTS KNOW . . .

Gretel, which is a form of the name Margaret, means "pearl." This girl's name is extremely common in German folktales, which the Brothers Grimm collected in 1810 and published. This name is the equivalent of the American "Jane Doe," a name used to symbolize every woman. Here, the poem reflects on both the sibling relationship between Hansel and Gretel, as well as the aftermath for any woman living with trauma.

Gretel killed to save her brother, but her guilt haunts her nonetheless. The trauma of her experience, her German name, the kiln, the "armed firs," and the allusion to spies may suggest the horrors of World War II, focusing particularly on those who killed to survive. Or it may suggest the recurring nightmare (now named posttraumatic stress syndrome) of soldiers and others who have experienced atrocities and who may have killed in legally justifiable circumstances. Comparisons with the use of the fairy-tale form in Gordimer's "Once upon a Time," Lawrence's "The Rocking-Horse Winner," or Sexton's "Cinderella" should prove fruitful.

LEONARD ADAMÉ

My Grandmother Would Rock Quietly and Hum

As the adult speaker looks back at his childhood relationship with his grandmother, he vividly contrasts his youth ("laughing greedily" at receiving a quarter, waking to sounds of cooking) with her age ("swelled hands," lost teeth, sweaters even in summer). As an adult, he realizes how much she gave him as she passed on her memories and traditions. Ironically, although he is now an adult, he still cannot see as much as his grandmother saw in her aged wisdom; yet as he hears the echo her feet and sees her fading calendar pictures, he remembers some of what she taught him. A comparison with Ortiz's "My Father's Song" and Ríos's "Nani" could lead to discussions of ethnic identity.

LANGSTON HUGHES

Negro

DO YOUR STUDENTS KNOW ...

Since 1989, U.S. Rep. John Conyers (D-Michigan) has reintroduced House Resolution 40, the Commission to Study Reparations Proposals for African Americans Act, requiring a study of slavery's impact. These reparations — the financial and/or land reimbursement to African-American citizens for the sufferings of an estimated 8 million enslaved from 1619 to 1865 — are likened to payments received by Holocaust survivors and those Japanese-Americans interned during World War II. Nearly 35 million African-Americans are the direct descendents of slaves.

Note Hughes's use of a repetitive stanza form and especially his repetition of the word "I," reminiscent of Walt Whitman's style. As in his poem "I, Too, Sing America," Hughes echoes Walt Whitman. Here, Hughes embraces his blackness and his homeland, Africa, much as Whitman embraces America and all humanity. See also Alexie's "Defending Walt Whitman," Angelou's "Africa," and other Hughes poems in the poetry casebook.

ROBERT BROWNING

My Last Duchess

The contrast between the duke's jealous arrogance and materialism and his young wife's natural innocence is underscored by what each values: his painting, sculpture, power, wealth, and family pedigree versus her enjoyment of the sunset, bough of cherries, and white mule. While she blushes and smiles at people, he "choose[s] never to stoop." Some students may believe the duchess has actually been unfaithful; they should look carefully for evidence.

LESLIE MARMON SILKO

Where Mountain Lion Lay Down with Deer

WRITING ACTIVITIES

1. In lines 13–15, the speaker says, "It is better to stay up here. . . ." Have students answer the question, "'better' than what?"
2. Ask students to write about the significance of the title. Why is past tense — not present — appropriate here?
3. Compare the images in lines 1–12 with those in lines 19–29. If the last ten lines tell the story of the speaker's birth, what are the first twelve lines about?

GROUP ACTIVITY

In lines 19–29, the speaker relates "the story of [her] birth." Have students work in groups to create similar metaphors for birth.

DISCUSSION

Silko's poetry embodies the Native American culture of Laguna Pueblo, New Mexico, where she grew up. Cultural tales and legends permeate her poetry and fiction. She tells stories as ceremony, as celebration, and as a means of defining herself. Students will be tempted to fuse speaker and poet, especially with this selection; encourage them, instead, to define the speaker ("I") in lines 1 and 4 as an individual persona, but to consider the "I" in line 9 as something else: the "I" of movement off the reservation into mainstream American life, the "I" who "swam away," the "I" of the ancestors.

In trying to recapture a true sense of her ancestry, the speaker moves from the role of "modern" woman to that of traditional Native American woman, returning from the present to the past, from "civilization" to a more peaceful natural existence (Q 1, 2).

The images of "black rock mountain," "grey stone cliff," "faded black stone," "freezing mountain water," "narrow mossy canyon," and "deep canyon stone" suggest a mystical, dangerous journey. These dangers, juxtaposed with the benign images of "pale blue leaves," "tall yellow flowers," and "mossy canyon," present a parallel to the lion lying with its natural prey, the deer. This phenomenon is associated biblically with the Messiah's arrival as predicted in Isaiah 11:6: "The wolf also shall dwell with the lamb, and the leopard shall lie down with the kid; and the calf and the young lion and the fatling together." But note that in this poem the peace is represented as in the past rather than the future: "the mountain lion *lay* down with deer." What does this suggest to your students? The rhetorical device of parallel structure gives the poem the suggestion of song: "I climb . . . / I smell . . . / Returning . . . / Returning . . . / How I danced . . . / How I swam. . . ." Students may equate this with a chant or a prayer of Native American rituals.

Silko's poem directly addresses cultural extinction in lines 16–19, and then suggests the possibility of regeneration through nature in lines 20–29. It is through nature that culture is preserved in "Where Mountain Lion Lay Down with Deer" (Q 4).

You may want to teach this with Erdrich's "Windigo" (ethnic identity) or with Plath's "Morning Song" to compare it with a mother's view of birth.

JANICE MIRIKITANI

Suicide Note

WRITING ACTIVITIES

1. Ask students to write the speaker a letter, telling her why she should not end her life.
2. Have students take on the persona of an academic advisor or college counselor and write the parents a letter, urging them to treat their daughter with greater sensitivity. Offer specific suggestions about how they should change their behavior.
3. Ask students to write a character sketch of the narrator.

GROUP ACTIVITY

Have students identify metaphors and similes and discuss why they are effective. Have a member of each group list patterns of figures of speech on the board: for example, snow and ice or birds. What similarities and differences do they find? This project could turn into a moving dramatic reading with one speaker as third-person narrator, one as the writer of the letter, and other group members as a parental chorus, chanting "not ___ enough."

DO YOUR STUDENTS KNOW . . .

One in four American women will experience depression during her lifetime, but Asian-American women have the highest suicide rate for women between the ages of fifteen to twenty-four and of those over the age of sixty-five. The stigma surrounding mental health and accessing psychotherapy is compounded with cultural barriers, discouraging seeking help when depressed.

DISCUSSION

The epigraph provides context and sets the tone for this "note." The speaker clearly says the note is an apology, and there is nothing to indicate insincerity on her part. She expresses an "if only" wish to have been a male — of vast importance, traditionally, in Asian-American cultures. She repeats that she has worked hard. And she offers to make a sacrifice, to offer penance. She has evidently written previous notes that have been shredded and that cover her like "whispers / of sorries / sorries" (ll. 50–55) (Q 1).

Although the speaker does not openly express anger, the thirteen repetitions of "not ___ enough" echo throughout the poem, too persistent to go unheeded, too strong to be denied. The introductory note tells us that the student had less than a 4.0 grade point average, suggesting that her parents were ambitious and demanding. The imagined son has shoulders as broad as a sunset; the speaker is a "sparrow / sillied and dizzied by the wind" (ll. 38–39). Other revealing phrases are "on the edge," "crippled wings," "bitter cloth." This mother Earth's breast is "white and cold and silent," a far cry from the nurturing, supportive embrace of a kinder mother Earth (Q 2).

It would be interesting to teach this with Tan's "Two Kinds" if you examine Asian-American cultures (ethnic identity). You may also want to compare the suicide in this poem with those in Robinson's "Richard Cory." If you prefer to explore the male/female theme, you might pair the poem with Kaplan's "Doe Season."

DEBORAH GARRISON

An Idle Thought

WRITING ACTIVITIES

1. Divide the poem at those places where you feel the speaker changes subject. Then, re-order the parts of the poem. Feel free to add a word or two in order to smooth out the transitions, but try not to change the wording more than is necessary. Once you have read through your new poem, write a paragraph on how it differs from the original.
2. Write a three-page research essay on the experiences of people who marry at an early age.

GROUP ACTIVITY

Divide the class into three groups. Then, assign each of the groups one of the people the speaker describes: the seductress, the second wife, and her husband. Each group should define the attitude of the speaker toward their character and be prepared to discuss ways in which the speaker's view may be biased.

DISCUSSION

Students will probably enjoy the humorous rhymes (Amis / famous, for example) and lighthearted tone of this poem. Although the speaker begins by lamenting her lack of sexual adventurousness, she and the reader see by the end of the poem that she and her husband are a perfect match. The phrase "an idle thought" refers to a thought one doesn't intend to do anything about (Q 20). The speaker's fantasies about being a seductress or wronged wife are not things she expects to come to pass (Q 1). Even in her fantasies, she quickly brings herself back down to earth, so it is likely that she is right in thinking she would not make a good seductress (Q 4). She is undoubtedly being unfair to both herself and her husband when she assumes that the only reason he doesn't leave her is that he is as timid as she is (Q 4). Ironically, when she imagined him leaving her, she was kinder to him than she is when she imagines he simply isn't *capable* of leaving her (Q 3).

"An Idle Thought" serves as a good example of poetic organization. As it currently stands, the poem is charming and entertaining. Imagine how different the effect would be if the order of the information were reversed, if the speaker began by touting her own fidelity and then moved on to disparage seductresses. The poem would still be humorous but considerably more barbed. Writing Activity 1 suggests having students reorganize the poem. You could have students read their new versions in class as a way of beginning the discussion. What do the students conclude about the effect that the order has?

You might teach this poem with "Cowboys Are My Weakness," "The Littoral Zone," "Happy Endings," and "A General Review of the Sex Situation." The first three selections are short stories that examine troubled romantic relationships, and the fourth is a poem that examines the tensions between the sexes in a humorous but rueful way.

JAMES TATE

Nice Car, Camille

WRITING ACTIVITIES

1. "Nice Car, Camille" lacks many traditional poetic qualities. Ask students to write an essay in which they argue that it should or should not be considered a poem.
2. Have students write an essay in which they are high school guidance counselors. How would they explain Camille's lack of interest in making friends?

GROUP ACTIVITY

It may be difficult for students to see the point of some of the details in the poem. Break the class into three groups and assign one of the following questions to each group:

1. Why does it matter that Camille speeds?
2. Why might it be important that Camille's father owned an oil company?
3. Why are we told that the man Camille's mother later married was a gambler?

DISCUSSION

This is an exceedingly easy poem to read, but discussing it may prove more difficult. Tate has chosen deliberately banal language, so students may assume that the poem's meaning — or perhaps lack of it — is self-evident. For this reason, "Nice Car, Camille" may be helpful in beginning a discussion of what constitutes the essence of poetry.

Camille is an "incredibly beautiful," unhappy, young woman whose chief asset is that she drives "a really sexy car." The speaker recalls that, "Camille didn't really make any friends in school. She didn't want any." The puzzle at the heart of the poem, then, is why someone who doesn't want friends bothers about the car she drives and, presumably, the way she looks. At some level, Camille must want the world's approval, even if she does not want its friendship (Q 1). Based on her personal history, it is easy to see why she would be wary of forming attachments.

The poem is as much about the speaker as it is about Camille. He sees her and her car as a symbol of the gap between a glamorous appearance and a sad reality (Q 3). He also feels guilty about not having reached out to her. The statement, "That was my contribution to making her life unforgettable" can be read a number of ways, but it is probably spoken in self-reproach.

You might teach this poem with "Sears Life," "Christopher Robin," "This Is My Letter to the World," and "Chin." Like "Nice Car, Camille," the first two selections may challenge students' assumptions what about poetry is. "This Is My Letter to the World" expresses the speaker's ambivalence, and "Chin" shows how a student's emotional problems are related to his abusive home life.

No — maybe / to suit / herself?

DORIANNE LAUX

The Shipfitter's Wife

WRITING ACTIVITIES

1. The shipfitter seems more like a force of nature than a person in this poem. Ask students to write an essay in which the shipfitter expresses his own feeling about his job.
2. Have students reflect on why the poem is in the past tense.

GROUP ACTIVITY

Divide the class into small groups and ask the groups to brainstorm reasons why Laux chose "shipfitter" as the husband's profession. Why did she not make him a carpenter or plumber or doctor?

DISCUSSION

There is something raw and elemental about the shipfitter as described by his wife. She compares his smell to that of the ocean, and she includes a succession of sensory images clustered around his work. For the speaker, to make love to another person is to experience what that person is and has known. The shipfitter is not simply himself but is also "the clamp, the winch, / the white fire of the torch." The Group Activity asks students to reflect on the meaning of the shipfitter's profession. If he had come home every night, his wife's statement that she "loved him most / when he came home from work" might indicate that all was well in the relationship. Given that he was away much of the time, however, the statement may well refer to problems in the marriage (Q 1). The entire poem is spoken in the past tense, which may indicate either that the shipfitter has died or that the marriage has ended (Q 3).

But the poem is about more than the expansion of self that can occur during lovemaking. It is also about gender differences as they relate to career. It is important to note that the wife does not tell us anything about her own day. At the same time, she is a more fully drawn character than her husband (Q 4). Note, too, that she says, "I'd open his clothes and take *the* whole day inside me [emphasis added]," as opposed to "his whole day." Note, too, the way in which various aspects of the husband's day — "the torch, the whistle / and the long drive home" become part of the couple's lovemaking (Q 2).

Consider teaching this poem with "Pitcher," "The Fireman," "How Do I Love Thee," and "When in Disgrace with Fortune and Men's Eyes." The first two selections examine the metaphoric possibilities of particular professions, and the third and fourth are among the most famous love sonnets in English.

ROBERT FROST

Fire and Ice

WRITING ACTIVITIES

1. Ask students to write briefly on which would be preferable, death by fire or death by ice. Why?
2. Students could do some research on "new" ways the world could end: movement toward the Sun / away from the Sun; the greenhouse effect; apocalypse or "nuclear winter"; return of an ice age.

DISCUSSION

A thorough discussion of this poem — especially of tone — can be found in the text. Metaphorically, the speaker seems to be saying that desire (l. 3) and hatred (l. 6) are both powerful.

THOMAS HARDY

The Man He Killed

WRITING ACTIVITIES

1. The last stanza begins with "Yes; quaint and curious war is!" Have students identify ways in which war is "quaint and curious"— and ironic.
2. Ask students to describe a situation in which they were morally, politically, or ethically at odds with someone with whom they could have been friends under different circumstances (a parent, a teacher, a coach or competitor, a political foe).
3. Ask students to write a letter from the speaker to someone back home, explaining the situation in the poem.

GROUP ACTIVITY

Create a dialogue between the narrator and his "foe" in a setting in which they meet and become friends. Perhaps they could discuss the moral dilemma that war creates.

DISCUSSION

The text includes a thorough discussion of tone in the poem. If necessary, remind students that the speaker is not the poet. Try to get them to see that the poet regards war as irrational and harmful; however, the speaker does not have the degree of insight the poet does. He enlisted because he was out of work and, trying to reconcile his own values with his having killed a man, can conclude only how "quaint and curious war is!" What do students make of "He" rather than "I" in the title? Discuss Hardy's attitude toward war and its influence on people's lives.

If you are teaching a unit on perspectives toward war, you may want to teach this poem with Owen's "Dulce et Decorum Est," Jarrell's "The Death of the Ball Turret Gunner," Reed's "Naming of Parts," and other poems about war in Discovering Themes in Poetry.

AMY LOWELL

Patterns

WRITING ACTIVITIES

1. Have students describe the speaker. What makes her seem warm and compassionate? Remote and unemotional?
2. Ask students to identify all the patterned items in the poem (garden paths, dress, etc.). How do they serve to reinforce each other?
3. Have students respond to the question in the last line, "What are patterns for?"

GROUP ACTIVITY

If you are interested in drama, you could have students dramatize this poem, turning it into a brief one-act play. This kind of group activity would also work with "My Last Duchess" and "Porphyria's Lover." If you choose this activity, you may want to tell your students that Amy Lowell was initially influenced as a poet by two actresses.

DISCUSSION

You will find a discussion in the text. You could connect "Patterns" to Jackson's "The Lottery" if you wish to examine the importance of ritual and pattern. You could also compare the speakers in this poem and in Hardy's "The Man He Killed" or in Lovelace's "To Lucasta, Going to the Wars."

ADAM ZAGAJEWSKI

Try to Praise the Mutilated World

WRITING ACTIVITY

1. This poem lists a number of positive and negative things about the world. Ask students to write about the things that they would have included if they had written this poem.
2. This poem appeared in *The New Yorker* shortly after the attacks of September 11, 2001. Have students write about another situation, either political or personal, in which they think this poem could be comforting (Q 4).

GROUP ACTIVITY

Divide the class into small groups and ask each group to come up with a phrase that could be used in place of the title and refrain. The phrase they choose should not include the word *praise*.

DISCUSSION

Although there is no mention of a deity, the poem has a decidedly religious feel. The speaker and listener are unidentified, and this fact helps give the poem the feel of a universal prophetic utterance (Q 1). More importantly, while we can certainly "praise" anyone or anything — an athlete, a musician, a sunset — this word is most frequently used in the context of worship. More specifically, the exhortation to "praise" is common in the biblical Psalms. One of the most prominent characteristics of the Psalms (aside from parallelism) is the repetition of selected words and phrases, a technique Zagajewski employs here. Note that each time the word *praise* is repeated, the speaker's instruction is slightly different. He begins by saying "Try to praise" and ends by simply saying "Praise." It is as though the speaker, having tried different formulations to persuade his listener, opts in the end for the simplest and most direct (Q 2). The differences between "Praise the Mutilated World" and the Psalms are just as important as the similarities, however. In the Psalms, the world is not praised but is presented as a reason for praising God. Not only does Zagajewski make no mention of God, but also the world we are told to praise is "mutilated."

This is a political poem, but not the sort that attempts to advance any narrow ideology. Rather, it examines politics with a skeptical eye and finds it wanting in comparison with moments of personal joy. Politics is associated with "exiles," "refugees," and executioners, whereas personal, individual experience is associated with a "park in autumn," a "gray feather," and "gentle light." As someone who lived through the years of communist dictatorship in Poland, Zagajewski is understandably reluctant to view the world in primarily political terms. The poem is ultimately positive in that it affirms that there are still things in the world (despite its mutilated state) that possess beauty and value (Q 3).

Consider teaching this poem with "Out of the Cradle Endlessly Rocking," "As I Walked Out One Evening," and "Desert Places." The first two selections are positive, visionary poems, one secular, one religious in nature. The second takes a darker look at reality.

FURTHER READING

Witkowski, Tadeusz, "Adam Zagajewski." *Twentieth-Century Eastern European Writers, Third Series*. Ed. Steven Serafin. *Dictionary of Literary Biography*. Vol. 232. Detroit: Gale, 2001. 398–402.

WILLIAM WORDSWORTH

The World Is Too Much with Us

WRITING ACTIVITIES

1. Have students write a brief essay in which they address how the world is too much with them in the twenty-first century.
2. The speaker begins by using "us" and "we" but changes to "I." Ask students how this pronoun shift changes the tone and mood of the poem. Why would the appearance of Proteus and Triton make the pagan speaker "less forlorn"?

GROUP ACTIVITY

Students are often more comfortable discussing rhyme, rhythm, and form in groups, where they can pool their resources. Have them identify the form (Petrarchan sonnet), chart the rhyme scheme (*abba abba cdcdcd*), and identify the meter (predominantly iambic pentameter). The harder question will be to address why Wordsworth chose this form: How (and why) does this subject work in a compressed structure?

DO YOUR STUDENTS KNOW . . .

Wordsworth's poem reflects the sense of alienation that has come to be associated with technology and urbanization that began during the Industrial Revolution. England was at the center of this technological revolution that moved many European countries from being primarily agrarian to industrial. This change led to the growth of the urban middle class, decrease in the authority of monarchies, and profound population shifts from rural to urban areas. By the mid-1850s, half of England's population lived in cities.

DISCUSSION

In lines 1–4, the speaker tells us that we have become too involved in contemporary society; lines 5–8 suggest that we have lost our harmony with nature. The speaker's impatience and frustration with the contemporary world build in lines 1–9 until he explodes with "Great God!" (Q 1). The irony of his expostulation becomes clear in the next few lines as he wishes to return to an earlier, pagan world that worshipped such gods of nature as Proteus and Triton (both gods of the sea). Not only does the speaker despair about a society lost in materialism, commerce, and industry, but (by evoking a mythic past) he also acknowledges a declining spirituality. He blames humanity for its own demise and sees hope for the future in the past (Q 2, 4).

If your class addressed the Group Activity, you probably will want to talk about the formal structure of this poem. The sonnet's condensed form, in this case, serves to emphasize the emotion of the speaker by understating it; his disgust and revulsion with the materialism and greed are restrained, barely contained within the lines. The Italian sonnet can be divided into two parts, an octave and a sestet. By ending his first point midway through line 9, rather than at the end of line 8, Wordsworth reinforces the idea of the encroachment of the modern world. The musical sound of rhymes and rhythm lull the reader into a false sense that the poem is presenting a pleasant concern, again reinforcing the notion of a society lulled away from nature. It is a direct contrast to line 8, "we are out of tune" (Q 3).

Your students may be interested in our contemporary desire to return to myth. If you assign research outside of class, you and your students might explore Robert Bly's Iron John (1990), Clarissa Pinkola Estés's Women Who Run with the Wolves (1992), and Rollo May's The Cry for Myth (1991). Each of these works examines the need for myth in our society.

You may want to teach this with Hopkins's "God's Grandeur" and Walcott's "Sea Grapes."

SYLVIA PLATH

Morning Song

WRITING ACTIVITIES

1. Have students write the "story" of this poem as a new mother's entry in her daily journal.
2. Ask students to write a descriptive essay about the mother or have them illustrate the poem.
3. Students could write a letter to the child from its mother, telling what its first morning was like.

GROUP ACTIVITY

Have groups choose the most effective image from each stanza and discuss/defend their choice. Compare answers with other groups.

DO YOUR STUDENTS KNOW . . .

Plath's poem, given the year of her child's birth, notes two trends in birthing and motherhood that became more popular for women during the 1950s. In America, 1939 was the first year that more babies were born in the hospital than at home; the current rate for hospital births is 95 percent. Bottle feeding rather than breastfeeding also became the norm in the later half of the twentieth century.

DISCUSSION

This speaker is a new mother, still "cow-heavy" after the birth, addressing her newborn child. She expresses affection, concern, and wonder (Q 1). Her respectful sense of awe and admiration are evident in stanzas 2, 3, and 4. She is realistic too, as is seen in stanza 1 with the slap and stanza 6 with the first cries (Q 3). The title also indicates her realization that every morning will be different for her now. Connect the title to the idea that this is the morning of the baby's life metaphorically (Q 2).

Your students may be familiar with Sylvia Plath and know that she committed suicide when her children were very young. Does such knowledge make the poem less valid? Students may have problems with lines 5 and 6: if they cannot decide whether "Shadows" has positive or negative implications, you may want to discuss Hall's "My Son, My Executioner." Stanza 3 may also be difficult in its suggestion that she is not responsible for this child (Q 5). But, in fact, the mother recognizes that the child is an individual as soon as she is born; she is no longer part of her mother; she has her own place in the universe. The clearest paraphrases of the elusive cloud/mirror image appear in Lynda K. Bundtzen's *Woman and the Creative Process* (Ann Arbor: U of Michigan P, 1983), p. 227:

> (1) "I am no more you than you are I. I am but a cloud, a vaporous distillation from a reflecting pool of water. You who carry my living image now also mirror my dissolution with the wind and time."
>
> (2) "I am like the creator, breathing life into a being in my own image. But this is breath on a mirror, eventually rubbed clean, effaced, to leave a new reflection."

See also Plath's "Mirror." This poem would be fun to teach with Plath's "Metaphors," a lighthearted yet realistic view of pregnancy. Or, to show the extremes of Plath's personae, teach it with "Daddy." Other possibilities are Hayden's "Those Winter Sundays" and Cofer's "My Father in the Navy: A Childhood Memory" (parent/child relationships).

ROBERT HERRICK

To the Virgins, to Make Much of Time

WRITING ACTIVITIES

1. In 1648, to "seize the day" meant to marry. Have students write about what it could mean now — for both males and females.
2. After reading stanza 3, students can write about how the meanings of words and phrases change: "rosebuds," "Old Time [. . .] a-flying," "flower," sun's "race be run," and "nearer he's to setting."

DISCUSSION

This poem is one of the better known *carpe diem* poems. The speaker is urging young, unmarried women to "go marry" while they are in their prime of youth and beauty. Opinions may vary on whether the speaker is a young man, trying to convince someone to marry him; a middle-aged man; or an older man giving sage advice (Q 1).

Obviously, the speaker's point is to make the most of time while we are young, because "the worse, and worst / Times still succeed the former" (ll. 11–12). According to the speaker, old age has no cure: Flowers die, the Sun sets, "Youth and blood are warmer." Once you are past your prime, the speaker argues, you can take your time and remember your past glory (Q 2).

The rhyme scheme is *abab cdcd efef ghgh*. This scheme lends a musical sense to the poem, undercutting its seriousness (Q 3).

This poem works well with Marvell's "To His Coy Mistress." Rich's "Living in Sin" is a feminist inversion of the *carpe diem* poem; you may want to use it, especially if you can find Richard Wilbur's "A Late Aubade" to teach love/sex relationships.

STEVE KOWIT

The Grammar Lesson

WRITING ACTIVITIES

1. Ask students to write an essay on the type of instruction that works best for them.
2. Have students write their own villanelle on a subject of their choosing.

GROUP ACTIVITY

Divide the class into small groups and ask them to discuss their own experiences of learning grammar. Do these experiences help them to better understand the poem?

DISCUSSION

This poem uses the villanelle form to teach a grammar lesson. In the process of repeating the refrains, however, the speaker makes the lesson progressively more difficult to follow. This would be a fault if the point of the poem were actually to provide an easily comprehensible rhyming guide to grammar. It is more likely, however, that the poet's intent was to reproduce the way that the typical grammar lesson sounds to the typical student (Q 1). In many cases, the line "A noun's a thing. A verb's the thing it does" may be the only thing that students are able to hold onto during a grammar lesson and the only thing they remember afterwards. The tone is lightly mocking because the poem is in part a critique of what the poet considers ineffective pedagogy (Q 2, 3).

This poem offers an opportunity to look at the villanelle form. If you teach it with "Do Not Go Gentle into That Good Night," students will begin to see the different ways in which the form can be used. Unlike Dylan Thomas, Kowit varies his refrains and does not always choose exact rhymes. As part of your discussion, ask students what impact these stylistic choices have on the poem.

You might also consider teaching "Grammar Lesson" with "Do Not Go Gentle into That Good Night," "The Waking," "In Memory of Donald A. Stauffer," and "The Value of Education." The first three selections illustrate different uses of the villanelle form, and the fourth gives the views on education of a not-too-diligent student.

ROBERT BROWNING

Porphyria's Lover

WRITING ACTIVITIES

1. Have students write a description of events that led up to the situation described in the poem.
2. Have students write an article for a daily newspaper, reporting the story of Porphyria's death.

3. Some students may be interested in doing research on psychopathic killers — their characteristics, behaviors, motivations. If so, have these students report their findings to the class by comparing the profile of the "typical" psychopathic killer with what they know of Porphyria's lover. The class could then respond briefly in writing to how these reports shed light on this poem.

GROUP ACTIVITY

Have students research the term *porphyria*, a hereditary metabolic disorder known to cause madness. Could Browning have been familiar with this meaning? If so, why might he have chosen to use the word?

DISCUSSION

The text provides a discussion of the irony in this poem.

Use this poem as an opportunity to talk about point of view, explaining that we see only through the narrator's eyes. Is he a credible narrator? Why not? If you use it in this way, teach it with Browning's "My Last Duchess."

You could talk about setting and examine what the storm contributes to the intensity of the poem and/or the mental state of the speaker. If you discuss setting, teach it with Chopin's "The Storm." This poem also works well with Faulkner's "A Rose for Emily" (love/sex theme). Students understand these "possessive love" scenarios because of the popularity of stalker films and news stories.

PERCY BYSSHE SHELLEY

Ozymandias

WRITING ACTIVITIES

1. Have students write a character sketch of Ozymandias or draw their perceptions of what the traveler saw.
2. Ask students to record their responses to each line as they read the poem the first time.
3. Have students write a story about someone who attempts to withstand the ravages of time.

GROUP ACTIVITY

Have half the groups research Ramses II, a tyrant who ruled Egypt in the thirteenth century B.C., and half research Shelley's England in 1817. In class discussion, try to arrive at an explanation for the appropriateness of Shelley's reference to Ramses II.

DISCUSSION

This poem's irony is discussed in the text.

Students will benefit from a discussion of narrative technique. Help them identify four characters: the narrator, the traveler, the sculptor, and Ozymandias. Readers go through four levels of narrative: the present speaker; the traveler, who reports his observations to the speaker; the artist, who speaks through the ruins; and Ozymandias, who hired the artist to record his "immortal greatness." You may want to discuss art's ability to endure: the sculptor's words remain; do the poet's and the writer's? Or is the ultimate message one of despair, of decay? "Ozymandias" contains an appeal to a "spirit of democracy" in its suggestion that death is the great equalizer. The reader — alive — can feel better than this king whose fame no longer lives.

See if your students can identify the progression of their emotions: confusion, curiosity, awe, despair, and satisfaction over Ozymandias's arrogance, pity for all of humanity. You might begin your discussion of the poem by asking students to do Writing Activity 2.

Compare the attitude here toward art and time with Shakespeare's view in "Not Marble, Nor the Gilded Monuments" and "Shall I Compare Thee to a Summer's Day?"

ARIEL DORFMAN

Hope

WRITING ACTIVITIES

1. Have students write about what life must be like for this parent, identifying other emotions shown in the poem.
2. The discussion accompanying the poem asserts "for most people, *hope* has positive associations," although it takes on a new meaning in the poem. Ask students to write about other situations in which hope is not so positive.
3. This poem demonstrates the political dimensions a poem may offer. Ask students to write a paragraph either defending or arguing against using political subject matter in poetry.

GROUP ACTIVITY

Have students do a group research project in which they search out more information about the military dictatorship in Chile after the assassination of Salvador Allende in 1973. How frequent was this type of kidnapping? What has happened in subsequent years?

DO YOUR STUDENTS KNOW . . .

Parents and family members continue to seek answers and justice for the over 1,100 "disappeared" and 2,095 murdered Chileans during the Pinochet regime. Augusto Pinochet began military rule in Chile following the 1973 overthrow of the elected Allende government. It is widely believed that this action was supported and instigated by American agencies like the CIA because Allende was a socialist.

DISCUSSION

The poem is discussed in the text. You may want to teach this poem with other "political" poems — for example, Soyinka's "Future Plans" and Forché's "The Colonel"— or with a story such as Valenzuela's "All about Suicide."

W. H. AUDEN

The Unknown Citizen

WRITING ACTIVITIES

1. Have students write about what it would be like to be married to an Unknown Citizen (male or female) or to be one of his or her children.
2. Ask students to write a paragraph about what Auden seems to think of this citizen. How does Auden's view differ from what the speaker thinks? From what you think? Is the speaker another "unknown citizen," or is he more aware? How do you know?
3. Have students identify the modern trends this poem satirizes.

GROUP ACTIVITY

Have groups make a list of what changes would be necessary if this poem were to be revised for contemporary readers. Then compare these lists to begin class discussion.

DISCUSSION

You may want to use the Group Activity to lead into a discussion of whether or not the poem seems dated. Students should be able to provide examples from modern life that illustrate how the poem holds true (Q 4).

Because the citizen is unidentified, he loses individuality; thus, he is unknown. His circumstance may remind some students of the Unknown Soldier monument at Arlington National Cemetery. Students will also comment on the numbers and letters in the inscription. Some will compare this inscription with our being known by our Social Security numbers. Some may mention the tattoos on the forearms of WWII concentration camp inmates (Q 1). These details contribute to our reading the poem as a political poem. You may want to have students discuss what Auden hoped to achieve by writing it (Q 5).

Students will most likely realize that the speaker is offering a funeral oration to the citizen. They may be divided on the question of the speaker's own self-awareness: Does he buy into the system and become similarly programmed and mechanical, or is he a spokesperson for the system, fostering its perpetuation?

Both positions are frightening. Either way, the tone of this monolithic speaker remains consistent until the last two lines. Have students talk about how these two lines represent relief for the reader, rather than intrusion. Some students will understand that these two lines probably suggest the poet's attitude (Q 2).

Your students should recognize the verbal irony in the last two lines and the situational irony of such a tribute to a nondescript person (Q 3). Ask students at what point they realize this is satire. How do they know?

Ask students if they believe "we" would have heard if anything had been wrong. Some will believe Auden has presented a totalitarian society in which Big Brother knows everything about every citizen; others will say that in a totalitarian world the citizen would be afraid to speak out. Some will argue the society is merely indifferent, and nobody would hear, even if the citizen complained.

If you are using films in this class, you could teach this in conjunction with Terry Gilliam's film *Brazil*. You might also teach this poem with Atwood's "The City Planners" or Piercy's "The Secretary Chant" (power/powerlessness).

ANNE SEXTON

Cinderella

WRITING ACTIVITIES

1. Ask students to write down what they know of the Cinderella story before reading the poem. How is their knowledge consistent — and inconsistent — with the story the poem tells?
2. Ask students if they find the poem humorous. Why or why not?

DO YOUR STUDENTS KNOW . . .

Scientists have found that the brain secretes a number of chemicals related to amphetamines when one falls in love. Oxytocin, sometimes called the "cuddling hormone," is released in small quantities when partners spend time together and is also found to surge into the bloodstream during intercourse, causing a kind of emotional bond between two people.

DISCUSSION

To best teach this poem, you need to be familiar with three Cinderella stories: Walt Disney's version — the one your students will most likely know; the version told by the Brothers Grimm — the one Anne Sexton knew; and the story in Sexton's poem. Unlike the traditional storyteller from childhood who rocks and reads soothingly, Sexton's speaker is cynical, jaded, and worldwise (Q 1, 4). By the fourth repetition of "That story" and after reading the many references to contemporary society (the Irish Sweepstakes, Dior, martinis at lunch, Bonwit Teller), students should recognize the irony and suspect the different slant of this narrator's version. This irony, usually suggested when the speaker seems to be talking directly to the audience, adds to the humor of the poem (Q 2). Ask students to identify these asides and assess their effectiveness.

The first four stanzas offer Horatio Alger rags-to-riches vignettes in a contemporary setting. The retelling of the tale begins simply with "Once," a shortened, modernized version of the familiar "Once upon a time. . . ." The poem contains many of the original elements (see the summary following this discussion) and much of the original diction of the fairy tale. However, by using contemporary, colloquial speech, Sexton conveys cynicism and the absurdity of a society in which children are still taught fairy tales while being bombarded by media that expose them to a sophisticated adult world. Students will enjoy looking for the similes and metaphors that illustrate modern speech and ideas: "like blackjacks," "a marriage market," "like a gospel singer," "Regular Bobbsey Twins" (Q 3).

Unlike many poets who began writing in their youth, Sexton never wrote a poem until she was twenty-eight. Like other confessional poets (such as Sylvia Plath), Sexton was encouraged to write as a means of expressing her suppressed anger as well as examining her own life. "Cinderella" is from *Transformations* (1971), in which Sexton adapts a number of the stories by the Brothers Grimm. The narrator in the poems is a "middle-aged witch" who retells the tales, offering no "happily ever after" (Q 1).

Most students will find the poem easy to understand but will be bothered by Sexton's bitterness. Some will, however, appreciate her dark and ironic sense of humor. It is this dark sensibility that enables us to read the poem as a fable about our own time, and the way we, in our cynicism, regard the ideas of love found in fairy tales (Q 5). Your students will probably be surprised at the violence in the version by the Brothers Grimm.

Summary of Grimms' Tale

Once upon a time, the wife of a rich man fell deathly ill and called her only daughter to her bedside. "Dear child," she said, "be good and pious, . . . and I will look down on you from heaven and be near you." Every day after her death, her daughter, remaining pious and good, went to her grave and wept. Soon, her father married a woman with two daughters who were beautiful but "vile and black of heart." They hated their stepsister and treated her badly, taking all her pretty clothes and forcing her to do hard work from morning to night. Because she had to sleep by the hearth in the embers, she always looked dusty and dirty, so they called her Cinderella.

Once when her father went to the fair, he brought back jewels and fine clothes for his two stepdaughters, but Cinderella asked only for "the first branch which knocks against your hat on your way home." When he gave her this twig, she went straight to her mother's grave, planted it, and watered it with her tears. As it grew into a lovely hazel tree, Cinderella visited it three times a day, weeping and praying. A little white bird sat in the tree and promised her any wish.

One day, the king ordered a three-day festival to which he invited all the beautiful young maidens so that the prince might choose a bride. As the stepsisters were preparing to go, Cinderella expressed her desire to go as well. But they only scoffed at her. Her stepmother threw a dish of lentils into the ashes, telling her that if she picked them out in two hours, she could go with them, whereupon Cinderella called to the white bird from the tree on her mother's grave. The bird called all the birds in the sky to come help, and Cinderella finished her task. But this time, the stepmother threw *two* dishes of lentils into the ashes. Again, the birds helped. But to no avail. The stepmother and stepsisters turned their haughty backs on Cinderella and went to the ball, laughing at Cinderella the entire way.

Cinderella went once again to the hazel tree and wished for a gown for the dance. Her wish granted, she went to the dance; she looked so beautiful that the prince danced only with her. When he tried to follow her home at the end of the first day, she hid in the pigeon house. The second day the prince danced only with Cinderella once again; this time she hid in the pear tree. The third day, the prince put pitch on the palace steps and when Cinderella ran away, her left shoe stayed behind, stuck on the stair.

The prince decreed, "No one shall be my wife but she whose foot this golden slipper fits," and he proceeded to Cinderella's house. The first sister, at her mother's bidding, cut her toe off to make the slipper fit, and the prince took her away. But two pigeons on the hazel tree told the prince, who saw blood trickling from the shoe and took her back home. The second sister cut her heel off to make the slipper fit, again at her mother's bidding, and again the pigeons advised the prince. Finally Cinderella tried on the slipper, which fit her foot perfectly; the prince looked closely at her and recognized her as the beautiful maiden of the dance, and he took her away to be his bride, with the two pigeons on her shoulders. Horrified and pale with rage, the two stepsisters nevertheless attended the wedding in hopes of sharing Cinderella's good fortune. The pigeons, however, plucked their eyes out for their wickedness and falsehoods, and the sisters remained blind for all their days. The prince and Cinderella lived happily ever after.

You may want to teach Glück's "Gretel in Darkness" or Lawrence's "The Rocking-Horse Winner" as a companion piece to illustrate how modern writers use fairy tales in a contemporary setting or to teach a modern moral. Also, have students read Plath's "Daddy." Sexton and Plath knew each other, read each other's poems in workshops, and probably shared ideas.

DUDLEY RANDALL

Ballad of Birmingham

WRITING ACTIVITIES

1. Have students research this incident. Some of the news magazines, such as *Time* and *Newsweek*, covered this event extensively. They should also check *Reader's Guide* for 1977 and 1978, when a former Klansman was convicted for planting the bomb.
2. Ask students to write a journal entry from the point of view of one of the parents, expressing the hopes he or she has for the child.

GROUP ACTIVITY

Have students "interview" parents or grandparents, asking such questions as "Where were you in 1963?" "Do you remember this incident?" "What else was going on in Birmingham at about that time?" "Do you remember the marches in Selma in 1965?" After these interviews, have students work in groups to compare what they learned. This exercise works well as a process: Students hand in the first step as an interview, then they turn the interview into an essay that includes setting and a character sketch of the person interviewed.

DO YOUR STUDENTS KNOW . . .

The deaths of four young girls preparing for church one Sunday morning in 1963 in Birmingham, Alabama, led to riots the same afternoon, leaving two more black youths dead. Although the deaths of the girls — Denise McNair, Carole Robertson, Cynthia Wesley, and Addie Mae Collins — outraged the nation, silence and fear prevented the perpetrators from being tried for over thirty years. Finally in 1977, 2001, and 2002, convictions were handed down for three men involved in the bombing.

DISCUSSION

The poem's first four stanzas present an imaginary dialogue that could actually have taken place between a mother and a daughter; a final statement by the mother appears in stanza 8 (Q 1). The narrator fills in the gaps: the mother expresses a typical mother's fear for her daughter; the daughter, wanting to go outside to join the activity, is not concerned for her safety. The mother's concern and the child's delight in being part of an activity are part of everyday life. But these were not normal times in the South, when even going to church could end in disaster.

Students will identify the irony of the situation. A church should be a "sacred place" where everyone is safe. Had the daughter gone on the freedom march (a potentially dangerous activity), she ironically would have been safer. Students may also recognize dramatic irony in the reader's knowing that the church has been bombed (Q 2). Some students may also note that only by participating in the march can the mother and her child help to achieve freedom from racially motivated church bombings — a freedom we are still seeking today.

The simplicity of the ballad form serves to emphasize the horror of the situation — another irony on which students may comment. Ballads are traditional oral forms that recount a dramatic incident in the life of a common person. They often memorialize actual events, as Randall's does (Q 3).

Compare this poem with Hughes's "Birmingham Sunday." It would also work well with Hughes's "Negro," and with Brook's "Ballad of Rudolph Reed," "Medgar Evers," and "The *Chicago Defender* Sends a Man to Little Rock."

If you wish to use films, teach this poem with the relevant section of the PBS *Eyes on the Prize* series. You may also want to use Spike Lee's film *Four Little Girls*, which is about this tragic Birmingham church bombing.

SHERMAN ALEXIE

How to Write the Great American Indian Novel

WRITING ACTIVITIES

1. Ask students to write a poem similar to Alexie's but using an ethnic group of which they are members or with which they feel a close connection.
2. Have students write a research essay on the current state of Native American literature.

GROUP ACTIVITY

Break the class into groups, and ask each group to brainstorm a list of stereotypes about Native Americans that they have received from movies or television.

DO YOUR STUDENTS KNOW . . .

In an effort to halt the cultural appropriation of Native properties, Congress passed the Native American Grave Protection and Repatriation Action of 1990. This act protects Native American human remains and funerary and sacred objects from being unearthed and taken by individuals or museums. Whether the items are recent findings or items already in museums, every attempt must be made to notify the culturally affiliated tribe. Items must be returned to the tribe or to the Secretary of the Interior.

DISCUSSION

The poem is ironic, in that the speaker clearly disapproves of the advice he is giving. The key is the insistent repetition of the word "must." The idea that a person "must" be a certain way because of his or her ethnic background is one of the misconceptions against which the poem is directed. Novelists — most of them presumably non-Native American — who write about Native Americans are lazy when they resort to the clichés enumerated in this poem rather than make an effort to develop well rounded-characters. They typically see Native Americans in clichéd terms, as either doomed or dangerous or both: the men are warriors, the women are healers, and both genders are endowed with exotic sexuality (Q 1, 2).

The most puzzling part of the poem for students will probably be its concluding couplet, where the speaker says, "all of the white people will be Indians and all the Indians will be ghosts." Although this statement at first appears illogical, it really follows from what has come before. The clichés listed in the poem have allowed whites to redefine Native American identity and then to co-opt it. The speaker implies that the reason whites do this is that they fear Native Americans even as they envy certain aspects of their culture. The kind of clichéd thinking demonstrated in the poem allows whites to become Native Americans — or what they think Native Americans should be — even as they supplant them (Q 3).

Consider teaching this poem with "Battle Royal," "Big Black Good Man," and "A Supermarket in California." The first two selections examine racial prejudice, and the third gives a modern response to the direction America has taken.

FURTHER READING

Bell, Madison Smart. "Native Son: Sherman Alexie Explores the Confusion and Anger Born of Oppression." *Chicago Tribune Books* 17 Nov. 1996. sec. 14, p. 3.

RACHEL ROSE

What We Heard about the Japanese

WRITING ACTIVITIES

1. The views that Americans and Japanese have of each other have historical roots. Ask students to write a research essay on the propaganda efforts conducted by both the American and Japanese governments during World War II.
2. Have students write an essay about preconceptions they feel Americans have about the ethnic or racial group(s) to which they belong.

GROUP ACTIVITY

Break the class into small groups and ask each group to discuss one of the preconceptions the speaker says Americans have about the Japanese.

DISCUSSION

The phrase "we heard" is repeated throughout the poem. The "we" is clearly meant to refer to Americans, and "heard" to emphasize the fact that these impressions of the Japanese are based on hearsay rather than direct contact (Q 1). Although the speaker never mentions a source for these ideas, it is likely that Americans have gotten them from the media and that some of them date back to the conflict between the two countries during World War II (Q 2).

Students may initially be puzzled by the last line of the poem: "We heard they were just like us under the skin." One could argue, after all, that such a statement asserts a common bond of humanity between the Japanese and Americans. The speaker's point throughout the rest of the poem, however, has been that Americans are unprepared to recognize such a bond. Saying that another group of people is "just like us under the skin" may be tantamount to saying that "we" represent an ideal form of humanity and that the other group must peel off the layers of its culture in order to become more like us and therefore more "authentic" (Q 3).

Consider teaching this poem with "What the Japanese Perhaps Heard," "Seventeen Syllables," and "Chin." The first selection was written as a companion piece to this poem. The second selection examines the life of Japanese immigrants in America, and the third deals in part with the misconceptions an American family has about their Chinese neighbors.

RACHEL ROSE

What the Japanese Perhaps Heard

WRITING ACTIVITIES

1. Ask students to write a research essay on the current state of relations between Japan and America.
2. Have students write about an aspect of American culture that people in other countries might be likely to misunderstand.

GROUP ACTIVITY

Divide the class into groups and have the groups brainstorm lists of the opinions of America that they would most and least like people in other countries to have.

DISCUSSION

This poem is intended as a kind of sequel or companion piece to "What We Heard about the Japanese." That poem was really a critique of the American lack of understanding of Japanese culture. "What the Japanese Perhaps Heard" does not simply present the reverse scenario, however. The criticism in this poem is still largely directed at America — in this case, at what the speaker sees as our lack of understanding and our violent tendencies. The speaker, an American, seems quite sympathetic to the Japanese in this poem (Q 1). The repetition of the word "perhaps" throughout the poem indicates that Americans, the speaker included, can really only guess what other cultures think about us (Q 2).

The conclusion of the poem contrasts Japanese grief, which is "perhaps" like "[o]ne island / bleeding into the next" with American grief, which is "an endless cornfield, silken and ripe with poison." This comparison suggests that American grief is the more expansive and dangerous of the two, whereas Japanese grief is more controlled and is more likely to be directed back on itself (Q 3).

Consider teaching this poem with "What We Heard about the Japanese," "The Third and Final Continent," "The Emigrant Irish," and "Immigrant Picnic." The first selection is the prequel to this poem, and the others all deal with the challenges faced by people moving between two cultures.

handwritten: new range poems fun

WORD CHOICE, WORD ORDER

SIPHO SEPAMLA

Words, Words, Words

South African poet Sipho Sepamla often addresses political issues in his poetry. This poem asks the question debated by proponents and opponents of political correctness: does changing the word for something actually change its connotation? If we cease to use the words *tribal wars*, will tribal identity fade into national and then multinational identity? Like George Orwell in his novels and essays, Sepamla seems to distrust politically motivated language changes and is suspicious of politicians taking poetic license and making words play new roles. Yet clearly words are powerful if they "stalk our lives."

WALT WHITMAN

When I Heard the Learn'd Astronomer

This poem, in which the poet feels sick in the lecture hall and is restored outdoors by gazing into the sky, might be discussed together with other Whitman poems. In "A Noiseless Patient Spider," the speaker is excited, enlightened, even elevated, by his examination of nature; in the selection from "Song of Myself," the speaker contrasts houses and rooms that are "full of perfumes" with nature, which is odorless and wholesome and restorative.

WILLIAM STAFFORD

For the Grave of Daniel Boone

Daniel Boone represents a time different from our own. Like the tire iron, saw, and rust in Gary Snyder's "Some Good Things to Be Said for the Iron Age," the "barbwire" carries with it negative connotations, suggesting that the past was better in some ways than the present. By placing a rock on Daniel Boone's grave (l. 24), the speaker connects Boone with "the land that was his"; but he also solidifies Boone's death (and the death of his era) by symbolically marking this grave as a permanent home for the wanderer who called so much of America home. The rock also serves as a memorial, indicating that someone has visited the grave.

JAMES WRIGHT

Autumn Begins in Martins Ferry, Ohio

WRITING ACTIVITY

1. Ask students to write about the images that come to mind when they think about a "small town." Have them compare and/or contrast these images to their notions of "city life" or "suburbia." Does "small town" life connote positive or negative qualities?

GROUP ACTIVITY

Ask groups of students to write collaborative paragraphs describing their own childhood towns or cities. How many came from small towns? What do students remember about their neighborhoods? Did any students attend a high school similar to the one that Wright describes in his poem?

DISCUSSION

You may want to begin by encouraging students to share their responses from the suggested writing activity. You will probably receive varied responses depending upon the area demographics and student backgrounds. Wright's word choice emphasizes his central theme of unfulfilled dreams and defeated lives in a small town (Q 3). Words such as "Polacks," "ruptured," "pullets," "suicidally," and "gallop" all contribute to mood and setting with their negative connotations. He is perhaps describing the "proud fathers" "ashamed to go home" in the first four lines of the poem. These are the "Polacks nursing long beers in Tiltonsville," the "Negroes in the blast furnace at Benwood," and the "ruptured night watchman of Wheeling Steel." Each is described negatively: the Negroes have "gray faces," and "the watchman of Wheeling Steel" leads a broken and "ruptured" life; similarly, "Polacks" are "nursing long beers in Tiltonsville," perhaps suggesting sadness or even alcoholism (Q 1).

A quiet desperation pervades the poem, with the men who are "Dreaming of heroes" returning home to their wives, who are "Dying for love" (Q 2). The people who inhabit Martins Ferry take pride in their sons who "grow suicidally beautiful" during football season in autumn. Even the women "cluck like starved pullets," and Wright creates in his simile a haunting image of an overpopulated henhouse where young hens are starved and "Dying for love." Critic Bonnie Costello aptly describes Wright as an "elegaic poet of place" as he indeed creates a distinct "sense of place" and haunting "spirit" in his poem (Q 4).

FURTHER READING

Elkins, Andrew. *The Poetry of James Wright*. Tuscaloosa: U of Alabama P, 1991.
Stitt, Peter. "An Introduction to the Poet James Wright." *Gettysburg Review* 3 (winter 1990): 35–48.

ADRIENNE RICH

Living in Sin

WRITING ACTIVITIES

1. Ask students if they remember ever seeing a milkman. Chances are they do not. Ask them to suggest a modern-day equivalent and have them write briefly on the role of the milkman in this poem.
2. Have students analyze the significance of the title by focusing on the concept of sin. What is the "sin" here, and what is the effect of the word on the reader? How does this title distance the writer from her subject?

GROUP ACTIVITY

Divide students into two groups and have each group discuss this poem from a different perspective (the woman's point of view and the man's point of view). This activity could take the form of presentations by each group or a debate between them.

DO YOUR STUDENTS KNOW . . .

Sociologist Arlie Hochschild initiated dialogue on the lives of working women and their families in her book *The Second Shift*. Although the women's movement of the 1970s allowed women to join the workforce in record numbers, Hochschild found that women still function as primary caretaker in the family. Hochschild calculated that being the primary caretaker adds an extra fifteen hours per week and an extra month of twenty-four-hour days to the work of most American women.

DISCUSSION

This poem is about love gone normal; it focuses on the gulf between the speaker's romantic, moonlit, naive notions of unconventional love and the harsh, revealing light of reality that morning sheds on this relationship.

Rich uses the past tense throughout the poem to show the reader that the woman is already disillusioned. This feeling, however, has not yet been translated into action, and the woman remains in the apartment, suspended between the romantic and the mundane. It would be "heresy" to wish anything different, even if the loud pipes, dusty furniture, dirty windows, and roaches were not what she expected when she first decided to move with the artist into his "studio." "Heresy" (l. 3) is perhaps the single most important word in the poem because it relates directly to the idea of an unfettered, Bohemian lifestyle implied in the title; it also shows that she refuses to come to terms with her feelings and renounce her initial belief.

She pretends to think the shawl in line 5 is "Persian" because she wants this relationship to be exotic, different. If there are mice in the "studio," they will be charming and will serve, of course, to amuse the cat (Q 1). These ideal descriptions contrast starkly with the empty, dry, "sepulchral bottles" left on the table from the night before. Morning reveals them coldly, just as it reveals her romantic artist-lover as a yawning, disheveled, beard-scratching boor. The second thoughts haunting her remain "minor" because she feels they are as of yet unimportant — as if they were merely slight inconveniences to an otherwise exciting relationship (Q 1). Even when asleep, she wakes only "sometimes"— not always — to dwell on these negative, relentless feelings.

Many words and phrases in the poem have negative connotations: "grime," "writhe," "tramp," "coldly," "sepulchral," "jeered," and "out of tune" are a few. Taken together, they suggest that the relationship itself is "out of tune" and that it is doomed to fail (Q 2). Rich deliberately uses words such as "dust," "boil," and "made" because they denote the everyday routine of housekeeping and, more important, suggest that the lovers' arrangement is settling down into nothing more than a routine, conventional existence (Q 3). Student responses will probably vary. Although Rich is rather subtle here and some might argue "cautious," her word choice is deliberate and, for the careful reader, not so "polite" (Q 5).

You might compare this poem to Shakespeare's sonnet "My Mistress' Eyes Are Nothing Like the Sun" and discuss how poetry focuses on realistic appraisals of love.

FURTHER READING

Rich, Adrienne. *Adrienne Rich's Poetry: Texts of the Poems: The Poet on Her Work.* New York: Norton, 1975.

E. E. CUMMINGS

in Just-

WRITING ACTIVITIES

1. Challenge the students to find the total number of times Cummings uses alliteration in the poem and ask them to write briefly about some of its effects.
2. For a more extensive written assignment, ask students to find some information on Pan, the Greek god of nature. Have them write a paragraph explaining some of the reasons why Cummings alludes to him here.

GROUP ACTIVITY

Have students work in groups to reorganize this poem into a paragraph of prose. Ask them what effect this rearrangement has on the poem and explain how spatial arrangement can give meaning to poetry.

DISCUSSION

Many students at first do not know what to think of Cummings's poetry. They will read and reread, not realizing that Cummings *arranges* words and that readers discover the deeper meanings in his poetry by studying this arrangement. For Cummings, space is very often more important than the words themselves. This poem is no exception, and if the students rearrange the poem into one paragraph, they will see how apparently simple Cummings's message is. However, the spatial arrangement is not simple here; the three variations of the refrain "far and wee" illustrate this complexity.

In the first instance (l. 5), "far" is separated from "and wee" because the balloonman is still quite far away, and the sound of the whistle is faint and distant (Q 2). This arrangement de-emphasizes "wee," making the sound seem even more distant. The word "wee" serves many purposes in the poem; here, it literally means "little," but the word also imitates the actual sound of both the whistle and the children's exuberance (whee!). In the second instance (l. 13), Cummings places the words "far" and "wee" equidistant from "and," which makes "wee" read far more like "we" than it did in the previous instance. Also, "wee" in this instance stands on its own, emphasizing the word — and, in turn, the balloonman's insistent, irresistible call. In the third instance (ll. 22–24), "wee" is clearly a cry of exuberance from the children. In short, the three words function in each instance as a refrain in the balloonman's song, but the different arrangements create different connotations (Q 2).

The balloonman here is Pan, the upper-half-man, lower-half-goat Greek god of nature whose pipe playing heralds the coming of spring. Instead of little forest creatures running to gather around him, however, here children come streaming from yards and across streets. Cummings originally called this poem "chanson innocente," for this poem is music celebrating the coming of new, innocent life. Many of his original word combinations express the children's innocent excitement and joy. The adjectives "mud-luscious" and "puddle-wonderful," for example, use assonance and consonance to mimic these emotions, while the playful word combination matches the children's play. Substituting "muddy" or "mud-filled," and "wet" for these adjectives would eliminate all the exuberance of Cummings's original choices (Q 1, 4).

Another effective way to introduce this poem is to read it in two or three different tones: playful, nostalgic, matter-of-fact, threatening, mysterious. In the last two, the balloonman (queer, old, lame, goat-footed satyr) becomes suspect — he may be a Pied Piper figure, a reminder of loss of innocence, a dirty old man, the side of Pan that causes panic, or a reminder of human mortality. By using different voices, you can illustrate how many ways a poem may be interpreted.

You may also want to call attention to the poem's present title. Many readers want to call it "in Just-spring" (when March turns to April), but Cummings has created a line break that should force us to think also that "in Just-" might imply injustice — the injustice of the old balloonman's reminding us of age in the middle of youth or the injustice of autumn at the start of spring. As in many of Cummings's poems, the wordplay and ambiguity here can lead to rich discussions.

FURTHER READING

Rotella, Guy, ed. *Critical Essays on E. E. Cummings*. Boston: Hall, 1984.

ROBERT PINSKY

ABC

WRITING ACTIVITIES

1. Ask students to write their own poem on mortality using the form Pinsky has devised.
2. Have students choose another poem in the anthology that addresses the issue of death (some suggestions are given at the end of the discussion section) and write a comparison/contrast essay.

GROUP ACTIVITY

Break up the class into small groups and ask them to consider why Pinsky chose this particular form in order to communicate his point.

DO YOUR STUDENTS KNOW . . .

The alphabet we use today originated in picture form and then gave way to the abstract symbols in use today. The alphabet, with ties to the Phoenicians, is largely made up of Latin and Greek elements. Although English borrows heavily from many languages, it is the official language of forty five countries in the world.

DISCUSSION

Students may not notice at first that each word of the poem begins with a successive letter of the alphabet. Part of the pleasure of reading the poem is simply noting the skill with which Pinsky has pulled off a difficult poetic feat. More important, this strategy is appropriate for several reasons. Our ABCs are one of the most basic things that we learn in school. Further, the song we use to learn them is it-self a rhyming poem, so that there is an early connection between poetry and the alphabet. In addition, however, the poem raises important questions about the connection between language, particularly written language, and such crucial topics as life and death.

The bulk of the poem states the obvious fact that everyone dies and that many die painfully. In this sense, it constitutes a lesson for children, as most adults will be aware of these hard facts. Students may be confused, however, by the last two stanzas. Here the poet addresses the "[s]weet time unafflicted" and the "[v]arious world"— phrases apparently meant to denote the moments of happiness or abun-dance in life. The final stanza/line moves us from the alphabet to mathematics. "X" is an unknown point, and "zenith" is the highest point something reaches. Unlike death, the moment of peak happiness is far less definite and far less easy to pinpoint.

Consider teaching this poem with "Do Not Go Gentle into That Good Night," "Group Photo with Winter Trees," or "I Was Taught Three." The first se-lection deals, according to most critics, with impending death; the second uses novel technical means to examine issues regarding mortality; and the third ex-amines the connections between language and life.

FURTHER READING

Kelly, Susan. "An Interview with . . . Robert Pinsky." *Writer* 112 (Nov. 1999): 18–20.

THEODORE ROETHKE

I Knew a Woman

WRITING ACTIVITIES

1. Challenge students to list four or five phrases used in everyday speech that have double meanings. Afterwards, discuss how this poem's sexual overtones help support its more general theme of love.
2. Ask students why the last line of each stanza is in parentheses. Are these lines essential?
3. Have students write a description of the speaker based on words or phrases in the poem.

GROUP ACTIVITY

Have groups of students work together to select words in the poem with double meanings or multiple connotations, especially those concerning sex and death. Ask them to explain the significance of their findings.

DISCUSSION

At first, many students may not grasp the tone of this poem, which is for the most part lighthearted and self-deprecating. Some of them will think the poem is completely innocent. However, if the poem's double meanings are pointed out, students should begin to understand clearly the speaker's humorous tone. The poem is filled with sexual overtones, for example, and numerous words with double meanings (Q 1, 2). While the dance terms "Turn, and Counter-turn, and Stand" are rough equivalents of the Greek words "strophe, anti-strophe, and epode," to which Roethke alludes in line 6, they may also suggest something sexual, given their close proximity to line 10, which discusses "Touch," and given the fact that the poem deals primarily with physical motion and the desire to transcend it. But the main metaphor of the poem, and the one that has the clearest sexual overtones, is the comparison of two lovers to a sickle and a rake. Because the word "mow" has obvious sexual connotations (in Scots dialect "to mow" means to have sexual intercourse, and Roethke is clearly aware of this connection since the poem alludes to Marvell's "The Mower's Song" in lines 12–14), the rest of this conceit becomes overtly sexual, and the "motion" mentioned in line 23 (and throughout the poem) is primarily sexual motion. There are more words with double meanings — even the word "Knew" in the title becomes, upon second reading, "to know" in a sexual sense (Q 1).

Roethke uses surprising words such as "container," "mobile," and "stone" because they focus the reader's attention on the physicality of the speaker's descriptions; after all, this love poem is about a lover surrendering to his lover's motion, and, in doing so, learning something of what eternity is like (Q 2). It is possible, however, to overemphasize the sexual connotations in this poem. Even though most of the poem can be interpreted this way, ultimately the sexual punning is not the main point.

This poem is successful because the delightful sexual connotations divert readers from the more serious overtones of the poem until even they may be swept up by the poem's motion. However, Roethke's main point here is the notion that through another's otherworldly motions (a *physical* union), a person can transcend the self and escape (albeit temporarily) the process of decay and death. The "old bones" image in line 27 alludes to the process of aging, an image contrasting directly with "lovely in her bones" in the first line, which suggests a pleasing, even sensual, shape and form (Q 3).

The subject then, suggested primarily in the last stanza, is the human inability to escape the natural cycle of life and death. Of course, there is a pun on the word "dying," which can be interpreted also in a sexual sense, but the more serious focus of the speaker's comments is his learning what "eternity" means. Only by intimately knowing these natural processes can we ever hope to transcend them.

Compare this to Roethke's "Reply to a Lady Editor" (in *Words for the Wind*), a poem written in response to an editor of a major magazine who had obviously missed the poem's sexual innuendo. "Reply to a Lady Editor" should make your students feel good about themselves by showing them that poetry is not always clear to everyone else except them. Also, compare Marvell's "The Mower's Song," to which Roethke alludes in this poem. You might also compare "I Knew a Woman" to Shakespeare's "My Mistress' Eyes Are Nothing like the Sun" and "Not Marble, Nor Gilded Monuments." Both of these love poems celebrate physical love and examine themes expressed in Roethke's work.

FURTHER READING

Stiffler, Randall. *Theodore Roethke: The Poet and His Critics.* Chicago: American Library Association, 1986.
Wolff, George. *Theodore Roethke.* Boston: Twayne, 1981.

MARGARET ATWOOD

The City Planners

WRITING ACTIVITIES

1. Most good poets avoid overusing adjectives, choosing instead to let the nouns and verbs carry the poem's weight. Ask students to respond to this statement based on their reading of this poem. Have them choose three adjective/noun combinations (such as "discouraged grass" or "sanitary trees") and comment on the effect of the adjectives in the poem.
2. Ask students to write their own poems complaining about a decision-making body they disagree with ("The Parents" or "The Teacher," for example).

GROUP ACTIVITY

Break students up into two groups named "us" and "them" (the City Planners). Ask each group to defend its position by drawing on details in the poem. Why is Atwood ("us") so offended? What have the city planners done poorly?

DO YOUR STUDENTS KNOW . . .

In 1947, architect William Levitt revolutionized house design and construction when his creation, Levittown, New York, became the archetype of suburban development. The assembly-line construction of small homes built on a concrete slab rather than over a basement became the perfect answer for returning servicemen who could obtain financing for houses through the GI bill. At the same time, urban planner Robert Moses designed highways from New York City to the new suburban areas. By 1951, 17, 447 homes had been built on the former potato fields of Long Island.

DISCUSSION

The first thing readers sense is the seeming cool-headed rationality of the speaker's proclamation. The second thing that comes subtly through is the underlying sense of violent resentment the speaker harbors toward the City Planners and these suburbs as a whole. Although the speaker gives the impression of avoiding emotional involvement by using the first-person plural and by choosing relatively formal diction, some other more disturbing elements of the poem serve to offset the speaker's detachment.

Readers must first ask why Atwood bothers to introduce an identifiable speaker at all. She could easily have written the poem without one, yet she chooses to introduce a speaker in the first stanza and to point out three rather important details about her: (1) the speaker, or the group she represents, is "cruising" through this residential neighborhood on a hot August Sunday; (2) she is offended by the all-too-sane, aseptic order of the place; (3) the car door is dented. Whether the speaker is from a gang, from the wrong side of the tracks, from the country, or just highly perceptive, Atwood's use of a first-person point of view makes it easier for readers to identify with the speaker than with the suburban residents. In lines 9–10, the speaker mentions shouting and breaking glass, suggesting that her world is not nearly so ordered and perfect as the one she is contemplating. Some students may not believe the speaker is different at first, but you might mention that in line 28 the speaker points out that no one from these suburbs "notices" the decay and disorder lurking beneath the surface, except for "us" — the speaker and her readers.

Atwood's word choice here is effective; it establishes a clear, rational, authoritative voice of reason. Any hint of informal diction — slang, for example — would upset the balanced tone and draw attention to the speaker and away from the argument. However, what lies beneath the calm surface of these suburbs and beneath the speaker's controlled description of them is an uncontrollable aversion. Look, for example, at these words: "hysteria," "avoidance," "sickness," "bruise," "vicious," "too-fixed stare," "insane," "concealed," and "panic." Together, these words offset the detached tone. In the end, the reader is left with more questions than answers, something that may be a strength or a weakness of the poem. Why is the speaker so offended and angry? How is *she* able to gain "momentary access to / the landscape behind" while no one else can? Is it because people want to order their lives and they cannot or because they resent having their lives ordered blindly for them?

You may want to teach this poem with Auden's "The Unknown Citizen," Piercy's "The Secretary Chant," and Updike's "A&P," three other works that deal with the theme of "us" (ordinary citizens) versus "them" (bureaucracy) (power/powerlessness).

FURTHER READING

McCombs, Judith, ed. *Critical Essays on Margaret Atwood*. Boston: Hall, 1988.

JIM SAGEL

Baca Grande

WRITING ACTIVITIES

1. Ask students to write an essay about their high school graduation, focusing on one aspect of it, such as the keynote speaker, and how they relate to it now that they are in college.
2. Ask students who the speaker is in this poem and how the viewpoint Sagel chooses makes them feel as if they too were in that graduating audience.

GROUP ACTIVITY

Divide students into two groups. Have one group make a list of the informal words in the poem and have the other make a list of the more formal words. In class, discuss the effect of these different levels of diction and why students think the poet has chosen these words.

DISCUSSION

The first thing readers notice here is the title, of course. The fact that it and the epigraph are Spanish shows us that the setting is probably an inner-city neighborhood somewhere in California and that the majority of these students — whose parents are probably immigrants or first-generation Americans — will fall far short of achieving the American Dream. James Baca, one of the very few who has escaped the neighborhood, seems anxious to distance himself from his heritage. He has gone East, has changed his accent, and has become quite willing to forget these people if given the chance. Since "Baca" and "vaca" sound alike in Spanish, the obvious pun on his name contributes to the linguistic tension present in the poem. Some of your students may point out that although the slick James Baca, through his name, is clearly identified with the braless cow, he also wears a moustache, like the rat. Perhaps Sagel here is suggesting that James Baca is very much like the little rats of the audience, since he shares the same hometown but has grown into a rather inflated cow.

You may want to discuss the poem's form to a certain extent, since it so obviously sprawls out across three pages and does not follow any traditional pattern. The line breaks here mirror the informality of the speaker's language. While some of the breaks are quite effective, the majority of them seem rather haphazard or hesitant. This helps create the cynical, suspicious tone of a speaker who can see through the insincerity of James A. Baca and into the reality of the future.

Word choice in this open form poem carries much of the poem's meaning; for every slang term such as "Big Bucks," there are more formal, mature words like "elegantly honed," "meticulously," and "emulate"— words the average high school senior probably would not use. This discrepancy, or juggling of word levels, distances the poem's speaker from both the main character and the audience. Also, it suggests the poet may be looking back at this scene, as the date of the poem's publication suggests.

This poem would work well with Cumming's "next to of course god america i," another poem in which a public speech reveals character.

WANDA COLEMAN

Sears Life

WRITING ACTIVITIES

1. Some of your students may work at stores like Sears or have family members who work there. Have students write a letter to Coleman in which they either agree or disagree with her evaluation of stores like the one described in the poem.
2. Ask students to write a short essay about the proliferation of malls in America.

GROUP ACTIVITY

Break the class into groups of three to five students and ask each group to discuss the personal qualities they think the speaker of this poem exemplifies.

DISCUSSION

The lack of capitalization in the poem is intended to convey some of the same informality as words like "goddamned" and "coondogging" (Q 1). You may be able to approach this issue by asking students under what circumstances they feel it is acceptable to dispense with capitalization. Whether it is in personal notes or in e-mails, chances are that most of the students will refer to fairly informal situations. In addition to its influence on tone, the lack of punctuation makes a larger point as well. Capital letters make the words they begin stand out from the rest of a given sentence. Since much of the speaker's anger is directed against the drab uniformity of modern stores, it makes perfect sense that no one word in the poem should raise itself above the others. It is especially appropriate, given the fact that the speaker feels the stores are dehumanizing, that her "i" is not capitalized (Q 2).

The diction of the poem is not uniform throughout. Phrases such as "neuron / pabulum" and "department / of object of conjecture" are considerably more formal than the language surrounding them. This raises a number of possibilities. Is the speaker talking above or below her normal register throughout the poem? If the former, she may be trying to raise herself out of this environment through the use of language she feels will make her sound more educated. If the latter, she may be a well-educated person adopting a lower level of diction in order to avoid sounding unduly snobbish (Q 3).

Consider teaching this poem with "The Lesson," "A Mown Lawn," or "A Supermarket in California," each of which is critical of American society.

FURTHER READING

Magistrale, Tony, and Patricia Ferreira. "Sweet Mama Wanda Tells Fortunes: An Interview with Wanda Coleman." *Black American Literature Forum* 24 (Fall 1990): 491–508.

MARK HALLIDAY

The Value of Education

WRITING ACTIVITIES

1. The speaker admits that his "definition of education" is only "negative." Have students write a positive definition of education.
2. Ask students to write a prose paraphrase of the speaker's position on education.

GROUP ACTIVITY

Break the class into three groups. Ask one group to present the case for the speaker's definition of education and another for a more traditional view. Ask the third group to act as a jury compiling a list of the reasons they felt were most convincing.

DISCUSSION

Students may enjoy this poem because of its informal voice and its relevance to their lives. The speaker, presumably a male college student, is clearly joking, but he just as clearly has a serious point (Q 2, 5). While keeping out of trouble is not the ideal goal of his being in a library, it is still, all things being equal, good that he is *not* in trouble. As long as he is in the library, he behaves more responsibly than he otherwise does (Q 1). Moreover, he has fairly convincing responses to the hypothetical objection of his audience, who are presumably educators (Q 2). Someone who is not at least self-educated would probably not say, "But this is merely a negative definition of / the value of education." In other words, the person who might raise the objection would show by doing so that he or she is educated. If the speaker, then, is able to anticipate what an educated person would say, he must already be somewhat educated himself (Q 3, 5). In other words, if he can both foresee and answer this objection, the speaker has proven that his approach to education can work. One of the organizing principles of the poem is the repetition of the word "library," and the phrase "I sit in the library." This repetition in the course of an evolving argument helps mirror the motion of the speaker's thoughts, which are moving forward even as he is sitting still (Q 4).

Consider teaching this poem with "School Letting Out," in which an idyllic after-school scene is described; "Scott Wonders if His Daughter Will Understand Tragedy if He Kills Rock and Roll," in which a father who is also an educator worries about his daughter; or "Chin," in which a father resorts to abuse in order to motivate his son academically.

FURTHER READING

Wilkins, W. R. "Little Star" (Review). *Library Journal* 112 (1987): 129.

BARBARA L. GREENBERG

The Faithful Wife

WRITING ACTIVITIES

1. Have students write a response to this poem from the husband's viewpoint. Or, have them go through the poem and change pronouns and other necessary elements to make this the husband's poem.
2. Ask students to write a few paragraphs describing the life of the speaker. What is she like as a person — strong and assertive? What are some of her interests? Is she a typical housewife (and is our idea of a "typical" housewife changing)?

GROUP ACTIVITY

Divide the students up by gender. Ask them to discuss the role of gender in the poem and to decide whether or not the speaker's statement in the final stanza seems justified by evidence found in the poem.

DISCUSSION

This poem is about gender stereotypes — the roles people are forced to assume — and the resulting effects. Early in the poem, the speaker seems to be addressing her husband, but as we read on, we begin to see clearly that she is not (Q 2). The final stanza, so different from the rest of the poem, tells us so for certain, but there are other, smaller details sprinkled throughout the poem that also seem out of place. It would be hard to imagine that such a faithful wife — who honors her imaginery husband even when speaking about adultery — would speak to him of bruising her lover's face or of taking long walks in fields of coarse, prickly weeds. As the poem progresses, the speaker's words become harsher and more accusatory toward her husband, and the tone reveals a woman who is angry both at her husband and at the role of faithful wife that she has played. The reader gradually sees that the speaker is speaking to herself — unable to commit adultery, but, more important, unable to reveal her thoughts to her husband, who may not understand her anyway (Q 2).

Because the speaker begins as if in midconversation and because some of the sentences are spoken as if in reply to questions, parts of the poem sound like everyday speech (Q 1). In addition, most of the words are fairly simple, and some of the descriptions — eating at Howard Johnson's, for example — refer to everyday events. Words such as "provident" and "heart's distress" are not common, although the syntax is quite formal. Line 2, for instance, would read "who couldn't take anything from you" if the diction were informal, and line 15, which reads "to which you are allergic," would normally be spoken with the preposition at the end: "which you are allergic to." Spoken language would also include contractions.

The title is highly ironic but also true: even though the poem is about an imaginary lover, the speaker takes pains not to "dishonor" her husband (Q 3). In this sense, she is "faithful." In addition, the notion that she would probably never reveal these thoughts to her husband also supports this contention. However, the mere fact that the speaker is discussing adultery gives the title its irony.

Notice that in the last line, the most important of the poem, the speaker states that her husband has "never asked to see" her "other body," instead of saying simply that he has "never seen" it. This sentiment turns the poem from a complaint into an accusation and implies that the speaker lacks the courage or opportunity to show her true self to her husband. If so, she is especially pitiful. The wife has had to play an unfulfilling role, and she clearly blames her husband for her situation (using the second person throughout the poem). The speaker depends heavily on oppressive male stereotype to gain the reader's sympathy in the final stanza, for the husband is a man who has never "asked" her (i.e., "let" her be more). Some students may be troubled by this assertion because nowhere in the rest of the poem has this stereotype been supported, and the reader is asked to assume that the husband is to blame. On the other hand, since the poem depends heavily on a stereotypical view of men and marriage, the poem indirectly criticizes all stifling gender roles, no matter who is to blame.

Nowadays, some students might ask why a woman would choose to play this role in the first place, but you might remind them that the poem was written in 1978, and the poet, being born in 1932, lived though an era when women had limited options, when a woman could never show her sexuality, let alone discuss it. Encourage students to put themselves in the speaker's place and time.

This poem can be taught with Chopin's "The Storm" or Rich's "Living in Sin."

FURTHER READING

Greenberg, Barbara. *The Spoils of August*. Middletown, CT: Wesleyan UP, 1974.

RICHARD WILBUR

For the Student Strikers

WRITING ACTIVITIES

1. Play the Crosby, Stills, Nash and Young song "Ohio," which, like "For the Student Strikers," was written in response to the 1970 shooting of four Kent State University students by National Guard troops. Have students read the lyrics of the song and write briefly on ways in which the song is similar to and different from Wilbur's poem.

2. Ask students to compare a recent event in history, such as the 1992 riots in Los Angeles, to similar events from another time period. Facts: This poem was written a few months after the killings; "Ohio" was released 31 days afterwards; "Peace in L.A.," by Tom Petty, was released only two days after the Los Angeles riots. What does this timing suggest? Students might also look into the 1999 rap CD *Price of Freedom* and Bruce Springsteen's 2000 song "American Skin," both responses to the fatal police shooting of the West African immigrant Amadou Diallo.

GROUP ACTIVITY

Divide students into four groups and assign each group a section of this poem to explicate and present to the rest of the class.

DO YOUR STUDENTS KNOW . . .

Following the murder of four Kent State University students during a protest against the war in Vietnam in May 1970, 441 colleges and universities experienced student strikes. Earlier, between 1936 and 1939, annual student strikes were organized by the American Student Union. This group, with 500,000 members, protested against war and in support of New Deal policies and social programs.

DISCUSSION

As the text notes, this poem is an exhortation, a form of discourse intended to incite or encourage listeners to take action. In the poem, the speaker asks students to react peacefully to an event that he believes will surely incite more violence. The Kent State University students were protesting President Nixon's decision to bomb Cambodia during the Vietnam War, and the speaker realizes that emotional, inflammatory rhetoric would simply worsen the problem. For this reason alone, Wilbur's diction must be formal and elevated: it is a single, objective voice of reason against a sweeping wave of violence (Q 3). But Wilbur employs a formal, somber tone for other reasons also. Poetically speaking, this poem is an elegy, a mournful song that reflects on death or the passing of time (Q 2). Here, the subject matter is the death of four student protesters killed by National Guard troops. The occasion is clearly somber and sad; any other tone for an elegiac poem written so soon after the killings would be inappropriate.

As an elegy, the poem uses many devices common to this form. Elegiac was the classical meter in which Greeks wrote their elegies. This meter consists of a line of classical hexameter coupled with a line of classical pentameter. Wilbur modifies this somewhat by writing in quatrains and ending each with a short two-foot, or dipodic line, but he succeeds nonetheless in capturing the elegy's somber, reflective spirit. Meter is a formal device, and it enhances and supports the formal diction Wilbur employs here with words such as "whom," "let," "evening," "discourse," and "rumored" (Q 1). His syntax is also formal, and the meter supports this solemnity. Look, for example, at the beginning of each line, and notice how often Wilbur begins with a stress, or a trochaic foot. The fact that many of these lines are exhortations and may be read as imperatives ("Stand on the stoops," "Talk with them") also contributes to the lofty, authoritative tone of the speaker's voice. The one full, exact end-rhyme used in each stanza adds to the poem's formality. Rhyme is a highly formal device that lends dignity, seriousness, and memorability to an utterance. Wilhur's careful use of rhyme lends even more dignity to the poem.

You may want to teach this poem along with newspaper clippings and/or news footage of the Kent State shootings. You may also want to tell students that a similar tragedy — which occurred at the same time at Mississippi's Jackson State University, a historically black school — received much less media coverage and is barely remembered today. Try to find news reports of this shooting as well because students will need the background.

FURTHER READING

Hill, Donald Lewis. *Richard Wilbur*. Boston: Twayne, 1967.
Turco, Lewis. *The New Book of Forms: A Handbook of Poetics*. Hanover: New England UP, 1986.

CHARLES BUKOWSKI

Dog Fight

WRITING ACTIVITIES

1. Discuss with students the concept of "road rage," particularly the violence occurring on the highways of California, where motorists have been shooting at one another mostly because of the frustration stemming from congestion and long delays. You might also mention the recent phenomenon of videotaped car chases. Is the geographic setting important to this poem? Ask the students to write a few paragraphs in response to this question.
2. Ask students to write briefly on whether this poem is meant to reflect a man's macho foolishness or to be seen as ironic.

GROUP ACTIVITY

Have groups go through the poem and underline phrases and words they consider slang or jargon. Discuss the effect these words have on the poem's diction.

DISCUSSION

What keeps this poem from being an exercise in macho indulgence is the mixture of informal and formal diction spiced with a healthy dose of jargon. When juxtaposed against informal phrases like "sucks upon a dead cigar," words such as "likewise," "upon," "nonchalance," and "perfect" seem unusually formal, especially in light of the speaker's emotionally charged state. This mixture of diction levels undercuts the speaker's seriousness (Q 1). Note, for example, that in line 14 the speaker could have more naturally said "on my bumper again," instead of using the more formal "upon" (a pun on "up on"). The poem's haphazard use of capitalization and disregard for the rules of grammar further undercut the seriousness of the situation. After all, the speaker romanticizes his situation somewhat by comparing a freeway commute to a WWI or WWII dogfight and commuters to fighter pilots; if the diction were overly formal, the poet would not have been able to distance himself from the speaker and impart the objective sense of humor that makes this poem successful (Q 2, 5).

Note also how many of the word choices and details in this poem are not arbitrarily chosen. "Draws up" (l. 1), for example, plays off the idiom "to draw a bead on" (to take aim at) and suggests immediately the image of a gunfight. In the same line, "fast lane" is chosen instead of the more conventional "passing lane" because this poem is about life in the fast lane. The fact that one of the speaker's adversaries has blue (Aryan) eyes and the other drives a Mercedes (a German car) suggests that he sees himself in the role of an Allied pilot sparring with the Germans, the two sides involved in WWI and WWII dogfights. Jargon, which helps lend a more informal tone to the poem, is also carefully chosen. The speaker "hits," "fires," "blazes," and "veers"— all of which a pilot does. Students may feel that the poem's macho sensibility reflects contemporary American life. The rugged individualism and self-aggrandizing fantasy of the speaker may remind students of their own identification with cinematic action heroes (Q 5).

FURTHER READING

Bukowski, Charles. *Run with the Hunted: A Charles Bukowski Reader*. New York: HarperCollins, 1993.

FAYE KICKNOSWAY

Gracie

WRITING ACTIVITIES

1. Have students look closely at some of the images (such as the bonnet, the apron, and the chicken) and write on how they are used and why they are repeated so many times.
2. Have students identify the speaker's age, origin, physical appearance, and personality by choosing one word or phrase from the poem that best communicates each; have students write briefly on how word choice helps to establish character.

GROUP ACTIVITY

There are two geographic parts to this poem: the city and the country. Have two groups of students analyze how these two parts differ.

DISCUSSION

"Gracie" is a poem of contrasts. The speaker is direct yet coy, uneducated yet complex, realistic yet imaginative, and naive yet sexual. Even the poem's structure is contradictory. Although it is filled with nonstandard grammar, colloquialisms, and dialect, "Gracie" is a sestina, one of the most complex and difficult of all traditional French poetic forms. Your students probably will not see this at first — even if they already know what a sestina is. In fact, this poem is a perfect one to turn to when they ask that inevitable question: "But did the poet really mean to do that?"

The poem is not a perfect sestina in the traditional sense: A traditional sestina contains thirty-nine lines and an envoi that belongs at the end of the poem. In addition, the end words in "Gracie" are not arranged according to the traditional pattern. Still, it is clearly a modified sestina. This form is not readily apparent for many reasons, primarily because of its humble, homely subject. Most readers would not expect to find such a formal, traditional pattern here, and you may want to ask your students why they think Kicknosway uses it. There are many possible reasons, but you might suggest to them that this form naturally repeats words and images, and this repetition mirrors the circular thoughts the girl is turning around in her mind. Also, the images in the poem (and in the girl's thoughts) come full circle — instead of her feeding the chickens at the poem's conclusion, they are feeding her. Instead of looking out from the chicken yard, she looks in at it from the city window. The images, emotions, and physical states at the beginning of the poem contrast with those at the end: coolness with heat, white with the dark of night, and country with city.

You may want to teach this poem with Walker's "Everyday Use" to compare the rural settings, or with Bishop's "Sestina."

ROBERT BURNS

John Anderson My Jo

WRITING ACTIVITIES

1. Ask students to write about their most important friend and the one event that made that friendship special. This assignment can easily be turned into a longer essay.
2. Have students compare this poem to a modern song about friendship or about a couple growing old together and discuss differences between sentimentality and moving expression.
3. Have students write a description of an aging couple they know.

DISCUSSION

Here is the poem written out in colloquial English, without simile or symbolism (Q 2):

> My dear John Anderson,
> When we first met,

> Your hair was dark black,
> Your handsome brow was smooth,
> But now your brow is bald, John,
> Your hair is white;
> But bless your white head,
> My dear John Anderson.
>
> My dear John Anderson,
> We have spent the best days of our lives together;
> And we've had many happy days
> With one another John:
> Now we grow old, John,
> And both of us will go,
> And be buried together,
> My dear John Anderson.

Clearly, Burns's use of dialect in this poem creates a sense of authenticity and sincerity not found in the overly sentimental colloquial English version above. Burns's poem illustrates the positive effects dialect can have on a poem: use of dialect allows him to avoid sentimentality by giving readers the impression that they are hearing the speaker's unedited thoughts. This poem is a good example of the definition of dialect: the pronunciation, grammar, spelling, and vocabulary are all distinctly Scottish in flavor, and they combine with the rhythm of the lines to create a moving, memorable reminiscence (Q 1).

The couple in this poem may be old friends or, more likely, a married couple. ("Jo" is most often used to signify a sweetheart.) The speaker alludes warmly to a lifetime of shared experiences and is accepting of both the changes that come with age and the inevitability of death.

GWENDOLYN BROOKS

We Real Cool

WRITING ACTIVITIES

1. Ask students to rearrange Brooks's poem so that the lines do not end with pronouns. What is lost in this arrangement?
2. Ask students why they think Brooks includes the information "The Pool Players. Seven at the Golden Shovel" underneath the title. Is it necessary? What does it add to the poem? How do these lines differ from the poem itself?

GROUP ACTIVITY

Discuss the elements of poetry used in this poem, addressing ways in which the alliteration, rhyme, and syntax used here resemble modern rap music. Have groups write their own rap versions of the story in this poem.

DO YOUR STUDENTS KNOW . . .

Although gangs have existed throughout American history, the 1950s marked the highest rate of gang membership in large American cities. At that time, female gangs, associated with larger and more powerful male gangs, were first reported. During the 1960s, gang membership fell to historic lows. The resurgence of gangs in the 1980s and 1990s saw increasingly brutal and business-like organizations supported by the production and sale of drugs.

DISCUSSION

The information given beneath the title is *not* written in dialect, and this prepares the reader for the final line of the poem, for it creates an aesthetic distance between the speakers and the poet that makes the final line so effective. Many students will probably see that, excluding the final sentence, there are seven sentences that represent the seven different pool players speaking to us from the Golden Shovel. What they may not see at first is that the final sentence is clearly not spoken by any of the men; rather, it is the poet's detached assessment of the previous seven speakers. Brooks ends each of the first seven lines with a pronoun that injects a dynamic rhythm in the lines, imitating the speakers' cadence. In addition, this arrangement lends additional weight and a sense of finality to the last statement. The fact that this last line does not end in a pronoun is fitting; the break in the pattern implies an abrupt, permanent end.

The poem's use of dialect — combined with strong rhyme — give authenticity to the voices in "We Real Cool," capturing the atmosphere of the urban bar and the dialect spoken there (Q 1). Even though this poem does not use natural speech patterns (the sentences are clearly too compact, the rhymes too regular and exact), it does suggest the speech patterns and mannerisms of the pool players. Without dialect, the poem would seem preachy and judgmental (Q 2, 4). You may want to discuss the elements of poetry used in this poem and the ways these elements (alliteration, rhyme, syntax) resemble modern rap music.

You may want to compare this poem to Sagel's "Baca Grande" or even to Wilson's *Fences* (ethnic identity).

FURTHER READING

Mootry, Maria K., and Gary Smith, eds. *A Life Distilled: Gwendolyn Brooks, Her Poetry and Fiction.* Urbana: UP of Illinois, 1987.

EDMUND SPENSER

One day I wrote her name upon the strand

WRITING ACTIVITIES

1. Have students discuss briefly the relationship between form and content in this poem. What makes it a sonnet, and what impact does this form have upon the poet's message?

2. Ask students whose argument they find more convincing, the speaker's or the woman's (i.e., will their love *really* live?).

DISCUSSION

Since this poem deals with the transience of the poet's expressions of love amid a tide of chaotic change and decay, it is fitting that it is written in a formal, ordered style — as a sonnet. However, this is a Spenserian sonnet, not a Shakespearean or Petrarchan sonnet. The poet's adjustments in syntax, perhaps motivated in part by a desire to preserve the sonnet's rhyme and meter, probably result from the difficult rhyme scheme: *ababbcbccdcdee.* There are few rhymes available (four), and although this presents little difficulty when writing in Italian (or in any romance language, for that matter), composing in rhyme-poor English is indeed a challenge. Also, note the regularity of Spenser's meter; in his time, poets adhered strictly to the rules of form, which also makes Spenser's task more difficult, perhaps accounting for the fact that only Spenser wrote sonnets in this form.

You may want to teach this with Shelley's "Ozymandias," another sonnet dealing with effects of time on people, or with Shakespeare's "Shall I Compare Thee to a Summer's Day?"

FURTHER READING

Bloom, Harold, ed. *Edmund Spenser.* Modern Critical Views. New York: Chelsea, 1986.

E. E. CUMMINGS

anyone lived in a pretty how town

WRITING ACTIVITIES

1. Have students rewrite Cummings's poem in colloquial English, paying special attention to word order. What is lost when they do?
2. Ask students to discuss in writing the extensive repetitions Cummings employs here, such as the seasons or the skies. Do they have a function? If so, is this function related directly to theme?
3. For a longer writing exercise, have students trace the life cycle of "anyone" and "noone" in a narrative essay.

GROUP ACTIVITY

Divide students into four groups and assign a season to each group. Have the groups search for imagery related to their season and then present their findings to the class.

DISCUSSION

Although students are often baffled by his poetry at first, they may be surprised to learn that beneath all of his extensive and witty wordplay, most of Cummings's poetry is quite standard romantic fare. For example, in this poem we are told the story of a generic "anyone" who lives in a small, beautiful town, falls in love with "noone," and dies one day, despite the strength and sincerity of this love. Eventually, the "noone" who mourned and loved him dies and is buried next to him, while all around, the cycle of life and death, sowing and reaping, continues. Certainly, this story is not unusual, which is part of Cummings's message here, for these people are *supposed* to lead ordinary and uneventful lives.

Much of the delight the reader finds in this poem, however, lies not in the story, but in the arrangement of the words. Rewriting this poem into ordinary language would be like filling a balloon with lead — the wordplay and inventive repetitions make the story interesting and memorable. For example, the names themselves ("noone" and "anyone") have double meanings throughout the poem, as in line 26. Line 2, "(with up so floating many bells down)," is repeated verbatim only once more (1. 24), but the line is echoed throughout the poem (ll. 10, 33), much like bells tolling the passing of time. In fact, Cummings plays off the patterns established in the first two stanzas, using variations of rhythm and word order much as a jazz musician improvises. The repetitions of seasons, weather, and light underscore the continuing cycle of life and death, as does the order of these words. Notice that the word order of line 8 changes during the poem, but toward the end, in lines 34 and 36, it settles back into the original pattern.

You might pair this poem with Gildner's "Sleepy Time Gal" or with another conventional (or unconventional) love story. Students who have read *Our Town* in high school may see some surprising parallels.

FURTHER READING

Kidder, Rushworth M. *E. E. Cummings: An Introduction to the Poetry*. New York: Columbia UP, 1979.

A. E. HOUSMAN

To an Athlete Dying Young

WRITING ACTIVITIES

1. Ask students to write an essay about their proudest accomplishment.
2. Housman asserts that, although the athlete's death is tragic, there is some comfort to be taken in the knowledge that the young man died before his glory had a chance to fade. Have students write an essay in which they agree or disagree with this viewpoint.
3. Have students write a poem of their own in which the young man (or woman) has achieved greatness in a field other than athletics.

GROUP ACTIVITIES

Break the class into small groups and ask each group to compose a one- to two-sentence summary of the poem. Then bring the class together for discussion.

Divide the class into groups and ask them to discuss why (aside from a possible basis in real life) the young man celebrated here is an athlete.

DO YOUR STUDENTS KNOW . . .

Housman wrote his poem in honor of the 22,000 British soldiers who died during the Boer War. This war (1899–1902) pitted the British Empire against the Dutch Boers Republics of South Africa. The British generals and politicians promised a quick and easy win, but the guerilla tactics of the Boers prolonged the war. Notable names in the Boer War included Sir Arthur Conan Doyle, creator of Sherlock Holmes and a physician, who ran a field hospital; Winston Churchill, later WWII Prime Minister of England, who was a soldier; and Mohandas (Mahatma) Gandhi, who served as a stretcher bearer for the British medical corps. Gandhi later defeated Britain through nonviolent means in India.

DISCUSSION

The poem's title prepares readers for the striking contrast between the cheers in stanza one for the victorious runner and the mournful silence at his premature death. In both cases, he is raised high above the crowd, honored for his achievements. The speaker, who cheered and mourned with the other townsfolk, is only partly ironic in addressing the dead youth as "smart lad"; he is acknowledging that youth fades and athletes' records get broken. By dying at the height of his success, the boy need not outlive his glory. Still, there is a poignancy to the poem at the idea of a life interrupted too early. You might compare the attitude toward the fading of youth in Herrick's "To the Virgins, to Make Much of Time".

EMILY DICKINSON

My Life had stood — a Loaded Gun

WRITING ACTIVITY

1. Have students brainstorm to explore all the ways in which their own lives might be like loaded guns. What can the loaded gun signify? In what ways are their lives "loaded"? When they have finished brainstorming, have them write poems about their own lives in the style of Dickinson, using her syntax and punctuation wherever possible.

GROUP ACTIVITY

A good way to initiate discussion of any of Dickinson's syntax is to place students in groups and have each group rewrite the poem as prose. Another effective way to begin discussion of any of Dickinson's most metaphorical poems is to present the poem as a riddle and ask students to work in groups to solve it. Although this poem is not quite as much fun as some of her more overtly riddle like poems, such as "I Like to See It Lap the Miles," students will enjoy debating the identity of the "Master."

DISCUSSION

This maddeningly inconclusive poem poses a challenging introduction for students to Dickinson's idiosyncratic syntax and punctuation. Although it can be argued that Dickinson deviates from conventional English syntax in the first stanza in the interests of rhyme and meter, elsewhere her aim seems to be to control the emphasis placed on individual words and phrases. For example, in stanza 4, which some critics have read as "erotic," the placement of the phrase "Deep Pillow" at the beginning of the line just before a trademark Dickinson dash seems to commandeer all the emphasis upon that phrase and to downplay the significant phrase "to have shared." The sharing of the eider-duck's deep pillow is what lends the stanza its erotic undertone; yet, the phrase appears to be a throwaway (Q 1, Q 2). Unsettling elements like this are what makes it difficult to identify the "Owner" or "Master" as God, which students will most likely wish to do.

The last stanza, too, departs from conventional syntax: this time, the emphasis is placed on the word "He." Of course, had Dickinson simply written, "Though I may live longer than He," her meter would have been disturbed; but more significantly, the structure of the sentence suggests a deference to the "Master" that goes beyond the servility one might expect from a personified gun. Indeed, the capitalization of the word "He" reopens the debate about whether the Master is indeed God, but only after tantalizing the reader with the intimacy of the fourth stanza (Q 1, Q 2).

The question of why the speaker might compare her life to a loaded gun hinges on several critical factors. Do we read the poem as "psychobiography," as some critics have? Do we read it as religious allegory? Or do we, along with Adrienne Rich, read it as a parable about the dangers of creativity in which the Master becomes a kind of demon — that is, an inspiring inner spirit or muse? It would be difficult to make an airtight case for any of these interpretations; however, in their journal entries, students can practice at making a case for their interpretations (Q 3).

FURTHER READING

D'Avanzo, Mario L., and Edgar P. Stocker. "Two Explications of 'Loaded Gun.'" *Dickinson Studies* 42 (June 1982): 40–50.

Dobson, Joanne, and Lillian Faderman. "Poem 754: Workshop Discussion." *Women's Studies: An Interdisciplinary Journal* 16 (1989): 133–48.

CHAPTER 20

IMAGERY

JANE FLANDERS

Cloud Painter

Students may want to consider this poem as a description of the painting process: first, the background "incidental, a drape, a backdrop" and then the middle ground details "an oak, a wall, water." As the painting takes on details, the artist then moves beyond "what we see around us" to "let us drift and remember" through the sensory images evoked by the words. Students might identify and share their personal responses to some of these images, such as "wash flapping on the line," "school books, smudged, illegible." Symbols found in the passages about the shrinking palette, the horizons, and the trees might also be discussed and examined in relation to a study of the maturation and chronological development of John Constable's art and how his wife's death affected his work.

WILLIAM CARLOS WILLIAMS

Red Wheelbarrow

DO YOUR STUDENTS KNOW . . .

The wheelbarrow, a staple of farm life, was developed in China in A.D. 132. This innovation, created during the Han Dynasty, translates to "the wooden ox." Despite its laborsaving potential, it was not developed in Europe until the Middle Ages.

Williams, who (with Ezra Pound, Amy Lowell and others) is associated with the imagist movement, concentrates on the wheelbarrow as a single object. This poetic technique is similar to a painter's focus on specific details to create an exact image from a specific perspective, drawing the reader beyond the object to the ideas it may convey. The poem adopts other painting techniques to develop this precise image: the contrasting colors of red and white and the reference to the wheelbarrow being "glazed." Employed in words, these techniques produce the same effect as in paint: they transform the ordinary into something new and different. The brevity of description focuses attention on the wheelbarrow alone, creating the opportunity for a unique perception of its importance. Then, when the chickens appear, they provide contrast in color and shape. Together, the chickens and wheelbarrow suggest a farm, where so much does depend upon them. Students might discuss what, literally and figuratively, depends upon them — on the farm, in the poem, in the image, in the world.

EZRA POUND

In a Station of the Metro

Pound's fascination with the "one-image poem" relies heavily on Japanese haiku. He does not strive as much for the perfect image of the object as for a concentrated combination of images to produce a central human response. Students might discuss how the juxtaposition of two very different images like those found in the two lines work together to form that central, concentrated response. Ideally, the petals in the second line transform the anonymous faces into something softer and more beautiful. Students might discuss the several meanings of the word "apparition" and how these contribute to the poem's overall effect.

GARY SNYDER

Some Good Things to be Said for the Iron Age

The strong aural images in this poem reverberate in the ear, and the imagined "taste of rust" lingers on the tongue, perhaps making the reader salivate. Together they create a strong emphasis not on the objects themselves, but on what is implied by the combination. Like Pound, Snyder is concerned with a central idea produced by a combination of images. Students might research Snyder's political and social views, tracing these to the messages in his works. Though he alludes to an earlier Iron Age, we too use iron in a way Snyder does not seem to like.

SUZANNE E. BERGER

The Meal

DO YOUR STUDENTS KNOW . . .

During the 1950s, most families dined together five to seven nights per week. Today, with many parents working and family members heading to separate activities, the number has fallen to one or two nights a week. In addition, family meals are frequently disrupted by telemarketer phone calls. In 1999, in an attempt to preserve some semblance of a family mealtime, Arizona enacted a state law banning telemarketers from calling homes between 5 and 7 P.M.

Berger's images of the perfect Sunday meal contrast with prevailing ideas of traditional family units and togetherness and may stimulate discussion of misconceptions about nontraditional families. Students might also offer symbolic interpretations of "eating together" to provide insights into the poem. Berger's images build upon each other, heightening tension, freezing the meal and the family in time, like a photograph, in the reader's mind. Students might note the use of the word "waiting" appearing in each but the last verse; however, instead of resolving the tension created by such repetition, Berger strengthens it with both subtlety and pathos in the closing line.

WILLIAM CARLOS WILLIAMS

The Great Figure

Unlike Berger's rigid images in "The Meal," Williams's images build one on another to create a sense of movement, much like a mobile, several objects in concentric motion: the "rain," the "lights," the "firetruck," the "gongs," the "sirens," and the "wheels." Students might identify and compare the images from the poems as static or kinetic. The reader's attention here is drawn from one image to another, but concludes in a unified, collective interpretation. Students might discuss the contrast in tone produced by these images and those in Snyder's "Some Good Things to Be Said for the Iron Age." Note especially the contrast between the effects of sounds. Finally, students might compare the effect of Demuth's painting (color insert) with the effect of the poem.

RICHARD WILBUR

Sleepless at Crown Point

WRITING ACTIVITY

Have students write a paragraph comparing Wilbur's approach to nature through the haiku to Basho's and Kizer's.

GROUP ACTIVITY

The central image of the poem is a bullfight. Ask students working in groups to list some words that they associate with bullfighting. Why is the poem effective even without the presence of these words?

DISCUSSION

In this haiku, the writer describes his sleeplessness by painting a picture of a piece of land jutting into the sky like a bull charging into the toreador's cape (Q 1). "Lunging" is a strong word, leading the reader to picture the rush of the bull. "Capework" also underscores this image by evoking the constant movement of the fighter's red cloak (Q 3). This image is active and dynamic, reminding the reader of the restless nature of sleeplessness. There are various ways of looking at the title in relation to this central image: the movement of nature may have kept the speaker awake, or nature may offer a mirror of the speaker's situation rather than acting as a cause of it (Q 2). Ask students if the sleeplessness is voluntary or an uninvited insomnia. Does such a distinction make a difference in the tone and effect of the poem?

All of the haiku in this chapter focus on natural images, although each writer approaches the subject a little differently. Students might wish to attempt a large-scale comparison among various haiku, drawing on those in Chapter 18 as well.

MICHAEL CHITWOOD

Division

WRITING ACTIVITIES

1. Ask students to write an essay comparing "Division" with "Digging."
2. Academic work can often seem detached and remote from real-life concerns. Have students write about an occasion when they saw a meaningful connection between material covered at school and their daily lives outside of school.

GROUP ACTIVITY

Break the class into groups and ask each group to make a list of all the possible meanings the word *division* might have in the context of the poem.

DISCUSSION

In the first stanza, the speaker describes the carpenter's shed and the carpenter's practice of making furniture during the winter months. The second stanza concerns the efforts of a child — most likely the carpenter's child — to learn division (Q 1). Some students may find the images in the poem — or, rather, the relationship between the images — confusing. One obvious similarity is that carpentry and division both involve calculations and require attention to detail (Q 2). There is more to the two images than that, however: division and carpentry have a great deal in common, in that the work the carpenter does, or rather his way of working, divides him from his child (Q 4). It may be that the carpenter has little choice in this, because there is some suggestion that money in the family is tight.

It is ironic that making furniture for other people's homes creates a strain in his own home. The child must be preoccupied with this lack of intimacy if he sees it expressed even in an equation on the blackboard (Q 3).

You might want to teach this poem with "Digging," "Those Winter Sundays," "My Papa's Waltz," or "B. Wordsworth." The first three selections all involve re-lationships between fathers and children, and the last involves a character who becomes *like* a father to a boy.

LAM THI MY DA

Washing Rice

WRITING ACTIVITIES

1. Ask students to write an essay on an everyday activity that has some special signifi-cance for them.
2. Have students write a research essay on the importance of rice to the Vietnamese cul-ture and economy.

GROUP ACTIVITY

The mother does not speak in this poem but expresses her feelings through the action of washing rice. Divide the class into groups and ask each group to draft a one-paragraph statement that the mother might make if she were to express her-self verbally.

DISCUSSION

This poem takes a domestic activity and describes it so that it becomes a comment on the relationships between parents and children. The speaker's mother is wash-ing rice in order to separate the ripe from the unripe grains (Q 1). The grains that are ripe, or mature, are the ones that do not drift away, that stay with the person who is washing them. They are also the grains that are fit to be eaten, thereby pro-viding life.

Just as it is impossible to tell a ripe grain from an unripe grain just by looking at them, so it is difficult to judge whether a person has reached maturity. If the mother has this in mind, it may explain why she spends so much time washing (Q 2). Unlike the grains of rice, young people often drift away from their parents when they mature. Note that the mother "is washing rice in the late morning." If one divides life into childhood, adulthood, and old age, then the "late morning" might well correspond to the end of childhood. This interpretation seems espe-cially likely if the speaker will literally "go out tomorrow."

Consider teaching this poem with "Those Winter Sundays," "The Gift," "The One Girl at the Boys Party," and "To See the World in a Grain of Sand." The first three selections deal with parent/child relationships and the transition to matu-rity, and the fourth finds vast implications in the smallest things.

CHITRA BANERJEE DIVAKARUNI

The Alley of Flowers

WRITING ACTIVITIES

1. Ask students to write about a place they feel is "in-between" two states of mind or be-ing. Possibilities include cemeteries, places of worship, and museums.
2. For the poem to have its full impact, the reader must either know or infer that the speaker is using a different cultural frame of reference from that to which most Americans are accustomed. Have students write a short research essay on Hindu funeral customs.

GROUP ACTIVITY

Divide the class into four groups. Assign one stanza from the poem to each group and ask the groups to discuss what the particular stanzas they have been assigned contribute to the poem as a whole.

DO YOUR STUDENTS KNOW . . .

The Hindu religion celebrates death as a movement of the spirit from one realm to another. For this reason, white is the color of mourning in the Hindu religion, and the body is cremated in order to allow the spirit to be released. Flowers and sweetmeats are left as offerings to the deceased, and bells and horns are rung. The spirit is then released in a joyful manner and moves toward Nirvana, or the next life, through reincarnation. Following is a thirteen-day period of grieving led by the male members of the family.

DISCUSSION

This poem is about a communion with the dead that, rather than making the living morbid, refreshes them. The alley is a place set apart from the rest of the busy city. It is cool, it is scented with flowers and earth, and it is filled with different kinds of flowers. The women there are not merely old, but have "eyes that have seen everything you can imagine." As the poem goes on, we can see that this alley is a place beyond time. The hands on the reader's watch have stopped, and the speaker tells us that it is "[a]s if the alley has no end."

The poem is rich in images: flowers, old women, light like rain, and "misted air like petals." Taken together, these images reinforce the idea of the alley as a place of light and delicacy, a place that is somehow between our own world and the world of the dead. It is helpful to know that flowers pay an important role in Hindu rituals for the dead and that Hindu widows traditionally wear white. Knowing this lends an added depth to the poem since the alley seems even more remote from the daily world. Students who do not keep these facts in mind may find the poem confusing. Even without this information, though, there are numerous hints about the poem's meaning. "The dead" are mentioned twice, and white is identified as the color "of female mourning." There is sadness in the poem, but there is also a profound calm and, as Divakaruni puts it, "a blessing."

You might consider teaching this poem with "Cathedral," "Monet's 'Waterlilies,'" and "Rainbow." Each selection includes a moment of transcendent beauty.

EDWARD HIRSCH

Man on a Fire Escape

WRITING ACTIVITIES

1. Ask students to write about a moment when they suddenly saw the world in a new way.
2. Have students write a continuation of the poem. What does the man do when he goes back to his "empty room"?

GROUP ACTIVITY

Break the class into small groups and ask them to discuss why the speaker of the poem finds this moment so important.

DISCUSSION

It is unclear from the poem itself whether the sudden brightening is a trick of the light or the result of some special receptivity on the part of the man. Since this was "just an ordinary autumn twilight / the kind he had witnessed often before," the latter possibility seems the more likely of the two. Although the man cannot remember why he is there, we are told that he was "propelled . . . onto the fire-escape." It would seem, then, that there was something on his mind, something troubling him that he perhaps wanted to consider (Q 1).

On a strictly literal level, the bright light of the setting Sun makes it appear as though the entire world is on fire. What the man himself sees, however, is a vision that goes beyond what could be literally possible. Although it is easy to see how the intense light could have made it seem as though there were "cars / burning on the parkway," it is unlikely that the man could have seen "steel girders / collapsing into the polluted waves" (Q 2). Part of what he sees, then, must be purely subjective.

The man has in a real sense had the world taken away from him and then restored, and this is undoubtedly why the speaker finds the experience important (Q 3). As part of your class discussion, you might ask students what they think it means when the speaker had seen "[n]othing" and gone "[n]owhere." Does this in any sense undercut the importance of what the man has seen?

The poem is interesting on a formal level in that it is written in a very loose iambic pentameter and follows — sometimes strictly, sometimes not — an unusual rhyme scheme. Because the meter is so flexible and because many of the rhymes are very faint, students may not notice this on a first reading. Having them read the poem out loud will allow them to pick up on the more obvious aspects of the pattern.

Consider teaching this poem with "The Fireman," "As I Walked Out One Evening," "Rainbow," "Desert Places," and "Try to Praise the Mutilated World." Each of these works contains a moment of visionary insight.

FURTHER READING

Boyle, Kevin. "An Interview with Edward Hirsch." *Chicago Review* 41.1 (1995).

MAXINE KUMIN

Vignette

WRITING ACTIVITIES

1. Ask students to write about a time when someone has made a mistaken assumption about them.
2. Emmet has probably had some difficulty coping with academic life, yet he seems to be well liked. Have students write a letter from his mother or father explaining what kind of a child he is.

GROUP ACTIVITY

Setting is an important element of this story. Break the class into groups and ask them to discuss ways in which they think the educational challenges faced by poor children are different in rural areas than in cities.

DISCUSSION

This poem gives a short sketch of the beginning and end of a school day for Emmet, a boy with attention deficit disorder (Q 1). Based on the condition of his road, we know that Emmet lives in a rural community, and given the fact that Emmet lives on "Poorhouse Road," it is likely that his family has little money (Q 4). There is an irony in the fact that the boy is picked up by the "Head Start van." Given his learning disability and his poverty, he already has two strikes against him and can hardly be said to be getting a "head start."

The poem as a whole, however, constitutes a warning against judging the quality of a person's life based on details like the above. When the speaker says that there is "[n]o attention deficit on either side," she means that Emmet and his dog Radar are completely focused and attentive in their interactions with each other (Q 3). Earlier in the poem, we see that Emmet "loves the schoolyard / slides and swings, lunchtime, and Sue, his driver." It is really an oversimplification, then, to say that Emmet has trouble paying attention. There are any number of things and persons to which he is able to devote himself with all his energy.

You might want to teach this poem with "Child's Grave, Hale County, Alabama," which describes the burial place of a poor child from a rural area, or "The Lamb," in which the title creature is an emblem of innocence. It would also work well with "In Memory of Jenny and Evelyn Who Were Playing When the Stoop Collapsed," a poem that examines the importance of place in the lives of children.

FURTHER READING

Shomer, Enid. "An Interview with Maxine Kumin." *Massachusetts Review* 37 (Winter 1996): 531–56.

MICHAEL McFEE

Valentine's Afternoon

WRITING ACTIVITIES

1. Have students write a poem of their own about a holiday other than Valentine's Day.
2. Like other holidays, Valentine's Day places a great deal of stress on some people. Ask students to write a short research essay on holiday stress.

GROUP ACTIVITY

Break students up into groups and ask each group to find an alternative symbol to the heart. Each group should be prepared to explain why the alternative symbol it has chosen effectively conveys the same themes and ideas that McFee expresses in "Valentine's Afternoon."

DO YOUR STUDENTS KNOW . . .

Although the Christian roots of Valentine's Day are debated, its pagan beginnings reach back to third-century Rome and the feast of Lupercalia. This feast on February 15 also honored the god Lupercus and the goddess Juno Februeta. During the feast, women put their names in a box that a man then drew out, and the two would be partnered for the next year. During the Middle Ages, the celebration of love was connected with February since it was understood that birds took a mate on or near February 14. Although several Christian martyrs with varying stories were named Valentine, the Church named the celebration St. Valentine's Day to remove the pagan association from this popular holiday.

DISCUSSION

This is not so much a love poem as a disillusioned look at love itself. The action in the poem takes place on February 14, Valentine's Day. This fact sets up in the poem in several ways. First, the fact that someone is driving along with a heart-shaped balloon is completely plausible on this day. Second, readers will more readily accept that the speaker, on seeing the balloon, would begin a meditation on the meaning of love. If students do not immediately see that the balloon is a symbol, emphasize the fact that it literally has the word *LOVE* written on it. Love is "a swollen word" literally because it is written on one side of an inflated balloon. Figuratively, it is "swollen" both because the experience of love can be wounding and because society has placed such expectations on romance that the word *love* may literally appear inflated.

You might teach this poem with "The Littoral Zone," "The Love Song of J. Alfred Prufrock," "Nice Car, Camille," and "Cathedral."

ROBERT FROST

Nothing Gold Can Stay

WRITING ACTIVITY

1. Ask students to use their dictionaries to look up what they consider to be five key terms in the poem. What connotative meanings do these terms have? What is the dictionary definition of *green*, and what does green suggest connotatively? What about *dawn*, *gold*, and so on?

GROUP ACTIVITY

Ask students in groups to brainstorm a list of things that have a brief moment of beauty and perfection, such as a sunrise or sunset, a rose's bloom, or a butterfly.

DO YOUR STUDENTS KNOW . . .

Although gold may have been mined as early as 6000 B.C., it was not used for monetary purposes until 700 B.C. in the kingdom of Lydia, in what is now western Turkey. Gold has great monetary value due to its scarcity. The world's holdings of gold account for only 120,000 metric tons, and even with mining, these holdings only increase by 2 percent each year.

DISCUSSION

You may want to begin discussion by asking students to identify "her" in the poem. Nature is personified and assumes a female identity. Ask students to consider why Frost might characterize nature as a woman. Students will probably consider the obvious and will mention "Mother Nature," but encourage them to consider additional possibilities. Frost's tone in "Nothing Gold Can Stay" is rather nostalgic, and some students might even characterize his mood as sad. The central idea of the poem is that most things reach their beauty and perfection early and hold it only briefly. The poem is about transient beauty, spring, youth, and love (Q 1). Line 1 reflects this notion and its inherent paradox is expressed by the idea that when leaves first bud in the spring, they take on a golden hue, but sadly, turn quickly, for gold is "her hardest hue to hold" (Q 2). Frost mentions four different images that reinforce his theme and prepare his readers for the last line. All have early, brief beauty: the foliage of trees, the flowers' bloom, the fall in the Garden of Eden, and the passing of a day (Q 4). In this context, the colors gold and green take on a symbolic significance. "Green" refers to the spring and birth in line 1, and "gold" perhaps symbolizes that brief perfection as "Nature's first green is gold / her hardest hue to hold." Similarly, "Eden," an obvious symbol of humankind's early perfection, "sank to grief." "Dawn," the "green" or birth of a new day, must always go "down to day" (Q 3).

You may want to help students understand and define Frost's theory of po- etry in his essay "The Figure a Poem Means" and work with his complex terms, such as "delight," "impulse," and the "melting ice" metaphor. Frost's theory of poetry does seem to hold true for "Nothing Gold Can Stay." The first line clearly reflects the central direction of the poem, and the last line simply asserts his main idea or "great clarification." Finally, each image takes his reader progres- sively to his main point or "surprise" in the last line of the poem: "Nothing gold can stay" (Q 5).

FURTHER READING

Marcus, Mordecai. *The Poems of Robert Frost: An Explication*. Boston: Hall, 1991.
Perrine, Laurence. "Frost's 'Nothing Gold Can Stay.'" *Explicator* 42 (1983): 38–39.

JEAN TOOMER

Reapers

WRITING ACTIVITIES

1. Have students analyze the use of sound and rhythm in this poem, looking particularly at the use of sibilants.
2. Ask students to analyze their responses to the images in this poem. How do they affect the tone? Could any of the images create a more positive tone if used in a poem about a different subject? Give an example.

DISCUSSION

The mood of this poem is dark and sinister. The first image, although dealing with a typically positive theme (harvest), has a negative tone as well, suggested by the Grim Reaper and his scythe (Q 2, 3). The speaker makes no comment about the first image other than to say that hones (stones used to sharpen cutting tools) are placed in pockets "as a thing's that done," alluding to the acceptability of this first image as a fact of life: reaping occurs as a fact on both the literal level and metaphorical level (Q 1).

The second image relates to the first in its literal and metaphorical connota- tions. Both images deal with cutting down life; however, in the second case, the lives lost are the lives of weeds and the useless field rat. The repetition of the word "black" in the poem suggests a dire situation for mankind in general (and perhaps for blacks in particular): People are cut down in two situations, both when death comes naturally and when people are dismissed as trivial. Student responses will probably vary. Toomer's poem is universal in its theme and subject and lacks direct reference to a "Negro" audience; however, students may mention the "black" repetition in the poem, possibly associating it with the black race (Q 4). A subtle comment on this fact of life appears in the last line: The mower continues even though he is blood-stained (Q 1). The rat is startled by the mower and the black horses, as the rhythm of line 6 suggests, but is helpless to do anything about the coming onslaught.

FURTHER READING

Bus, Heiner. "Jean Toomer and the Black Heritage." *History and Tradition in Afro-American Culture*. Ed. Gunter H. Lenz. Frankfurt: Campus, 1984. 56–83.
Jones, Robert. "Jean Toomer as Poet: A Phenomenology of the Spirit." *Black American Literature Forum* 21.3 (Fall 1987): 253–73.

WILFRED OWEN

Dulce et Decorum Est

WRITING ACTIVITIES

1. Ask students to comment in a paragraph on whether the sentiment that sparked this poem (the glory of dying for one's country or for a cause one strongly believes in) is evident today.
2. Have students compare the story in this poem to a recent movie about war such as *Saving Private Ryan*.

GROUP ACTIVITY

Divide the class into groups and distribute photographs of a different war — the Vietnam War, the Persian Gulf War, and so on — to each group. What descriptions in Owen's poem apply to wars in general? What details would each group add to make the poem more relevant to its own particular war?

Ask the students in each group to take the role of a different type of reader: an eighteen-year-old eligible for the draft, a businessman with no military experience, a middle-aged housewife, a Vietnam vet, a WWII vet, or some other specific person. How would each respond to the poem? How would age and background influence each person's reading of the poem?

DISCUSSION

This poem is told from the point of view of the soldier in WWI, who includes himself in the misery he describes ("we" in l. 2). The soldier has no sense of glory or honor in regard to his service; rather, he is moving as a robot, going on without an understanding of where or why. His attitude is one of horror, disillusionment, and fatigue (Q 1). Through this attitude and through the experiences he describes, the speaker reminds the reader that war has nothing to do with "sweet" or "fitting" aspects of life.

Three central images appealing to the senses of both sight and sound reinforce the idea of unnaturalness and horror. In the first eight lines, we see images of physical impairment and old age: "bent double," "limped," "lame," "blind," "drunk," "deaf," and "tired." The images suggest that the soldiers plod forward with great difficulty, much as the physically impaired or elderly do. The irony is that these are young men who should be in the prime of life; instead, they are forced into premature frailty (Q 2).

The second eight lines illustrate the fishbowl effect of a gas attack and vision through a gas mask. The scene, although blurred by chemicals and the shield of the mask, is powerful enough to recur in all the speaker's dreams. Again, through the use of the "green sea" imagery, we sense the lack of connection between the war and anything solid, natural, or real. In the final section of the poem, the speaker draws readers even further into a world detached from reality, asking us to consider the situation in "some smothering dreams." The images here are both visual ("white eyes writhing," l. 19; "his hanging face," l. 20) and auditory ("gargling," l. 22) (Q 3). The poem's movement from control to confusion reinforces the theme that war is inglorious and unreasonable like the solders' lack of understanding and sense of purpose. The poem's structure takes on a chaotic and "blurry" nature in the second half (Q 5).

The striking images of the last section may seem very harsh ("bitter as the cud / Of vile incurable sores on innocent tongues," ll. 23–24); however, they reinforce the poem's theme: War is neither sweet nor fitting. Owen's argument against war, then, is conveyed not so much in the logic of his words as in the pictures that he presents as a contrast to the traditional maxims about war.

As a postscript to this poem, you might mention that Owen wrote it while recuperating from shell shock he experienced at the Battle of the Somme. After leaving the hospital, he returned to the trenches and ironically was killed a week before the end of the war. The knowledge that Owen died in WWI will probably heighten the reality of the experience for students, but the imagery alone is compelling enough for most (Q 4).

This poem might be appropriate in the context of a larger unit on the theme of war in general. In such a framework, you might compare the poem with Jarrell's "The Death of the Ball Turret Gunner," Owen's "Anthem for Doomed Youth," and some of the other poems in the section on war in Discovering Themes in Poetry.

FURTHER READING

Griffith, George V. "Owen's 'Dulce et Decorum Est.'" *Explicator* 41.3 (1983): 37–39.

Quinn, William A. "Multiple Metrics in Wilfred Owen's 'Dulce et Decorum Est.'" *English Language Notes* 21.2 (1983): 38–41.

CHAPTER 21

FIGURES OF SPEECH

WILLIAM SHAKESPEARE

Shall I compare thee to a summer's day?

Ask students if they think the speaker's comparison of his beloved to a beautiful summer's day remains effective some four centuries later. Perhaps they can suggest analogies of a loved one to inanimate objects or abstract ideas and then explain their reasoning for these associations. You might also compare this poem with Shakespeare's other sonnets — especially "Not Marble, Nor the Gilded Monuments," in which the speaker also promises to immortalize the beloved in verse.

LANGSTON HUGHES

Harlem

DO YOUR STUDENTS KNOW . . .

Lorraine Hansberry drew the title of her play, A Raisin in the Sun, from Hughes's poem. The play was based on her family's experiences with Chicago's restrictive covenants that kept neighborhoods white and African-Americans out. Hansberry's family won a court battle to ensure their right to purchase property in a restricted neighborhood.

Students might discuss their own dreams (careers, marriage, graduate school) and how they would react if someone told them they would have to put the dreams off for years. You may also want to go beyond the list of six answers to the question "What happens to a dream deferred?" by considering how other writers have treated the suspension or the death of dreams — for example, Miller's Death of a Salesman. Students might discuss whether or not society has progressed much in race relations in the decades since Hughes wrote about explosive tensions in the African-American community. Is this theme still a concern today in their communities? See also "Dream Boogie" and other Hughes poems in the poetry casebook, as well as Brooks's "Ballad of Rudolph Reed" and "Medgar Evers."

LAWRENCE FERLINGHETTI

Constantly Risking Absurdity

Students can explore still other imaginative comparisons involving poets, or even depict themselves as writers or express the act of writing itself in figures of speech. One student, for example, compared writing to eating chicken noodle soup — the noodles (ideas) kept slipping off her spoon (pen) before they got to her mouth (paper).

AUDRE LORDE

Rooming houses are old women

DO YOUR STUDENTS KNOW . . .

To aid the homeless, rooming houses and single-room occupancy (SRO) buildings were established to provide safe, clean places to live. The Lakefront SRO nonprofit organization of Chicago has renovated numerous local hotels to SRO buildings. Rent for these rooming houses and SRO buildings is based on annual income and ranges from $90 to $250 per month.

Compare the juxtaposition of images here (rooming houses/old women) with Pound's very different juxtaposition of white faces on a metro in "In a Station of the Metro" to petals on a bough. In both, the unexpected similarly challenges readers to revisualize — to revise their customary responses to the ordinary.

ROBERT BURNS

Oh, my love is like a red, red rose

WRITING ACTIVITIES

1. Have students compare the effect of the exaggeration here to that in Marvell's "To His Coy Mistress."
2. Have students locate some song lyrics that rely on hyperbole and — in writing — evaluate the use of hyperbole.

GROUP ACTIVITY

Students might enjoy coming up with some of their own hyperboles: "My love is like a . . ." or "I will love you until. . . ."

DISCUSSION

Students will know that roses symbolize love. Another simile, "My love is like the melody," demonstrates the "harmony" of true love (Q 1). The harmony in lines 3 and 4 is easily understandable. Also, hyperbole in a pronouncement of love is hardly unusual. If students have sought out lyrics (Writing Activity 2), look at them in class.

The exaggeration in this poem will be obvious to most of your students. It begins in stanza 2 (he will love her until the seas go dry); it continues in stanza 3 (he will love her until the Sun melts rocks); and it is carried through to stanza 4 (he will go ten thousand miles for her) (Q 3). The similes seem a little more believable than the hyperboles, but hyperbole is a traditional device that has long been accepted (and one that works). The poem progresses from conventional similes to grandiose claims of devotion. If the similes came last, the effect would be anticlimactic (Q 2).

You may want to teach this poem with Marvell's "To His Coy Mistress," which uses hyperbole in much the same way, or with Marlowe's "The Passionate Shepherd to His Love."

JOHN UPDIKE

Ex-Basketball Player

WRITING ACTIVITIES

1. Have students write two paragraphs about Flick Webb: one focusing on his life in 1946, one describing his present life.
2. Ask students to consider why Flick Webb did not become a successful pro-basketball player and have them write an essay or a fictional story that explains what happened to his dreams.

GROUP ACTIVITY

Have students work in groups to brainstorm about what associations the proper names have: Flick Webb, Pearl Avenue, Colonel McComsky Plaza, Berth's Garage, The Wizards, Mae.

DISCUSSION

Stanza 2 has a wonderful extended example of personification: "idiot pumps," "bubble-head," "rubber elbows," and the facial features with the word *ESSO* (Q 1). (Your students may need to be told that ESSO was the former name of EXXON — it is still used in Europe.) A photograph of an old gas pump will be helpful.

The gas pumps that Flick stands among are compared to members of a basketball team. "Five on a side" refers to the team on court, and their "rubber elbows" connote the flexibility needed for passing, dribbling, and shooting. They also suggest images of gangling, leggy young men.

Students will also comment on the personification in lines 29–30: The applauding tiers of snacks behind Mae become the fans in the bleachers, cheering behind the cheerleaders, a reference to Flick's earlier glory days on the court with the team (Q 1). Have students give you their sense of the simile "His hands were like wild birds" and the metaphor "Grease-gray and kind of coiled" (Q 2). What do they make of "The ball loved Flick"? In addition, students may wish to argue about whether the stereotype of athletes' not being very bright (having more brawn than brains) is accurate in their experiences. Do they enjoy Updike's poking fun at basketball players ("bubble-head" glass tops of the "idiot pumps")— or at the even dumber football players (no head at all)? Will they be able to identify Necco Wafers, Nibs, and Juju Beads as kinds of candy?

Students who like this poem might be encouraged to read Updike's novel *Rabbit, Run*, published two years later. The theme of early promise followed by failure is explored in many other works of literature as well. Students will probably be able to name films that treat this theme and point to athletes whose careers were cut short by academic failure, drug use, or injuries.

You may want to teach this poem with Updike's "A&P," Hughes's "Harlem," or Miller's *Death of a Salesman* (American Dream/nightmare); you might contrast it with Housman's "To an Athlete Dying Young."

RANDALL JARRELL

The Death of the Ball Turret Gunner

WRITING ACTIVITIES

1. Have students do the Journal Entry as an in-class writing activity.
2. Ask students to write briefly about the birth images in this poem. Are they effective? Why or why not?

DISCUSSION

This young soldier in World War II compares himself to a newly born animal, which helps to explain his innocence, naïveté, and youth. Students will have little trouble locating the important phrases: "from my mother's sleep," "hunched in its belly," and "wet fur" (Q 1). His lack of control of the situation contributes to his feeling like a helpless cub. Students may suggest that he goes from one womb to another (Q 2). Point out the irony of this comparison. (The womb is a place of security. In this case, however, the womb is a place of violence and death. Instead of being born, the gunner is washed "out of the turret with a hose," as if aborted.) The vulnerability of the gunner's position, along with the title, reinforces the fate of this soldier. A photograph of a B-17 or B-24 (the bombers equipped with ball turrets) helps students understand the gunner's vulnerability.

As students compare this poem with "Dulce et Decorum Est," they will experience various reactions. Some will probably have a stronger reaction to "Dulce et Decorum Est" because of its extremely graphic imagery (Q 3). Encourage students to consider theme and purpose with regard to the brevity of the gunner's life.

You may want to teach this poem with Reed's "Naming of Parts" and Hardy's "The Man He Killed" (perspectives on war) or with Dickinson's "Because I Could Not Stop for Death" (perspectives on death).

MARGE PIERCY

The Secretary Chant

WRITING ACTIVITY

1. Have students write about the use of metaphors in the poem. What assumptions about women and secretaries do these comparisons satirize?

GROUP ACTIVITY

Have each group of students create a profile of a worker in another occupation: medical doctor, firefighter, nurse, lifeguard, coach, police officer, lawyer, student, factory worker.

DO YOUR STUDENTS KNOW . . .

In 1986, the *Wall Street Journal* coined the term *glass ceiling* as a metaphor for women who are allowed to reach some success in American business without the chance of promotion or advancement to positions of authority. Although the worker can go no higher, the glass ceiling ensures that she can see clearly above her. One survey in 1999 noted that 95 percent of managers in U.S. companies are men.

DISCUSSION

Once students realize the significance of the metaphors, they will easily identify the other comparisons (Q 1). It is the metaphorical nature of the comparison — as opposed to simile — that makes the secretary's transformation into an object seem so powerful. If you use the Writing Activity, use students' responses as a way to begin discussion. The onomatopoeic words ("Buzz. Click. . . . Zing. Tinkle.") may be harder to identify.

Talk about point of view. This woman's perception of herself is based on the way she is treated as a secretary. What does the "wonce" say about her sense of humor? About her ability to laugh at herself? Do students believe secretaries — or other workers — are dehumanized, as the poem suggests? Or do they see the speaker's description as humorous hyperbole? Since some of your students may actually be secretaries, they may find Piercy's indictment of a dehumanized work-place a trifle bombastic. On the other hand, they may agree with Piercy's condemnation (Q 3).

You might teach this poem with Neruda's "The United Fruit Co." or Blake's "The Chimney Sweeper" (power/powerlessness).

JOHN DONNE

A Valediction: Forbidding Mourning

WRITING ACTIVITIES

1. Have students choose two or three of the comparisons and write about their effectiveness.
2. Ask students to attempt a description of the narrator in the poem and/or to describe what they think the relationship is like.

GROUP ACTIVITY

After you explain a metaphorical conceit and examine the last three stanzas, have students work in groups to come up with one or two conceits of their own.

DISCUSSION

You may want to begin by explaining the kind of compass to which Donne is referring. (Bringing one to class is a good idea.) Also, comment on the appropriateness of a compass drawing a circle, the symbol of unity and perfection. Demonstrate the way the compass works, literally and figuratively: a compass is joined, yet it has the capability to separate to perform individual duties. Students may also recognize the "flexibility" as one leg "leans and hearkens after" the other. Yet the speaker also refers to stability, to reliability, to being two in one, to completion (Q 2). Your students may be interested to learn that Donne wrote this poem to his wife before he left for a trip to France. What kind of mourning is he "forbidding"? Students may find Donne's figurative speech more appropriate when they consider that, in Donne's day, such a separation was a serious matter. It is the gravity of the separation underlying this poem that gives it its emotional power (Q 4).

Some students will have difficulty in recognizing both spiritual and physical love in stanzas 1 and 2. Stanza 3, with its reference to an earthquake and the "trepidation of the spheres," further comments on the contrast between the two types of love.

The movement of the spheres indicates both separation and union. And "dull sublunary lovers" represents those who rely on physical presence. The speaker's love is more refined, as is gold.

You may want to teach this poem with Browning's "How Do I Love Thee?" or Bradstreet's "To My Dear and Loving Husband" or Burns's "Oh, My Love Is like a Red, Red Rose" (love/sex).

E. B. WHITE

Natural History

WRITING ACTIVITIES

1. White uses an unusual simile to describe his connection to the one he loves. Ask your students to come up with an alternate simile.
2. Have your students write a letter in reply to the poem.

GROUP ACTIVITY

Break the class into small groups and ask them to list the advantages and disadvantages of the simile White has chosen.

DISCUSSION

In this short poem, the speaker uses the metaphor of a spider at work to explain the way in which he is connected to the woman addressed (Q 1). A spider's web is a complicated construction, as is the life of any individual. The speaker realizes that, just as the spider needs a stable base and point of return in order to function, he himself needs his connection to Katherine (Q 3). The title "Natural History" suggests that contemplation of the natural world is an appropriate way to learn about ourselves. The different types of language in the poem — "rig" as contrasted with "silken," for example — also suggest that the scientific intellect and the heart are not necessarily irreconcilable (Q 2). Some of your students may have read White's children's book, *Charlotte's Web*, or seen the film based on it. If so, they may be predisposed to like this poem. The biggest challenge may be the feeling on the part of some students that spiders are repulsive and therefore not appropriate for use in a love poem.

You might want to teach this poem with "The Swing," "A Valediction: Forbidding Mourning," "For Once, Then, Something," or "A Noiseless Patient Spider." The first two selections address issues of separation, the third looks at nature in an attempt to find meaning, and the fourth, as will be evident from the title, uses a spider as a metaphor.

FURTHER READING

Sampson, Edward C. "E. B. White." *American Humorists, 1800–1950.* Ed. Stanley Trachtenberg. *Dictionary of Literary Biography.* Vol. 11. Detroit: Gale, 1982. 568–83.

BEI DAO

A Bouquet

WRITING ACTIVITIES

1. Ask students to pick the one metaphor they find most powerful and explain why.
2. Have students write their own poems in which they use multiple metaphors.

GROUP ACTIVITY

Break the class into five groups and assign each group a stanza from the poem. Ask each group to share their impressions of the cluster of images in their stanza.

DO YOUR STUDENTS KNOW . . .

Bei Dao, a pseudonym for the Chinese poet Zhao Zhenkai, writes poetry in the "menglong shi," or "misty school," style. These poems, which focus on the intimacies of love and friendships, have elusive, oblique subjects and use a grammatical style and syntax that are elliptical or unclear. Dao's poetry was written on many banners carried during the 1989 pro-democracy demonstrations in Tiananmen Square in Beijing. The political power of his poetry led to his exile in 1989.

DISCUSSION

Students may initially find this poem overwhelming because it contains metaphor on metaphor. In addition, the title may strike them as misleading. After all, there is only a brief mention of flowers in one line. You may want to point out to them that the word *bouquet* is itself a metaphor, that the poem is a "bouquet" of metaphors (Q 1).

   While particular metaphors may be beautiful and meaningful, the whole is greater than the sum of its parts. It is possible to detect a kind of connection between the different metaphors in a given stanza. In the first, metaphors suggesting transport by ship ("a bay, a sail / The faithful ends of a rope") and natural forces ("a fountain, a wind") are combined. In the second stanza, the metaphors all seem to cluster around a particular house in a particular landscape. In the third stanza, the addressee is compared exclusively to things that provide guidance. One of these, "[a] preface that comes at the end," may puzzle students at first. The metaphor is not all that complicated, however. "A preface that comes the end" would be one that gives readers the information they have needed all along. A lover often feels that finding in the beloved he or she has found the explanation to everything. The metaphors in the fourth stanza have a very different emphasis from those in the third. Here, the beloved conceals meaning rather than revealing it. In the fifth and final stanzas, the metaphors again become consistent enough so that readers can identify a landscape — in this case, a dramatic one.

It may be best to identify the patterns of metaphor in each stanza during discussion and then go on to talk about the poem as a whole (Q 2).

MARTÍN ESPADA

My Father as a Guitar

WRITING ACTIVITIES

1. Ask students to write an essay in which they compare and contrast "My Father as a Guitar" with "Why I Went to College."
2. Have students write a short research essay on the connection between stress and heart disease.

GROUP ACTIVITY

Break the class into groups and ask each group to discuss why Espada chose to compare his father to a guitar. Why did he choose a musical instrument? Why did he choose a guitar as opposed to another instrument?

DO YOUR STUDENTS KNOW . . .

Heart disease remains a killer across ethnic groups in the United States. Coronary disease is the leading cause of death for Latinos living in the United States. Research also shows Latin-American men also have the tendency to develop obesity two and a half times more quickly than their European counterparts. Poverty and little access to quality medical care contribute to this high rate of cardiac deaths.

DISCUSSION

This poem makes skillful use of metaphor, simile, and personification. In the first stanza, the speaker says, "The heart pills are dice / in my father's hand / gambler who needs cash / by the first of the month." In the second stanza, he introduces a simile that is thematically related to the metaphor in the first. Finally, in the third stanza, he brings in the metaphor that has been promised all along by the title.

Metaphor is sometimes preferable to a simile or a simple statement of fact. In the case of the final stanza, a simile just would not work since the speaker could not strum his father's strings if his father were only *like* a guitar. Nor would the simple statement, "I feel guilty because my father has to work so hard even though he has a heart condition" be very effective. It is certainly clear, but it is not very memorable, nor does it convey the idea with the same economy as the metaphor of the guitar does.

There is an element of guilt in both of the dreams. The speaker's father no doubt feels guilty that he is not with his mother when she dies. The speaker, though he never mentions it, is aware that he himself is, or at least was, one of the reasons his father has had to work so hard. The metaphor of the father as a guitar indicates that the speaker sees some connection between music and the dangerous predicament in which his father finds himself. It is dangerous to assume that the speaker and writer are one and the same, and you may already have warned your students against this danger. We cannot therefore say with certainty that the speaker is a poet or artist of any kind. It is quite possible, however, that the speaker is pursuing an artistic life and feels that he is doing so at his father's expense (Q 3).

Consider teaching this poem with "Hold Tight," "The Carnival Dog, the Buyer of Diamonds," "Aguantado," or "Do Not Go Gentle into That Good Night". All selections deal either with death or with troubled parent/child relationships (some deal with both).

FURTHER READING

Rivas, Marguerite Mari. "'Lengua, Cultura, Sangre': Song of the New Homeland." *Americas Review* 21 (Fall/Winter 1993): 150–63.

MARY JO SALTER

Kangaroo

WRITING ACTIVITIES

1. Ask students to write an essay in which they observe the behavior of an animal.
2. Have students write an essay in which they argue that the similes Salter uses in describing the kangaroos are either successful or unsuccessful.

GROUP ACTIVITY

Divide the class into small groups. Ask each group to speculate on why Salter chose to describe the kangaroos in human terms.

DO YOUR STUDENTS KNOW . . .

Kangaroo Mother Care — developed in Bogota, Colombia, in 1983 by Drs. Neos Edgar Rey and Hector Martinez — has helped to decrease the high mortality rate among preemies. When the mothers carried their low–birth weight babies all day in slings, the mortality rate fell from 70 percent to 30 percent. This international program took a cue from kangaroos, the Australian mammal famous for keeping its young safe in its pouch until old enough to care for itself. Inside the warm pocket are four teats that feed the joey, or baby kangaroo, which lives in the pouch for up to six months.

DISCUSSION

In the first lines of the poem, kangaroos are described as being "[l]ike flustered actors / who don't know what to do / with their hands." You might begin the discussion by asking students how this simile affects their reading of the poem and whether they find it effective (Q 1). The poem includes relatively few physical details about the kangaroos, so students' ability to judge the fitness of the simile will depend in part on their having seen footage of kangaroos standing around.

The simile used to describe the joey in the last stanza is surprising in several ways: first, it does not have any apparent connection with the idea, mentioned earlier, of the kangaroos as "actors." Second, it is a very everyday, humdrum image. Finally, it does not seem immediately appropriate to a description of a baby animal. Despite these difficulties, the simile succeeds, on a purely visual level, at describing the joey's action.

On careful reflection, some of the above difficulties disappear. Salter is not trying to carry through an extended metaphor in which the kangaroos are seen as actors or women. Rather, she is trying to humanize the animals in two different ways. Nor does the fact that we do not expect a baby to be "rummaging in a purse" ultimately detract from the poem. Instead, it allows the poet to show that the animals are very like us but still very different.

You might want to teach this poem with "Natural History," where the speaker compares himself to a spider; "Alligator Poem," where the alligator becomes a symbol for the destructive power of nature; or "The Fish," a poem in which the line between detailed description and meditation is blurred.

FURTHER READING

Darling, Robert. "Mary Jo Salter. *American Poets since World War II, Third Series.* Ed. R. S. Gwynn. *Dictionary of Literary Biography.* Vol. 120. Detroit: Gale, 1992. 273–75.

SYLVIA PLATH

Daddy

WRITING ACTIVITIES

1. Have students make a list of the images this speaker uses to characterize her father and write about the appropriateness of each comparison.
2. Ask students to write a letter from the speaker to the father, outlining her grievances without the anger apparent in the poem.
3. Have students write a letter from the father, answering the speaker's accusations and defusing her anger, rather than generating more.

GROUP ACTIVITY

The date of composition for this poem is given as October 12, 1962, although it was published posthumously in 1965. As students compare "Daddy" with "Wreath for a Bridal" (1956), "Morning Song" (1962), and "Metaphors" (1960), they might speculate about what might have been happening in the life of this confessional poet. Assign questions to each of three groups: What poetic devices do you find in these poems? What are the themes of each poem? Characterize the persona in each; can the anger in "Daddy" be found in the other three?

DISCUSSION

Your text discusses this poem. Read the poem aloud before you discuss it so that students can see the intrusion of the nursery rhyme scheme that — along with the title — suggests a return to childhood. The temptation to make autobiographical connections will be very strong here, especially given certain particulars. For example, Plath's father was a college professor at Boston University — thus the reference in lines 51–52. In fact, students can actually see Otto Plath (with the prominent cleft in his chin) standing at the blackboard in a 1930 photograph published in *Letters Home by Sylvia Plath: Correspondence 1950–1963*, edited by her mother Aurelia Schober Plath (Harper, 1975), p. 17. The infection in his toe turned to deadly gangrene (ll. 9–10); he died when she was a child (eight, not ten) (l. 57); she attempted suicide when she was a college student (l. 58). Although these details may refer to Plath's own life, she also makes a number of comparisons to the general experience of oppression. Does she progressively lose her identity throughout the piece? What do students make of the love/hate relationship in the speaker's memory? Does this help to explain in any way Plath's attempts at suicide? Several of your students will be able to respond to these questions, especially if they have read Plath's novel *The Bell Jar*.

While Plath is a confessional poet, this poem certainly shares a personal experience with an impersonal audience. What justifies Plath's doing so? Does she identify any universal themes that make this "confession" more acceptable or accessible?

You may want to teach this poem with the other Plath poems in the text (see the Group Activity) or teach it with Olsen's "I Stand Here Ironing" and Hall's "My Son, My Executioner" (parent/child relationships).

DAVID HUDDLE

Holes Commence Falling

WRITING ACTIVITIES

1. Have students write a letter to the editor of the Austinville newspaper from the point of view of the speaker in the poem encouraging some community action or have them write a letter as the CEO of the lead and zinc company, explaining the business's position and how the company benefits the people of the community.

2. Have students write an objective article that presents an unbiased account of the situation depicted in the poem.
3. Compare this poem with Neruda's "The United Fruit Co.," another indictment of a business's exploitation of the land and the people.

GROUP ACTIVITIES

Have students research different methods of mining and look at some of the problems associated with them.

Have students develop a skit based on the poem. They can create characters and dialogue to suit a small or large group. You may even have them offer a solution.

DISCUSSION

This poem is discussed in the text. You may want to explain that owning mineral rights means that the original owner keeps and has responsibility for the land, but the buyer gets profits from mining the minerals.

Talk with students about the departures from "literary language" in the poem. Have students comment on these "departures." Do they work here? How? Why?

You may want to teach this poem with Auden's "The Unknown Citizen."

ANNE BRADSTREET

To My Dear and Loving Husband

WRITING ACTIVITIES

1. Ask students to look at this poem from the feminist point of view and write about whether they think the speaker is a weak or strong figure.
2. Have students analyze the meter of this poem and its effect on the meaning of the poem.
3. Ask students to write a reader response analysis of this poem. Ask them to what extent the use of an earlier form of English ("thee," "ye," "thy," "doth," etc.) influences their reaction to the poem.

GROUP ACTIVITY

Divide the class into two groups. Ask one group to play a believing husband who takes his wife's poem at face value. The other group will play the role of a suspicious husband who doubts the seriousness of the poem. Discuss which parts of the poem make it believable and convincing and which parts suggest otherwise. Have students discuss what assumptions about love influence their judgments and to what extent those beliefs reflect contemporary values.

DISCUSSION

Although the language of this poem departs from contemporary English, the use of hyperbole to make declarations of love should be familiar to students. In fact, the poem makes use of several common strategies for proving affection, strategies that are exploited (or implicitly ridiculed) by other poems in the text. For example, the poem begins with a series of conditionals that set up standards against which the love between husband and wife may be evaluated (ll. 1–3). The speaker here feels that her own marriage matches, if not exceeds, those standards. This is the same strategy that Shakespeare inverts in "My Mistress' Eyes Are Nothing Like the Sun" ("If snow be white, why then her breasts are dun").

The second section of the poem (ll. 5–8) uses hyperbole, just as Marvell does for more lascivious purposes in "To His Coy Mistress." The use of the hyperbole fits the gushing tone established in the first part and thus fits into the whole scheme of the poem (Q 1). Moreover, whereas the first section refers to a love that exceeds standard assumptions about marriage, the hyperboles in the second allow the speaker to show that her love is also beyond standard bases for physical value. In other words, there is no price sufficient for this love.

In the last section, Bradstreet moves into religious imagery, equating the love of the husband with a more divine love that is impossible to requite fully. In fact, she suggests that the only just response would be divine favor (l. 10). The final two lines complete the religious imagery by asserting that love in life will lead to life everlasting.

Students should note that the final couplet, although perhaps strongest in its assertions about the value of the love in this marriage, also is the only part of the poem to end with weak syllables. They might discuss how this change in meter affects their willingness to believe the woman fully. Does her love really extend as far as she would claim, or does the last line reveal a weakness?

You may want to teach this poem with Campion's "There Is a Garden in Her Face" or Donne's "A Valediction: Forbidding Mourning" (love/sex) (Q 2).

ANDREW MARVELL

To His Coy Mistress

WRITING ACTIVITIES

1. Have students discuss the structure of this poem as an argument.
2. Ask students to write a letter (or poem) from the "coy mistress" responding to the lover's requests.
3. Students could analyze this poem from a feminist perspective and analyze the speaker's attitudes, explicit or implicit, toward women.

GROUP ACTIVITY

In groups, brainstorm to come up with a list of expressions or types of arguments that might be used today to accomplish the purpose of persuading a woman to become a lover. How are they different from Marvell's devices? How are they similar?

In groups, have the students "stage" the poem as a monologue from a play. Which actor would play the part? What actions would he take at various parts of the poem? Will the woman be seen? If so, how will she respond? Where will the tone be more serious? Where will it be lighter?

DISCUSSION

The most striking feature of Marvell's poetry is its use of figures of speech, especially hyperbole. As you begin your discussion of the poem, you might put three columns on the board representing the three sections of the poem, and in each have students list hyperboles and other figures of speech as they find them. Once these have been listed, the students should consider how each section exploits the figures of speech to contribute to the overall structure of the poem.

For example, the first section, which introduces Marvell's "argument," takes the form of a hypothetical situation characterized by hyperbole. Thus, the time frame of the opening section ranges from "before the Flood" (l. 8), a reference to biblical beginnings, to the "conversion of the Jews," a reference to biblical frames for the end of time. Within such a span, exaggerated times may be spent for adoration: a hundred years (l. 13), two hundred (l. 15), and thirty thousand (l. 16). The spatial limits of the speaker's fantasy world range from the close ("Humber," l. 7) to the most exotic and remote rivers ("The Ganges," l. 5).

The second section abruptly ends the vision of the first part, and the use of "but" in line 21 signals this change. Students will see that the figures of speech change as well. The romantic hyperboles of the first part become more realistic and blunt: the eternity before them is now a "desert" (l. 24), and the speaker predicts that worms will be able to violate the woman's virginity despite her refusals (Q 1).

Having established the contrast between the hypothetical and the real, the speaker brings his argument to a close with a call for action. "Now therefore" (l. 33) signals this shift. The poet uses similes to illustrate the request: "like the morning glew," (l. 34), "like amorous birds of prey" (l. 38). The second simile carries through to the end, with "time" personified as the victim of the hungry birds, and the sun, also symbolizing time (l. 45), is put to flight.

As the students see the poem as a whole, they should notice that the tone of the poem is fairly light, especially in the beginning. Using the hyperboles allows Marvell to create such a tone while still dealing with some very heavy and potentially depressing topics: old age, death, and decay. In addition, the poem may be seen as a reprimand for the "coyness" of the woman; Marvell avoids making the reprimand too strong by setting the tone of the argument through hyperbole, which is less direct (Q 2).

Students might wish to compare the strategies employed by Marvell to those in some other "love" poems: Browning's "How Do I Love Thee?," Shakespeare's "My Mistress' Eyes Are Nothing like the Sun," Campion's "There Is a Garden in Her Face," or other love poems in this chapter.

FURTHER READING

Crider, Richard. "Marvell's Valid Logic." *College Literature* 15 (1988): 224–32.
Duyfuizen, Bernard. "Textual Harassment of Marvell's Coy Mistress: The Institutionalization of Masculine Criticism." *College English* 50 (1988): 411–23.

ROBERT FROST

"Out, Out —"

WRITING ACTIVITIES

1. Ask students to analyze the punctuation in this poem. What does Frost do with dashes?
2. The basic form of the poem is a narrative. Ask students to analyze the poem in terms of the traditional divisions of a story: exposition (with foreshadowing), climax, denouement. What source of conflict drives the poem forward?
3. Ask students to write either an objective newspaper account of the incident, giving only the facts, or a subjective letter to the editor that argues against having children do dangerous work.

GROUP ACTIVITIES

Ask students to form groups, each of which will analyze one of the following oppositions in the poem: boy versus man, dead versus alive, light versus heavy, day versus night.

Have groups analyze the sensory images in the poem: sight, sound, and smell.

Ask the groups to choose a minor character in the poem (the doctor, the sister, the "I" [l. 10], or "they") and argue that their character is central to the poem.

DISCUSSION

You might begin your discussion of the poem by having students identify the theme of the poem: how people respond to the knowledge that life is brief and senseless. Frost makes a reference to a more passionate expression of this theme in his allusion to the tragedy *Macbeth* in the title (Q 1). However, rather than using metaphor to convey the theme (as Shakespeare does in the excerpt cited in the text), Frost uses understatement and the events of ordinary life to emphasize the fact of death and its unpredictability. Death need not come with the emotional fanfare of *Macbeth*; in fact, it normally does not.

Encourage students to find examples of understatement in the poem. For example, in line 18, Frost personifies the saw and says that neither it nor the boy's hand "refused the meeting." The event happened so quickly that the boy did not have time to pull away, but Frost makes the accident seem less tragic by characterizing it as a simple personal encounter. In line 25, the boy "saw all spoiled." Here again, the immensity of the consequences of the accident is minimized by a simple statement. Have the students think about the range of things "spoiled": the boy's job, his usefulness, his ability to do everyday things, his chance to hold hands with a girl, and ultimately, his life.

In line 32, the boy, who was so much alive at the beginning of the poem, is dead: "that ended it" (Q 4). Neither grief nor shock nor agonizing questions are dealt with; the life is simply ended. Finally, in line 33, the last rather callous but practical understatement occurs: "no more to build on there." There is nothing that can be done, and life will go on (Q 2).

Students may be disturbed by the apparent indifference of the others in the poem; let them explore that response. Ask them also to explore their response to the death of the boy. Were they prepared for it? The use of "snarled and rattled" in lines 1 and 7 foreshadows an attack by the saw, and there are other warnings as well: references to sunset suggest a coming death (l. 6), as does the comment that "day was all but done" (l. 9). These lines are suggestive, but at the same time, they represent events that occur every day; Frost thus makes the climax more power-ful by suggesting that painful or tragic events may come out of the most ordinary and banal situations, without any embellished warnings. In line 27, the simple one-word sentence "So" sums up the wait between the boy's plea for his hand and the arrival of the doctor. All those details, all the agony, all of this is left to the reader to infer from the single word (Q 4).

You may want to teach this poem with Wilbur's "For the Student Strikers," Jarrell's "The Death of the Ball Turret Gunner," or Gordimer's "Once upon a Time" (perspectives on death).

FURTHER READING

Locklear, Gloriana. "Frost's 'Out, Out —.'" *Explicator* 49 (spring 1991): 167–69.
Schakel, Peter. "Frost's 'Out, Out —.'" *Explicator* 40 (summer 1982): 47–48.

DONALD HALL

My Son, My Executioner

WRITING ACTIVITIES

1. Have students write a letter from the son's point of view, assuming that he finds this poem as an adult.
2. Ask students to analyze the tension between immortality and death created in the poem.

GROUP ACTIVITIES

Divide the class into two groups, and ask them to debate whether or not the speaker's reaction to his son is natural.

Ask groups to discuss different ways Hall could have developed his theme without using hyperbole.

DISCUSSION

You might begin your discussion of this poem by asking students to describe their initial reaction to the poem and to the comparison that Hall uses in line 1. What would they expect to hear from a father holding a newborn son? Hall violates those expectations in order to achieve a calculated effect: to show readers that passing life on inevitably means losing one's own life, a sentiment that shocks us a bit (Q 1).

Students should also note the use of the past tense in line 10: "seemed." The time of immortality, as well as freedom, is ended. The parents have made a transition into a different stage of life, and they cannot return to the earlier stages. In this sense, the baby is indeed an executioner: he has killed the young married couple and put them permanently into the state of parenthood. For the rest of their lives, they must be parents, responsible for the child in terms of time, health, money, education, and the like. Their provision for the child's living will be the precursor to their own deaths (ll. 11–12); the child will "consume" their lives (Q 2).

You may want to teach this poem with Plath's "Morning Song" or Olsen's "I Stand Here Ironing" (parent/child relationships), or you may want to teach it with Frost's "'Out, Out —'" or Wilbur's "For the Student Strikers" (perspectives on death).

FURTHER READING

Barney, D. "Happy Men in Desert Places: An Interview with Donald Hall." *Southern Humanities Review* 22 (summer 1988): 225–37.
Hall, Donald. "Donald Hall on His Poetry: Looking for Noises." *American Writing Today*. Ed. Richard Kostelanetz. Washington, DC: U.S. International Communication Agency, 1982. 129–39.

MARGARET ATWOOD

you fit into me

WRITING ACTIVITIES

1. Discuss with students the complete absence of mechanical conventions (punctuation, capitalization) in this poem and then have them write this single sentence in prose.
2. Ask students to explore as many connotations as possible for the last two images, the fishhook and the open eye.
3. Ask students to compare the situation between the man and the woman in this poem to that described in Donne's "A Valediction: Forbidding Mourning." How are the two poems different in tone?

GROUP ACTIVITY

If possible, work on this poem without having assigned it for reading at home. Divide the students into four groups and give each group a portion of the poem: one group gets line 1 only, the next gets lines 1 and 2, the next gets lines 1–3, and the last gets lines 1–4. Ask students in each group to discuss what they think about the poem based on what they see. Compare responses.

DISCUSSION

Students will pick up on the sexual image of the first line of the poem rather quickly, but they may not recognize the hook-and-eye images of the second line. The hook and eye refer to a fastening device used in dressmaking or for fastening (with a buttonhook) Victorian-style shoes (Q 1). It would be helpful to bring an example of this type of hook and eye to class or draw one on the board. Many women's bras have such fasteners.

The simile created in the first two lines takes on a violent and shocking reading in the last two lines, an exaggerated expression of the pain involved in a relationship. Thus, the hyperbole is meant not only to shock the reader but also to illustrate pain and anger on the part of the speaker (Q 2).

You might end your discussion by asking students to characterize the emotional state of the speaker in this poem. Is she angry only? Does she see herself as victim, or is she in some way partially responsible for the situation?

You might want to teach this poem with Donne's "A Valediction: Forbidding Mourning," Faulkner's "A Rose for Emily," or Ibsen's A *Doll House*.

SHEROD SANTOS

Spring Elegy (1998)

WRITING ACTIVITY

1. Have students write down their initial reactions to the poem. Have they ever had an experience that was similar to what the poet describes? Have them imagine themselves as the poet. What other feelings might the poet have that are not described in the poem?

DO YOUR STUDENTS KNOW . . .

The forsythia has small, delicate, yellow flowers, which bloom in early spring before the leaves appear on the plant. For this reason, the flower is associated with anticipation and hope. These small shrub bushes, a member of the olive family, originated in eastern Asia and eastern Europe.

DISCUSSION

Frank Vincent's death has profoundly affected the speaker. Why, then, does he not focus exclusively on that death? Why are the first three lines of the poem even there? One answer is that they give a sense of how Vincent's death has affected the speaker's life as a teacher (Q 1). His realization "of how little / we are left to say" has several meanings. It applies, of course, to the difficulty one experiences, when someone close has died, in finding something appropriate to say about the departed person to his or her family and friends. The statement also demonstrates, however, how the speaker has begun to question the value of his work (Q 2).

The turn comes at the words "and then" in line 2. When the speaker discovers these three objects on his desk, it is almost as though they have been placed there in response to his musings in the classroom (Q 3). The fact that he does not seem to know who left them adds to the sense that he has been answered by a more-than-human agency. The answer he receives, however, is not an unambiguous or entirely comforting one. The photograph (presumably of Vincent) is black and white and therefore does not fully capture the dead man as he was in life. The forsythia is no doubt beautiful, but as an early-blooming flower, it serves as a poignant reminder of a life that ended too soon. The "tenth share of his ashes" is a reminder of how close the speaker and the deceased must have been and of the small community of people who now share his physical remains (Q 4).

Students may at first read the tone as detached and strangely calm. We know from the title and epigraph, however, that this poem was written a year after the events it describes. The fact that the speaker still recalls the events leading up to the discovery of these three objects, coupled with the fact that he was not immediately able to translate the experience into poetry, suggests that the death had a very powerful effect on him (Q 4).

Consider teaching this poem with "Do Not Go Gentle into That Good Night," "To an Athlete Dying Young," "In Memory of Donald A. Stauffer," "Midterm Break," or "After Great Pain, A Formal Feeling Comes." All of these poems, except the last, are responses to death; "After Great Pain, A Formal Feeling Comes" uses physical death as a metaphor for the death of the emotions.

RICHARD LOVELACE

To Lucasta Going to the Wars

WRITING ACTIVITIES

1. Have students write a paragraph explaining what the speaker might mean in the poem's final two lines.
2. Ask students to list the other uses of metonymy and/or synecdoche in this poem and to write briefly on why they think these figures of speech are (or are not) effective.

GROUP ACTIVITY

Using the text's discussion as an illustration, students can practice using metonymy and synecdoche to enliven their own writing. Ask them to supply two or three well-chosen words to represent ideas such as "going to college" or "going to work."

DISCUSSION

Although written well over three centuries ago, this love poem is relevant to any society that still sends its young people into battle. Students might discuss the antithesis of this poem, a speaker arguing *against* leaving a lover to go to war. What valid reasons come to mind as a counterpoint argument for going to war to defend honor? Compare with Amy Lowell's "Patterns."

THOMAS LUX

Henry Clay's Mouth

WRITING ACTIVITIES

1. Ask students to write an essay about why, based on the poem, they would or would not vote for Henry Clay.
2. Ask students to write a short research essay on Henry Clay.

GROUP ACTIVITY

Divide the class into three groups. One group will argue, based on the poem, that Clay would have made a good president. Another group (again, based on the poem) will argue the contrary. The third group will decide the winner and present reasons for its decision.

DISCUSSION

"Henry Clay's Mouth" is about an expansive, energetic man whose large mouth serves as a symbol of his expansiveness. This is an example of synecdoche, in that a part of Clay's anatomy stands in for the whole man and his character (Q 2). Although this would not necessarily be apparent to the reader before beginning the poem, Lux establishes the connection throughout. Clay eats, drinks, kisses, and talks with his mouth, and his enthusiasm for all of these activities implies that they are related in a more than coincidental way (Q 1). Although one gathers from the poem that Clay had his failings, the poem's attitude toward the politician is positive.

The form of the poem helps support the points it makes about Clay's character. The syntax is extended and flowing in several places, and the poem is printed without stanza divisions. Dividing the poem into stanzas would break the rhythm significantly and detract from the poem's meaning. Lux, after all, is making two points: the first is that Clay was a sprawling, larger-than-life personality; the second is that his personality was a unified whole and that no one part of it can be looked at in isolation (Q 3).

You might want to teach this poem with "A Supermarket in California," the excerpt from "Song of Myself," or "For the Grave of Daniel Boone." All three poems address issues related to the American self, the last by meditating on the legacy of a famous pioneer.

SONIA SANCHEZ

On Passing thru Morgantown, Pa.

WRITING ACTIVITIES

1. Ask students to write briefly on the tone of this poem. What do they think the speaker's frame of mind is?
2. Ask students to write a paragraph on what the speaker might mean in the poem's final four lines. Why do the "red indian / hills" beckon (and to whom do they beckon)?

GROUP ACTIVITY

Divide students into two groups; one group argues that Sanchez's poem is an effective Petrarchan sonnet, and the other argues that it is not.

DISCUSSION

To encourage students to connect this poem with the inspiration of Van Gogh's paintings, bring some pictures that are representative of his art. If possible, find works that suggest the "exploding" colors of Pennsylvania's green cornfields and red hills. Besides being an excellent example of apostrophe, this poem seems to be a good illustration of imagism, appealing more to the visual imagery of the scene than to an intellectual concept. Note, however, that Sanchez has transplanted Van Gogh from Europe to America, where she tricks the reader into thinking black people and red Indians will appear — only to have them become "black birds" in a cornfield and "red indian hills" in the background.

ALLEN GINSBERG

A Supermarket in California

WRITING ACTIVITIES

1. Ask students to write an essay, based primarily on this poem, about Ginsberg's attitude toward America.
2. Ask students to write a research essay on Walt Whitman.

GROUP ACTIVITY

Walt Whitman never acknowledges the speaker's presence or speaks during the course of the poem. Divide the class into small groups and ask each group to brainstorm possible reasons for this poetic strategy.

DISCUSSION

This poem is rooted in Ginsberg's enormous respect for Walt Whitman and his work (Q 1). Though Ginsberg is typically thought of as a nonacademic poet, his meeting with Whitman owes something to Eliot's encounter with "some dead master" in "Little Gidding" and, farther back, to Dante's journey with Vergil. Significantly, we never get to hear what Whitman thinks. When Dante encounters Vergil, the dead poet acts as a guide. Here, however, Whitman remains silent while his companion poses questions. The poet has come "shopping for images"—that is, searching for poetic material—in the supermarket because he sees it as a microcosm of contemporary America (Q 2).

The poem's greatest strength is its balance of humor and pathos. The sight of Walt Whitman wandering half in a daze through the aisles of a twentieth-century supermarket could have been merely silly. Perhaps this is one of the reasons why Whitman does not speak in the poem. As long as only his contemporary companion speaks, the incongruity of the situation does not become too comical (Q 4).

The title, with its indication of the location of the supermarket, is also important. When the poem was written in 1956, California was the westernmost extreme of the United States (Alaska and Hawaii had not yet been admitted to the Union). It is appropriate, then, that Walt Whitman, a poet closely linked to America and to questions of American identity should, when he returns, come to California. It is the ideal place for him to observe what the country he celebrated has become.

Any attempt at paraphrase in this case is likely to fail or to be longer than the poem itself. The poem is about Walt Whitman, but it is also about America in the 1950s and the poet's place in it (Q 3). Finally, it is a relatively unassuming way for Ginsberg to assume Whitman's poetic mantle. This is another reason for Whitman's silence in the poem: Ginsberg does not really expect his questions to be answered, and there is no indication that Whitman hears them. Rather, he is posing the questions that he knows he will have to answer for himself (Q 1).

Consider teaching this poem with the excerpts from "Song of Myself" and "Out of the Cradle Endlessly Rocking," "To Brooklyn Bridge," or "A Mown Lawn." The first two poems are by Whitman and will give students a clearer sense of the poet to whom Ginsberg refers. Hart Crane's "To Brooklyn Bridge," owes a great deal to Whitman's vision of America. Whitman and Crane are essentially optimistic about America, but Lydia Davis's "A Mown Lawn" presents an almost entirely negative view of the country.

FURTHER READING

Thurley, Geoffrey. *The American Moment: American Poetry in the Mid-Century.* New York: St. Martin's Press, 1978. 172–86.

CHAPTER 22

SOUND

WALT WHITMAN

Had I the Choice

In typical Whitman fashion, art takes second place to nature in this poem. Whitman would much rather learn the secret of how the sea manages its perfect rhythm than be granted the gifts of the greatest of all artists. As in "When I Heard the Learn'd Astronomer," Whitman reveres the natural world, of which he is an integral part and from which he gains energy and health as well as inspiration and knowledge. His apostrophe to the sea is also reminiscent of Shelley's "Ode to the West Wind."

GWENDOLYN BROOKS

Sadie and Maud

Sadie may have lacked a college education and a husband, but she lived life fully and raised her daughters to do the same. When she dies, they are ready to strike out on their own. The poem begins and ends with Maud, who "went to college" but is "a thin brown mouse . . . living all alone"; the rest of the poem, however, is about Sadie, "one of the livingist chits in all the land." The sing-song rhythm and regular rhyme (lines 2 and 4 of each stanza) keep this poem light, despite the loneliness of Maud in the last two lines. The reader does not pity her because she seems to have chosen her path, as Sadie has chosen hers. Alice Walker also contrasts two African-American sisters in her story "Everyday Use," and the college-educated one is less sympathetic there too.

EMILY DICKINSON

I like to see it lap the Miles

Students enjoy comparing the words and phrases that suggest a horse (lap, feed, step, crawl, neigh, stable) with those suggesting a locomotive (tanks, [going around] a pile of mountains, hooting). Although the rhythm of this poem suggests the movement of the train or the horse, it is also (like many Dickinson poems) in hymn meter; the poem can be sung to the tune of "A Mighty Fortress Is Our God" or "Oh God Our Help in Ages Past."

ADRIENNE RICH

Aunt Jennifer's Tigers

WRITING ACTIVITIES

1. Aunt Jennifer may be seen either as a specific person or as a type. Ask students to write on the characteristics that define Aunt Jennifer and her situation. Can they think of other characters in stories or poems who are "Aunt Jennifers"? In what ways do they handle their situations similarly? Differently?
2. Ask students to write about Aunt Jennifer's creation. How has it helped her cope (or hindered her from coping) with her "terrified" existence?

GROUP ACTIVITY

Ask groups of students to practice reading the poem aloud with different meters. How does changing the meters (i.e., forcing a strict iambic pentameter without using anapests) affect the meaning and the impact of the poem?

Have groups try to analyze the poem as seen by different readers: someone like themselves as students, a woman over forty-five, a man over forty-five, a person from a different culture.

DISCUSSION

This poem allows the readers to experience the way in which a contrast in metrical form can support a thematic contrast in a poem. Specifically, students will see the ironic differentiation between a woman (oppressed by her marriage) and tigers (fierce, strong, and free). The basic meter of the poem, reflecting the bounds and strictness of Aunt Jennifer's life, is iambic. The steady monotony of this rhythm suggests the constraints her reality holds (Q 1).

In contrast, however, anapests are interposed throughout the poem ("Still ringed with ordeals she was mastered by") that suggest the lightness and freedom that Aunt Jennifer creates in the screen and in the tigers. Aunt Jennifer thus vicariously lives out the life she might wish to have, and the meter of the poem reflects the tension between those two worlds. In the same way, the poet's use of end-stopped lines in stanza 1 suggests the strictness of Aunt Jennifer's life, but ironically the stanza describes the created tigers, who are not bound by men. In stanza 2, the run-on lines indicate a desire for freedom, but the words suggest the burden of being dominated. It is clear that the speaker feels that the "massive weight" of "Uncle's wedding band" has impinged upon Aunt Jennifer's freedom (Q 4). The combination of the techniques, again in stanza 3, emphasizes the concluding theme of the poem: even though her own life with its hardships will die, the legacy of the woman will endure in the strength of her creations (Q 2).

The final theme is also underscored by the breaking of the rhythms with caesuras in the first and fourth lines of the last stanza (Q 3). The first draws the reader's attention to the finality of Aunt Jennifer's death, whereas the last caesura centers attention on the continuity and confidence that will remain in the tigers. The tigers are, as Keyes states, "gorgeous" and "compelling" in a way that Aunt Jennifer can never be (Q 5).

If you are including this poem in a larger section on feminist issues, you might want to compare it to Glaspell's *Trifles*, Faulkner's "A Rose for Emily," Sexton's "Cinderella," or Gilman's "The Yellow Wallpaper" (these also work for power/powerlessness).

ETHERIDGE KNIGHT

For Malcolm, a Year After

WRITING ACTIVITIES

1. Have students describe the kind of poem that this poet might have created if his topic were Martin Luther King, Jr., rather than Malcolm X.
2. Have students analyze the use of repetitions and sound in the poem. How do they create tension?

DO YOUR STUDENTS KNOW . . .

When Malcolm X (1925–1965) led the movement for black power, he was drawing on the legacy and words of abolitionist David Walker (1785–1830). Both men fought for the rights and self-determination of black Americans. Walker, who lived as a freed black because his mother was white, is considered the father of black nationalist thought. His calls for slave revolt and violence as a means to emancipation were described in his pamphlet, "Appeal to the Colored Citizens of the World." Walker was wanted in the South —$10,000 was offered for his capture alive and $3,000 if dead.

DISCUSSION

This poem, like "Aunt Jennifer's Tigers," illustrates the importance of meter in the interpretation and analysis of a poem, especially in creating ironic contrasts. Here, the poem chooses a strict iambic pattern with end-stopped lines as a mark of the conventional and constrained life that Malcolm X certainly did not lead. Had Knight wanted to mimic the sound and power of Malcolm X, he might have chosen a freer rhythm, or even an erratic rhythm, using run-on lines to create the effect of the rushing of Malcolm X's words (Q 1, 2).

The choice of meter is ironic for the poem, but this irony makes the poem powerful. By trying to force the message into a form for which it was not meant, the speaker makes a comment about the medium versus the message; the "verse will die" (l. 15), because it will have been robbed of the passion with which it was originally uttered (Q 4). Line 15 uses a strong caesura as well, emphasizing the fact that the verse form of "empty anglo tea lace words" (l. 11) will not survive, but the message that Malcolm X uttered will (Q 3).

The reader further senses this contrast between message and medium in the word choice that Knight uses. The power of the message, and the angry tones in which Malcolm X uttered it, are described in lines 2–10. In line 6, alliteration of the initial *dr* imitates force in Malcolm X's rhetorical style. In addition, the use of repeated negatives in lines 7–10 reminds the reader that a constrained or reserved form is not appropriate to express Malcolm X's ideas. Rather, it offers only "dead white" words (l. 12) (Q 2).

If students discuss this poem in the context of a larger unit on race issues, you might suggest that they see Spike Lee's movie *Malcolm X* as background, and the poem might be taught with McKay's "The White City."

FURTHER READING

Hill, Patricia L. "'Blues for a Mississippi Black Boy': Etheridge Knight's Craft in the Black Oral Tradition." *Mississippi Quarterly* 36.1 (1983): 21–33.

Pinsker, Sanford. "A Conversation with Etheridge Knight." *Black American Literature Forum* 18.1 (1984): 11–14.

ALFRED, LORD TENNYSON

The Eagle

In this *tour de force*, the reader begins by looking up at the eagle high on a craggy cliff, framed by lonely mountain, Sun, and blue sky. Against this panorama, the solitary eagle's strength is emphasized as he clings to the crag with his strong, "crooked hands." Then, in stanza 2, the reader is with the eagle up on the cliff, looking down at the sea far below. Suddenly, the reader falls with the eagle, whose strength and power are reiterated as he dives (perhaps sighting prey) like one of Zeus's pitched thunderbolts.

N. SCOTT MOMADAY

Comparatives

Native American author of the highly respected *The House of Dawn*, Momaday here creates an appealing seaside scene, an idyll of bobbing boats, into which death intervenes. The planks may suggest pirates or a place to sit while fishing;

the fossil fish later on implies that the earlier death (the "agony twice perceived") may have been a fish as well. Despite the pleasure of the "sunlit sea," (l. 1), "a shadow runs" (l. 14), and the speaker is twice reminded of death.

ROBERT HERRICK

Delight in Disorder

The speaker prefers artlessness to art in a woman — or at least in her clothing. If she is too neat and carefully groomed, he fears she may be too precise a person, perhaps lacking in spontaneity. Instead, he is beguiled and excited by a seeming carelessness — a shawl thrown over the shoulder rather than carefully pinned there, a shoelace unevenly rather than perfectly tied. By using words like "wantonness," "disorder," and "tempestuous," to describe the clothing, the speaker implies that the woman wearing such clothing is sensuous and sexually responsive. In any case, her clothing seems to seduce him into such a belief.

OGDEN NASH

The Lama

The short lines, unexpected rhymes, and surprise ending all contribute to the whimsical tone of this typical Nash nonsense rhyme. Nash loves to play with language and often makes up words that seem as if they should exist; here, he rejects a word. He first distinguishes between two words that sound alike but have very different meanings — a common occurrence in English. Then he presents a word that even he rejects as improbable: lllama — though it seems not much odder than a "two-l llama" when he describes it that way, alluding to the apparent arbitrariness of language.

RICHARD WILBUR

A Sketch

DO YOUR STUDENTS KNOW . . .

The contemporary holiday of Christmas may owe as much to the god, Saturn, as to the Christian figure, Jesus Christ. Saturn, the god of fertility and agriculture, is said to have fled Greece to escape the wrath of his son, Jupiter. He escaped to Latium, now Italy, where his reign is viewed as the "golden age" of ancient Italy. Saturn, envisioned as the figure of Father Time, was celebrated during Saturnalia, a winter feast of seven days marked by feasts, merriment, and gift giving.

The speaker tries to frame the goldfinch as in a painting, but the bird will not sit still and pose. Each time the speaker tries to paint a word picture, the bird moves into a new light, so its color changes as well as its position. The speaker is left with a series of mental "sketches" of the bird and cannot choose one. As the bird flits, so too do the lines of the poem, both visually and aurally. The shifting bird becomes a metaphor for the difficulty of the poet's task: in a world of constant change, no description can ever be definitive.

GERALD MANLEY HOPKINS

Pied Beauty

WRITING ACTIVITIES

1. Have students analyze the form of the poem on the page. How does it relate to the theme of the poem?
2. Ask students to write a response to Hopkins's poem from the point of view of an atheist.
3. Have students compare Hopkins's description of nature to Basho's treatment of nature in his haiku, "Four Haiku."

GROUP ACTIVITIES

Have students look at Hopkins's habit of creating words with hyphens. Rewrite the poem as prose, substituting single words for his compounds. What effects are lost in the paraphrase?

Have groups brainstorm about the kinds of things Hopkins would describe were he to write the poem in the place where these students are now. What kinds of compound words might he invent?

DISCUSSION

Hopkins's fascination with sound makes this poem exemplary for many of the concepts introduced in this chapter. For example, the phonetic stops in "dappled," "stipple," and "freckled" suggest a lack of continuity or smoothness, so that sounds here reflect meanings (onomatopoeia). Hopkins also uses alliteration to enhance meaning: the repeated f sounds (fricatives) (l. 4) suggest the whistle of falling chestnuts or flapping wings. Similarly, the repeated p sounds in line 5 reflect a choppiness that is evident in the broken and divided land. (Also note "couple-color" [l. 2] and "fathers-forth" [l. 10]) (Q 1).

Hopkins uses assonance in the poem, as in the compound "rose-moles" (l. 3), and in "finches' wings" (l. 4). It is interesting that Hopkins chooses to reflect the diversity and change that he sees in nature with vowel choices. In line 9, for example, a succession of different vowels, both long and short, illustrates the variation of form and sound in nature (Q 1).

Imperfect rhyme occurs in line 8, with "fickle" and "freckled" having the same initial consonant *f*, followed by different short vowels (*e*/*i*), and the same consonant cluster (*ckl*). The final words of each line are examples of perfect masculine rhymes ("things-wings," "cow-plow," "swim-trim") (Q 3). The combination of such a variety of techniques emphasizes the poem's theme: nature is varied, changing, and fascinating. The complexity created by these techniques contrasts with the simplicity of the centered last line: "Praise him." The second part of Hopkins's theme is evident here — all the variety of nature flows from one single, immutable divine source (Q 2).

You may want to teach this poem with Donne's "Batter My Heart, Three-Personed God."

W. H. AUDEN

As I Walked Out One Evening

WRITING ACTIVITY

1. Have students write a love letter in which — instead of making extravagant promises to their loved one — they describe more accurately exactly what they will do (e.g., "I will sit on the couch drinking a beer until the Bullets make the playoffs").

GROUP ACTIVITY

Have students in groups list all the popular songs they can think of in which the singer makes promises like those of the lover in Auden's poem (e.g., "Baby, I'm yours until the stars fall from the sky," or "until two and two is three"). What is their response to these promises? Are they believable? If not, why do so many songs contain them?

DISCUSSION

Auden himself described "As I Walked Out One Evening" as a "pastiche of folksong," and the poem clearly owes much to ballad form. It is fitting that Auden's rhyme scheme, while relatively consistent, avoids a commitment to using only perfect rhyme because the poem is an attack on popular notions of perfect love. The difficulty of rhyming in the imperfectly rhymed lines suggests the difficulty of the kind of love the poem ridicules (Q 4). Indeed, were Auden's rhyme scheme or his meter more regular, the poem would lose the sense of instability, of fracture, that is introduced by the song of the clocks (Q 1, 2).

It is no wonder that Auden uses alliteration and assonance here, musical effects that underscore the poem's balladic quality. The poem's assonance and alliteration are more pronounced in the lover's section of the poem. Alliterative lines like "the salmon sing in the street" and "seven stars go squawking / Like geese about the sky" and the assonance of "till the ocean is folded" suggest the perfect harmony and ease of the lover's view of love. When we get to the clocks' harsher dose of reality, the poem's use of sound changes: Although there is still some alliteration ("the beggars raffle the banknotes / And the giant is enchanting to Jack"), it is less consistent, and its overall effect, given the content of the lines, is more cynical. The clocks' section of the poem relies on repeated words for its musical effects ("look, look," "stare . . . stare," "blessing . . . bless," "stand, stand"); this repetition suggests the relentlessness of the clocks' message and the futility of resisting it. Here, as throughout the poem, Auden's sound effects mirror the content of the poem (Q 2, 3). He plays with ballad structure, the form of popular music, only to deconstruct it (Q 4).

FURTHER READING

Fuller, John. *A Reader's Guide to W. H. Auden*. London: Thames and Hudson, 1970.
Mendelson, Edward. *Early Auden*. New York: Viking, 1981.

KELLY CHERRY

Nobody's Fool

WRITING ACTIVITIES

1. Ask students to write an essay comparing and contrasting "Nobody's Fool" and "For Once, Then Something."
2. In this case, the speaker uses the metaphor of a well in order to describe the journey she has taken into herself. Ask students to write about a thing or place that has a similar meaning for them.

GROUP ACTIVITY

Break the class into groups. Ask each group to agree on an actress they think should play the speaker of the poem and to list reasons why they would cast her.

DO YOUR STUDENTS KNOW . . .

What will one suffer in the name of love? According to statistics released in 2000, ten percent of violent-crime victims were injured or killed by an intimate partner, and eighty-five percent of that number were women. Children under the age of twelve lived in forty-three percent of the homes where intimate-partner violence occurred.

DISCUSSION

"Nobody's Fool" is composed in two-stress lines and has an *abcb* rhyme scheme (Q 1, 3). There are exceptions to each of these rules. In the first stanza, line 4, "A good-looking man pushed me," has three stresses, as does the poem's concluding line (Q 3). And in the fifth stanza, line 1 rhymes with line 4 of the preceding stanza (Q 1). It is important to note, too, that most of the lines in the first four stanzas are trochaic — that is, they alternate strong and weak stresses, beginning with the strong. This is especially appropriate at this point in the poem because trochaic is referred to as a "falling" meter, and the speaker herself is falling. The meter becomes predominantly rising only in the last two stanzas, when the speaker has begun to take stock of her situation. Also in the last two stanzas, the rhymes become faint (forever / fever) and then almost inaudible (fools / hells) (Q 2). It is as if the speaker, who was emotionally excited and falling out of control in the first four stanzas, has restrained herself.

It is clear from the title and from clues provided in the first and last stanzas that the speaker was driven into herself by a man, perhaps one with whom she had a romantic relationship. The speaker adjusts to living within herself and even threatens not to come out again. It does not seem, though, that she views this situation as an ideal solution. In fact, she equates "her own depths" with "hell's." And yet the pain of isolation may be preferable to being "pushed" again. She is determined to be "Nobody's Fool" (Q 4).

You might teach this poem with "Diving into the Wreck," "The Yellow Wall-Paper," and "For Once, Then Something." The first two selections explore the oppression of women, and the third uses the metaphor of a well as the basis for a meditation on the difficulty of discovering meaning in life.

LYDIA DAVIS

A Mown Lawn

WRITING ACTIVITIES

1. Ask students to write a poem in the same style on another series of words and addressing another cluster of issues.
2. This poem does not so much make an argument as proceed by a series of associative leaps. Have students write a brief summary of what they believe Davis's position to be. Then, ask them to write an essay either agreeing with or disagreeing with that position.

GROUP ACTIVITY

Break the class up into groups. Ask one person in each group to function as a note taker. Then, ask each group to compose a one-paragraph paraphrase of Davis's points.

DISCUSSION

"A Mown Lawn" is a prose poem because it is clearly intended to be read as a poem yet lacks line breaks (Q 2). Unlike many prose poems, however, it makes abundant use of some of the resources of more traditional poetry. Having said that, there is very little exact rhyme in the poem. Rather, it makes use of similarities in sound — primarily assonance and alliteration — and spelling to move from one word to the next, from one idea to the next (Q 1).

Based on her free associations, the speaker generates a cluster of words and phrases: *long moan, woman, man, Nam, lawman, more lawn, lawn mower, lawn mourn and lawn moron* (Q 3). It is clear that the speaker views the United States as an oppressive country where citizens are more concerned with order and appearance than with freedom and authenticity (Q 4). The poem thus raises important questions about language in general and political speech in particular. Is Davis presenting an argument that could persuade a reader with a differing point of view, or does one have to share her political views in order to find the poem convincing?

You might want to teach this poem with "The Grammar Lesson," which has some of the same playful attitude toward language; "The World Is Too Much with Us," which rebels against what the speaker perceives to be inauthentic experience; and "A Supermarket in California," which examines American society.

FURTHER READING

Ziolkowski, Thad. "Lydia Davis." *American Short-Story Writers since World War II.* Ed. Patrick Meanor. *Dictionary of Literary Biography.* Vol. 130. Detroit: Gale, 1993. 104–108.

ROBERT FRANCIS

Pitcher

WRITING ACTIVITIES

1. Ask students to rewrite the poem in such a way as to eliminate any end rhymes. Then, ask them to write a paragraph explaining how the poem is helped or hurt by this change.
2. "Pitcher" uses the movements of an athlete as a metaphor for the work of a writer. Have students write an essay about another activity they feel could function as a metaphor.

GROUP ACTIVITY

Divide the class into small groups and have each group find an activity (aside from writing) to which they feel Francis's metaphor applies.

DISCUSSION

Although the poem provides a fairly accurate explanation of the principles of pitching, it is important that the students understand that it is about more than baseball (Q 4). It is also about the arts in general and poetry in particular. Poetry often operates in a less direct way than prose, and part of the pleasure in reading a poem can be in understanding "too late." This would be an excellent poem to teach early in the poetry unit since it may help students be more open to work that is not immediately comprehensible.

The poem acts much like a pitcher trying to fake out a batter. The first two lines would both end with "aim" if it were not for the word "at" in the second line, and the effect resembles rhyme. The next four lines are unrhymed. Then, in lines 7 and 8, there is an off rhyme on "wild" and "willed." The only perfect rhyme occurs in the last two lines, and the rhyme itself is only clinched on the last word of the poem, "late" (Q 1). Only at the end does the reader realize that the poem has been moving toward rhyme, just as the batter realizes "too late" that he has been pitched a strike. There are other stylistic aspects of the poem that also serve to reinforce its meaning. The repetitions ("— aim / aim at,"—"throw / throws") and oppositions ("comprehended / misunderstood," "[n]ot to / yet still") help convey the idea of the pitcher as someone who needs to temporarily mislead others in order to succeed at his task (Q 2). The frequent use of alliteration and assonance throughout the poem serves to distract the reader from the line endings, thereby making the final perfect rhyme all the more surprising.

Consider teaching this poem with "The Fireman," "The Shipfitter's Wife," and "Please Fire Me," each of which examines a work situation.

FURTHER READING

Stambuk, Andrew. "Learning to Hover: Robert Frost, Robert Francis, and the Poetry of Detached Engagement." *Twentieth Century Literature* 45 (Winter 1999): 534–53.

ALAN SHAPIRO

A Parting Gift

WRITING ACTIVITIES

1. Have students research one of the metaphysical poets and write an essay comparing one of that poet's poems with "A Parting Gift."
2. Bird song is one of the recurring auditory images in the poem. Have students write an essay in which they analyze its importance.

GROUP ACTIVITY

Break the class into four groups and assign one stanza of the poem to each group. Ask the groups to be responsible for raising questions about the stanzas they have been assigned.

DO YOUR STUDENTS KNOW . . .

Although the song of a bird sounds harmonious to the human ear, birds produce songs for important evolutionary reasons. A bird either wants to attract a mate or uses the song as defense of his territory. Within the song range of a bird, many dialects, like in spoken language, exist. A recent study of the greenish warbler in the Himalayas documents that, in this large territory, greenish warblers will sing in different dialects, causing the birds to not recognize some of their own species.

DISCUSSION

"A Parting Gift" is an attempt by its speaker to call up and transform into song his last night with his lover. Given that the poem is about music, it is fitting that Shapiro would have chosen to rhyme portions of it. The use of run-on lines creates a fluid music appropriate to a description of a birdsong, while the stanzaic form is complex enough yet regular enough to mimic that song (Q 3, 4). As important as the sonic elements are, it is important to not lose sight of the fact that this is a love poem and may therefore appeal to students who as yet have no interest in the technical aspects of verse.

The basic rhyme scheme of the poem, as established in the first stanza, is *abcbdc*. Students may at first have difficulty seeing the pattern, both because it is reasonably complex and because Shapiro sometimes uses very faint rhymes — "pleasure / another," for example. The rhyme scheme is abandoned entirely in the last stanza, unless one accepts "ago / you," as a ghost rhyme (Q 1). Instead, "you" rhymes with "do" in the middle of the third line. The effect of this technique is to break down the stanza while continuing the music. Shapiro is matching form and thought here in a way that is reminiscent of George Herbert, and in fact the stanzaic form he has devised resembles that of a poem by Herbert or Donne or one of the other metaphysical poets. The absence of rhyme leaves the reader somewhat unsatisfied, but that is only fitting, since the memory of what has ended cannot fully satisfy the writer (Q 1).

You might consider teaching this poem with "How Do I Love Thee?," "When I Have Fears," "Nothing Gold Can Stay," and "The Shipfitter's Wife." The first two are among the most famous love poems in English, and the third is a lyric dealing with the passing nature of everything worthwhile. The final selection is a very modern love poem.

MONA VAN DUYN

The Beginning

WRITING ACTIVITIES

1. Ask students to write a one-page essay on why they feel Van Duyn chose the sonnet form for this poem.

2. Have students summarize the poem's argument in prose and then a write a one-page response to that argument.

GROUP ACTIVITY

"The Beginning" is written in lines of rhymed dimeter. Break the class into small groups and ask them to discuss how the rhyme and line length affect the poem's tone.

DISCUSSION

"The Beginning" is one of Van Duyn's "minimalist sonnets," which are tightly rhymed and written in extremely short lines. The poem makes the point that the end of a passionate, and presumably physical, relationship can be not only an "end" but it can also be a "beginning." The heart is afraid to move from romantic love to friendship, but the soul welcomes the change. That friendship is purer and more ennobling than sexual love is an old idea, one that Van Duyn here gives new poetic life.

Consider teaching this poem with "Minimalist Sonnet," Collins's "Sonnet," and "Rainbow". Each selection is an example of a different variation on the standard sonnet form.

LEWIS CARROLL

Jabberwocky

WRITING ACTIVITIES

1. Ask students to retell the story of the Jabberwock in ordinary prose.
2. Have students pick two or three of the nonsense words in the text and try to decide what they mean, based on context and sound. Have them write a dictionary entry for each word, including a guide for pronunciation, a part-of-speech classification, and a meaning. (This can also work as a group activity.)

DISCUSSION

The basic story of "Jabberwocky" centers on the development of a young boy. In this way, it is a typical initiation story. The boy is issued a challenge when he is warned about the existence of a mysterious creature, which he must face. The boy seeks the dangerous creature, and when the opportunity arrives, he kills it. He then returns home to his proud father (Q 3).

Students should not have any trouble understanding the basic action of the poem, although they may become frustrated by the use of nonsense words. They might be interested in knowing that Lewis Carroll provided some hints to the meanings of the words in *Through the Looking Glass*. For example, "brillig" refers to four in the afternoon, when "you begin broiling things for dinner." "Slithy" is a combination of *lithe* and *slimy*. A "wabe" is an area of grass around a sundial, and its name refers to the fact that it goes "a long way before it, and a long way behind it." Aside from these definitions, students will guess that "toves" are creatures and that "gyring and gimbling" are activities that these creatures do. Some words, such as "jubjub," "whiffling," and "burbled" are examples of onomatopoeia; their sounds suggest the sounds of the poem's actions (Q 2). As students discuss their reactions to and impressions of each word, you might comment on what information can be gleaned from grammatical clues (pluralization, verb endings) and what comes from context or sound (Q 1, 4).

The rhyme scheme of the poem, generally linking the second and fourth lines, and usually the first and third as well, suggests the unity of a single heroic event. In addition, the rhyme scheme allows the poem to exploit the sound relationships between unusual words. Finally, the repetition of the first stanza at the end forms a frame for the story (Q 3).

You may want to teach this poem with other initiation works in the text, such as Ríos's "The Secret Lion."

FURTHER READING

Alkalay-Gut, Karen. "Carroll's 'Jabberwocky.'" *Explicator* 46.1 (1987): 27–31.

CHAPTER 23

FORM

JOHN KEATS

On the Sonnet

Keats uses this sonnet, which follows a complex rhyme scheme (different from that of the Shakespearean or Petrarchan forms) to argue for the use of form in new ways. Instead of adhering to old forms because they are traditional, Keats suggests that poets keep the idea of a regular form alive but base their rendition of the form less on what has already been done and more on what creativity and divine inspiration (the "Muse" of line 13) provide. Although he plays with the rhyme, he does still follow a fixed form, and he also includes such traditional figures of speech as allusion (to Andromeda and Midas), alliteration, and metaphor.

BILLY COLLINS

Sonnet

DO YOUR STUDENTS KNOW . . .

Known for perfecting the Italian sonnet form of Petrarchan sonnets, Francesco Petrarch (1304–1374) was an Italian poet, historian, and scholar. According to his sonnets, he was the victim of unrequited love for a woman known only as Laura. Some believe she was a real woman and the wife of another man, whereas others theorize Laura is a stand-in for the Virgin Mary. Other critics believe she personified intellectual pursuits; the name Laura has origins in the word *laurel*, a symbol for classical thought.

Students will be better able to respond to this poem if they are already familiar with the traditional sonnet. Collins, a poet who writes primarily in free verse, uses several of the conventions of the sonnet form — that it should have fourteen lines and a turn after the eighth line — in order to write a poem that mocks this traditional form. One could argue that the poem is intended as an affectionate send-up rather than an all-out attack. A fair number of lines in the poem are in fact iambic. If one pronounces "medieval" with four syllables, for example, then the last two lines are both iambic pentameter.

WILLIAM SHAKESPEARE

When, in disgrace with fortune and men's eyes

This sonnet is much more traditional than Keats's "On the Sonnet," and students may benefit from a comparison between the forms of the two poems. You may want to review with students the text's comments on Petrarchan and Shakespearean sonnets and then perhaps compare this poem with a Petrarchan sonnet, such as Keats's "On First Looking into Chapman's Homer" or Wordsworth's "Composed upon Westminster Bridge. . . ."

CLAUDE McKAY

The White City

WRITING ACTIVITIES

1. Ask students to write a short response from McKay's point of view explaining why they think he chose to use traditional form for such a nontraditional subject. You may want to point out to them that, traditionally, most sonnets deal with love, while McKay's deals with hate.
2. Have students compare "The White City" to a rap song that deals with the same subject.

GROUP ACTIVITY

Ask students to research different influences on McKay (in particular, the Harlem Renaissance). Have student groups give short reports centering on how these events in McKay's life may have affected his poetry.

DISCUSSION

Students should not expect modern poets to restrict themselves to traditional themes simply because they write in traditional, closed forms; McKay's "The White City" is a case in point. Sonnets have traditionally dealt with love, and some students will immediately see that McKay's use of the sonnet form to express his hatred is deeply ironic (Q 1, 4). At the beginning of this poem, the speaker's mood is similar to that of the speaker in Shakespeare's "When, in Disgrace with Fortune and Men's Eyes," but toward the end of McKay's poem there is none of the hope and satisfaction we find in the Shakespeare sonnet (Q 1). Whereas the speaker in Shakespeare's poem finds comfort and strength in others, McKay finds strength only through hatred — his constant companion. It veils everything he sees with a mist and makes the surrounding city seem harsh and forbidding (Q 1).

There is no "lark at break of day arising" in McKay's poem; in fact, the city is a hostile setting that prevents nature from appearing in benign forms. The only animals here are the people who live in the "dens" the speaker contemplates in the third quatrain. This comparison is consistent with the emotions he expresses earlier, because his hatred drives him on in the same way that all things — from the people, to the ships, and finally to the tides themselves — are driven by natural, elementary forces. For the speaker, hatred has become a basic, fundamental force, a "dark blood" that beats through his heart (Q 2). This is, in part, McKay's point: for the black person at this time in American history, the white city is *not* a nurturing, friendly environment.

You might point out here to the students that, although the closing couplet of "The White City" may sum up the sonnet's concerns, it certainly does not lead to any satisfactory resolution (Q 3). Perhaps McKay leaves his speaker's dilemma unresolved to reflect the hopelessness of the situation: the city is a "wanton love" for the speaker because it is cruel and unjust, yet the city is singularly attractive as a source of hope to the speaker as well as to the great mass of African-Americans who immigrated to the great Northern cities from the poorer, agricultural South. You may want to provide some background to students about the migration of African-Americans from the South to northern cities during the early and middle parts of the twentieth century. You might also ask students whether they believe the poem's ambivalence toward the city is still an appropriate one.

One final observation: McKay's relationship with the white city mirrors his relationship with his poetry. Just as he must live as an outcast in the white world, so too must he write as an outcast, using the white culture's traditional forms as the framework for his poetic protests. Therefore, when the speaker says: "I muse my life-long hate, and without flinch / I bear it nobly as I live my part," he is indirectly speaking of his writing and of how he fulfills the demands of forms provided him, such as the sonnet, without stumbling or "flinching" (Q 5).

You might want to compare "The White City" to another one of McKay's poems on the same theme, "If We Must Die," published in 1919; or you might compare it with Wordsworth's "Composed upon Westminster Bridge . . ." for a different view of a city in a sonnet.

FURTHER READING

Gayle, Addison. *Claude McKay: The Black Poet at War*. New York: Broadside, 1972.

JOHN KEATS

On First Looking into Chapman's Homer

WRITING ACTIVITIES

1. Ask students to compose an essay reflecting on a time of great discovery in their lives. Have them mirror the form of this sonnet by first discussing their exploration and what the discovery has since meant to them.

2. Assign students to write a one-paragraph response to Keats's historical inaccuracy in line 11. Does this inaccuracy ruin the poem or in some way render it less effective?

GROUP ACTIVITY

Assign different groups of students to research different facets of Keats's life (and, specifically, the background to this poem). Have each group report its findings to the class. In class discussion, consider Keats's well-known comment that he wrote this poem after staying up all night reading Chapman's new translation of Homer. Do they believe Keats?

DISCUSSION

You may want to begin by discussing who Homer is and explaining that he wrote about discovery and exploration. His two best-known works are *The Iliad* and *The Odyssey*; ask students what they know of these epic poems.

This is a Petrarchan (or Italian) sonnet: The octave deals with the process of exploration, and the sestet relates the experience of discovery (Q 1). The word "Then" in line 9 shifts the reader from the extended metaphor of traveling (reading) to the two similes in the sestet that express the emotion, the thrill of discovery itself (Q 2). If you have discussed Keats's historical inaccuracy, some of your students may have pointed out that this poem deals not so much with history as with emotion. Although he focuses on one historical incident, the discovery of the new world, Keats's main theme here is self-exploration and its relative importance. Since Keats uses this particular incident as a symbol for all forms of discovery, his historical inaccuracy is not important.

Students have a tendency to overextend metaphors (as do critics), to read things into lines that simply are not there, so you may want to suggest that the "realms of gold," the "goodly states and kingdoms," and the "many western islands" found in the octave do not necessarily stand for any specific ideas. For example, many students might pick up on the word "western," suggesting that it might have some historical significance (explorers sought gold in the West Indies), but it is probably used in a more general sense — the journey to the New World for the Europeans was a westward one, and it is the direction toward which Cortez stares. Cortez was searching for gold (thus "realms of gold" makes sense), and for Keats, the west seems to signify the New World and opportunities that Chapman's Homer seeks. Still, Keats's subject here is discovery itself, not geography, and Homer's world was definitely not near the West Indies. Homer and Cortez were both on voyages of discovery, so there is (in Keats's mind) a connection between them.

In an Italian sonnet, the sestet traditionally resolves a problem or question raised in the octave, and in many ways the sestet here does so (Q 2). After reading the first eight lines, the reader naturally asks what the significance of this discovery is, and Keats answers this question in the sestet. The fact that Cortez (more accurately, another explorer, Vasco de Balboa) himself can only guess at the significance of his discovery serves to convey accurately the awe and excitement we all feel during the initial moments of any important discovery — whether it is of personal or of universal significance. Line 10 is especially effective, for "ken" means both "range of vision" and "perception" or "understanding." It is this first simile that prepares the reader for the final comparison with the discovery of the Pacific: like all significant discoveries, it opens up a new world to us and vastly expands the world we know — just as Chapman's translation of Homer does for Keats.

Students may find Keats's language more like Pope's than Chapman's; however, it was certainly Keats's intention to capture the "loud," "bold" freshness of Chapman's translation (Q 3).

Mark Twain's frequently anthologized essay, "Reading the River" (from *Life on the Mississippi*), which contrasts innocence and experience, works well with this poem. It can help introduce a discussion of what is *lost* (not just what is gained) when we discover new knowledge. Other initiation stories can also work well with this poem (Updike's "A&P," Ríos's "The Secret Lion," Kaplan's "Doe Season," and Carroll's "Jabberwocky," for example.)

FURTHER READING

Barnard, John. *John Keats*. New York: Cambridge UP, 1987.

GWENDOLYN BROOKS

First Fight. Then Fiddle

WRITING ACTIVITIES

1. Have students turn to "We Real Cool" and write a brief comparison of the two poems. In what ways are they different? Similar?
2. Assign students to write a few paragraphs about the subject of this poem. Is Brooks really writing about music, or is this a metaphor for something much more serious?

GROUP ACTIVITY

Ask groups of students to discuss this poem's form. How does this sonnet differ from more traditional sonnets, such as Keats's "On First Looking into Chapman's Homer" or Shakespeare's "When, in Disgrace with Fortune and Men's Eyes"? How does it compare to other, less traditional, sonnets such as McKay's "The White City"? Assign a different sonnet to each group, and examine the group's conclusions in class discussion.

DISCUSSION

If you begin the class by discussing the subject of Brooks's sonnet "First Fight. Then Fiddle," do not be too anxious to narrow down the list of possibilities (Q 1). For example, it would be easy — not knowing anything of the history of this poem — to infer that because Brooks is black, this poem is about African-Americans struggling to make art in a white world. To do so would be an injustice to the poem, for the metaphor is not that limited. Looking at the date of publication, 1949, a few years after the end of World War II, the reader could conclude that the poem is about violence and hatred of all kinds from all people. Another interpretation might focus on the process of creating art, with Brooks speaking to artists of all races and nationalities, or the poem could be about the conflict between art and "real life." The word "they" in line 3 could mean "white people," but it could also be a general term for classical composers of music — or any artists, for that matter. After all, the reader should not limit the depth of a musical metaphor to only music; the poem is also about art as a whole — whether that be music, writing, or any other art.

Regardless of the author's intentions, students should devote as much attention to *how* the poem speaks as to *what* it says. Notice, for example, how Brooks begins with the word "fiddle" and ends with "violin." This change in diction mirrors the message: hate and pain are necessary to all art, but we should wrestle with and control these more savage feelings before we create art; otherwise, we will leave behind hate instead of harmony — just the opposite of what Brooks asks. "Fiddle" is a rustic, informal name for "violin," a word that suggests civility and grace. Her regular rhyme scheme reinforces the ideas of civility and harmony (Q 2).

Notice how almost every sentence after the first two begins with a verb in the imperative mood; then notice the progression of these verbs: "Ply," which means "To use diligently as a tool or weapon," as well as "To perform or work diligently," and, in a nautical sense, "To work against the wind in a zigzag course"; "Qualify"; "Devise"; "Devote"; "Be [remote]"; "Carry"; "Be [deaf]"; "Win"; "Rise." Brooks uses a similar verb progression in her poem "We Real Cool." Taken together, the verbs map out the direction of the poet's exhortation, and the fact that they are all capitalized lends them even more importance (Q 3). You should ask students what we are supposed to conclude about the progression of the verbs.

Enjambment is a common device in modern poetry. Brooks ends many of her sentences in midline because this allows her to emphasize words such as "thing" and "hate," which, if embedded within a line, would have little impact (Q 3).

You may want to compare this poem with Frost's "Stopping by Woods on a Snowy Evening," which is often interpreted as an expression of the conflicting demands of life and art, or with Heaney's "Digging" for another perspective on art.

FURTHER READING

Shaw, Harry B. *Gwendolyn Brooks*. Boston: Twayne, 1980.

MONA VAN DUYN

Minimalist Sonnet: Summer Virus

WRITING ACTIVITIES

1. Have students write an essay about an illness they have had.
2. This poem expresses a longing for self-transformation. Ask students to write about an event that has changed them.

GROUP ACTIVITY

Divide the class into groups and ask each group to discuss whether Van Duyn's central metaphor, in which the virus is regarded as a power source that might illuminate her, is effective.

DISCUSSION

This poem provides an example of how even time-honored forms can be used in fresh ways. Most modern variations on the sonnet have loosened it in one way or another, but Van Duyn tightens it by shortening the lines and by linking the four quatrains together with a shifting rhyme scheme. One of the chief pleasures of the poem, in addition to its metaphysical conceit, is the skill with which Van Duyn negotiates these self-imposed limitations.

Students may at first be confused about why the speaker wants her fever to increase. It is important for them to understand that she does not want to become sicker, but rather to become so hot that she glows. Although this is not literally possible for a human being, we see examples of it —"a lampbulb's wire," for instance — around us every day. The question still remains, though, as to why she would want to become "more and more light." The answer lies in the first stanza: "let my fever aspire / to transfigure me." The speaker wants not simply to be changed in appearance but to be made glorious. In the New Testament, the transfiguration of Christ occurs shortly before his crucifixion, so there is a biblical precedent for connecting suffering (in this case an illness in already hot weather) with transfiguration.

Consider teaching this poem with Keats's "On the Sonnet," Collins's "Sonnet," or Hopkins's "God's Grandeur." The first poem is a meditation on the ways in which the sonnet form can be used effectively, the second parodies the form as outdated and fussy, and the third experiments with the form's meter.

FURTHER READING

Howard, Ben. "Masters of Transience." *Poetry* 163 (Dec. 1993): 158–70.
Logan, William. "Late Callings." *Parnassus* 18 (Feb. 1992): 317–27.

ALBERTO ALVARO RÍOS

Nani

WRITING ACTIVITY

1. Ask students to write a paragraph in which they analyze the female character in this poem. What is her relationship to the speaker? In the absence of dialogue, how is she characterized?

DISCUSSION

Ríos is of Hispanic origin — born in Nogales, Arizona, on the U.S.–Mexico border — and the students most likely will see the Hispanic influence in his poetry. What they may not understand at first is the cultural conflict inherent in the speaker's mind. In fact, it is the speaker's duality of mind and culture that lies at the heart of this sestina. The speaker has another cultural heritage, and his one link to this heritage is the character he calls "Nani," who speaks the language he only vaguely remembers. Clearly, "Nani" has raised the speaker, but she is not his mother. Lines 22–25 most explicitly reveals her importance:

> I see a wrinkle speak
> of a man whose body serves
> the ants like she serves me, then more words
> from more wrinkles about children [. . .].

The reader sees here that "Nani" provides the speaker with sustenance. More important, the speaker realizes this relationship, and the poem itself, is a direct result of her work. When the speaker writes, he is using words the only way he knows how, and although he cannot speak her language, this poem — these words — are hers. Looking closely at the six words repeated throughout the sestina, we can see that they fall logically into two separate groups, as shown in the envoi (conclusion). "Me," "words," and "speaks" are connected to the speaker, while "more," "her," and "serves" are associated with "Nani."

This sestina is nontraditional in two ways. First, as the text notes, the stanzas are arranged differently, in two groups of eighteen lines. The second unconventional feature of this poem is its line lengths: A traditional sestina has a single line length, whereas Ríos's line length varies.

You may want to teach this poem with Yamamoto's "Seventeen Syllables," Tan's "Two Kinds," or Adamé's "My Grandmother World Rock Quietly and Hum" (ethnic identity).

ELIZABETH BISHOP

Sestina

WRITING ACTIVITIES

1. Ask students to try writing a poem about one of their own grandparents.
2. Have students choose an unusual word from the poem, such as "equinoctial" or "inscrutable," and define it. Then, have them write one or two paragraphs about the word's importance in the poem.

GROUP ACTIVITY

Separate the students into six groups and have each group trace the changing meanings and uses of one of the six repeated words in "Sestina."

DISCUSSION

Bishop begins her sestina by revealing to the reader both the time of year and the mood of the poem: "September rain falls on the house." There are subtle, repeated words that add additional weight: the grandmother is an "old" grandmother, someone who has lost her husband, someone who knows the seasons. This poem is about loss, and the character of the grandmother — in fact, the entire poem — is filled with a quiet, resigned emptiness. This whisper of emptiness, of cycles coming to an end or beginning — the poem's theme — is controlled by the six repeated words of "stove," "almanac," "house," child," "tears," and "grandmother" (Q 3). Taken alone, these six words in themselves tell a short story, but when repeated in six different patterns throughout the poem, they become engines, pulling the reader on while delivering the theme. How these words function together is what in fact makes "Sestina" such a remarkable poem. The child and the grandmother, two of the six objects, are connected by the other objects — by the stove, by the almanac, and by the house. They are also connected through the tears, and perhaps these tears play the most noticeable role in the poem. For example, in the first stanza, they reveal the grandmother's state of mind. In the second, they introduce the theme of cyclical change. In the third, they are objectified by the teakettle, and in the fourth and fifth, the "old" grandmother drinks them up while the boy draws tear-shaped buttons on his figure of the absent grandfather. Finally, the tears fall from the almanac in the shape of "little moons" — pieces in the irreversible cycle of time — and they become planted seeds destined to sprout again someday, in the child's future.

Although these key words function meaningfully throughout the poem, they do so without strain (Q 1). A sestina is one of the most demanding of all forms, and very few read as naturally as this beautiful and delightful piece. Perhaps one measure of Bishop's success is the fact that the reader barely notices the repetition throughout the poem; when we do, we are delighted, not bothered, for her imaginative recycling keeps the words fresh. In addition, Bishop manages to pull the reader into her poem with her deeply personalized diction, which creates such simple, yet universal images.

All sestinas use alliteration and assonance simply because of the heavy repetition involved. However, Bishop employs these techniques even more frequently (Q 2). For example, in the fourth stanza, she repeats the long *o* sound in the words "open," "old," "more," and "stove," while repeating other, shorter *o* sounds in words like "brown," "wood," "hovers," "on," and "above." Clearly, this repetition supports the somber, pensive tone of the piece, much as a painter might use browns, greys, and other dark colors to create a distinct mood in a painting.

You may want to teach this poem with Frost's "'Out, Out —'" or Hayden's "Those Winter Sundays" (perspectives on loss/death).

FURTHER READING

Stevenson, Anne. *Elizabeth Bishop*. Boston: Twayne, 1966.

THEODORE ROETHKE

The Waking

WRITING ACTIVITY

1. Ask students to choose one line and try to paraphrase it. Try to assign a different line to each student.

GROUP ACTIVITY

Divide students into groups of three, according to the lines they worked on in the Writing Activity. Have each group work further to revise the paraphrases. In class discussion, consider what is lost between the original and the paraphrased poem. Is anything gained?

DISCUSSION

Do not expect your students to reach a consensus about the meaning of "The Waking." One of the poem's strengths is that it suggests so much without stating anything in specific terms. Basically, the tension in this poem is between life and death, or "waking" and "sleeping." The speaker "cannot fear" death, for the simple reason that he knows nothing of it. If it is true that we are sentient creatures who cannot know what we cannot feel, then "we learn by going," and our instinct leads us. Notice, for example, that in line 5 the speaker states that he "hears" his being "dance from ear to ear." The two verbs here represent physical, unthinking processes. Later in the poem, when the speaker notes the world and beings that surround him, he sees that so many of even the simplest things are ultimately unknowable — how "Light takes the Tree," for instance.

In lines 10–11, Roethke suggests that the secret of all life can be found even in the "lowly worm," but we must travel back down the difficult "winding stair" of evolution to know for sure — something we cannot do with certainty. We lie at the top of this stairway, and what is in store for us is something with which we should not concern ourselves. Once we accept this notion, once we deny the intellectual notion of life after death (giving up the comforting notion of heaven makes us tremble with fear), of life beyond what we can feel, our perception of time must change. "Always" falls away because the speaker no longer thinks about time but feels it: he lives in the present, the more immediate world.

You may want to teach this poem with Donne's "Death Be Not Proud" or Thomas's "Do Not Go Gentle into That Good Night" (perspectives on loss/death).

FURTHER READING

Stiffler, Randall. *Theodore Roethke: The Poet and His Critics*. Chicago: American Library Association, 1986.

Wolff, George. *Theodore Roethke*. Boston: Twayne, 1981.

WILLIAM MEREDITH

In Memory of Donald A. Stauffer

WRITING ACTIVITY

1. Ask students to write an essay or a poem about a teacher they remember from high school.

GROUP ACTIVITY

Assign students to work in groups to list similarities and differences in the diction and syntax of Meredith's villanelle and Roethke's "The Waking."

DO YOUR STUDENTS KNOW . . .

Oxford University, located in England, is the world's oldest English-speaking university. Although the actual year of its beginning is unclear, records show that teaching occurred in Oxford as early as 1096. When English students were banned from the University of Paris in 1167, Oxford grew rapidly. International students have been welcomed since 1190, whereas women have been admitted only since 1920.

DISCUSSION

You may want to begin discussion of this poem by having students identify Donald A. Stauffer's outstanding qualities. What makes him such a memorable character? What other qualities might a good teacher possess?

Meredith's poem expands the possibilities of the traditional villanelle by changing parts of the two repeated lines (Q 1). Because the villanelle is one of the more rigid and difficult forms in which to write, the poet must usually choose rhymes that are simple and plentiful. Meredith does this, using words such as "go" and "light." However, within the two repeated lines are two rather difficult, multisyllabic words (one reason that this villanelle sounds so completely different from "The Waking"): "indiscriminate" and "obvious." By varying certain words within these two lines, Meredith makes his task easier and the lines more engaging. If we were to change this poem to make it conform absolutely with the prescribed form of the villanelle, we would discover that this process is relatively simple: only the two repeated lines would need to be modified (Q 2). In addition, students may be surprised to learn that these lines could be repeated in their original form without much change at all. This tells us that the poet modified the lines because he wanted to make them more effective and evocative, not simply to make them fit.

Perhaps the most interesting, effective word in this poem is "anthology." Not only is the word unusual and denotatively correct, but also its connotations fit perfectly with Stauffer's vocation. Certainly, lines 16 and 17 are two of the most moving lines in the poem, which raises another point: because in the villanelle two lines are so heavily repeated and must carry so much weight, these two lines should be extraordinary, like Thomas's "Do not go gentle into that good night / Rage, rage against the dying of the light," or at least provocative, such as Roethke's "I wake to sleep, and take my waking slow. / I learn by going where I have to go." You may want to ask students how Meredith's two lines measure up to these others. Do they have to, or is Meredith's poem attempting something different (Q 3)?

Consequently, it might be useful to teach this poem with Thomas's "Do Not Go Gentle into That Good Night" and Roethke's "The Waking."

FURTHER READING

Rotella, Guy L., *Three Contemporary Poets of New England*. Boston: Twayne, 1983.

SAMUEL TAYLOR COLERIDGE

What Is an Epigram?

This poem is especially significant because Coleridge is doing what Keats does in "On the Sonnet": he is writing what he is writing about. He defines the epigram within these two short lines, but at the same time he is creating the kind of epigram he defines. Have students compare his definition to the one given just above this poem in the text itself. Students should be able to discuss how accurate Coleridge's "definition" is, while also finding the "soul of wit" in the representation of the epigram's qualities.

WILLIAM BLAKE

Her Whole Life Is an Epigram

This poem in some ways works on the same principles as Coleridge's "What Is an Epigram?," for it also defines the epigram while being an epigram. Blake's poem, however, defines the epigram through metaphor, comparing the epigram structure to a woman's life. The "twist" at the end of this epigram is the "sliding noose," and it adds a macabre tone to the end of the poem, suggesting perhaps this unknown woman's life is more complicated than it seems, for her tidy, organized life apparently comes to a sudden end. The epigram is the same, for the last few words are meant to suddenly complicate the seeming smoothness of the work itself. In the sense that the epigram was once to be carved on a monument, the circumstances described within this epigram also fit the established form of the poem. *Note:* A common variant of this text has no comma in the second line, so one could imagine the woman has "platted" her life into a noose to catch applause; nonetheless, the noose still suggests hanging — but in this reading she has perhaps caused her own downfall.

MARTÍN ESPADA

Why I Went to College

WRITING ACTIVITIES

1. Ask students to write a personal essay about why they have come to college.
2. In this poem, the speaker's father does not give much explanation for his insistence that he attend college. Have students write a letter from the father to the son in which he explains his reasons.

GROUP ACTIVITY

Divide the class into groups and have students discuss why they think the speaker went to college instead of defying his father.

DISCUSSION

Unlike the epigrams by Coleridge and Blake, this poem constitutes a brief personal narrative told in the first person. Like them, however, it is short and pithy and depends in part on rhyme for its effect (Q 1). The title is essential to a proper understanding of the poem. Without it, one might see the speaker's father simply as a threatening figure. With the title in place, however, we understand that the father in fact had his son's best interests at heart and that the speaker lacked the foresight to see how college might help him (Q 2, 4). It may be that the father did not attend college himself and wanted a better life for his son, although it is impossible to say for sure based on the poem (Q 3).

Consider teaching this poem with "The Carnival Dog, the Buyer of Diamonds," "The Value of Education," "Desert Island," and "My Father as a Guitar." The first selection is a story about a young man pressured by his father to take a certain educational path. The second and third selections both take lighthearted looks at students' motivations. "My Father as a Guitar" is another poem in which Espada examines his relationship with his father.

FURTHER READING

Rivas, Marguerite Mari. "'Lengua, Cultura, Sangre': Song of the New Homeland." *Americas Review* 21 (Fall/Winter 1993): 150–63.

RICHARD BRAUTIGAN

Widow's Lament

Have students compare Brautigan's haiku to the standard haiku form. The subject matter, as the text suggests, is not strictly an image, but other differences exist as well, even in the number of syllables (6-7-4 instead of 5-7-5). Discuss why Brautigan might have chosen this subject instead of a traditional one and have students experiment with the form on their own or in groups, conforming to the structure in various ways and building upon it in others. Note that once we have read the title, this haiku's emotional impact can be as strong as a typical haiku's sensory impact: The widow's loneliness is almost palpable.

MATSUO BASHO

Four Haiku

WRITING ACTIVITIES

1. Have students pick one or two of the haiku and paraphrase them into ordinary prose. They should also compare the effect of their paraphrases with the original translations. Which are more powerful and why?
2. Ask students to use the first lines of each haiku and write their own endings, focusing on nature and the seasons.

DISCUSSION

The impact of haiku is associated with its brevity, and you might begin your discussion of the poems with an explanation of the type of imagery used in haiku. The images tend to be single, stark motifs that offer a holistic interpretation of a more general theme. For example, the first haiku uses an unidentified hill to capture the pleasant and mysterious nuances of early spring. There is an emotion within the single image as well; the hill is unnamed and veiled, perhaps suggesting a woman and the sense of expectancy of good things to come.

In the same way, the second haiku presents the image of the sea and the rice paddy, both emerald green. Here again, only one word is necessary to turn the image into a positive experience, and "emerald" does so for the second haiku. The third haiku paints a chestnut tree blowing in the wind. "Yet still green" is the positive image here, suggesting that the death associated with the arrival of winter has not yet come. Finally, the last haiku is an aural image; the cry of a heron breaks the gloom much as a flash of lightning pierces darkness (Q 1).

Students should note that all the poems are built up from images of the land and nature, following Basho's own advice to begin art with "the depths of the country / and a rice-planting song" (Q 2). In addition, like a rice-planting song, the poems reveal a cultural link to nature, as lives and emotions are organized around the cycles of the passing seasons. As students consider poems about nature in general, they might compare these to a more detailed poem, such as Whitman's "A Noiseless Patient Spider." Whereas Whitman looks at nature to analyze and reflect, haiku seeks only to capture a single effect (Q 3). Students may also wish to compare these haiku to Pound's "In a Station of the Metro." Pound's debt to haiku is clear; however, noting the poems' differences may help underscore some of the important characteristics of haiku, such as reference to season (Q 4).

FURTHER READING

Hamill, S. "Basho's Ghost." *The American Poetry Review* 18.6 (1989): 49–54.
Miner, Earl. "Basho." *Textual Analysis: Some Readers Reading*. Ed. Mary Ann Caws. New York: MLA, 1986. 91–111.

CAROLYN KIZER

After Basho

WRITING ACTIVITIES

1. Ask students to paraphrase the haiku into ordinary prose and discuss in writing which version they think is more effective and why.
2. Have students write a paragraph comparing their responses to this haiku to their reactions to the four by Basho.

DISCUSSION

Kizer's haiku is "after" Basho, not only chronologically, but also in the sense that Basho set the standard and the style for haiku as poetic form (Q 1). Kizer's purpose, then, is to meet that standard in modern English. Like Basho, she illustrates a facet of nature and its cycles — namely, the rising of the Moon. However, the mood of this haiku is a bit different, suggesting fatigue and weariness. The Moon is "tentative" and "pallid," implying perhaps an agedness in its presence (Q 2). The reader may feel that the Moon is a tired stage actress, famous but worn thin by repeated performances (Q 3). Because she is famous, she is expected to perform. Thus, the cyclicity of nature is seen as something that wears down, a habit that grows tiresome, whereas in Basho's work, the cycles are seen in a positive light.

You should of course compare Kizer's poem to Basho's "Four Haiku."

CARL SANDBURG

Chicago

As a prose poem, this work functions in several ways. You can discuss first with the class why this prose poem differs from prose fiction, examining the line endings, beginnings, indentations, and so on. In free verse, the first words of lines (and the pauses created between them and the last word of the previous line) become ways to emphasize the most meaningful or important element of the poem itself. Although "Chicago" is not written with rhyme, its lines express the cohesiveness and repetition that focus the poem on the sprawling, dynamic nature of the city itself. Many of the words and line beginnings, like the repetitive use of "and" and the extraordinary prevalence of progressive verbs ("flinging," "shoveling," "wrecking,") show an active city with hard edges. Sandburg uses numerous metaphors to describe the city, and these images, whether of the "Tool Maker" or the "fierce" dog "lapping for action," portray the city with the same conciseness of language that closed forms use. This should serve as an excellent example of free verse which still fulfills many of the expectations we hold for poetry, without a rigid structure. Have students examine the structure for its parts, for the poem shifts through several movements, and many of them are reinforced by changes in line length and message.

LOUISE GLÜCK

Life Is a Nice Place

To help students understand the effect of the unusual line endings (with the punctuation usually occurring somewhere within the line), read the poem aloud, pausing where punctuation occurs, but also paying attention to line endings as Glück has written them. Then have students write the poem out into prose, leaving the punctuation intact but removing the line endings. They should notice that even with the words set down in prose, the parenthetical words, which take up the majority of the poem, still fit uncomfortably within the rest of the poem, and the line structure reinforces the randomness of the ideas expressed by the persona.

E. E. CUMMINGS

the sky was can dy

A discussion of syllables may be a good beginning for dealing with this poem. Concentrate also on the lines themselves, for some words set by themselves on a line encapsulate the color or image present in the word, and the movement of the description down the page implies the gradual accumulation of colors, sensations, and movement in a slow way, unlike what would be suggested if the words were placed together on two or three more traditional lines. Have students examine how their eyes follow the letters and words down the page, and show them how the breaks, especially within words, slow the reading of the poem down to add to its overall effect.

WALT WHITMAN

from "Out of the Cradle Endlessly Rocking"

WRITING ACTIVITIES

1. Tell students that Whitman once titled this poem "A Word Out of the Sea" (1860). Ask students to write a paragraph discussing how and why this title is appropriate for the poem. How does it differ from the later title? Which do they prefer?
2. Ask students to analyze the role of the mockingbird in the poem.

DISCUSSION

You may want to begin by having each of the students read a small part of the poem — one or two lines — aloud. In many ways, this chorus of voices will help students understand what Whitman was trying to do in much of his poetry: reflect the great diversity of North America.

This poem has three main elements: the boy (who is now a man), the bird, and the ocean waves. The poem is a reminiscence because as a boy the man wandered the shore, searching for meaning in the mysterious cycle of life, death, and rebirth. While there, the boy saw a pair of birds mating and heard their songs of love. Later, the female disappeared, apparently killed, and the male sang his lonely song to the wind, waiting for her to be blown back to him. The story of the two mockingbirds is not included in this excerpt, but knowledge of it will help clarify the appearance of the bird here. Of course, the only answer to the bird's lament was the sound of the ocean's waves crashing on the shore; it was at first an unintelligible answer, but before daybreak, the poet discerned the waves' whispered answer: the "delicious word death." Since all life comes from death, Whitman in this poem eventually celebrates the triumph of eternal life over death — for this reason, death can be "delicious." The poet's focus in "Out of the Cradle" moves from bird to boy to the sea. Poetry, Whitman suggests here, is the resulting fusion in the memory, on the page, of all three.

Many elements give this poem its form (Q 1). Most students will readily pick out the groups of similar prepositional phrases that begin most lines. Point out to students that Whitman depends heavily on assonance and alliteration, with many phrases repeated and mixed with words that echo previous sounds ("wander'd" and "shower'd," for example). In addition, every line except the last is end-stopped, and almost every line is a complete image or observation. Students will recognize these tropes from Whitman's "Song of Myself" (Q 3). Although the lines vary widely in length, they are almost completely dominated by dactylic and trochaic feet. With a falling foot, Whitman tries to imitate the motion of the waves breaking on the shore. The poem's lines vary widely in length because they are imitating the varying sounds of the sea, and this musical aspect, the idea that the poet is "singing," or "chanting," his pains and joys, demands that the lines reflect the wide range of emotions in the poem (Q 2). Like the phrasing of a singer, Whitman's lines attempt to embody the melodic, rhythmical patterns in the cycle of life and death of which we are all part. Students may find some of Whitman's language archaic. However, if this poem is taught in the context of poets of Whitman's own time, students generally recognize the uniqueness of Whitman's form (Q 4).

You may want to compare this poem's use of repetition, alliteration, and assonance with Sandburg's use of these strategies in "Chicago."

FURTHER READING

Allen, Gay Wilson. *A Reader's Guide to Walt Whitman*. New York: Octagon, 1975.

DIANE WAKOSKI

Sleep

WRITING ACTIVITY

1. Ask students to write about Wakoski's choice of animal. Why a mole? Why not some other creature — a mouse, for example?

GROUP ACTIVITY

Have groups of students rearrange Wakoski's poem into one or two sentences and have the class compare the different revisions. In class discussion, consider what Wakoski's arrangement of words adds to the poem.

DISCUSSION

If students have done the Writing Activity, begin by discussing it. Be sure that they know that moles are blind. The form of this poem conflicts with the logical divisions suggested by syntax and punctuation because the poem mirrors the division between sleep and action, unconsciousness and consciousness (Q 1). Essentially, the poem is indented because Wakoski apparently wants to suggest a pause, the sudden, sleepy nodding off of the tired mole who, dozing off temporarily in his snug hole, awakens from the pressure of "the fine grit" pressing in against him. Notice that in the aligned section of the poem no action takes place — all the action verbs are in the other section of the poem (Q 2). It is as if this middle section has been pushed aside to make room for something, suggesting perhaps the mole's condition in his tunnel, with the fine grit constantly falling, pressing in on him. Wakoski seems to draw a parallel between the condition of the mole and the poet's constant search for the proper form of a poem.

What is interesting about this poem is that the lines can be combined in many different ways and still make a certain sense. Reconstructed without the parenthetical comment and with clear punctuation, the lines make perfect sense: "The mole / lifting snouts- / full of strained black dirt / . . . must keep bringing out. / the fine grit / to keep size / for even one day." The parenthetical section, which reads "his perfect tunnel / sculptured / to fit / the fat / body," also makes sense. Ask students about the title and its relationship to the body of the poem. The title, "Sleep," is repeated (l. 8), and the lines, "Sleep / fits tight," (ll. 8–9) also make sense but suggest that sleep itself is a sort of tunnel into which one descends. Clearly, the form of this poem generates meaning. For example, the arrangement of the words "Sleep / fits tight" implies movement. Instead of suggesting merely that sleep is a tight fit, the kinesthetic motion of the words (suggested by the necessary motion of a reader's eyes across the page) implies an awakening, a continuing of the action that begins the poem (Q 3).

You may want to teach this poem with Cummings's "l(a" and "next to of course god america i," Herbert's "Easter Wings," or Swenson's "Women" (to compare form).

FURTHER READING

Wakoski, Diane. *Waiting for the King of Spain*. Santa Barbara: Black Sparrow, 1976.

ROBERT HAYDEN

Monet's "Waterlilies"

WRITING ACTIVITIES

1. Assign students to select a painting and write about it, analyzing their responses to it.
2. Have students write a paragraph or two about what they know of the civil rights movement. Is Hayden's poem still relevant? What recent event(s) does the poem bring

to mind? You probably should follow this exercise with a class discussion that gives students necessary background and then ask what recent events the poem suggests.

GROUP ACTIVITY

Ask groups to brainstorm about this idea: Is the fact that Hayden is African-American important to the poem? Is it even relevant? Can it ever be completely irrelevant?

DO YOUR STUDENTS KNOW . . .

Monet spent the last thirty years of his life attempting to capture the beauty of waterlilies in a series of paintings. One painting in the series, completed in 1908, sold at the auction house Sotheby's, for $20 million (U.S. dollars). The record sale of a Monet was another in the series, which sold in 1998 for $29.7 million (U.S. dollars).

DISCUSSION

You may want to bring to class, or have students bring, a picture of Monet's painting and discuss its distinguishing characteristics.

Hayden chooses not to use the soothing rhythms and comforting shapes of closed form in this poem for the simple reason that these elements would undercut the speaker's disturbed state of mind (Q 1). After all, in this poem Hayden takes temporary refuge from the world; he does not leave it behind altogether. He goes to see the painting not to escape the world but to reassert the timeless joy we can find in great art, art that brings us closer to that unspoiled, innocent Earth "each of us has lost." Great art does not allow escape from the world; it brings the world closer to us.

This poem deals with perception, with seeing the world as it could be, not as society itself has made it. This poem is not simply about black people's civil rights; the fact that Hayden is African-American has little to do with the poem's ultimate message. If Hayden's main concern here were the condition of black people, he would have focused entirely on Selma — or compared the two situations and explored their relationship in order to make some point about Selma. Instead, he seems to have selected Selma and Saigon because they illustrate "man's inhumanity to man" in a common historical period.

The poem's structure illustrates its theme: the contrast between the joyful, beautiful world of art as it embodies aesthetic experience and beauty and the painful, poisonous world of everyday experience. Hayden indents lines 3, 7, 10, and 13 for several reasons (Q 2). First, they indicate a turn in the direction of the speaker's thought, much as indenting the first line of a paragraph does. Second, this indenting isolates the lines and further emphasizes them — something that lines 10 and 13, at least, clearly deserve. Finally, indentation highlights the division between two worlds: the sublime world of art and the real world of violence.

Art, Hayden suggests, mirrors the joy that the violence of everyday existence has destroyed.

The final section of the poem reads much like an envoi, summarizing the speaker's perceptions. In this second section, the poet focuses wholly on the painting itself, interpreting its "illusive flesh of light" mentioned in the first part. Note here that the poet sees the painting's light "as through refracting tears." "Tears" is doubly accurate and meaningful here, for it describes not only Monet's technique, but also the speaker's state of mind. The speaker views the painting *through* the sadness of his modern world, not as an escape from it. Great art is timeless for precisely this reason (Q 3).

You may want to compare this poem to Auden's "Musée des Beaux Arts," focusing on how poets use paintings as starting points for observations about the world around us. Alternatively, it can be compared with other "political" poems, such as Wilbur's "For the Student Strikers," Brooks's "The *Chicago Defender* Sends a Man to Little Rock," or Randall's "The Ballad of Birmingham."

FURTHER READING

Fetrow, Fred M. *Robert Hayden*. Boston: Twayne, 1984.

WILLIAM CARLOS WILLIAMS

Spring and All

WRITING ACTIVITIES

1. Williams was a physician. Ask students to write a paragraph explaining how this biographical information might hold the key to interpreting the poem.
2. Have students list the verbs in the poem and write a paragraph describing their number, placement, and significance.
3. For a more ambitious writing assignment, have students look at the entire volume entitled *Spring and All*, of which this poem is but a small part ("Red Wheelbarrow" is also in this volume). Ask them to write an essay explaining how "Spring and All" develops the themes of the work.

DISCUSSION

You might start a discussion of "Spring and All" by asking students about the poem's setting and speaker. Is there a speaker? If so, is the speaker going to the hospital or simply observing the road leading up to it? Most of the students will not know that Williams was a doctor, and some may conclude that the speaker (if there is indeed a speaker) is going there simply to visit someone, not to work.

After hearing that Williams was a physician, what do your students now think about the poem? Make sure students understand that readers cannot take for granted that a poem is autobiographical. Even if this poem were a personal account, there is no evidence that it is strictly autobiographical. In truth, there may not even be a speaker in the poem. Williams often tried in his poetry to communicate directly with the world—leaving the speaker out of the poem. Williams's statements about poetry echo this idea. "No ideas but in things," he says in *Paterson*. Later in this volume, he states: "The poet does not . . . permit himself to go beyond the thought to be discovered in the context of that with which he is dealing." "The poet thinks with his poem," Williams later adds. Even in *Spring and All*, he states: "There is a constant barrier between the reader and his consciousness of immediate contact with the world."

As a result, this poem is not so much about the world of a particular consciousness as it is about the world itself. Clearly, the hospital may contrast with the world around it (if we take the hospital as a symbol of death or stagnation), but it is also similar to it. Neither world — neither the hospital nor the nature surrounding it —lies outside the cycle of life and death, and although many people come to the hospital to die, we also enter life there, just as every year spring enters in the form of a plant sprouting through the frozen ground.

Many elements of this poem are found in traditional closed form (Q 1). The poem is in clear divisions, and the lines are, for the most part, of similar length. Many of the lines contain a distinct trochaic meter (Williams employed what he called a "variable foot"). In addition, the lines echo each other, often using alliteration (Q 3). Williams describes the lifeless, stagnant roadside, for example, repeating the harsh consonant sounds such as *b* and *d* in lines 4–6: "Beyond, the / waste of broad, muddy fields / brown with dried weeds, standing. . . ." And in lines 7–8, he repeats *t*: "patches of standing water / the scattering of tall trees. . . ." This alliteration not only slows the rhythm — it is impossible to read these lines quickly without slurring the words together — but these harsh, difficult sounds also reinforce the harsh description. Williams uses assonance in lines 2–3 to achieve an opposite effect: softness. The repetition of *u* in the words "under," "surge," "blue," and "clouds" reinforces the image of soft, billowy clouds. Williams even repeats entire words, such as "standing" (ll. 6–7), to emphasize the ubiquity of the puddles. Sound is clearly one of the most important elements in Williams's poetry, and throughout much of his work, sound imitates meaning.

As a whole, though, this poem lacks traditional form. There are no even stanzas to this poem, and the meter certainly is not regular throughout. The lines are not linked by rhyme, either. Williams's isolation of two separate sets of lines emphasizes them as well as their differences from the other descriptions (Q 2, 4, 5). The tall trees and the water are separate, and spring is personified as an actor — sluggish and dazed by the light —entering through the ground, the stage for the poem.

You may want to teach this poem with Cummings's "in Just" or Basho's "Four Haiku" (to compare form).

FURTHER READING

Guimond, James. *The Art of William Carlos Williams*. Chicago: U of Illinois P, 1968.
Weatherhead, A. Kingsley. *The Edge of the Image*. Seattle: U of Washington P, 1967.

CAROLYN FORCHÉ

The Colonel

WRITING ACTIVITY

1. Have students research conditions in El Salvador in the late 1970s. Ask them to write a paper on what could possibly have been the fates of the people whose ears were cut off.

GROUP ACTIVITY

Place students in groups and have them reformat "The Colonel"—first in paragraphs, and then in conventional poetic form. What effects do these different formats create?

DISCUSSION

Forché has said of "The Colonel" that it was "almost a *poeme trouvé*" (a "found poem"): "I had only to pare down the memory and render it whole, unlined, and precisely as recollection would have it" (quoted in Smith 22). The horrific nature of Forché's subject matter has led her to abandon poetic form and to present the story of dinner with the colonel unadorned, in a prose form. The poem can indeed be divided into paragraphs: one for the opening description of the house; one for the description of the dinner itself; one for the discussion that takes place after dinner; one for the colonel's return with the sack; and so on. It would also be possible to restructure the prose poem in poetic lines:

> "What you have heard is true. I was
> In his house. His wife carried a tray
> Of coffee and sugar. . . .

However, it is important to explain to students that to make these changes would be to call attention to the craft, the form, of Forché's story. An attention to form, and not to content, in a story like this — and we have no reason to believe that it is not a true story — would distract the reader from the poem's main point, would dilute its powerful effect (Q 1, 2).

Whether we consider "The Colonel" to be poetry or prose is determined by our view of what the function of poetry should be. Forché's own view is that her poetry is a "poetry of witness," grounded in the belief that it is her role as poet to testify to the horrors that she was made aware of during her time in El Salvador. This philosophy underpins the theme of "The Colonel" in which the most important point — and most powerful image — involves the role of the bag of human ears that the Colonel spills onto the table and then sweeps onto the floor with his arm. Clearly, although these are the ears of dead people, the fact that when the colonel speaks, "some of the ears on the floor caught this scrap of his voice" while others are "pressed to the ground" indicates that the ears are in some figurative way alive, and that they are involved in the process of communication and, perhaps, retribution. It is Forché's poetry that breathes life into these ears; in acting as "witness," Forché is able to render the ears — and the people to whom they belonged — immortal. Questions of form seem secondary to this powerful message (Q 3, 4).

You might try teaching this poem alongside Dorfman's "Hope" or Valenzuela's "All about Suicide."

FURTHER READING

Montenegro, David. "Carolyn Forché: An Interview." *American Poetry Review* 17 (Nov.–Dec. 1988): 35–40.

Smith, Leonora. "Carolyn Forché: Poet of Witness." *Still the Frame Holds: Essays on Women Poets and Writers*. Ed. Sheila Roberts. San Bernandino: Borgo P, 1993.

PAT MORA

Immigrants

WRITING ACTIVITIES

1. The parents in this poem desperately want their children to become Americanized. Ask students to pretend they are emigrant parents writing up wish-lists of things they want for their children.
2. Have students write a short research essay on the challenges faced by the children of emigrants from a particular country.

GROUP ACTIVITY

Divide the class into groups and ask each group to make a list of the positive and negative consequences that are likely to result from the desire of these parents to Americanize their children.

DO YOUR STUDENTS KNOW . . .

More than 100 million Americans today are directly related to 12 million emigrant ancestors who arrived in the United States through Ellis Island. Emigrants from Europe were processed at Castle Garden, New York, until 1892, when the Ellis Island facility was opened on an island in New York Harbor. Until 1954, most emigrants arriving in New York from Europe were medically and legally inspected at Ellis Island, now a museum dedicated to America's emigrant past.

DISCUSSION

The emigrant parents in this poem want their children to be fully assimilated into and accepted by the broader American culture. To this end, they speak to their children in heavily accented English and buy them toys that, in some cases at least, resemble children of a different, presumably more acceptable, ethnic background. At the end of the poem, however, the speaker implies, through the use of a lower case "a" in "american," that the children will not achieve the complete acceptance hoped for by their parents (Q 3). This is the parents' "dark / parent fear" (Q 1).

This poem is an example of the way in which older forms, such as the sonnet, exert a continuing influence even on free-verse poetry. While it is not rhymed or metered, this poem makes a nod to the sonnet form in that it has fourteen lines and a turn after the first eight lines (Q 4). For the most part, the lines are broken at places where there would be a rhetorical pause, however slight. One of the few exceptions to this rule is in lines 4 and 5, where there is no pause between "blue" and "eyes" (Q 2).

Consider teaching this poem with "Immigrant Picnic," "Chin," or "How to Write the Great American Indian Novel." The first two selections address the emigrant experience from different points of view, and "How to Write the Great American Indian Novel" deals with some of the long-term consequences of European immigration to North America.

FURTHER READING

Kanellos, Nicolás. "Pat Mora": *Chicano Writers, Third Series.* Ed. Francisco A. Lomelí and Carl R. Shirley. *Dictionary of Literary Biography.* Vol. 209. Detroit: Gale, 1999. 160–163.

CZESLAW MILOSZ

Christopher Robin

WRITING ACTIVITIES

1. Ask students to write an essay in which they reflect on a book they enjoyed when they were children.
2. "Christopher Robin" is an example of a prose poem. Have students break it up into lines of verse and reflect on how this formal change affects their reading of the poem.

GROUP ACTIVITY

Split the class into three groups. Ask one group to argue that "Christopher Robin" is poetry, and another that it is not. Ask the third group to decide which group's interpretation is correct and why.

DISCUSSION

This poem is an unconventional elegy for Christopher Robin Milne (Q 2). The speaker is Winnie the Pooh, the fictional Christopher Robin's closest friend, referred to as "old bear" (Q 1). Pooh is the ideal narrator because, being "a bear of little brain," he has no preconceptions about what has happened to his friend. None of the other characters mentioned is as close to Christopher Robin, and no real person would have had the experience of actually living in this fictional world. Death, in this case, is a result of the character's having stepped out of the fictional world that Pooh and his friends inhabit and into "Time," or our own world (Q 4).

In addition to writing an elegy, Milosz is making points about the value of literature and about the difference between fiction and reality. Not only does a work of literature create a timeless world, but literature can seem even more real than the "real world" itself. The real Christopher Robinson may have died in 1996, but his fictional counterpart remains alive to anyone who reads his father's books.

Students will immediately be struck by how different "Christopher Robin" looks from most of the other poems in this book. The question of what a prose poem is remains an open one. Without meter, regular use of rhyme or even line breaks, prose poems might be indistinguishable from notebook jottings, parables, or, as in this case, very short stories. In a prose poem, more than in any other type of poetry, the formal expectations the reader brings to the work are crucial (Q 3).

Consider teaching this poem with "On the Death of Friends in Childhood," which focuses on the way that those who die young remain unchanged; "Once Upon a Time," which uses the form of a fairy tale to make a political point; or "A Mown Lawn," a more obviously "poetic" prose poem.

FURTHER READING

Baranczak, Stanislaw. "Milosz's Poetic Language: A Reconnaissance." *Language and Style* 18 (Fall 1985): 319–33.

Lazer, Hank "Poetry and Thought: The Example of Czeslaw Milosz." *The Virginia Quarterly Review* 64 (Summer 1988): 449–65.

MAY SWENSON

Women

DO YOUR STUDENTS KNOW . . .

American feminism, often seen as an offshoot of the civil rights movement of the 1960s and 1970s, actually is described as having three "waves," or phases. The first wave crystallized during the nineteenth century as women like Susan B. Anthony and Elizabeth Cady Stanton became involved in a number of social reform movements that supported the abolition of slavery, temperance, and the right to vote. The second wave broke new ground for women legally and professionally during the 1960s and 1970s, following the publication of Betty Freidan's book *The Feminine Mystique*. The third wave recognizes feminism's current focus balancing the gains of the past with the power of personal choice.

The visual effect of the two columns is especially interesting in this poem, for it suggests two ways to read the text: down each column individually or along the lines themselves. Swenson adds other patterns to this. The two adjoining lines that link the columns together may also divide the poem into three stanzas; or the lack of punctuation at the end of each column might suggest a continuous repetition from the end of one column to the beginning of the next, and then back to the first one. The last few lines of the second column reinforce this, for they present the same three lines that begin the first column of the poem. You might see how many different ways students can discover for reading the poem — and then discuss whether the meaning or tone changes at all from one pattern to another. You might also discuss the images used to describe what women "should be," especially noting how the meaning of the longer lines changes from one column to the next, yet somehow the overall meaning of the poem remains the same. Let students examine the more traditional version of this poem, "Women Should Be Pedestals."

GEORGE HERBERT

Easter Wings

WRITING ACTIVITIES

1. Have students write briefly about the poem's structure. Why are there two separate stanzas?
2. Ask students to write a paragraph about the idea of writing an emblem poem. Is this arrangement a gimmick, or is it as valid as any other form?

GROUP ACTIVITY

Divide students into two groups and have them explicate each section of this poem. When they are finished, have them discuss their findings with the other group.

DISCUSSION

The shape of "Easter Wings" clearly reinforces the poem's themes and ideas (Q 1). Most obviously, the two winged-shaped stanzas visually embody the speaker's subject, found in the title. There are two sets of wings because the speaker asks God ("sings" to him in the form of this poem) to let him rise "harmoniously" with him. Man's sins, which have resulted in "the fall," may be repaired, or "imped" (literally, to "imp" means to graft new feathers onto the wing of a bird to repair damage), which will allow man to lift himself up — with God's help, of course — toward heaven, toward victory. The varying line lengths help trace man's plight before and after this fall. The first few lines are full and long, reflecting the "wealth and store" of Eden. Then, after the fall, man's situation becomes most poor as he is cast out of the garden.

This idea is echoed in the second stanza, when the speaker traces the path of his own life, which becomes "Most thin" when he is furthest from a righteous path. As the speaker accepts God, combining with him like feathers grafted onto a great wing, the lines increase in length again, expanding as the speaker uses his sufferings to spur himself on and climb higher. Not coincidentally, the lines are shortest where the speaker is most poor or thin, where humankind has strayed furthest from God.

The repeated rhyme scheme of *ababa cdcdc* reflects the progression of ideas within each stanza while also uniting them (Q 2). Each stanza is divided into two parts that are made more distinct by rhyme. The first five lines, which focus on man's shortcomings, share two rhymes, while the second five lines, which focus on a union with God, contain a different set of rhymes. The two stanzas are linked by repetition, and since the speaker seeks to "combine" with God, this union of sound patterns reinforces the poem's main theme. Note here that if the white space between these two stanzas were closed, the emblem would change into one set of wings with a large body in the middle, rather than two separate sets of wings.

You may want to teach this poem with Wakoski's "Sleep," Swenson's "Women," or Cummings's "l(a" to compare form.

FURTHER READING

Vendler, Helen. *The Poetry of George Herbert*. Cambridge: Harvard UP, 1975.

GREG WILLIAMSON

Group Photo with Winter Trees

WRITING ACTIVITIES

1. Ask students to write three prose summaries: one of the bold lines, one of the fainter lines, and one of the poem as a whole.
2. Have students write their own poems in the form Williamson has invented.

GROUP ACTIVITY

Break the class into small groups and ask them to discuss the use of rhyme in this poem. Would it be more or less effective if it were in blank verse?

DISCUSSION

Good poets put their individual stamps on the forms they use. Relatively few, however, invent their own forms, let alone forms as complicated as Williamson's. This poem is part of a series titled *Double Exposures*. In each case, the bold lines can be read as one poem, and the fainter lines as another; the rhyme scheme for both is *aabbcc*. One can (and should) also read the two together as one poem, rhyming *abab cdcd efef* (Q 1, 2).

The bold lines, taken by themselves, describe a group of neighbors posing for a photograph. The fainter lines describe the winter trees in the background (Q 4). Taken together, the poem is a mediation on the mortality not only of the leaves but also of the people posing for the photo. It is impossible to say whether this is one poem or three: each way of reading the poem is true (Q 3). We obtain the fullest picture, however, when we look at the people in the context of their environment and observe how each is necessary to a full understanding of the other.

Consider teaching this poem with "The Hongo Store 29 Miles Volcano Hilo, Hawaii," "For the Anniversary of My Death," "Do Not Go Gentle into That Good Night," or "Christopher Robin," all of which reflect upon mortality.

CHAPTER 24

SYMBOL, ALLEGORY, ALLUSION, MYTH

WILLIAM BLAKE

The Sick Rose

Most students will identify the rose as female and the worm as male; some will recognize the sexuality in these symbols. As the text indicates, the rose is also a symbol of beauty, love, passion. The worm is identified with death — worms feed on dead matter and can bring diseases to plants; although they can also aerate the soil, this worm does not bring life or joy — he destroys both. He is invisible and flies through the stormy night — like a vampire or howling phantom — perhaps a satanic figure. He is associated with darkness, night, destruction; she with crimson (bloody? royal? passionate?) joy. The rose has been happy in her ("flower / conjugal") bed. Is the worm a jealous lover? A rapist? One insightful student suggested that the rose may be associated with upper classes, the worm with lower classes they would like to keep under foot — but that may destroy them if they continue to treat these masses as invisible. This is an interesting reading in relation to "The Chimney Sweeper" and other Blake poems.

ROBERT FROST

For Once, Then, Something

Like the speaker in the poem, poets are traditional seekers of meaning and truth. Critics of Frost's poetry have sometimes argued that his "messages" are too pat, too obvious. In this poem, however, Frost suggests that truth is not obvious or easy to find — that one must look beneath the water in the well and that only occasionally and only with great effort will that truth or meaning be discernible to the seeker. Notice the traditional, symbolic identification of whiteness (presence of light?) with truth.

JIM SIMMERMAN

Child's Grave, Hale County, Alabama

The poignancy of this poem lies in the speaker's imagining the father's pain at burying his child in "hard" (cruel, "rock-ridden") land, alone on a cold, windy night. The father's isolation and poverty are emphasized by his need to "steal" quietly across the farm — to avoid waking anyone — and to "steal" the wood, to bury his child. The simplicity of the wooden half-cross also underscores his poverty, his sacrifice, and his grief.

EMILY DICKINSON

Volcanoes be in Sicily

"Vesuvius at Home" may well allude to creative powers — or to the emotional upheavals in life — the potentially destructive eruptions that may create craters in a family or community, but that are a natural part of human existence.

LANGSTON HUGHES

Island

WRITING ACTIVITIES

1. Ask your students to write for a few minutes on what they think the island represents. This exercise will show them how poetry can be at once both public and private.
2. Discuss Hughes's ethnic background and then ask students to write briefly on how this knowledge of Hughes influences their interpretation of the poem. Should it?

GROUP ACTIVITY

Divide students into groups and ask each group to explore one possible "meaning" of the island — that is, one possibility for what the island symbolizes (e.g., a paradise, a shelter, peace, equality). Groups can then argue which interpretation is the best.

DISCUSSION

Interpreting the island merely as a symbol of freedom or equality would limit the poem's broad range of possible interpretations. The poem does not have to deal solely with black issues just because Hughes was black. In addition, no poet ever wants to limit a symbol's range; a poem such as "Island" has a wide range of implied meanings. The island in this poem is a universal symbol because it cannot (and should not) be limited to one culture. Notice that Hughes barely describes the island — the only significant detail he provides is found in line 6: "And its sands are fair." We each have our own personal island, a place where we will realize our dreams, or simply find peace (Q 1).

The fact that Hughes begins with a metaphor describing a negative state of mind is important: the island seems to be more of a shelter than a paradise (Q 2). The rhythm of the poem supports this interpretation. Since all but one line (l. 6) begins with a stress, the poem reads like a plea, a prayer for relief or help. The speaker, riding waves of sorrow, does not control his own destiny; he must ride the waves where they lead. Perhaps the most important word in the poem after "sorrow" is "fair," a word with many possible meanings.

Among other interpretations, the island could represent peace or equality (Q 3). It could also connote something much more personal, such as escape from trouble. Finally, it might suggest art (specifically poetry), since so much art begins with sorrow.

FURTHER READING

Miller, R. Baxter. *The Art and Image of Langston Hughes*. Lexington: UP of Kentucky, 1989.

THEODORE ROETHKE

Night Crow

WRITING ACTIVITIES

1. For a more extensive writing assignment, ask your students to look closely at the adjectives in this poem. How important are they, and which are unusual?
2. Ask students to write about the significance of the crow. Why does Roethke choose a crow instead of some other bird? You may want to mention Poe's poem "The Raven" as you discuss their responses.
3. Have students write a few paragraphs on the two birds in this poem. Do they represent two sides of a coin, or is one of them a symbol and the other just a bird?

GROUP ACTIVITY

Ask groups of students to present oral reports on poems in addition to "Night Crow" that use animals as central metaphors, such as Wakoski's "Sleep" or Hopkins's "The Windhover." Ask students to focus on the significance of the animal in each poem.

DISCUSSION

The title of this poem is significant because it focuses on the second image and not on the "clumsy crow" of the first line (Q 1). In doing so, Roethke shifts our attention away from the literal, denotative crow to the symbolic, connotative image, which appears later in the poem. On one level, the "clumsy crow" differs from the night crow flying "Deep in the brain" simply because the first is real, the second imaginary (Q 2). Unlike the foreboding, swift, imaginary bird, the first crow is a clumsy creature who "flaps." On a deeper level, the physical difference between the two birds is not important, for the speaker in this poem seems more interested in their similarities. Perhaps on one level this poem is a commentary on the difference between reality and imagination — the second bird is clearly more suggestive than the first and therefore is more symbolic. However, ultimately the poem is more about the process of symbolization (how things become symbols) than about the symbols themselves (Q 3).

In many ways, "Night Crow" exemplifies Jung's theory of archetypes. The speaker has seen a specific image that in turn triggers something in his subconscious. Whether the crow or the crow together with its surroundings is responsible for the evocation of the night crow remains to be seen. Notice, however, that the first, or daylight, crow is taking off from "a wasted tree." In a poem of so few words, this detail must have significance. Indeed, in the dream, the sky is "moonless," a detail that perhaps mirrors the wasted-tree image of the second line. Significantly though, the night crow is far more frightening and impressive than the real crow. If this poem comments on the difference between reality and imagination, we can see clearly that the imaginary bird, the one triggered in the speaker's subconscious, is much greater than the real thing. In other words, the imagination is much greater than reality. The fact that this "tremendous bird" is receding back into the brain's dark pool of archetypical images further supports the notion that the poem is dealing also with the process of universal symbolization. Also, keep in mind that the Moon itself is a symbol for the imagination, and the night crow is flying "further and further away" from the light of the speaker's conscious, deep into the "moonless" depths of the subconcious. The term "far back," which ends the poem, can be interpreted to mean not only "far back" into the subconscious, but also far back into time itself, to the timeless image at the bottom of a whole mass of catalytic images.

FURTHER READING

Kalaidjian, Walter B. *Understanding Theodore Roethke*. Columbia: U of South Carolina P, 1987.

CHRISTINA ROSSETTI

Uphill

The allegory of life as a journey is a common one. Compare Rossetti's approach, for example, with Dickinson's in "Because I Could Not Stop for Death." Both comment on the length of the journey and portray the grave as a roof in the ground. Rossetti's speaker seems to be on foot and alone until stanza three, whereas Dickinson's is accompanied by the gentlemanly (personified) Death, who accompanies her in a carriage. Dickinson's speaker is too busy to stop for Death — she finds her life interrupted by him; Rossetti's is moving constantly uphill toward death. Dickinson also addresses eternity more directly.

ADRIENNE RICH

Diving into the Wreck

WRITING ACTIVITIES

1. Have students write about the diver. Why does Rich use this figure, and why does she compare herself to Cousteau?
2. Ask students to write briefly on the significance of the wreck. What might the wreck represent?
3. For a more extensive writing assignment, ask your students to research Rich's life and write an essay showing how certain events in her life appear in this poem.

GROUP ACTIVITY

Since this poem is supported by an allegorical framework, assign each group a particular image for interpretation. For example, ask them to examine the significance of the diver, the shipwreck, or the sea itself.

DISCUSSION

"Diving into the Wreck" is clearly an allegory, but its allegorical framework is anything but clear. At the most rudimentary level, the poem is about a deep sea diver's exploration of a wrecked ship, but many details suggest Rich is attempting much more than just realistic imagery (Q 1). The "book of myths," the ladder, the focus on the "mask"—these details all infuse the poem with deeper, parallel meanings, the literal significance of which are secondary. The allegorical framework is at once highly personal and universal (Q 2).

Knowing a few basic facts about Rich's life and poetry allows readers to understand the more puzzling elements of this poem. Much of Rich's poetry, for example, is written as dialogue. Sometimes this dialogue is with another character, as in "Face to Face" (1966), and other times it is with herself, as in "Planetarium" (1971). In "Diving into the Wreck," the woman writing the poem and the woman in the poem are the same. Often, through her poetry, Rich attempts to come to terms with her life; for example, she calls "Orion" (1969) "a poem of reconnection with a part of myself I had felt I was losing." For Rich, the personal *is* political, and very often her poetry deals with private, personal issues. Knowing that Rich identifies herself as a radical lesbian feminist, readers can interpet the merging genders of the pronouns toward the end of "Diving into the Wreck."

If we look at this poem as personal testimony, then the two most important words must be "wreck" and "diving." There are events from her life which could be categorized as "wrecks" or "psychological wreckage"— Rich's husband, for example, committed suicide — and Rich may be "diving" into her past (descending into the subconscious) as a costumed diver looking for meaning beyond the conscious masks we all wear. As she looks for truth —"the wreck and not the story of the wreck"— she moves closer and closer to her real self, becoming more understanding of how her own sexual identity was constructed (Q 4). For this reason, the sex of the diver at the end of the poem is not only uncertain but also not important. The diver gradually becomes the wreck, identifying with it, and finding a nameless, "maskless" truth.

Of course, we should not limit our interpretation of a poem to biographical sources. For example, the diver could simply be a poet (writer) who dives down into "the hold" of history, the depths of mythology, and tries to find the truths behind centuries of "masks." "The words are maps," Rich says, and the poet is the mapmaker. Using this interpretation, the reader can see that the gender of the writer would be irrelevant and that the names, our name, would be absent. Notice that in this interpretation the reader takes an active, important part —"We are, I am, you are . . . / the one who finds our way"— in the search.

The poem could also be a more general, objective statement about our relationship to all history — both personal *and* private. After all, as the speaker descends the ladder of time, she is reverting to a more primitive, insectlike stage, and whether she means to or not ("by cowardice or courage"), she, like the reader, must search within this wreck of the past for meaning (Q 5).

Ultimately, we should not limit a poem's possible meanings simply because we favor any one viewpoint; in fact, we should allow and encourage students to find their own appropriate, justifiable allegorical framework for this poem. "Diving into the Wreck" can fit a variety of interpretations, any one of which might fire that spark of recognition in the student's mind.

FURTHER READING

Rich, Adrienne. *Adrienne Rich's Poetry.* Ed. Barbara C. Gelphi and Albert Gelphi. New York: Norton, 1975.

WOLE SOYINKA

Future Plans

WRITING ACTIVITIES

1. Ask students to make a list of the people mentioned in this poem. What things do they all have in common? Have them write a paragraph about this. If you do this after the Group Activity, you might assign a longer paper.
2. Have students write on this poem's aesthetic merits. Is this more of a political statement than a poem? What elements common to poetry does this poem contain? Should all poetry please the eye and ear?

GROUP ACTIVITY

Assign each group of students one political figure or pair from among those Soyinka mentions. Using encyclopedias, other reference books, or the Internet, each group can read about and then elaborate on the political roles of these figures. They may explain, attack, or defend Soyinka's implications, explaining whether they believe he is generalizing about politicians, speaking metaphorically, or actually alluding to events in the political lives of the figures he mentions.

DISCUSSION

Not only does this poem parody an agenda for a meeting, but also it parodies "coming attractions," previews of entertainment to come in a movie theater or on television. The meeting's chair is described as "a dark horse, a circus nag turned blinkered sprinter," and the poem ends with the invitation common before station breaks on television: "*and more to come.*" The sexual suggestions about Arafat, Meir, and the Pope, plus the allegation of Nixon and Castro getting drunk, sound like tabloid journalism. The grimness of the humor comes from the knowledge that such world leaders hold the fate of humanity in their corruptible hands. Compare with Sepamla's "Words, Words, Words" and Valenzuela's "All about Suicide."

WILLIAM MEREDITH

Dreams of Suicide

WRITING ACTIVITIES

1. Ask students to write about the title of this poem. Why might the speaker be dreaming about these particular people?
2. Have students analyze in writing the speaker's attitude toward his subjects. Does he admire or condemn these writers?
3. Ask students to write on the mythological allusions in this poem. How do these allusions tie the three parts together?

GROUP ACTIVITY

Divide students into three groups and ask each group to present an oral report on the life of the writer mentioned in one section of the poem.

DISCUSSION

Although the epigraph says this poem is in "sorrowful memory" of three writers who took their own lives, the tone of the poem is more mystical than depressing. Meredith translates the writers into dream figures and honors their uniqueness by turning them into unicorn, totem, and Icarus of myth. Thus, they are transformed from sad figures to mythic ones — artists and muses at once.

FURTHER READING

Rotella, Guy L. *Three Contemporary Poets of New England*. Boston: Twayne, 1983.

DELMORE SCHWARTZ

The True-Blue American

WRITING ACTIVITIES

1. Have students look up the four names that appear at the end of the poem. Then have them write about what they all have in common.
2. Ask students to write about the poem's tone. How important is it to our understanding of the poem?
3. For a more extensive writing assignment, ask your students to respond to this poem in an argumentative essay. Do they agree with Schwartz, or do they think that his argument is more emotional than factual?

GROUP ACTIVITY

Ask groups of students to focus on the name "Jeremiah" and to find an instance of its use in the Bible. What might the significance of such an allusion be?

DO YOUR STUDENTS KNOW . . .

Throughout much of the twentieth century, the five-and-dime store was a fixture of Main Street businesses in American cities and towns. F. W. Woolworth opened the first five-and-dime stores in New York state and Pennsylvania in 1879, where one could purchase clothes, food stuffs, and household goods and get a quick meal at the lunch counter. By 1911, the Woolworth company had opened over 1,000 stores across America. Although the last of these stores closed in 1998, the popularity of department stores with low prices live on in stores like Wal-Mart and Target.

DISCUSSION

The phrase "true-blue American" conjures up a wide array of emotions in any reader, but Schwartz uses the phrase ironically in his poem (Q 1). A "typical" North American, Jeremiah Dickson believes it is his right to have everything he wants. In addition, he believes that America's resources and greatness are unlimited. Unlike the philosophy of Kierkegaard and other "Europeans" (as North Americans so casually refer to people from a wide variety of different cultures), our free will as Americans is expressed by attaining material things, by having or buying anything we may desire (Q 2). The name "Jeremiah Dickson" is not necessarily an allusion, but it gives the poem both authenticity and universality. It suggests the religious fervor (and perhaps intolerance) of the Pilgrims and blends it with the blind devotion to materialism that seems to characterize contemporary society. An ethnic name would not have the generic significance that this distinctly "American" name has. In a way, this name not only denies ethnic individuality but also ignores the fact that all of us — except for Native Americans — are descendants of immigrants (Q 3).

The places and things mentioned in lines 19–22 have all been commercialized to a certain extent. "Vulgarity" and "Grandeur" are mixed together, as in the case of Niagara Falls (the grandeur of the falls and the vulgarity of the commercial establishments that surround it), and our particularly American sense of enterprise and appetite affects all aspects of our lives. For Americans like Jeremiah, Christmas no longer teaches humility and reverence; instead, it serves as a catalyst for an "infinite appetite" (Q 4).

The names at the end of the poem illustrate and celebrate aspects of the American spirit (Q 6). Columbus, the great explorer and adventurer, fuels our infinite hope that our resources and frontiers are inexhaustible. Barnum exemplifies the great entrepreneurial spirit behind not only the circus but also all enterprises ("there's a sucker born every minute" is his most famous statement). Edison illustrates the practical application of the imagination and shows us, according to the speaker, that we can invent what we do not have. Finally, Jeremiah Dickson represents the combination of all these people put together, as he proceeds to order both the chocolate sundae and the banana split — two very typical North American creations (Q 5).

You may want to teach this poem with Hughes's "Harlem," Oates's "Where Are You Going, Where Have You Been?," or Miller's *Death of a Salesman* (American Dream/nightmare) or you may want to pair it with Cummings's "next to of course god america i" to discuss clichés about American life.

FURTHER READING

Atlas, James. *Delmore Schwartz: The Life of an American Poet.* New York: Farrar, 1977.

COUNTEE CULLEN

Yet Do I Marvel

WRITING ACTIVITIES

1. Have students write about this poem's form. What kind of sonnet is it? Why do you think Cullen chose this form, and how does it reinforce the poem's theme?
2. Compare this poem to McKay's poem "The White City." How does the focus of these two poems differ, despite their similar subjects?

3. For a longer assignment, have students study the myths of Tantalus and Sisyphus and write an essay comparing or contrasting one of these myths to an aspect of their own lives.

GROUP ACTIVITY

Assign each group one sonnet to compare with this one in form, tone, style, and subject matter. (Writing Activity 1 might grow out of this activity.)

DISCUSSION

In the first two lines of this sonnet, the speaker pretends to believe God is kind and well meaning, yet suggests the same arrogance Browning portrays in the duke of "My Last Duchess": he will not "stoop to quibble." In the rest of this first quatrain and in the second one, Cullen's speaker poses questions about God's ways. In the first, he asks about mole blindness and human mortality; in the second, he questions the punishment of Tantalus and Sisyphus, figures from myth whose situations often represent the sufferings and frustrations of the human condition. In the third quatrain, the speaker ironically suggests that we humans are incapable of understanding God's "awful" (awe-inspiring, terrible) brain. Finally, in mock awe, the poet "marvels" at his own role as a black poet — a seeming oxymoron in a racist society.

LOUISE ERDRICH

Windigo

WRITING ACTIVITIES

1. Have students write on this poem's point of view. Why does Erdrich write this poem from the creature's perspective? What is gained by this? Is anything lost?
2. Have students discuss the significance of the Windigo. Why does Erdrich choose this mythological creature, and what symbolic overtones does he have?

GROUP ACTIVITY

Many students will know the Disney movie *Beauty and the Beast*. Discuss the story first and then have groups compare and contrast this poem with the Disney version of the fairy tale. In what ways are they similar? What are the important differences?

DO YOUR STUDENTS KNOW . . .

The Windigo personifies the madness, cannibalism, and death that famine and starvation can bring. For the Native American tribes in contemporary America, the Windigo legend reflects a troubling reality. According to the U.S. Department of Agriculture, twenty-two percent of Native households are hungry or live on the edge of hunger due to poor employment and educational opportunities and poverty.

DISCUSSION

Because she does not expect her readers to be familiar with this Native American myth, Erdrich supplies the reader with some necessary background information in the epigraph, which becomes a kind of prologue (Q 1). Having read this information, the reader in turn expects to see it illustrated or acted out; we expect the story to focus on how the girl forces the boiling lard down the beast's throat. But Erdrich departs from the prologue's account and presents an ironic coming-of-age story (Q 4).

Assuming the persona of the beast in this poem, Erdrich reveals the "man buried deep inside" the beast — in the process, we see how he changes from beast to man (Q 2). By telling this story from the beast's perspective, Erdrich can be more objective while providing unusual, refreshing, even ironic insights. For example, although the girl seems to be coming of age here, the beast himself undergoes a similar transition, changing from demon to lover, from beast to man. In addition, the speaker's point of view "humanizes" the beast. At the beginning of the poem, we see the beast as a one-dimensional creature ruled by uncontrollable urges, but as the poem progresses, he gradually assumes the character of a lover, someone who himself is caught up in the act of love, vanquished and tamed, almost, by the very thing he himself sought to vanquish. In line 14, for example, instead of laughing, he murmurs and licks the soles of the young woman's feet. Later, his fur "melts," and he notices his own body: "steam rolled from my wintry arms." At the end of the poem, the young woman herself seems to take over, and the beast passively notices her hands as they now grasp him ("ice and snow") and sees breathlessly that morning comes "at last."

Instead of retelling the myth, Erdrich revitalizes it by changing the focus of the story and therefore its major theme (Q 3, 5). The girl herself becomes the catalyst for the creature's transformation, and her passion becomes the "boiling lard" of the myth. Many students may miss the subtle sexual imagery of this poem. The word "Hackles," in line 6, for instance, describes a location while suggesting two important qualities: fright, a state of mind ("hackles" are erectile hairs at the back of an animal's neck); and male sexual arousal, a physical state ("hackles" are the colorful feathers found on a cock's neck). The phallic suggestiveness of line 11 ("The sumac pushed sour red cones through the air") combines with the shivering "naked" surroundings, and the obvious connotations of "spill" (1. 21), to convey the idea of passion without overtly limiting its significance.

FURTHER READING

Erdrich, Louise. *Baptism of Desire.* New York: Harper, 1991.

WILLIAM BUTLER YEATS

Leda and the Swan

WRITING ACTIVITIES

1. Have students research the myth of Leda and the swan and write a brief response explaining what happened as a result of this union.
2. Ask students to write about the significance of the poem's final question. How many questions are in this poem, and in what ways are they related?
3. For a longer writing assignment, have students read about Yeats's life and political involvement. In what way could this poem illustrate certain ideas and events from his own life in Ireland?

DISCUSSION

Ultimately, this poem is not so much about the act of rape as it is about the consequences of rape. Readers should not forget that, despite Zeus's "feathered glory," Yeats portrays a violent, crude, deceitful, sordid attack on someone. The term "feathered glory" is used because the god-swan is glorious — not because the act is glorious (Q 2). The fact that a god in the form of a swan commits this act makes it no less heinous, nor, for that matter, is it psychologically different from any other rape. There is, for example, no love involved. After sexual climax, Zeus drops Leda and is wholly indifferent toward her (Q 2). However, because a god and a mortal princess are involved, because immortal power and knowledge have been mingled with the mortal, the consequences are surely greater than Zeus's indifference suggests.

Yeats's allusion to the Trojan War in stanza 3 develops the theme of this poem because it is the one major event that results from the rape, and "knowledge" about this result is something only the gods have (Q 3). The offspring of this union were Helen and Pollux (Polyduces). Because Helen was so beautiful (and therefore tempting), all her suitors (almost all the young princes in Greece) swore a solemn oath to champion the cause of whichever of them would become her husband if any wrong were done to him through this marriage. Years later, when Helen and Paris ran off to Troy together, her husband Menelaus and many of his countrymen — all sworn to defend his marital honor — went off to destroy Troy. Thus began the Trojan War, the war in which Agamemnon was killed (Q 1).

Answering the three questions Yeats asks in this modified Shakespearean sonnet will help students grasp the poem's central message. The answers to the first two questions are clearly negative: Leda cannot escape Zeus's grip, nor can her body help but feel the "strange heart beating where it lies." That these answers are negative, however, does not imply that the third answer is also negative. In fact, Yeats leaves the question unanswered, and it may ultimately be unanswerable (Q 4). Clearly, Leda attains some level of power from this union, simply because she carries Zeus's child. But does she also gain Zeus's knowledge? That is, can she also foresee the significance of the rape? Does she attain both power and wisdom despite her mortality? These are some of the "opposites" that attracted Yeats to the myth of Leda (Q 5).

Let the students come to their own conclusions because critics themselves differ as to whether or not Leda attains some insight into the future. Ask them to consider these questions, though, when they try to decide: Do humans ever foresee the consequences of any — not just sexual — violent passions? Have not most political and social upheavals throughout history been triggered by violence? Have the protagonists ever understood the consequences of their acts? If gods do transfer some of their power to humans, where can we find instances of this? In art? Politics? If so, perhaps Zeus fathers more than just a child — perhaps Leda, in this moment, understands the consequences, loosens her thighs, and seizes immortality (Q 2).

FURTHER READING

Rosenthal, M. L. "Introduction." *Selected Poems and Three Plays of William Butler Yeats*. 3rd ed. New York: Collier, 1986.

Unterecker, John Eugene. *A Reader's Guide to William Butler Yeats*. New York: Octagon, 1983.

DEREK WALCOTT

Sea Grapes

WRITING ACTIVITIES

1. Have students write about the last line of the poem. Who do they think needs consolation and why?
2. Ask students to write about how Walcott's allusions to the *Odyssey* deepen this poem's meanings. Do these allusions hurt the poem in any way?

GROUP ACTIVITY

Have four groups of students each look up one allusion to the *Odyssey* and present reports on how Walcott uses each allusion in his poem.

DISCUSSION

The twin poles of this poem are passion and responsibility. They are the two forces that tug at Ulysses (Odysseus), and they are the two that tug also at the heart and mind of "the one on shore," the adulterer who must decide between his lover (passion), and his wife and family (responsibility).

Although the setting of "Sea Grapes" is Caribbean, the poem evokes Ulysses traveling through the Aegean Sea (Q 3). To understand the poem fully, the reader must know something of the *Odyssey*, which Walcott adapts for his own purposes. In the poem, Walcott refers to the Trojan War, which was fought essentially because of adultery. Troy was destroyed because Helen, an unfaithful wife, ran off with Paris. Menelaus (her wronged husband) and his countrymen laid siege to Troy because they were sworn to defend marital honor. As a result, Ulysses himself was forced to leave his family, join the army, and fight — all for the sake of a faithless woman. "The classic war" Walcott mentions, then, is not only the ancient struggle between "obsession and responsibility," but also the Trojan War itself (Q 1). The *Odyssey* is the story of Ulysses's voyage home from this war, during which he tarries with several women who bewitch him in one way or another. Walcott refers in particular to the episode where he lands, naked and exhausted, on the shores of Scheria. He takes shelter under an olive tree and covers himself with leaves. The sea grape is the Caribbean version of the olive tree and further connects the poem to Ulysses's story. Nausicca is the princess who inadvertently wakes Ulysses and who then leads him to the city, modestly directing him to enter on his own, so that citizens would not see them together and gossip. Once there, Ulysses meets her father, King Alcinous, who expresses an interest in having Ulysses marry his daughter; but this time, Ulysses resists temptation and remains determined to return to his wife and country.

Standing in his way for some time, however, has been Neptune, god of the sea. Ulysses explains why as he recounts the Cyclops episode to King Alcinous; Walcott refers to it in line 17. In one of their adventures en route home from Troy, Ulysses and his mariners must blind the Cyclops, who has been keeping them prisoner and devouring them, and then escape by boat. However, before they can sail out of range, the Cyclops throws a huge boulder at them, which misses and helps thrust them towards the island where they have left the other ships. The Cyclops then pleads to Neptune, his father, to bring hardship upon Ulysses and let him find trouble in his house. Needless to say, Neptune hears the Cyclops's request, and this is how, in lines 16–18, the giant's boulder creates the *Odyssey's* lines of dactylic hexameter. This incident brings new temptations and hardships to Ulysses, and he must endure Neptune's wrath before reaching home. Like ripples from a great boulder, these lines "finish up as Caribbean surf" because this classic war, Ulysses's war, the war between passion and responsibility, takes place in everyone's heart, as it is now taking place in the heart of this man on the shore of his island (Q 2).

Ultimately, the last line carries the weight of the poem's message and serves as a reminder: like Ulysses, we all may face making such a decision in our lives. If so, we must resolve the problem personally — the classics, although they may help to guide us, cannot make this decision less difficult than it is (Q 4).

A comparison with Tennyson's "Ulysses" should prove interesting.

W. H. AUDEN

Musée des Beaux Arts

WRITING ACTIVITIES

1. Ask students to write about the tone of this poem and how it reinforces the theme. Does this tone reveal a certain attitude in the speaker's voice?
2. What does Icarus's position in the painting (he is in the lower right-hand corner) imply?

GROUP ACTIVITY

Bring reproductions of the three paintings alluded to in the poem to class (see discussion below). Have three groups of students each take a painting and develop ideas about how their painting supports Auden's statement, "About suffering they were never wrong."

DISCUSSION

Understanding one basic difference between the "Old Masters" (superior artists and craftsmen of the sixteenth, seventeenth, and early eighteenth centuries) and earlier artists will help students grasp Auden's initial allusion: their view of nature was markedly different from the medieval (fifth to fifteenth centuries) conception. In their works, the Old Masters often portray nature as a splendid, indifferent presence, in the context of which human suffering — including Icarus's — seems normal and insignificant (Q 2).

The title of the poem refers to the Musée Royaux des Beaux-Arts, the museum in Brussels, Belgium, where *Landscape with the Fall of Icarus* hangs, but the generality of the title implies that the images could come from any museum containing similar paintings. In the poem, Auden points out details from three different paintings, all by Brueghel. Two of these paintings, *The Fall of Icarus* and *The Census in Bethlehem* (often referred to as *The Numbering at Bethlehem*), are hanging in the Brussels museum. The other painting, *The Massacre of the Innocents*, is in the Kunsthistorisches Museum in Vienna. These three paintings are the key to understanding this poem, and even though it can be understood without seeing the actual paintings, showing them to the students will help clarify their understanding of the Old Masters and the poem's theme.

In lines 5–8, Auden refers to *The Numbering at Bethlehem*, a painting that illustrates a passage from the Gospel according to St. Luke. Brueghel depicts the arrival of Joseph leading an ox and ass. His pregnant bride, Mary, riding the ass, is wrapped in a gray blanket and clutching a basket. Like Icarus, they too are tucked away in the lower part of the composition, and no one notices their arrival. Except for his saw (Joseph was a carpenter) the couple would be indistinguishable from the other minor figures in the painting. The focus of the painting is the tax collector, who has decided to collect his tithe. The townspeople surround his window and huddle against the cold. In the background sits the local inn, which we can see is full (which is why Joseph and Mary had to sleep in a barn). The Sun is setting, and children are skating and throwing snowballs on the frozen pond.

In lines 10–13, Auden refers to *The Massacre of the Innocents*, a painting that was probably a companion piece to *The Numbering at Bethlehem*. It depicts the slaughter of the first-born by Herod, and the soldiers, wearing the Hapsburg double-headed eagle, are slitting the children's throats. The villagers are pleading with a mounted herald, who can only shrug his shoulders and spread his hands in a helpless gesture.

The second stanza of this poem deals entirely with Brueghel's *Landscape with the Fall of Icarus*. The poet separates the discussion of this poem from the rest of the poem because it presents the definitive, most obvious example of the poem's message and Auden's inductive conclusion — that human suffering is ultimately insignificant to the majority of human beings. Auden alludes to three details in the picture: the plowman, Icarus's white legs (he has been reduced to two legs and a hand — not wing —jutting slightly above the surface of the water), and the merchant ships (Q 3). Both the plowman (the largest object in the picture) and the ships are turned away from Icarus, as are all of the other animals and people in the painting.

Other details are equally revealing. For example, students may notice that the Sun is setting — implying that Icarus must have fallen a tremendous distance and taken half a day to reach the ocean. Next to the plowman, a shepherd glances wistfully into the sky, but somehow has not seen Icarus falling. His dog, seated calmly next to his master, is also oblivious to the sight, and even the sheep — more than seventeen of them — are all turned away from the sight. In addition, a sailor and a fisherman are absorbed in their work and also fail to notice. If they look closely enough, students might even notice in the distance under some bushes what appears to be a man lying down or a skull that has been turned up by the plow, an idea supported by an old Flemish proverb to which Brueghel may have alluded — "the plow passes over corpses." Students may also notice a partridge perched directly beneath Icarus; this partridge is from Ovid's *Metamorphoses*, but instead of beating its wings in joy, it is looking at us — the only thing in the entire painting facing our direction (Q 3).

Auden's use of these events reinforces his theme: suffering, even on a grand, mythological scale, has its place in the world (Q 1). Monumental events occur as people, animals, all things perform their everyday business; even after Icarus falls, Jesus dies, and children bleed to death, the plow continues, life continues.

Indeed, Auden's tone supports this conclusion. He speaks matter of factly and avoids the notion (as the Old Masters themselves did) that suffering occupies a central position in our lives. He is concerned not with interpreting what suffering means but with revealing our relationship to it. The poem's irregular rhyme and line length also support this conclusion. The rhymes come unexpectedly (most students do not even notice the rhyme) and never settle into any easy, predictable pattern —just as suffering itself is unpredictable.

FURTHER READING

Classens, Bob. *Bruegel*. New York: Alpine, 1982.
Johnson, Richard. "W. H. Auden." *British Poets, 1914–1945*. Ed. Donald E. Stanford. *Dictionary of Literary Biography*. Vol. 20. Detroit: Gale, 1983. 19–51.

T. S. ELIOT

Journey of the Magi

WRITING ACTIVITIES

1. Ask students to write an essay in which they compare and contrast Eliot's poem with the narrative in Matthew 2: 1–18.

2. Have students write a letter home from one of the men traveling with the Magi. What would be his attitude toward the journey?

GROUP ACTIVITY

Break the class into two debating teams. Ask one team to argue that the poem is a statement of faith, the other to argue that it is skeptical.

DO YOUR STUDENTS KNOW . . .

The Christmas story includes the Star of Bethlehem, which helped lead men to Bethlehem where Jesus was born. This story included three kings, Caspar, Melchoir and Balthasar, who brought precious gifts of gold, frankincense, and myrrh to the child. In many countries, January 6 celebrates the kings' arrival and completes the Christmas season. Beginning in the third century, this feast was tied to baptism, the Christian rite through which one claims membership in a Christian faith and belief in Jesus Christ.

DISCUSSION

This is a challenging poem for students for a number of reasons. Those who are familiar with the story of the Magi may have seen idealized versions of it and so be surprised by such realistic details as "the camel men cursing and grumbling / And running away and wanting their liquor and women." They may also be surprised by the tone of the speaker. Whereas one might expect him to be overjoyed at having found Jesus, he seems unhappy and ill at ease (Q 1). This retelling of the biblical story adds many details about the journey, but it leaves out others, such as the meeting of the Magi with King Herod and their decision (Q 4).

To grasp the poem's meaning, students will have to be alert to subtle word choices and symbolism. They will have to see, for example, how the crucifixion, with its three crosses, is foreshadowed by "three trees on the low sky." They will have to recognize the enormous implications of the word "satisfactory." According to Christian doctrine, Jesus' eventual death on the cross was for the "satisfaction" of sins (Q 2).

The most challenging portion of the poem will likely be that from lines 35–43. Students may be puzzled about why the Magi experienced the birth of Jesus as "hard and bitter agony" and why the speaker concludes by saying, "I should be glad of another death." Again, some knowledge of Christian doctrine is necessary. Salvation only became possible after the death of Jesus on the cross, a death that would not occur until more than thirty years after the Magi visited the child. It is this death to which the speaker looks forward (Q 3). On returning home, the Magi are "no longer at ease" because they realize that they are living in a transitional period, one in which the old order of things is passing away while the new has not been fully realized.

You might consider teaching this poem with "Araby," "The World Is Too Much with Us," "On First Looking into Chapman's Homer," and "The Love Song of J. Alfred Prufrock." All the selections include moments of realization and discovery, and "The Love Song of J. Alfred Prufrock" is one of Eliot's most accessible poems.

FURTHER READING

Mason, David. "Rehabilitating Eliot." *Sewanee Review* 109 (Fall 2001): 628–35.
Paulin, Tom. "Many Cunning Passages." *Times Literary Supplement* (Nov. 2002): 14–16.

ELIZABETH HOLMES

The Fathers

WRITING ACTIVITIES

1. Have students write a poem based on a children's story other than Peter Pan.
2. Ask students to write a short essay in which they explain what is lost if the same actor does not play both Mr. Darling and Captain Hook.

GROUP ACTIVITY

Break the class into small groups and ask each group to draft a list of words — both positive and negative — that they associate with fathers.

DISCUSSION

In noting that the same actor who plays Mr. Darling typically plays Captain Hook, Holmes establishes a comparison that provides the framework for her poem. Children laugh at Hook because it is a relief for them to see someone who seemed both powerful and dangerous be hurt or embarrassed. There is an obvious connection to real life: since most parents do not outlive their children, there is a sense in which, from a child's point of view, each father is being chased by time and mortality.

You might consider teaching this poem with "Gretel in Darkness," "Cinderella," "Christopher Robin," and *Tender Offer*. The first three selections are based on well-known children's stories, and *Tender Offer* examines the reconciliation of a father and daughter.

CHAPTER 25

THE POETRY OF EMILY DICKINSON: A CASEBOOK FOR READING, RESEARCH, AND WRITING

USING THE CASEBOOK

In addition to twenty-five of Dickinson's poems, the casebook includes biographical and critical material, selections from Dickinson's letters, and a sample student paper. You could ask students to write a short research paper based exclusively on the materials in the casebook, or you could require that they find additional sources. Even if the sample paper does not entirely reflect the assignment you have in mind, it can still serve as an example of how to develop and support an argument. It will also give students a clear idea of how to integrate and cite sources using the MLA format.

Dickinson's work is examined in the casebook from several different perspectives. Allen Tate's essay on Dickinson, written at a time when she was not as firmly established in the literary canon as she is today, provides a good general introduction to the poet's work. In addition, it also presents an argument for Dickinson's greatness, something more recent writers may take for granted. It may be best to have students begin with Tate's piece before moving on to essays that are more narrowly focused. Because Tate minimizes the importance of biography to an understanding of the poetry, his essay may also serve as a springboard for discussion of different critical schools.

Given her position as one of the most influential women writers in American literature, Dickinson's life and work are natural subjects for feminist criticism. "Emily Dickinson's Feminist Humor" by Juhasz, Miller, and Smith examines the subversive uses to which Dickinson puts humor. This source will be helpful for students who might miss the humor in the poetry. It might also be used as the starting point of a discussion on satire and political humor.

Two of the essays focus exclusively on Dickinson's distinctive use of language. Judy Jo Small's selection from *Positive as Sound* concentrates on the ways in which the poet uses aural imagery. Small sees this imagery as related to Dickinson's sense of herself as a singer or musician. E. Miller Budick's essay concentrates on what the critic calls the "wild animation and vital energy" of the language in Dickinson's poetry. Each of the two pieces provides examples of the type of close reading you will want students to do.

READING AND REACTING

1. What is Dickinson's attitude toward solitude? Is it something she seeks or avoids? Look primarily at her poetry in trying to answer this question, but feel free to refer to her letters as well.

2. Dickinson makes frequent references to God in her poetry, and she uses other religious terminology as well. Based exclusively on the poetry, how would you characterize her religious beliefs?

3. What do you think are the most striking aspects of Dickinson's technique? Some of these will be immediately obvious when you see the poems on the page. In other cases, however, you may need to read the poems out loud in order to fully appreciate what the poet is doing.

WRITING ACTIVITIES

1. Write a letter form the head of a British University inviting Emily Dickinson to do a reading. Your letter must convince this reclusive poet that such a long journey and such a public appearance will be to her advantage. It should also demonstrate that the person writing the letter has read Dickinson's poetry and is capable of identifying its most important themes.

2. Imagine that you are writing the introduction to a volume of Dickinson's poetry intended for high school students. Which aspects of the poet's work would you stress? What about the poetry would appeal most to your audience? What would need the most explanation?

GROUP ACTIVITY

Select several poems that illustrate the distinctive qualities of Dickinson's verse technique. Divide the class into small groups and assign one poem to each group. Then, assign one student in each group to read the poem out loud. Before the reading, however, allow the student ten minutes to practice the reading and to receive feedback from the other members of the group. After the student from each group has read the assigned poem, ask the class as a whole for feedback and suggestions.

DISCUSSION

Dickinson's poetry is distinctive — too distinctive apparently for her first editors, who regularized her punctuation and eliminated her famous dashes. Even as late as 1968, Yvor Winters and Kenneth Fields took this approach when editing Dickinson's work for their anthology, *Quest for Reality* (Q 2). Since Dickinson's punctuation (or lack thereof) and her use of dashes are the first things that will strike most readers, it is worth taking time to discuss these elements with students. The Group Activity includes suggestions about how to address this issue (Q 1 in Reading and Reacting). The dashes force the reader to linger on each unit of sense and then pause before going on, but the capitalized words are given more prominence and an added sense of importance (Q 6).

A less obvious but equally important aspect of Dickinson's style is her use of rhyme. Although there are many cases where she uses full rhymes, an unusually high percentage of her rhymes are slant or even fainter, what some might call, "ghost rhymes". You might take a poem where the majority of the rhymes are not full — "Heaven is what I cannot reach," for instance — and ask students to identify the rhyme scheme. Although most or all will recognize the tree / me rhyme in the first stanza, many will (quite understandably) fail to recognize land / found or decoy / yesterday as rhymes. Rhymes in other poems are even fainter. Having students read some of the poems out loud in class will help them gain a better sense of the subtle music of Dickinson's verse (Q 1 in Reading and Reacting).

Religious and philosophical issues are central in Dickinson's work, as evidenced by the many references to "God," "Paradise," "Heaven," "Resurrection," and "Eternity." Although these references are easily spotted, it is not always so easy to decipher them. One of the chief obstacles to an accurate reading is the fact that students may have very strong ideas about what each term means. You might begin a discussion of Dickinson's religious references by working with the class to define each term in the context of the poems themselves. It is important for students to keep in mind that Dickinson's poems are not theological tracts and that the poet is under no obligation to remain consistent throughout her body of work (Q 2 in Reading and Reacting).

In "'Faith' is a Fine Invention," Dickinson is openly skeptical about the efficacy of "Faith," as indicated in the first line by her use of quotation marks around the term. Familiar as she was with the Bible, she would undoubtedly have known that Paul defined faith as "the evidence of things unseen." To argue that faith only works "[w]hen Gentlemen can *see*," is to reject Paul's definition. Also, to call faith an "invention" is to raise the possibility that it is something invented by humans, opposed to a gift given by God.

Despite such skepticism, it is clear that Dickinson had a religious sense of life. "Some Keep the Sabbath Going to Church" demonstrates how the poet's views differed from those of some of her more conventional contemporaries. There is some similarity of viewpoint between this poem and "I Taste a Liquor Never Brewed —."Although the speaker is a person in the first poem and a bird here, both view the transition from Earth to heaven as an ongoing process rather than a sudden transition. Although the bird is literally "going to heaven" each time it takes to the air and although it would be inappropriate for it to actually go to church, Dickinson intends the bird's statement to be applicable to human life as well. Put simply, the poem's message is that it is better to find God through nature than in the confines of a church.

Closely connected with Dickinson's religious beliefs is her preoccupation — some might say obsession — with death. Of the twenty-five poems in the casebook, almost half make some reference, either direct or indirect, to death (Q 5). "I Heard a Fly Buzz — When I Died —" is one of Dickinson's best and best-known poems, and it may appeal to students because it is a short narrative. Note that the most important things in the poem are left unsaid. We know from the first line that the speaker is dead and that the rest of the poem concerns the moment before she died. Strangely, though, there is no attempt to describe life after death.

Nor do we have any clear sense whom the speaker is addressing. What we do know is that the speaker places a great deal of importance on the moment of her death. What initially appears a straightforward poem in fact has great depths. It is important for students to consider who "the King" is in stanza 2. This is one of the terms frequently applied to Christ, but here it more probably refers to death. Note, too, that just when death is expected, the fly appears. It is quite likely that the fly is in some sense death and has some connection to Beelzebub, the "Lord of the Flies."

There are two drafts of "Safe in their Alabaster Chambers" included in the casebook. These two versions of the same poem offer an excellent chance not only to deal with Dickinson's feelings about death but also to discuss her stylistic development and attitude toward revision. The most obvious differences are formal: the poet has tried to regularize the form by condensing it to two stanzas of five lines each and by adding many more of he characteristic dashes. There are also telling differences in content. Although the first five lines of the two drafts are nearly identical, "the meek members of the Resurrection" "[s]leep" appears in the earlier draft and "[l]ie" appears in the later. The first choice indicates a speaker who is more confident that the dead will eventually awake. This sense of diminished hope becomes even stronger when one compares the second half of the poem, which Dickinson completely rewrote. Whereas the first draft concludes with the line, "Ah, what sagacity perished here!" the second makes no mention of the dead being particularly wise or noteworthy.

Isolation is another important issue, both in terms of Dickinson's work and her biography. In some poems, she seems to present her withdrawal from the larger society as something liberating. In other places, a tragic note is struck, and one has the sense that there was a part of the poet that longed for closer relationships with others. Readers can approach this issue from a number of angles, of course, and it is perfectly valid to introduce biographical information into a discussion of this or any of the other themes in Dickinson's poetry. There are some serious disadvantages, however, to placing too much emphasis on this aspect at first, one of the chief being that students may try to use biographical data to interpret any passages with which they have difficulty. In that case, they will not be reading as closely as they should. It may be best to see what conclusions the students draw about the speaker (or speakers) of individual poems before introducing information about the poet's life (Q 3 in Reading and Reacting).

"The Soul Selects Her Own Society" is one of the poems that addresses Dickinson's dual needs for solitude and companionship. This poem is essentially about friendship and love, whether romantic and otherwise. The soul is pictured as a noblewoman deciding who will be admitted to her company. It is significant that it is the soul, and not the heart or mind, that makes the decision. This implies that the other person or persons who are admitted are allowed into the innermost part of the speaker's being. It is clear from the second stanza that position and rank have no impact on the soul's choice. Although much of the poem might be read as a touching tale of how one finds one's "soul mate," the ending is somewhat unsettling. "Like stone" almost implies the closing of a tomb, thus the decision of the soul to cut herself off entirely from the rest of the world (Q 10).

"This Is My Letter to the World" is another short, relatively direct poem that expresses two of Dickinson's most cherished themes: separation from society and love of nature. If there is any difficulty for students, it is in distinguishing between "the World" and "Nature," and in the punctuation of the second paragraph. In this case, "the World" is used, as it often is in the New Testament, to refer to society, whereas "Nature" refers to the physical universe itself. In the last two lines, it is not entirely clear whether "Sweet" refers to "Her" or to "countrymen." It is more likely that the speaker is referring to nature, but the ambiguity remains, and it may be intended to convey the speaker's affection for the society despite its disregard. Many of Dickinson's poems, perhaps all of them, are communications with the world from which she was withdrawn. That world is not monolithic, however, and it is often addressed in very different terms from poem to poem (Q 7).

Finally, it is important to note the many poems that deal in one way or another with the imagination and art. "The Brain — Is Wider Than the Sky —" is a good example of such a poem, although there is a chance that students may find the image of a brain absorbing the sea comical. Ask students how the various statements the speaker makes about the brain might be literally true. If necessary, point out that although the brain can contain the thought of anything that exists in the sea, the sea cannot contain everything of which the brain might think. The first and last stanzas are relatively easy to parse, but students may have difficulty with the third, which introduces challenging theological ideas about the connection between and possible identity of the brain and God. One of the most remarkable things about the poem is how much Dickinson is able to covey with simple, ordinary language. "Syllable," a very plain word, is the only word in the poem that has more than two syllables, and it is not introduced until the last line (Q 8).

FURTHER READING

Diehl, Joanne Feit. "Selfish Desires: Dickinson's Poetic Ego and the Rites of Subjectivity." *Women's Studies* 31 (Jan./Feb. 2002): 33–53.

Lachman, Lilach. "Suspense Is His Maturer Sister." *Gothic Studies* 3 (Apr. 2001): 61–75.

McNair, Wesley. "Discovering Emily Dickinson." *Sewanee Review* 108 (Winter 2000): 117–24.

Mitchell, Domhnall. "The Grammar of Ornament: Emily Dickinson's Manuscripts and Their Meanings." *Nineteenth-Century Literature* 55 (Mar. 2001): 479–515.

Vendler, Helen. "Emily Dickinson Thinking." *Parnassus: Poetry in Review* 26. 1. (2002): 34–57.

CHAPTER 26

THE POETRY OF LANGSTON HUGHES: A CASEBOOK FOR READING, RESEARCH, AND WRITING

USING THE CASEBOOK

The most obvious use for the casebook is as a resource for students learning to write research papers. Students have available not only a representative sample of poems and essays by one writer, but also critical essays about that writer, plus a sample research paper. You might assign a short research paper on Langston Hughes, like the sample paper in the casebook, for which the students could rely on the materials in this casebook alone, as a kind of practice for a longer paper requiring more research about Hughes or another author. Students could each select one poem, for example, and explicate it, relying on their own ideas, supplemented by quotations from several of the professional writers. Or students could select two or three poems, such as "The Weary Blues," "Dream Boogie," or "Ballad of the Landlord" and compare the use of music to convey social commentary. In so doing, students might incorporate into their papers ideas from Hughes's essays about the social function of poetry, as well as the ideas of one or more critics.

The casebook also provides background on Hughes's life. Besides the biographical introduction, the casebook presents additional biographical information on Hughes in his own essays, in Rampersad's, and occasionally, in other essays.

Fourteen poems by Hughes are part of the casebook. The publication dates of these poems range from 1925 to 1967, a period of enormous social change. You might use these poems to demonstrate how Hughes's poetic subjects change over time, although he remains committed to his belief in himself as a "social poet," one who works for social change through his art. Despite changes that have occurred, racial, social, and economic injustices continue to exist, and Hughes continues to address them. Studying Hughes's poems within historical contexts could make the poems more meaningful to students. Several Web sites and most encyclopedias provide information about African-American and civil rights history, should you wish to supplement the casebook with such material. The video *Eyes on the Prize* is an excellent resource for a longer examination of the civil rights movement. Comparisons between Hughes's poems from different periods might sharpen critical and historical awareness.

You can also use the casebook to help students see the range of critical responses to literature, from Rampersad's biographical approach to Tracy's genre criticism. Beavers refers to both Rampersad and Tracy as he examines the sounds of Hughes's work, and Ford cites many other writers. Students may learn from them as well as from the student essay how to quote and paraphrase appropriately from sources. Hutchinson's essay can help students see how other writers' works, in addition to life experiences, may influence an author. You may also want to select two or three passages from the critical essays and encourage students to disagree with the writers, using evidence from Hughes's poetry and prose selections to support their own interpretations. This would help them recognize their right to develop their own insights, even if these differ from published ones.

READING AND REACTING

1. Langston Hughes calls himself a "Negro poet," insisting that to say only "I am a poet" implies a rejection of his blackness. He adds that most of his poems are "racial in theme and treatment, derived from the life I know." Which of his poems best fit this description? Are there any that do not? If so, why not?
2. Does Hughes's insistence on identifying his voice as black imply an intention to exclude nonblack readers? Who do you think his audience is? Look at his essays as well as his poems for answers.
3. As a "social poet," Hughes is dedicated to social change. What kinds of changes does he most hope to see? What kind of world would be his ideal? Give examples from his poems and essays to support your views.

WRITING ACTIVITIES

1. Choose one of Hughes's social poems and write a letter to a present-day newspaper editor on the topic of that poem. For example, African-Americans no longer eat in the kitchen (as in "I, Too"), but do they sit at the same tables as whites — or Asians — or Native Americans? Think about the college dining hall or local pizza place. What has changed? Other situations to consider appear in "Ballad of the Landlord," "Harlem," and "Birmingham Sunday."
2. Imagine that you are a poet who disagrees in some way with Hughes's ideas about the role of the poet as expressed in his essays. Write a response, one to three pages long, outlining your own views about the poet's role in the world.

GROUP ACTIVITY

Give the class a description of the traditional ballad form: a narrative poem, often based on a well-known story, usually told simply, using dialogue and direct descriptions of action. Like epics, ballads often jump right into the action, assuming the listener-reader knows what happened before or can figure it out. Ballads may begin by introducing a central character, who will participate in the telling of the story. Ballads make use of repetition, refrains, stock descriptive phrases or metaphors (blood-red lips; blood-red wine; night-dark hair), and sometimes inverted sentence structure (And slowly, slowly, raise she up). Often, they are in the four-line ballad stanza, with alternating lines of four feet and three feet, rhyming *abcb*. Common themes in ballads include betrayal, especially by lovers or comrades; political or social oppression; murder(s), particularly gruesome or shocking ones; and mysterious or inexplicable events.

Divide the class into groups and give each group a copy of a ballad. (You can use "The Ballad of Rudolph Reed," "Ballad of Birmingham," or "Bonny Barbara Allan.") Ask them to compare the ballad you have given them with "Ballad of the Landlord," noting not only how each follows the traditional form, but also how each departs from it. Have each group share its observations with the class. If you have time and your students enjoy creative activities, you may want to ask each group to write a ballad on a recent local or world event that seems appropriate for the ballad.

DISCUSSION

This section responds to most of the Reading and Reacting questions in this chapter of the text as well as to the questions raised in this manual.

When he calls himself a "Negro poet," Hughes is expressing pride in his heritage and acknowledging the importance of his own experiences in forming both his personal and his literary identity. He discusses why he insists on this designation in "The Negro Artist and the Racial Mountain." But he also acknowledges, especially in "My Adventures as a Social Poet," that his experiences are sometimes shared by people of other racial groups (Q 1 in Reading and Reacting). In fact, the personae in his poems vary considerably. In "I, Too," the speaker is a black servant (students sometimes think he is a slave, despite the poem's 1925 date) who believes in his right to greater respect from and equality with whites and has confidence in a future that ensures both. In "Ballad of the Landlord," the first speaker is a black tenant demanding repairs to his home before he will pay his rent — but the narration shifts to the voice of the landlord, then to a disembodied voice, and finally to newspaper headlines in which the original speaker is identified first as a man, then as a tenant, and finally as a Negro (Q 9).

In "The Negro Speaks of Rivers," the persona is larger than life, a mythic Negro who speaks for all blacks (across historical and geographic boundaries) of the profundity of their shared experience (Q 1). In "Theme for English B," the speaker is a specific college student, "twenty-two, colored, born in Winston-Salem [. . .] the only colored student" in his class at City College in New York, "on the hill above Harlem." While the mythic speaker links rivers with bloodlines and emphasizes almost transcendentally the shared black experiences in Asia, Africa, and North America, he also alludes to the empathy of a white man — Lincoln. The college student speaks much more personally to his white instructor, suggesting that they are irrevocably linked by their relationship at the college, in his paper, and as Americans. They have become part of one another's experience and have been changed by one another, learning from one another — whether either of them wishes it or not. Neither of these speakers is precisely Hughes, born in Missouri in 1902; yet both share with him aspects of the black experience, and both acknowledge at least the possibility of positive interaction with whites, despite very clear differences in their lives (Q 4).

In other poems, perhaps in "Island," the persona is more ambiguous. Hughes echoes Walt Whitman in becoming all Americans — black, red, Old World immigrant. In "Park Bench," Hughes focuses on the largest gap, in his time or ours, in American society: that between the homeless and the very rich. In "Harlem" and in "Dream Boogie," the voice is again more clearly black (Q 1 in Reading and Reacting).

Hughes is careful to acknowledge his influences, both poetic and political. In "Old Walt," he talks directly about his predecessor, Walt Whitman. Here, the emphasis is on Whitman's "seeking and finding," by which Hughes means Whitman's search for the ideal America. In "Ballad of Booker T.," Hughes honors the memory of Booker T. Washington (1856–1915), a prominent African-American educator. The poem praises Washington for what he was able to accomplish, given the racial situation during his lifetime, while lamenting the fact that circumstances prevented him from forming a bolder vision.

Not only do Hughes's personae shift, but his audience seems to do so as well (Q 2 in Reading and Reacting). His comments in "To Negro Writers" (1935) make clear that he is, in general, addressing both "Negro masses" and "white masses," for different reasons. He calls upon other black writers to "reveal to the Negro masses . . . our potential power to transform the now ugly face of the Southland into a region of peace and plenty." He also writes to encourage black pride, to encourage blacks to begin to think "Why should I want to be white? I am a Negro — and Beautiful." (See "The Negro Artist and the Racial Mountain.") The poem "Negro" is clearly a poem designed to encourage such thinking, as are "The Negro Speaks of Rivers" and "I, Too." These poems also "reveal to the white masses those Negro qualities which go beyond the mere ability to laugh and sing and dance and make music, and which are a part of the useful heritage that we place at the disposal of a future free America." He also urges his peers, in "To Negro Writers," to help "unite blacks and whites" as part of a "working-class struggle to wipe out . . . inequalities." This is clearly his goal in such poems as "Ballad of the Landlord" and perhaps even "Harlem." These aesthetically effective poems of social protest use the power of art — the ballad form, image, musicality, metaphor, repetition (Q 3) — to make readers aware of injustice (Q 10). Perhaps some readers will merely appreciate the artistry, but Hughes clearly hopes to inspire them to join with other people who are appalled by social conditions to "help . . . change come."

At times, Hughes examines his own role in the political life of America. In "Un-American Investigators" he rails against the House Committee on Un-American Activities, The speaker of "Dinner Guest: Me" is a prominent African-American (perhaps Hughes himself) who is being consulted by well-intentioned and well-heeled whites on the racial situation in America. The poem is shot through with irony: because the speaker is able to express the situation of his people, he is elevated above the rest of them. And even though the whites consult him, little is done about the "problem" of which he is a representative.

Hughes's ideal world would be a just, egalitarian one, a world in which racial differences would result in individuals enriching rather than belittling one another

("Theme for English B") (Q 3 in Reading and Reacting), Riches would probably be redistributed ("To Negro Writers"), violence would have ended, and people would treat one another with respect. Even the deeply ironic "Birmingham Sunday" holds out hope for the day Christians will "implement the Golden Rule," something the missionaries in China and the church bombers in Birmingham did not do. Hughes subtly but irrevocably links these two groups and two cultures through references to dynamite, "Red" politics and red blood, and Christian Sunday schools in China and Birmingham. Allowing readers to gradually recognize the connections, Hughes delivers a more powerful message than if he had made a direct statement linking bombers of children to Christian missionaries — a comparison to which many readers might object (Q 7).

Sometimes Hughes delivers his messages musically, as in "The Weary Blues" and "Dream Boogie" (Q 2). Steven Tracy discusses Hughes's use of boogie, and Hughes himself writes about jazz as an "inherent expression of Negro life in America — the eternal tom-tom beating in the Negro soul — the tom-tom of revolt against weariness in a white world. . . ." ("The Negro Artist and the Racial Mountain") "Ballad of the Landlord" combines elements of the ballad form with the rhythm of the street rhyme or jump-rope chant, an effective merging of two folk traditions to tell the story of social and racial inequality and injustice on the streets of America. The poem begins abruptly, in the manner of ballads, with the tenant directly addressing the landlord. Using the ballad stanza (abcb), but in shorter lines and a less even meter than in a traditional ballad, the tenant conveys a sense of urgency and outrage as he chants his complaints. Finally, in a single italicized stanza, the landlord calls upon the police, after which the rhyme scheme and meter shift as the ballad turns into a staccato report on the action, and then a series of newspaper headlines. The frantic nature of life on the edges of society comes alive in the rhythms of this poem.

Hughes alludes to music and singing in nearly all of his poems (Q 2). In "Lenox Avenue: Midnight," Hughes says that "[t]he rhythm of life / Is a jazz rhythm." "Genius Child" not only alludes to music but is itself insistently songlike. In "The Negro Speaks of Rivers," the speaker refers to "the singing of the Mississippi when Abe Lincoln went / down to New Orleans." Here the singing river suggests metaphorically the slaves' songs; Lincoln was said to have become determined to end slavery during his trip down the Mississippi. In "I, Too" the speaker, like Walt Whitman, "sings" America — but a darker, less democratic America in need of change for the darker-skinned singer.

Comparing Hughes's poems with those of other minority writers who hope for social change (e.g., Brooks, Erdrich, Welch, or Valdes) might be a fitting end to a discussion of a poet who calls himself a "social poet," particularly as these writers continue to address issues Hughes raised many years ago.

FURTHER READING

Berry, Faith. *Langston Hughes, Before and Beyond Harlem, A Biography of Langston Hughes*. New York: Wings, 1996. 112–32.

Bloom, Harold, ed. *Langston Hughes*. Modern Critical Views. New York: Chelsea, 1988.

Miller, R. Baxter. "Langston Hughes." *Afro-American Writers from the Harlem Renaissance to 1940*. Ed. Trudier Harris. *Dictionary of Literary Biography*. Vol. 51. Detroit: Gale, 1987.

———. "Langston Hughes." *American Poets, 1880–1945, Second Series*. Ed. Peter Quartermain. *Dictionary of Literary Biography*. Vol. 48. Detroit: Gale, 1986. 218–35.

CHAPTER 27

POETRY FOR FURTHER READING

SHERMAN ALEXIE

Defending Walt Whitman

The word *defending* offers two interpretations: (1) speaking up for an appreciation of Whitman (with the innuendo of his supposed homosexuality); (2) making basketball moves on the defense. This wildly imaginative free-verse poem offers wonderful comparisons with Whitman's "Song of Myself"—for example, the strong appeal to visually detailed images, the fast-paced rhythm, the celebration of the body, and the inclusion of all groups within American culture. Here, Alexie focuses on beardless Native Americans who react strongly to Whitman's beard. You might compare Alexie's poem with Soto's "Black Hair," which celebrates how brilliantly the Mexican-Americans play baseball and uses similar images of brown skin and black hair.

MAYA ANGELOU

Africa

DO YOUR STUDENTS KNOW . . .

Africa was still nominally colonized by European powers well into the nineteenth century. In 1884, the Berlin West Africa Conference was held—fourteen white European nations decided how to control black Africa. At that time, 80 percent of the continent was under local or tribal control. Since only the coasts were colonized, the interior of the continent and all its resources was up for grabs. Having little to no regard for ethnic or tribal affiliations causing turmoil within the African countries, the European ambassadors carved up these areas.

By describing the topography of Africa in terms of a woman's sensuous body — the hair, feet, breasts, tears — Angelou humanizes the abstract concept of the rape of a continent through centuries of slavery and colonization. The obvious contrast with Wheatley's poem is that Angelou, having the historical perspective of slavery's horrors, is much more bitter than Wheatley, who perhaps felt an obligation to her white master to justify slavery as an institution that brings Christianity to the heathens. Compare how Langston Hughes's "Negro" depicts Africa as a homeland.

ANONYMOUS

Bonny Barbara Allan

Sir John Graeme dies after ignoring Barbara Allan when making a toast ("health" in 1.9) at the tavern. Some readers believe witchcraft kills him; others suggest Barbara Allan rejects him over the thoughtless toast and he pines away. Students might be interested in hearing someone sing this Scottish ballad and in learning more about the way narrative poetry evolved from the oral ballad tradition. The other ballads in the text will offer interesting comparisons.

ANONYMOUS

Western Wind

This haunting lyric reaffirms the oral tradition of singing about nature's elements to express human emotions. The reader can compare this short lyric with Shelley's famous "Ode to the West Wind" with its promise of springtime ("If Winter comes, can Spring be far behind?"). By addressing the western wind, the speaker begs for the sweet spring showers that also bring the promise and anticipation of love.

MATTHEW ARNOLD

Dover Beach

DO YOUR STUDENTS KNOW . . .

The white cliffs of Dover have been immortalized in literature, in song, and by Hollywood. The cliffs, from which France can be seen on a clear day, have been the site of fortifications since the Iron Age. These nearly 300-foot high cliffs of chalk were nicknamed "Hellfire Corner" during World War II for the heavy attack they underwent from the German air force and long-range guns in France.

The opening scene is peaceful and appealing, but in line 7 the mood begins to change. As the speaker observes the English Channel (a branch of the North Sea), he hears "the eternal note of sadness," which he recognizes as the "ebb and flow of human misery" that the Greek tragedian Sophocles heard on the Aegean. Human misery, mortality, battles, and the sea's ebb and flow remain constant in a world of change. The sea imagery merges into the central metaphor, the "Sea of Faith," which the speaker fears is ebbing in this era of confusion. Discoveries by Darwin and others had led to conflicts between science and religion. The speaker suggests that the joys and beauties we perceive are illusions, and he leaves the reader with these questions: Is this poem hopeful or hopeless? If the sea of faith ebbs, will it flow again? Can love help us face confusion and doubt? Is misery an inevitable part of life, like mortality? You might want to use Anthony Hecht's much-anthologized parody, "The Dover Bitch."

JOHN ASHBERY

Myrtle

DO YOUR STUDENTS KNOW . . .

The name Myrtle has Greek origins and may have come into use from the myrtle tree. This small evergreen tree or bush, growing primarily in southern Europe and Greece, has white flowers, a distinct smell, and is known since ancient times for its medicinal uses.

This is a poem to teach toward the end of the semester once students have gained confidence in their abilities as readers. In a sense, Ashbery's poems are well suited to analysis precisely because they resist it so successfully. It is not that the language itself is difficult; on the contrary, it is colloquial and unforced, and students may find the voice appealing. The difficulty arises when one attempts a paraphrase of certain key points. What does the speaker mean, for example, by saying, "How funny your name would be / if you could follow it back to where / the first person thought of saying it"? Is he referring to the name of anyone reading the poem or to someone named Myrtle? And why, in either case, would the name be funny? Would it be comical or merely strange? The metaphor of the river and the assertion that "[r]ivers have no source" might suggest that searching for the origin of language or even of a particular word is an attempt doomed to failure. There are other questions: What does the image of the girlfriend on stage mean? Are we to assume that the sharing of a name by two things has the power to change them?

ELIZABETH ALEXANDER

Apollo

DO YOUR STUDENTS KNOW . . .

An estimated 1 million people jammed on the Florida coast to watch the departure of the Saturn 5 rocket that helped launch *Apollo* to the Moon. When the lunar landing module of *Apollo*, the Eagle, was about to hit boulders and a crater on the Moon's surface, astronaut Buzz Aldrin calmly looked for a clearer landing site and touched down in the aptly named Sea of Tranquility. When he landed, he only had a few minutes of landing fuel left.

This poem achieves its effect by not revealing the fact that the speaker and her family are black until almost the end of the poem. Consider asking the students why the poet waits so long, since race is obviously one of the poem's central concerns. At least one reason may be that as readers we see the family accepted as part of the road shack's temporary community before we have any reason to suspect that they might not ordinarily be. The poem's conclusion is double-edged: on the one hand, it is good that the *Apollo* landing has brought people of different races together; on the other hand, it is tragic that an event of this magnitude was needed to make people look past issues of race.

MARGARET ATWOOD

This Is a Photograph of Me

Like "You Fit into Me" and many of Atwood's other poems, this one begins with a matter-of-fact statement in a calm, ordinary tone, offering images we think we already know: the lovers fitting one another, the blurred photo of a country scene. But then suddenly, the reader is shocked by an intensely personal and painful twist: the fishhook in one's eye, the knowledge that the speaker has drowned. As in reading Kafka, we are not sure whether to gasp, laugh, or grimace. The mocking tone forces the reader to feel fooled. But who or what is mocked here — the reader's ready acceptance of the conventional? The idea of photography as an art or a version of reality? The nature of reality itself? Our conceptions of death? The ambiguity fascinates and frustrates many readers. Others may decide the poem is about the ambiguous state of adolescence. Note the images in lines 1–14: blurred photo, tree branch emerging, small frame house, something that *ought* to be a gentle slope, lake, low hills — the emerging scene suggesting the emerging self, growing painfully from child into adult. The evasions in lines 15–26 then suggest the confusion of adolescence, rather than the actual death of the speaker. Note especially the speaker's uncertainty about "where precisely" or "how large or small" she or he is.

ROBIN BEHN

Whether or Not There Are Apples

In this poem, the dress the speaker takes off the line is a reminder of a dead loved one, perhaps her mother. The dress still retains the scent of the dead woman, and when it is just off the line it is warm as well, and so seems to radiate body heat. The dead woman smelled like apples, and so there is the scent of apples on the dress even when they are out of season. The dress has been a source of comfort for the speaker for years, but now she is getting old enough to begin thinking about her own death.

ELIZABETH BISHOP

The Fish

This poem provides an example of detailed description and the uses to which it can be put. Toward the end of the poem, Bishop openly declares her feeling of "victory," but she has really been preparing us for this declaration all along. Through her detailed description of the fish, she makes us see it as something both precious and powerful. We therefore understand the speaker's excitement better and admire her compassion all the more. The descriptive language of the poem is expertly handled — "irises backed and packed / with tarnished tinfoil" is a particularly striking example — and the short, loosely metered lines provide an example of the flexibility a good poet can achieve working in the gray area between metrical and free verse.

WILLIAM BLAKE

The Chimney Sweeper

Blake's ironic contrast between the relentless cheerfulness of the child narrator and the misery of his life makes readers angry at a society in which impoverished parents sell into apprenticeship children small enough to creep into coffinlike chimneys. Like lambs, they are shorn and sacrificed to adult avarice. Only in dreams are the boys set free by an angel to play in a sunny, Edenic world. They awake to darkness and cold, warmed by promises of a heavenly father who will bring them joy if they are good — but apparently only after they die. The boys may believe the last line, but Blake and the reader do not, in this chilling selection from *Songs of Innocence*.

WILLIAM BLAKE

The Lamb

The child speaker (like the one in "The Chimney Sweeper") uses repetition, simple words, and simple sentence patterns. He addresses the lamb directly, asking childlike questions (Who made thee?) and answering them, like a child pretending to be a teacher. Despite the warm, safe, sunny world of stream and meadow, the potential sacrifice of the unwary innocent is suggested in the explicit identification of the lamb and child with Christ: "he calls himself a Lamb" and "He became a little child."

In a more sophisticated voice and more complex language than the previous Blake poems, the following three selections from *Songs of Experience* portray a darker world.

WILLIAM BLAKE

London

The city is a place of moral and mental weakness, illness and misery. Men and infants cry, and their minds, like the streets and river, are narrow and manacled. No green, sunny fields or streams (the real or dream settings in *Songs of Innocence*) greet city dwellers. The churches are not uplifting, nor are soldiers courageous, as the oxymorons make clear. Sexual immorality leads to sexually transmitted diseases, such as syphilis, which infect infants and spouses, in effect linking marriage to death.

WILLIAM BLAKE

To see a World in a Grain of Sand

Students may initially feel that there is not enough material in this quatrain to discuss. For that very reason, however, the poem is an ideal text for a close reading. You might look, for example, at why Blake writes "a Heaven" as opposed to simply "Heaven." What difference does the indefinite article make? Look, too, at the statements in the last two lines. How are these two statements similar?

WILLIAM BLAKE

The Tyger

If the voice in "The Lamb" is childlike, this voice is clearly adult. Students will notice the complex language and intricate sentence structure. Reading the two poems aloud, then asking how each makes listeners feel, generates good discussion. The contrast between feeling calm, cozy and safe, and feeling fear or awe leads to discussions of setting and word choice. In answering the poem's central question, some readers will say God made the lamb while the devil (fire, anvil, dread) made the tiger. Others see the Old Testament God of Justice (or Anger) and the New Testament God of Mercy (or Love). Some say an omnipotent God could certainly create both lamb and tiger.

EAVAN BOLAND

The Emigrant Irish

DO YOUR STUDENTS KNOW . . .

Irish immigration to America existed since the colonial era but peaked during the ten years (1845–1855) of the Great Famine in Ireland. Desperate to leave starvation and poverty, the Irish secured passage on ships bound for America and

Canada. These ships came to be known as "coffin ships" due to the great numbers of Irish who died on board or shortly after arrival in the new land. Mortality rates of twenty to forty percent aboard the "coffin ships" was common, with 17,465 documented shipboard deaths in 1847 alone.

The speaker looks to the Irish who emigrated to the United States and Canada as an example of admirable qualities: "Patience. Fortitude. Long-suffering. . . ." The contemporary Irish, she maintains, need these qualities, need to learn from those who left to make a life in "the New World." The poem, then, is a plea to the people of modern Ireland to derive power from those in the past who were, paradoxically, the least powerful. Some people try to disown the past, while others hold to it uncritically. This poem argues for an approach that makes use of what is valuable yet overlooked in history.

ANNE BRADSTREET

The Author to Her Book

The speaker, Bradstreet herself, addresses her book of poems. Her sister's husband took her manuscript volume and had it published (*The Tenth Muse Lately Sprung Up in America * * * By a Gentlewoman of Those Parts*) in London in 1650 without her permission. Since she did not have the opportunity to correct her work for this initial unauthorized publication, she recounts here her attempts to correct the deficiencies in her "child," her creative work. She revised her poems around 1666, and they were published posthumously in 1678. While the tone is playful, the anguish suffered is genuine.

GWENDOLYN BROOKS

The Ballad of Rudolph Reed

Like Dudley Randall in "Ballad of Birmingham," Brooks adapts the traditional ballad form to address contemporary social issues. Though her meter is uneven, she adheres to the ballad's *abcb* rhyme scheme and its traditional tragic subject matter, in this case combining social oppression and murder. She begins by introducing the central character of her narrative both by name and by a distinguishing metaphor: "Rudolph Reed was oaken," dark-skinned, strong, solid, rooted. The word "oaken" will appear throughout, providing the poem's unifying repetition. In other stanzas, the words "hungry" and "dark" serve a briefer, similar function. In this poignant tale of a man who hungers to fulfill the American Dream of a safe, clean home for his family, Brooks demonstrates how racist violence transforms that man from proud endurance to murderous outrage. Using dialogue to allow Reed to speak heroically of his quest, and balladlike syntax and alliteration ("up did rise our Rudolph Reed"; "Nary a grin grinned Rudolph Reed / Nary a curse cursed he") to make his plight seem age-old, Brooks leaves the reader shocked and saddened by the ugly attack on a child, her father, and their family's dignity. Although Reed is a fallen hero, his wife remains "oak-eyed" at the end, a conclusion that may suggest either the continuation in her of Reed's strength and determination — or a silent, numb emptiness in the face of the terrible destruction of their dream.

GWENDOLYN BROOKS

The *Chicago Defender* Sends a Man to Little Rock

The journalist-narrator, witnessing the historic attempt in 1957 to integrate Little Rock public schools, suffers writer's block upon discovering that the racist villains attacking "brownish" boys and girls are just ordinary folks, "like people everywhere." The first forty-four lines of the poem describe the mundane daily lives of people who have babies, burn toast, sing hymns, drink tea, play baseball, love, open "themselves in kindness," answer telephones, and so on. Then suddenly, these same people are "hurtling spittle, rock, / Garbage and fruit," and otherwise "harassing." boys and girls because they are brown rather than white. The narrator deplores the behavior, identifying the victims with Jesus, "the loveliest lynchee," and suggesting alliteratively that such actions are un-Christian. Brooks overwhelms readers with the ordinariness of people just like themselves, who nonetheless become a mob, a "scythe of men," attacking girls who wear bows, barrettes, and braids as symbols of their innocence and making at least one boy bleed. Beyond the theme of racism, Brooks addresses the question of whether villains are in fact different from the rest of us, and she challenges our assumptions about the nature of evil. One is reminded of research by Stanley Milgram and others on obedience, showing that most normal adults in an experimental setting will give what they believe are painful shocks to human subjects in a laboratory. Research on ordinary Germans' reactions to concentration camps leads to similar unsettling conclusions about human nature.

GWENDOLYN BROOKS

Medgar Evers

DO YOUR STUDENTS KNOW . . .

On the night Evers was killed, June 11, 1963, President John Kennedy addressed the nation on civil rights and his plan to urge Congress to pass legislation ensuring equality for all Americans. Kennedy noted that an African-American child born in 1963 had many disadvantages a white child did not: one-half the chance of finishing high school, one-third the chance of completing college, and one-half the salary of what a white child would earn during his or her lifetime.

The complex syntax, absence of rhyme, and heavy dependence upon sometimes oblique allusions make this poem quite different from much of Brooks's work.

Though her usual straightforward lines are missing, repetition and alliteration remain important unifying devices. Brooks presents Evers as a down-to-earth, uncorrupted hero, a man fed up with the "old styles, old tempos"— the evils inherent in a society that tacitly accepts (or fails to prevent) a pattern of assaults on the bodies and the dignity of his people. The "tight whistlings" (1.7) may allude to Emmett Till, lynched for allegedly whistling at a white woman (see Emanuel's "Emmett Till"). "The mothballs in the Love" (ll. 7–8) may be a rejection of the kind of Christianity that puts off action or turns the other way in response to bigotry. (See also Brooks's "Ballad of Rudolph Reed" and "The *Chicago Defender* Sends a Man to Little Rock.") Written after Evers's assassination, the poem opens with an apparent allusion to an Evers speech a few days before his death, in which he acknowledged death threats and fears that he would be killed, but added, "I love my children and I love my wife with all my heart. And I would die and die gladly if that would make a better life for them." Rejecting the past, this civil rights martyr nonetheless "leaned across tomorrow," seeking to move his people forward.

GEORGE GORDON, LORD BYRON

She Walks in Beauty

Instead of sunshine, roses, lilies and cherries, we find this woman compared to the cloudless, starry night. Hers is a cooler, richer beauty, more somber and less "gaudy." The opening lines of the poem are stately, like the woman, instead of sprightly. She is raven-haired instead of blonde, with bright, dark eyes. Her character is beautiful too: serenely sweet, pure, calm, smiling and good. Her mind is at peace with all on Earth (below), and the speaker's admiration seems detached and pure.

SHULAMITH WECHTER CAINE

Intellectual Heritage

This poem describes the experience of an emigrant from Vietnam as he tries to make sense of *Oedipus Rex*. In some ways, he is able to relate to the work better than his American counterparts. After all, he is familiar with "[m]urder, blindness, / wandering, disaster and great suffering." What he is unable to comprehend is Oedipus's patricide. Not only did this young man's father "sacrifice his life" for him, but he comes from a culture that reveres ancestors. Obviously, the speaker could explain to him that Oedipus never intended to kill his father, but it is not clear that this would make the play any less disturbing for him.

RAFAEL CAMPO

Oysters

DO YOUR STUDENTS KNOW . . .

Although oysters have been regarded as aphrodisiac, their taste and inherent beauty have also made them popular. Roman emperors are said to have paid for them by weight in gold. In the United States, oyster fishing has hit hard times, but this shellfish still remains a strong export, with sales of $8.6 million in 2000, mainly to Canada and Hong Kong.

This poem's mixture of sexuality and violence seems particularly well suited to the sonnet form. As a reputed aphrodisiac, the oyster has the potential to awaken the speaker's sexuality. The violence that is needed to pry the shell open, however, disturbs him. The cook's work is "grim" in several senses. It is grim in that he takes no pleasure in it, but grim also means cruel, and there is certainly something cruel about opening an animal's protective shell in order to eat it. The last line — "I see what is left: bone-white, hollow shelled"— signals the speaker's disillusionment both with the activity and with sensual pleasure. Even pleasures that are more en-during than this one end in death.

PHYLLIS CAPELLO

In Memory of Jenny and Evelyn Who Were Playing When the Stoop Collapsed

DO YOUR STUDENTS KNOW . . .

The front stoop of an apartment building was the center of neighborhood life for the emigrants, especially the Italians, who flooded American cities. Between 1880 and 1920, 4 million Italians emigrated to the United States to escape the poverty and political woes in Italy. Every neighborhood was broken down by street according to the sections of Italy the new arrivals came from. This group of immigrants came for work, and between twenty to thirty percent would eventu-ally return to "Bella Italia."

The speaker describes the stoop in such a way that it becomes the focal point not only of the girls' lives — or rather, of "what should have been" their lives — but of the universe as a whole. It is at the poem's midpoint, in the fourth stanza, that the "older brother points out the constellations." In fact, the entire poem seems to flow into and then back out of this midpoint. The first stanza establishes that the stoop is where the girls "dream [their] li[ves]," the second lists the people they see from the stoop, and the third introduces the hypothetical first boyfriend. After the fourth stanza, this order is more or less reversed, though there is no mention of the boyfriend. In the fifth stanza, the people in the neighborhood are mentioned again, and the concluding stanza ends with "lives."

LUCILLE CLIFTON

the mississipi river enters into the gulf

DO YOUR STUDENTS KNOW . . .

The Mississippi River, which begins as an outlet stream for Lake Itasco in northern Minnesota, crosses all or parts of thirty-one states and flows for 2,350 miles. It ends in a bird's-foot delta south of New Orleans. The powerful rush of this river is 612,000 cubic feet of water per second, causing coastal Louisiana to have the highest rate of land loss in the United States. The delta area covers 13,000 square miles.

This poem argues that we are too quick to see particular times and places in our lives as unique. If "every water / is the same water coming round" and if what is true of rivers is, by analogy, true of the world, then everything is one. This is either depressing or transcendent, depending on one's point of view. The paradoxical aspect of the poem is that the speaker comes to her conclusion about the unity of all waters by observing one particular body of water and then meditating on its connections with all others.

SAMUEL TAYLOR COLERIDGE

Kubla Khan

Coleridge claimed to have written this under the influence of opium, having had a vision that he lost when he was interrupted by a caller at the door. The poem does not read like a fragment, however. In fact, it includes all the elements of Coleridge's best poems. The incantatory first stanza sets the scene in an exotic, mysterious land of measureless caverns and sunless sea. The second stanza continues the description of the "holy and enchanted place" where the "mighty fountain" and "sacred river" begin. Soon the shadow of the pleasure dome is floating on the waves; then the image of the pleasure dome disappears, and a new vision — a damsel with a dulcimer — appears (l. 36). Like Wordsworth's solitary reaper in "The Solitary Reaper," she sings a haunting melody — but the speaker cannot remember it. He longs to revive it within himself so he can create with words that pleasure dome of his vision; with the damsel as his muse, he would be a Dionysian figure, with "flashing eyes" and "floating hair." Ironically, as he bemoans his inability to revive the song or re-create the pleasure dome, he *has* created the poem he longs for and become a master poet.

BILLY COLLINS

Lines Lost among Trees

According to the Romantic view, the woods would have been the ideal place to write a poem. The poem we have, however, was written on returning home. The obvious irony is that in the process of describing how he lost six or eight lines, Collins writes a poem thirty-six lines long. The speaker has mixed feelings about the loss in any case. Stanza six, in which he describes the poem with its "little insight at the end / wagging like the short tail / of a perfectly obedient spaniel / Sitting by the door," is affectionate, but it is also patronizing. It would not be unreasonable to conclude that the speaker is happier with the poem about the lost poem than he would have been with the original. The experience in the woods was analogous to his "fugitive dreams" and his return from the woods to "waking up." This is really a poem about the pleasures of disenchantment.

HART CRANE

To Brooklyn Bridge

One of the joys of Crane's poetry is the way in which an extravagant Elizabethan diction is married to the things of the modern world. Here, in particular, this method lends a mythic dimension to the poem's subject matter. This approach is also, however, the thing that students will find most confusing about "To Brooklyn Bridge." The dilemma, then, is whether to paraphrase the poem, stripping it of its beauty in the process or to leave it beautiful but incomprehensible. It is probably best to read the poem aloud several times before beginning the discussion. Ask students to concentrate on the sound rather than the sense. Then, ask them to choose lines or stanzas they enjoy and begin a discussion about what makes these parts of the poem work and what they mean. Once enough passages have been elucidated in this way, you can move toward an understanding the poem as a whole.

E. E. CUMMINGS

Buffalo Bill's

By running the words together, especially in line 6, Cummings visually creates the rapid-fire rifle shots breaking the targeted clay pigeons. Students will be interested in examining this creative experimentation with language, reminiscent of the way Whitman plays with the poem's rhythm by breaking lyrical lines with the cadence of words and phrases. This way Cummings uses words instead of end rhyme to provide emphasis. Breaking the traditional rules of syntax allows for a bold statement. Discussion of the poet's choice of "defunct" to connect to the last line

("Mister Death") should provide interesting ways of expressing the same idea but with different shades of meaning.

E. E. CUMMINGS

next to of course god america i

DO YOUR STUDENTS KNOW . . .

The "happy heroic dead" of Cummings's poem were men he may have known as a veteran of World War I. Cummings volunteered as a member of an ambulance corps in France. But over 4 million American men were called up in a universal draft of all American men between the ages of eighteen to forty-five. In 1917, when America entered the Great War, only 200,000 men were in the army. With a total male population at the time of 54 million, 26 million men were registered from 1914 to 1918. At the war's end, 136,516 were dead and 4,452 were listed as Missing in Action.

The speaker in this satire of phony patriotism is probably a politician making a speech at some ceremonial occasion honoring the war dead — perhaps a holiday such as Memorial Day or Veterans Day. Students can easily identify all the clichéd, patriotic buzz words and stereotyped phrases that politicians still use. The irony of alluding to God, America, "My Country 'Tis of Thee" (l. 2), and the "Star-Spangled Banner" (ll. 2–4) is that the speaker has no real compassion for the war heroes and no real respect for the audience's intelligence. Using sparse punctuation and no capitals, Cummings floods the reader with a rushing flow of words that reflect the speaker's insincerity and jingoism ("by jingo by gee by gosh by gum" in l. 8).

CHITRA BANERJEE DIVAKARUNI

The Brides Come to Yuba City

The unpleasant Prufrock-like images (yellow, smoke — compare this poem with T. S. Eliot's "The Love Song of J. Alfred Prufrock") of the opening suggest sickness and vomiting ("The train heaved us from its belly"), an unpropitious beginning for a poem about brides. But these women have traveled long distances to join men they may never have met — or may barely remember. The negative imagery continues: "the tracks gleam dull," "heavy air," "ladder to eternity," "smell of vomit," "damp palms," "broken smiles." Not surprisingly, the wedding trunks are black. Yet, to this uninviting landscape, the women bring with them from India the sounds of home in their litany of words for food and clothing; and they bring seeds of hope — seeds they will plant to grow vegetables, spices, and perhaps — in their "new soil"— babies. These women are sick with fear — the hands of one woman shake (l. 41), and others cannot breathe (l. 36). They are frightened, not happy, as they approach the strangers who are to be their husbands; they will be "opening their legs," but not their hearts. The final line ("We cannot recognize a single face") is not encouraging, despite the seeds that promise, in lines 32–33, "to burst from this new soil / like green stars." Divakaruni tells a similar tale about arranged marriage from the husband's point of view in "The Disappearance." Contrast this poem with Wheatley's "On Being Brought from Africa to America." For a different view of a marriage between an older man and a younger woman, see Pound's "The River-Merchant's Wife: A Letter."

GREGORY DJANIKIAN

Immigrant Picnic

This poem is in some ways so playful that students may miss its deeper meaning on first reading. The fact that the speaker's family members do not have a full command of idiomatic American English is the chief source of comedy. At the same time, however, their use of English is unintentionally poetic. When, at the poem's conclusion, the speaker's uncle says, "You could grow nuts listening to us," the speaker surrenders to the possibilities of the new phrase rather than fighting it. Most students will be able to identify with the speaker, who at different points is embarrassed by, or frustrated with, his parents. The Fourth of July, as the national holiday, is an ideal time for a meditation on the immigrant experience.

JOHN DONNE

Batter My Heart, Three-Personed God

The speaker's ambivalent relationship with God is characterized not only by various words suggesting violence —"batter," "knock," and "break"—but also by words suggesting salvation —"breathe, shine, and seek to mend." Students might be interested in an autobiographical reading of this poem by learning more about Donne's own early ambivalence toward God and commitment to service in the Anglican Church before he became dean of St. Paul's. As in "Death Be Not Proud," students will find evidence of the sonnet's rough rhythms that express a highly charged emotional state.

JOHN DONNE

Death Be Not Proud

Because the speaker looks forward to eternal life after death, there is no fear of death, and therefore, death should not be proud of its "mighty and dreadful" power. The rough rhythms of this sonnet's lines reinforce the speaker's uneven emotional state in coping with the anguish of death. The paradox in the poem's conclusion ("death, thou shalt die") is based on the affirmation of the afterlife. This poem supplies the title of the biography that John Gunther wrote about his son's early death.

JOHN DONNE

Song

The speaker seems to have lost a woman's love and now wonders if there even exists a woman capable of true love and faithfulness. He exhorts the listener to attempt several impossible tasks and predicts that even if the listener could accomplish these, he would never find a true and fair woman. Then the speaker decides that his listener should not even bother, for even if such a woman did exist, she would be false before the speaker could meet her. This antilove song is filled with cynical wit.

MARK DOTY

A Display of Mackerel

This poem is an example of how what seems like an utterly unpoetic subject can reveal hidden depths. In the first five stanzas, Doty limits himself to a description of the mackerel. Once he has described them vividly, he moves into the meditation on identity that is really the heart of the poem. To be a person is to be an individual, an "I." The fish, however, represent a kind of life in which each creature is identical with the others in terms of both physical appearance and consciousness. Doty goes on to make a connection between the selflessness of the fish and the particular kind of beauty they posses. The poem's concluding sentence — "How happy they seem, / even on ice, to be together, selfless / which is the price of gleaming" — is ambivalent. It might, on the one hand, suggest that transcendence of self is ennobling. On the other hand, it might mean that the extinction of the self is too high a price to pay for "gleaming." These last lines in particular should provide material for class discussion.

RITA DOVE

The Satisfaction Coal Company

DO YOUR STUDENTS KNOW . . .

The use of coal for heat and industry goes back thousands of years. Archeologists have found evidence of the use of coal by the Romans in England between A.D. 100 and 200 and by the Hopi tribe in America. European explorers found coal in

America as early as 1673, but mining did not begin until the 1740s. Over thirty-eight states have coal deposits that contribute to the 1 billion tons of coal mined in the United States each year.

Although the poet does not name the "he," students can assume he is Dove's grandfather because the work comes from a collection of poems about her grandparents, *Thomas and Beulah* (1980), which won the Pulitzer Prize for poetry. By reading more of the poems in this collection, students can get a better picture of this man's life. The title expresses the ironic conflict — the old man had spent an unsatisfying life working hard doing manual labor at the Satisfaction Coal Company. The lack of purpose ("What to do with a day") now consumes him in old age.

STEPHEN DUNN

Waiting with Two Members of a Motorcycle Gang for My Child to Be Born

DO YOUR STUDENTS KNOW . . .

Although the motorcycle was first manufactured in America in 1902, the rise of motorcycle gangs did not begin until after World War II. In 1969, the Rolling Stones hired Hell's Angels, a notorious motorcycle gang, to provide security at an outdoor concert. Although the legend is wrong that they were paid in beer for their efforts, the Angels' security actions resulted in violence that left three people dead.

The central irony of the poem is that the speaker's daughter is born — added to the world, as it were — even as the speaker is talking to two "Eliminators." The speaker sees in this juxtaposition an ironic contrast between the creative action that the women are performing by giving birth and the violence-laden name the men have adopted. He ends with a kind of prayer: "May you turn stone, my daughter / into silk. May you make men better than they are." It is important to note that this prayer has already been answered, since the news of his daughter's birth prompts the two men to treat the speaker with kindness.

PAUL LAURENCE DUNBAR

We Wear the Mask

Students can offer different interpretations of the concept of the mask, perhaps thinking about masks they themselves wear. "Mask" suggests not only a synonym for the speaker in a poem but also a rich tradition of ritual and ceremony in many cultures around the world. The speaker seems to criticize not the wearer of the mask but rather the racist society that makes necessary this masking of true feelings in order to survive. With the allusion to the martyr Christ, the speaker characterizes those who are masked as tortured souls, grinning on the outside but crying on the inside. The idea of the happy, singing "darky" is debunked here too.

T. S. ELIOT

The Love Song of J. Alfred Prufrock

The age-old conflict between action and indecision lies at the center of this poem. Similar in theme to Eliot's "The Hollow Men," this poem focuses on the inability to feel or act. The speaker's world lacks meaning, purpose, and spirituality, and he has become ineffectual—incapable of the acts of Prince Hamlet (finally moved to action), Lazarus (raised from the dead), or John the Baptist (decapitated head served on a platter). The speaker seeks some resolution to his spiritual paralysis, emotional indifference, and trivial existence.

He longs to be romantic and have mermaids sing to him, but he is paralyzed by fears and lack of confidence. Students enjoy playing with the title: discussing what kind of love song this is, who sings it to whom, and also what Prufrock's name suggests (prudence, prudishness, prunes, proof, frock-coat, frock, rock).

JAMES A. EMANUEL

Emmett Till

DO YOUR STUDENTS KNOW . . .

Till's torture and murder illustrates the use of violence to keep black Americans silent and oppressed, particularly in the South. In 1921, the NAACP reported that from 1889 to 1918, 3,224 lynchings occurred. Of that number, 2,522 were black. During this time period, however, there was never a single conviction of the perpetrators. Despite confessing to the crime, Till's murderers were found not guilty on September 23, 1955—the anniversary of the signing of the Bill of Rights.

This poem includes the sort of personal, historical, and mythical allusions that require knowledge beyond the poem. Fortunately, students have the footnote about the fourteen-year-old black youth murdered in Mississippi in 1955 for talking to and perhaps whistling at a white woman. Students may comment about the speaker's sympathy for the victim of this racist murder. Or, they may recognize that the child speaker wants a bedtime story of the fairy River Boy to erase the nightmarish image of the tragically brutalized Emmett. Bob Dylan wrote a ballad called "The Death of Emmett Till," and the murder and trial are recounted on many Internet sites. Till's killers were acquitted.

LOUISE ERDRICH

Indian Boarding School: The Runaways

From the 1870s to the 1960s, many Native American children were educated at off-reservation boarding schools run by the government or by Christian groups. One goal of these schools was to make the children more "American" by forcing them to abandon traditional tribal languages, dress, and culture. One such school was in Wahpeton, North Dakota, the area where Erdrich grew up among the Turtle Mountain band of the Chippewa; her grandfather was tribal chair of the reservation. Tales of abuses and brutality such as those to which the poem alludes ("scars," "welts of ancient punishments," "shame," "long insults," humiliating labor) abound in newspaper articles and in books such as Zitkala-Sa's *American Indian Stories* (Reprint ed. University of Nebraska Press, 1986). Erdrich links the children to the land, suggesting the mistreatment of the children through descriptions of the scarring of the tribal lands by railroads, highways, and sidewalks. Compare these children's dreams to little Tom Dacre's dream in Blake's "The Chimney Sweeper" and compare the abuse of the children.

ROBERT FROST

Acquainted with the Night

Having suffered from depression himself, Frost depicts in this sonnet a speaker familiar with despair, loneliness, guilt, and helplessness, as suggested by images of the depressing rain, sad city life, and someone's cry. The "night" in the title, as well as in the opening and closing lines, implies the dark night of the soul — the plight of the solitary wanderer. Offering no solace, the moon ("luminary clock") reminds the persona that time is relative and nature is indifferent to human suffering. Thus, Frost uses the traditional fourteen-line format to depict the problem of despair but does not offer solutions.

ROBERT FROST

Birches

DO YOUR STUDENTS KNOW . . .

In many countries, the birch tree, of which there are over fifty species in the world, is thought to have mystical properties for fertility and healing. For this reason, well into the 1980s, a punishment for criminal behavior in England was to be flogged with a birch switch. The belief was that the birch tree's magic could rid the body of evil spirits. Birch was also often used to make cradles in order to keep children healthy.

Frost often presents two opposing viewpoints (thesis and antithesis) and then suggests a certain truth, a middle position (synthesis). Here the "Truth" is that Mother Nature, in "all her matter-of-fact," is not concerned with humanity or damage done to the birches by fierce ice storms. However, the speaker prefers to imagine that a boy, needing a diversion from work, bent the trees instead. Opposites of earth/sky, work/play, and adulthood/childhood merge as the speaker imagines "a swinger of birches." This unity of contraries allows one to escape earthbound worries and return refreshed, more capable of love. Students might compare their own "escapes" (getting "away from earth awhile") with the speaker's and consider why swinging from birches might be so invigorating.

ROBERT FROST

Desert Places

The speaker's despondency ("I am too absent-spirited to count") compares with the despair in "Acquainted with the Night" in the truth that the human heart can be as desolate as any desert place. Reinforcing the initial images of snow and night, Frost uses the words "loneliness" and "lonely" four times, along with other words that connote an absence (whiteness, nothing, empty). The speaker cannot be scared of the unknown emptiness in outer space because he feels an even greater emptiness within. Pervasive long *o* sounds (snow, oh, no, nothing) convey the anguish of this lonely heart.

ROBERT FROST

Mending Wall

Criticizing his neighbor's assertion ("Good fences make good neighbors") yet initiating the wall mending, the speaker is willing to do whatever it takes to resolve conflict. Actually, Frost presents a well-balanced argument, matching the neighbor's saying (ll. 27 and 45) with his own stubborn belief ("Something there is that doesn't love a wall," ll. 1, 35). Even though the speaker's apple orchard will not invade his neighbor's pine forest, the wall gives them a chance to get together for this annual ritual — a necessary process of repairing their boundaries and renewing their friendship.

ROBERT FROST

The Road Not Taken

The choice of roads represents the choices faced throughout one's journey in life. Often people must choose between equal yet unknown alternatives. Significantly, the speaker accepts full responsibility for following that one path — "and I — / I

GARRISON: PLEASE FIRE ME **313**

took the one less traveled by" (ll. 18–19), though he admits they are worn "really about the same" (l. 10). Certainly, the speaker feels ambivalent about the choice. The speaker knows this decision between two equally viable alternatives made a difference, so it is only human to speculate where the other road would have led. The title, focusing on the road *not* taken, expresses the speaker's thinking about what might have been.

ROBERT FROST

Stopping by Woods on a Snowy Evening

The woods attract the speaker's sense of spirituality. The voice is that of a laconic rural New Englander who senses the mystery of life yet confirms commitment to responsibilities. This most famous poem by Frost fuses the idea and form — the sense and sound — of human awe of nature. The tone is quiet and meditative, and the form is structured and controlled. The third line of each of the first three quatrains serves as a link, moving the reader forward by rhyming with lines 1, 2, and 4 of the next stanza. The final stanza's uniform rhyme scheme and repeated final line reaffirm the speaker's choice to continue the journey.

FREDERICO GARCIA LORCA

Arbolé, Arbolé

Although Lorca is a modern poet, this poem has some of the feel of a folk ballad. Each time the girl receives an offer, it is from a man or men who ought to be more appealing — they are certainly more colorful — than the wind with its "grey arm." By remaining where she is, the girl has chosen a more austere lover. The wind is literally loftier, since it is a "playboy of towers." It is also often a metaphor for the spirit. The poem as a whole is the story of a girl who chooses duty and spirit over pleasure and the world.

DEBORAH GARRISON

Please Fire Me

Garrison mixes two metaphors together here, describing the males as predatory animals and the females as hens. Although the poem is laid out in quatrains, the rhymes that occur — "liquor / sicker," "eyes / sympathize" — fall in such a way that they undermine rather than reinforce the stanzaic form. You might ask students to find all the rhymes and half-rhymes in the poem and then ask them why they think the poet arranged them as she did. In the last stanza, the speaker says, "I'd like to go / somewhere else entirely / and I don't mean / Europe." Raising the question of where the speaker really wants to go will help students get at the poem's central point, which relates to a longing for a better society.

NIKKI GIOVANNI

Nikki-Rosa

DO YOUR STUDENTS KNOW . . .

Childhood memories sustain many adults, but many memories prior to the age of five are hard to remember. Psychologists have termed this phenomenon "childhood amnesia" to explain the great difficulty people have in remembering events younger than age five. Psychologists believe that during the years of early childhood the brain can capture implicit and unconscious memory with ease, and only later in childhood, do we remember explicit, conscious memories.

The absence of punctuation in this autobiographical poem heightens the narrator's stream of consciousness and conversational quality. Students might agree that "childhood remembrances are always a drag" because they can be boring or even inaccurate. But Giovanni's remembrances of things past accentuate the positive, while acknowledging the negative memories; for example, she had a happy childhood despite her family's poverty and her father's drinking. Looking back at the child Nikki-Rosa she was, the poet sees her as happy. "I really hope no white person ever has cause to write about me / because they never understand Black love is Black wealth . . ." (ll. 24–25) might strike some readers as a racist comment and thus could lead to fruitful class discussion.

JORIE GRAHAM

I Was Taught Three

Among other things, this poem tackles the difficult subject of the relationship among names, the things they designate, and the perceiving mind. It is not that the *actual* tree is being contrasted with the *idea* of a tree. Rather, the speaker asks, "What is the idea / that governs blossoming?" Whether it is "the human tree / clothed with its nouns, or this one / just outside my window," the process is still seen as being governed by an idea. Students will likely see that the poem is concerned with language, but they may be puzzled about exactly what is being said about language. These issues are perhaps impossible to resolve. Philosophers have always been concerned with the distinction between subject and object. Because human beings have consciousness, they can make a distinction between themselves and the world around them, yet they also feel that they are part of that world. Because language is one of the most important components of consciousness, it will have an important bearing on this question. By the end, the speaker cannot determine whether mind gave rise to nature or nature to mind.

H. D. (HILDA DOOLITTLE)

Heat

In the opening apostrophe and the closing lines, the speaker implores the wind to "rend open," "cut apart," "rend to tatters," "cut," "plough through" the hot, humid air. Repetition of these powerful verbs emphasizes the heaviness of the heat and creates an image of heat as a solid entity, like a field or a suit of clothing. Students who have walked out of air conditioning into summer's humid heat will recall the sense of being met by such a wall. The middle stanza describes the heat's effects on fruit — which cannot fall through such thickness. Though solid and heavy, the heat is nonetheless air, which rises to meet the falling pears and grapes until the collision squashes them, changing their shape. H. D., an Imagist, presents a tightly concentrated tactile image. Compare this poem with those in the chapter on Imagery.

H. D. (HILDA DOOLITTLE)

Helen

Aphrodite (goddess of love and beauty), competing with other goddesses for a golden apple, promised Paris, Prince of Troy, that she would grant him the most beautiful woman on Earth if he would give the apple to her. Unfortunately, the woman (Helen) was already married, and her abduction led to the Trojan War. Helen of Troy is sometimes portrayed sympathetically as a victim of the gods or as a woman worth fighting for. At other times, she is the faithless, fallen woman who caused massive death and destruction. H. D. suggests Helen's beauty and innocence with words like "white," "still," "lustre," "born of love." Yet Greece, unmoved by her suffering (wanness), hates her nonetheless, holding her responsible for the loss of so many heroes in the terrible war. Note how the whiteness becomes ash — the Greeks will forgive Helen only when she is dead. Other poems related to the Trojan War include Yeats's "Leda and the Swan" and Walcott's "Sea Grapes."

MARILYN HACKER

I'm four, in itchy woolen leggings

Here, an apparently unremarkable event — the failure of a child to recognize her father at a distance — is invested, in retrospect, with great significance. Although students will have little difficulty paraphrasing the action, they may have difficulty articulating its deeper meaning. The fact that the speaker's memory of the event is so clear indicates that it had, and continues to have, great emotional importance for her. When the speaker was young, the fact that she did not see her father was due to her own lack of vision. Now, even though she can see her father clearly in memory, he is not there.

RACHEL HADAS

Thick and Thin

The human experience of time is always bittersweet: it brings new people and experiences into our lives even as it takes familiar ones away. To complicate matters, the events and influences we would most like to see undone are inextricably bound up with those we cannot bear to lose. In the first stanza, Hadas introduces the metaphor of a substance "[s]ticky, taffy brown" that it is shaped like dough "by a succession of urgent hands." Here, time is seen as something too substantial, too "thick." In the second stanza, this substance thins, becoming less substantial. Note that the two conditions are not sequential and that each lasts "a lifetime." Students will likely be familiar with the feeling of wanting time to move more quickly yet at the same time wanting it to stop.

JOY HARJO

Morning Song

DO YOUR STUDENTS KNOW . . .

Although nautical folklore warns sailors to be wary of a red sky at dawn, this phenomena suggests dry weather. Because the Sun is low in the sky in the morning, its rays travel a longer distance. The red color indicates that there are a large number of dust particles in the atmosphere that are being pushed ahead of a high-pressure system.

The language in this poem is deceptively simple, and students may feel they have understood it more thoroughly than they actually have. They may miss, for example, the complex metaphor developed in lines 4–6: "Each sunrise a link in the ladder / The ladder the backbone / Of shimmering deity." They may also miss the layers of meaning in the line "Child stirring in the web of your mother." However one interprets this line, it is a startling image. If the child is being compared to the spider's prey, then its birth struggles are the antithesis of the prey's death struggles. If the child is being compared to a spider, then the implication is that the child has created the mother, which may be emotionally true even if it is causally false.

THOMAS HARDY

The Convergence of the Twain

Advertised as the largest, safest ship in the world, the *Titanic* symbolizes the vanity and pride of mankind, in contrast to the indifference and power of nature. The "unsinkable" ship sank on its maiden voyage (April 14, 1912), suggesting to

Hardy the sexual imagery and hence the ironic convergence of two halves (an "intimate welding" and "consummation"), like a couple on their wedding night. "The Immanent Will that stirs and urges everything," also called "the Spinner of the Years," represents Hardy's deterministic philosophy. This Will, be it Fate or some vengeful god, has arbitrarily snuffed out at least 1500 lives and mocked the overweening pride in human progress. Notice how the unusual line lengths make the stanzas look like ships.

ROBERT HAYDEN

Homage to the Empress of the Blues

The speaker pays tribute to Bessie Smith (1894–1937), famous jazz and blues singer in the 1920s. Feathered and beaded, she dressed extravagantly and sang mournful blues about unfaithful love so beautifully and powerfully that she allowed her audience to ease fears in their lives riddled by the "riot-squad of statistics." The title suggests giving someone publicly some special honor and respect, especially paying allegiance to a feudal lord by a vassal — someone in a subordinate or dependent position. The speaker acknowledges Smith's bringing solace to people's lives.

SEAMUS HEANEY

Mid-term Break

Students may become confused in stanza five when the ambulance brings the body of the speaker's brother home for the wake. American wakes are typically held in funeral homes, but in Ireland it is still common to have them in the home. Aside from this detail, the events of the poem should be easy for students to follow. Much of the poem's emotional impact derives from the fact that the reader doesn't know how old the dead boy is until the last word of the poem, though we already know that he must have been young. You can look with students at the technical means — repetition, rhyme — that Heaney uses to give this moment an additional emotional charge.

VICTOR HERNÁNDEZ CRUZ

Anonymous

It is possible that "Anonymous" is not only the title of the poem but also the name of its speaker. Many of the great works of literature were written by anonymous authors. In some cases, these authors were members of a group (e.g., women) that the majority of society did not believe should be producing literature. By not attaching their names to their works, these authors were able to engage the dominant tradition even as they remained outside it. It is obvious that the speaker knows something about the canon of English poetry. He knows the name of Henry Howard, Earl of Surrey, and knows that older poets used words like "alas" and "hath." He has also reflected on the purpose and technique of rhyme. It is equally obvious, based on his nonstandard English and the fact that he spells Chaucer as "Choicer," that he is not a member of a group for whom these authors are considered an automatic inheritance. Like some of the anonymous writers of the past, he is engaging the English canon from the outside.

GERARD MANLEY HOPKINS

God's Grandeur

The internal rhyme of "seared," "bleared," and "smeared" emphasizes the speaker's dislike of how "trade" and "toil" have destroyed people's lives. In addition to a reliance on rhyme, Hopkins's repeated use of alliteration creates language with a sense of balanced unity, dynamic energy, and smooth rhythm. "God's grandeur" is found in nature. As opposed to the commonplace, workaday world of trade and toil, nature offers intense beauty and pleasure. In turn, this profound sense of natural beauty reflects a sense of an unseeable yet knowable divine presence, the Holy Ghost. Thus, revealed in nature, the image of God offers hope to a brooding world.

GERARD MANLEY HOPKINS

The Windhover

The speaker admires the windhover (a small European falcon) so much because this remarkable bird, which hovers in the air against the wind, has mastered the seemingly impossible. In expressing delight in the windhover's beauty, valor, and sheer power, the speaker also describes the awesome mystery of the universe and praises Christ, to whom the poem is dedicated. The poet's "sprung rhythm," which breaks away from standard metrical feet and fixed syllables, offers a more flexible, rhythmic beat. This rhythm, along with assonance and consonance, effectively reproduces the bird's movement.

GARRETT KAORU HONGO

The Hongo Store 29 Miles Volcano Hilo, Hawaii

In essence, this is a poem of gratitude and a recognition of the fragility of life. A connection to religion and ultimate things is made early in the poem when the sound of the volcano is compared to "the bell of the Buddhist Church." Note, too, how the description of "that greenhouse world behind the store" makes it seem as though the volcano is threatening Paradise. The photograph that prompts the poem thus documents a reprieve or moment of grace. This reprieve is only temporary, of course; in a sense, the existence of death makes every reprieve temporary.

ANDREW HUDGINS

Desert Island

The challenge in teaching this poem is to analyze it without killing its humor. The speaker in "Desert Island" knows his teacher and is able to manipulate her by telling her what she wants to hear. Students who haven't done this themselves have certainly seen it done and will probably enjoy this humorous presentation of it. Much of the poem's humor derives from the fact that the end is unexpected, although the notice the speaker takes of the teacher's bra provides *some* foreshadowing.

TED HUGHES

Visit

DO YOUR STUDENTS KNOW . . .

No poet's personal life has been more criticized, perhaps, than Ted Hughes, whose name was chipped off Sylvia Plath's (his first wife) headstone by angry Plath admirers who blamed Hughes for Plath's death. Both of the women Hughes married committed suicide by carbon monoxide poisoning. Nearly six years after Plath's death, Assia Welvill, the woman for whom he left Plath, killed herself and their daughter, Shura.

Students interested in reading more about the Sylvia Plath–Ted Hughes marriage, from his point of view, will find this poem interesting and perhaps painful. It may also make Hughes seem more sympathetic to readers of "Daddy" and other Plath poems in which he is cast as villain. More personal and confessional than earlier Hughes poems, this one is more like Plath's (though without her patterns of myth and symbol) and like his own "A Pink Wool Knitted Dress," which it also resembles structurally. In both, a recounting of an early, happy time is overshadowed by the knowledge of events to come. A discordant note interrupts the playful beginning in which the speaker remembers a time of youth and hope (blind man's buff, throwing clods at a window): "Nor did I know I was being auditioned / For the male lead in your drama" (ll. 25–26). Soon he is comparing himself to very conventional puppet on strings or (much more attention-getting) to "a dead frog" whose legs are "touched by electrodes." As he recounts reading his dead wife's journal, his emotions rise and fall as he imagines their "future trying to happen," only to realize she is "ten years dead," and he is reading a story. Does this mean it is untrue, only a story? "Your story. My story," he adds at the ambiguous conclusion. Hughes did not tell "his" version of "their" story until he published *Birthday Letters* in 1998, shortly before his death.

DONALD JUSTICE

On the Death of Friends in Childhood

DO YOUR STUDENTS KNOW . . .

Cancer remains the second highest killer of children, but rates of death from cancer have dropped significantly. Death rates in children have declined by 62 percent since 1960, due to improved treatments. Although cancer in children is often diagnosed at a more advanced stage than in adults, up to 70 percent of all children with cancer can be cured.

An analysis of Justice's technique will show how much he accomplishes here, and how subtly. It's best to begin, though, by asking students what sorts of feelings or emotions the poem calls up for them. Once they've responded, you can move on to a discussion of technique. What words does Justice use to end his lines? Why did he choose these particular words? Do students feel the poem would have been more or less effective if it had been longer? Point out, if students don't notice it themselves, how the rhyme on "games" and "names" mimics the sound of a rhyme children might recite during a game.

DONALD JUSTICE

School Letting Out

Like "On the Death of Friends in Childhood," this poem achieves its effects with a great deal of subtlety. The epigraph, "Fourth or Fifth Grade" is given in parenthesis and so may not seem immediately important, an impression reinforced by its vagueness. Think how much less evocative the poem would be, however, if the poet had chosen a more defined time period. Justice grew up in Florida, and this may well explain the reference to "young fruit trees and winter flowers." Since poetry in English has traditionally viewed winter as a time of torpor, the mention of "winter flowers" carries with it a suggestion of eternal youth. Also important is the fact that the tense of the poem as a whole is uncertain, so it seems poised between past and present.

JOHN KEATS

La Belle Dame sans Merci: A Ballad

The narrator questions this knight who has met a lovely woman and fallen under her fatal spell. Like the typical protagonist in the Romantic tradition, the young man is a solitary, pale wanderer in this wintry, deathlike landscape. The concept of a beautiful woman without pity or mercy brings to mind other literary and mythic images of the temptress, the femme fatale, who has the power to attract, delight, and then destroy unsuspecting, entrapped men. The plentiful images of sexuality foreshadow death, as does the dream of death-pale men who have also fallen victim to La Belle Dame's fatal attraction. This poem can be compared with Blake's "Song" and Heine's "The Loreley" (not in this text) or with other ballads such as "Bonny Barbara Allan."

JOHN KEATS

Bright Star! Would I Were Steadfast as Thou Art

This sonnet in the Shakespearean form addresses a popular topic: the permanence of love. While wishing to be as steadfast as the star, the speaker rejects in the first quatrain the solitary, celibate (hermitlike) nature of the star. Nor does he want to stare at Earth's beauties as the star silently does. The "No" that opens the sestet introduces the lover's desire — he wishes to remain permanently united with his love. If that is impossible, he wishes to die at his moment of ecstasy (a very Elizabethan idea). Keats wrote in an 1818 letter to his brother Tom that scenes of natural beauty in the Lake Country "refine one's sensual vision into a sort of north star which can never cease to be open lidded and stedfast [sic] over the wonders of the great Power."

JOHN KEATS

Ode on a Grecian Urn

Addressing the urn, the speaker contemplates art and life, permanence and change, the real and ideal. On the urn, he sees leaves and people "overwrought" (a reference both to their emotions and to the technique of raising figures onto the surface of the urn). At first, he envies the urn: its pipers pipe unheard melodies that are better than heard ones as the imaginary is always richer than the real; the lovers stay forever young and just about to kiss; the trees never lose their leaves. Later, he realizes that the urn's pastoral world is cold and lifeless. Immortal, it remains a friend to each generation of mortals, reminding us that we must experience life rather than imagine it, or our lives will be as empty as the desolate town on the urn — or as the urn itself. Some students enjoy discussing the much-debated line about beauty and truth.

JOHN KEATS

When I Have Fears

Keats (the apparent speaker) uses the Shakespearean sonnet form to discuss his fears about an early death from the tuberculosis that plagued his family. In the first quatrain, he worries about all the poems he might not live to write. In the second, he imagines the high adventures he would miss. In the last quatrain, he realizes he would never see his beloved again, nor share love. The progression from poet to adventurer to lover is suddenly interrupted, midline, when he stops imagining and recognizes how isolated he is in his mortality. Like Dickinson in "Because I Could Not Stop for Death," Keats illustrates how a sudden confrontation with eternity makes all else seem insignificant.

ARON KEESBURY

On the Robbery across the Street

Rather than describing a scene or presenting an argument, this poem is a dramatic monologue spoken by an eyewitness to one of the most famous bank robberies in American history. Ask students if they think the speaker's use of nonstandard English is convincing. Point out that although the poem purports to be spontaneous speech, it is carefully constructed: the first two lines of the final stanza are essentially variations on the first line of the poem, thus drawing attention to the fact that the speaker has been talking in circles. The irony, of course, is that the speaker, who is complaining about "kids" who "think they can get away with murder," may be withholding evidence about a major crime.

JANE KENYON

A Boy Goes into the World

DO YOUR STUDENTS KNOW . . .

Although equality for men and women remains a goal in education and employment, psychologists, researchers, and physicians confirm that profound biological differences between men and women affect all aspects of life. Variances in gender begin when a fetus is only six weeks old, as the brain begins to develop. Brain chemistry and hormones also create differences in genders.

Ask students if they notice any patterns in the line breaks. If they do not see one, you can point to the second and second-to-last lines. In each case, the lines ends with, "but." In the first instance, it signals the fact that the speaker's societal assumptions are conflicting with her desires. In the second, it indicates that she is now able to triumph over those assumptions. By adult standards none of the things the speaker's brother brings back is a prize. And this fact constitutes the poem's tragedy: by the time the speaker can "claim" these things as her own, it is too late for her to experience them in the way she once would have.

PHILIP LARKIN

Aubade

"Aubade" is not only instrumental music or a song suitable for greeting the dawn but also a poem or song about lovers separating at daybreak. The word *aubade* comes from the Latin *albus*, meaning "white," so it would be interesting to compare the sky, which Larkin describes as "white as clay" (l. 48) with other images suggesting death, indifference, and desolation. Instead of the promise of a new day, the speaker ironically feels closer to death. The sadness of lovers parting fits the sense of the poem's gloom.

LI-YOUNG LEE

The Gift

To help another person cope with an injury, however small, is to help that person face his or her mortality. If students miss this point entirely, they will have difficulty with the final stanza. It may seem perfectly reasonable to them, for example, that the speaker, as a child, did *not* call the piece of metal "Little Assassin" or "Ore Going Deep for my heart." It would be unusual for a child to think of either name. In retrospect, however, the speaker sees this early injury as an attempt that the world made on his life. He also sees his father's actions as an example of how one should meet pain and danger with kindness and gentleness.

PHILLIP LEVINE

Llanto

"Llanto" is a very faintly rhymed, loosely metered Shakespearean sonnet. It is also an elegy that spends more time on nature than on its supposed subject, who is not even mentioned, until the sonnet's sestet. Part of the discussion might focus on why Levine chose this approach. One reason may be that to one poet it seems the most honest or accurate method. He sees that the elements that made up his friend have returned to nature. To write about him in the present tense, then, he must write about nature. It may also be that the poet's feeling of loss makes writing about the dead man as if he were present seem inauthentic. Finally, much of the poem's power comes from its restraint, a restraint that would be more difficult to maintain if the dead man and his personality were the sole or primary focus.

HARRY MCCABE

Evening at the Shack

Students may have difficulty determining the poem's tone at first, but most will realize that it is tongue-in-cheek by the time they reach the concluding couplet. There are clues before this, of course: some of the rhymes are forced, the meter is awkward in places, and articles are frequently omitted to smooth out the meter. This may also be an attempt to imitate the syntax found in some translations of Chinese classical poetry. Li Po, one of China's most revered poets, was as fond of writing about nature and of wine, as is the speaker of this poem. It seems clear, then, that one of McCabe's intentions is to poke gentle fun at this poetic tradition and at the speaker's place in it.

CLAUDE MCKAY

If We Must Die

Knowing that McKay wrote this sonnet in response to the 1919 Harlem race riots allows students to put the defiance in the context of social protest. The speaker calls for retaliation to violence even though it appears futile. He is resigned to death in a racist society but urges bravery in fighting to the last moment of life. The depiction of people as animals reinforces the inhumanity of the struggle — whites are like "mad and hungry dogs" attacking outnumbered blacks, slaughtered like hogs. Compare this poem with McKay's "The White City."

JAMES MERRILL

Page from the Koran

Merrill's poem is a meditation on the relationship between religious faith and violence. The violence, though latent, is introduced in the first stanza, where the speaker compares the script used in a valuable copy of the Koran to "[s]corpions." The danger contained in the holy book is contrasted with the "mild winter morning" when it is sold for "six hundred Swiss francs." Switzerland is a neutral country, and its nickname is "the country of a thousand years of peace." The second stanza introduces an actual armed conflict that has its roots in religious differences. In the third stanza, the poet wonders how it is that an individual — in this case, a muezzin — who conveys words that do such damage is himself unhurt.

W. S. MERWIN

For the Anniversary of My Death

It is difficult for anyone to imagine his or her own death. Merwin tries to do this by the novel means of noting that he has already lived a number of times through the date that will one day be the date of his death. It is important to note, however, that the speaker talks more about life than death and that life is regarded as a great mystery. The speaker is reverent but not fully certain what it is he reveres when he is "bowing not knowing to what." You might have several students read the poem out loud before discussing its tone and the ways in which the lack of punctuation affects that tone.

JOHN MILTON

When I consider how my light is spent

This autobiographical sonnet expresses Milton's acceptance of his blindness. The word *spent* in the title can be construed in two ways — in the sense of acknowledging that his eyesight is gone as well as explaining how he spends his remaining intellectual light in service to God. Milton's imaginary dialogue with God suggests a beneficent, understanding deity, one who asks only that a person live as meaningfully as possible.

PABLO NERUDA

The United Fruit Co.

The speaker's attitude toward the United Fruit Co. is clearly one of contempt and anger. This rage is obvious, for example, in his description of the corporation's support of political dictators who are "bloodthirsty flies." Like the fruit flies that suck out the life of citrus, bananas, and other fruits, the company and the dictators have sucked out the life of "succulent" central America — called "Banana Republics" by those who ravished Latin America. The ironic tone of the first nine lines satirizes the way American businesses considered it their divine right to exploit less developed countries. Neruda accomplishes this satire by combining biblical language and allusions with the names of large American corporations that played God.

DANIEL NESTER

Pay-Per-View Étude

According to Nester, viewers watching "old actors play roles past their prime" do not pity the actors because the viewers themselves are in some cases past their prime. To feel sorry for the actors, then, would be to start down the road to self-pity. This is not the only reason audiences are indulgent; they know that creative people — Monet is given as an example — sometimes produce exceptional work late in life. Although it is not necessary to know the term *etude* in order to understand the poem, students without a musical background will need it explained. An *etude* is a piece of music composed to help its player in the development of a particular technique. In many cases, the piece is merely a glorified exercise, as are most of the appearances by actors "past their prime." In other cases, however, an etude can be a work of genuine artistic merit.

SHARON OLDS

The One Girl at the Boys Party

The fact that the speaker's daughter is obviously different from everyone else at the party, coupled with the fact that this difference is a matter of gender, gives her a presence that the boys lack. Besides this obvious difference, she views the world differently. The boys dive into the pool while she treats it as something to be analyzed, something to be brought into her own mind. The power of her intellect and her awareness of her own difference are intimately related to her emerging sexuality. Each boy there is a potential future lover. Because none of them yet is her lover, the possibilities remain endless. In her, we see the union of innocence and calculation.

SHARON OLDS

Rite of Passage

The mother of the birthday boy appears both amused and horrified at how boys as young as six and seven are already playing macho games and are well versed in the language of war. The irony is that another year of the child's life is celebrated with talk of fighting and killing. A "rite of passage" is a ritual or ceremony that commemorates an important event in a person's life or indicates the transition from one stage to another. Thus, Olds uses the birthday party of a first-grader to represent ironically the transition from small child (*"We could easily kill a two-year-old"*) to boy. At the advanced age of seven, this boy is looking toward the adult world of "playing war."

FRANK O'HARA

Autobiographia Literaria

Much of the poem's effect is achieved by the juxtaposition of the solemn Latin title and informal tongue-in-cheek poem. In the poem, the speaker pokes fun at the trajectory that the lives of many artists (perhaps his own) follow. The list of writers who have had (or imagine they have had) unusual childhoods is a long one. Students who have not developed an ear for tone may believe, based upon the final stanza, that the speaker is an egomaniac and take literally his claim to be "the / center of all beauty."

MARY OLIVER

Alligator Poem

Although one of the great strengths of this poem is its vivid descriptions of nature, these descriptions, and the narrative into which they are woven, are intended to convey an important truth. Many of us, after an encounter with our own or another's mortality, view life in a fresh way. Oliver's poem conveys this sense of a new beginning so powerfully because it is so dramatic and so elemental. What happened to the speaker in modern-day Florida could have happened to a human being tens of thousands of years ago. Examine the physical details of the poem with your students. As the discussion progresses, help them see how the physical descriptions are charged with meanings beyond the literal. Look at "blue stars / and blood-red trumpets,"—for example. In addition to being flowers that the speaker actually picked, they also allude to the stars in the heavens and the blood in human veins.

MICHAEL ONDAATJE

Dates

Whereas the date of the speaker's birth was not marked by a significant event (Winston Churchill's wedding anniversary can hardly be called a momentous occasion for the world), something marvelous was happening on the other side of the world when the speaker was an eight-month-old fetus whose mother was living in Ceylon (now Sri Lanka). Wallace Stevens's act of creating a poem in Connecticut is just as miraculous as the creation of life. Words grow to sentences that grow to pages —just as a baby grows in the womb and flowers grow in the garden. The dates of conception, gestation, and finally birth for both baby and poem represent a sense of harmony for the poet.

GREGORY ORR

Once the two of us

This poem is an extended metaphor in which the speaker and his wife or lover are described as having been "a single stream / flowing over / and around itself." A separation has occurred, and the woman is being destroyed, possibly dying. The unanswered question is how and why this destruction is occurring. If the woman "flee[s] alone" is she fleeing from the speaker or from some other person or power? The fact that she is "shattering on the rocks below" makes it unlikely that she is simply leaving the speaker. The most probable explanation is that some tragedy has occurred.

JUDITH ORTIZ COFER

Claims

The speaker seems to agree with her grandmother that sex and childbearing are impositions on a woman's individuality. There is a brief mention, in line 6, of the "gift of comfort" that sex can bring. Otherwise, the attitude toward reproduction is bleak. The grandmother introduces the metaphor of herself as an ocean when she refers to her three miscarriages. This image is crucial to an understanding of the poem. One might initially think of the grandmother as having been powerless. The sea, however, is an immensely powerful force, and when it inundates the land, it washes away everything in its path. The grandmother made her choices and dealt with the consequences; she also made sure that her daughters knew what the consequences of motherhood would be. Now she is choosing a different way.

LINDA PASTAN

Ethics

DO YOUR STUDENTS KNOW . . .

Ethics, or moral thought, has been studied by a number of psychologists. In his studies of men and women and morality, Lawrence Kohlberg found that women scored consistently lower on moral questions. One of his students, Carol Gilligan, published her own groundbreaking theories on female moral development in 1982 in the book, *In a Different Voice*, which theorized that women and men have different conceptions of morality. Men are likely to be focused on the rules that need to be followed, whereas women focus on the needs of the individual.

The speaker's attitude toward art and its relationship to life has changed over the years as she has matured. The young will care little about a hypothetical question about saving either a priceless Rembrandt painting or an old woman soon to die anyway. However, the speaker, now nearing old age herself, finally realizes that woman and paintings and seasons all fade sooner or later. Thus, the hypothetical question is irrelevant because "all are beyond saving by children." Furthermore, young people do not fully appreciate the complexities of art, education, or even ethics.

LINDA PASTAN

Marks

The detached, sardonic tone of this poem prepares the reader for the last line. The speaker, a wife and mother, imagines her family grading her performance, as if she were a schoolchild. The insensitivity of their evaluations suggests that they have no idea about her feelings or about the relative value of her tasks: her performances at cooking, ironing, and lovemaking are given equal importance, for example. Titling the poem "Marks" rather than "Grades" suggests that such evaluating may bruise. In the end, the speaker notes that her family has something to learn. Is she actually leaving them, or merely "dropping out" of the grading game? The ambiguous conclusion might suggest either a Nora Helmer exit (see *A Doll House*) or a decision to seek approval from within rather than from her family. As in Piercy's "Barbie Doll," we encounter a woman who has sought validation from others, but the woman in this poem seems ready for a change.

LUCIA MARIA PERILLO

Scott Wonders if His Daughter Will Understand Tragedy if He Kills Rock and Roll

DO YOUR STUDENTS KNOW . . .

When *Carmen* premiered in Paris in 1875, the opera was criticized for many of the same reasons that rock and roll was attacked when it first appeared. Critics complained that the music was undistinguished and the story was so obscene that it was an assault on law and order. The response left its composer, Bizet, so depressed that he died three months later. Soon after Bizet's death, and continuing today, *Carmen* became a popular opera. Both its populist forms and the character of *Carmen*, like the rock-and-roll generation later, lived and died by her own rules, despite the standards of the society in which she lived.

A number of different themes are woven together in this poem. One is the struggle between high culture and low. Scott is convinced that the rock and roll his daughter listens to is to blame for the poor choices she has made. By the end of the poem, though, he realizes that he would probably destroy the music he loves if he killed rock and roll. High culture cannot be preserved by destroying low culture; they are simply too closely related to each other. Although this point becomes clear by the end of the poem, it has been prepared for throughout. Scott feels that his daughter does not understand tragedy because she does not appreciate *Oedipus Rex*. If we look at the text of one of the songs she listens to, however, we realize that he may be wrong. Granted, "Inna Gadda Da Vida" sounds like pure gibberish, but the lyrics are — according to rock-and-roll legend — a garbled version of the phrase "in the garden of Eden." The few lyrics we know Scott's daughter sings, then, are related to the tragic story of paradise and the fall. And what does her interest in astrology signify if not an interest in the intersection of fate and free will, one of the central themes of *Oedipus?*

MARGE PIERCY

Barbie Doll

Bitterly ironic, this poem satirizes society's unrealistic expectations of physical beauty for girls and women, as symbolized by the Barbie doll, which has become a cultural icon after more than four decades. This image of plastic perfection brainwashes young girls into accepting false values (playing coy, dieting, smiling, wheedling to attract boys) instead of appreciating their natural strengths (health, intelligence, sexuality, dexterity). Piercy, an ardent feminist, exaggerates how a girl sacrifices herself to the "ideal" Barbie-doll look by cutting off her nose and her legs, and in death, finds the fairy-tale "happy ending." Note the allusion to the Grimms' story in which Cinderella's sisters cut off parts of their feet to fit into the slipper and win the prince. Socialization encourages women to re-shape their bodies to achieve perfection, so some women do so with rhinoplasty, liposuction, breast implants, even anorexia and bulimia. Compare with Piercy's "The Friend" (self-mutilation and sacrifice for acceptance) and with Sexton's "Cinderella" (use of the fairy tale).

MARGE PIERCY

The Friend

As in "Barbie Doll," Piercy's direct, simple sentences deliver an ironic punch, forcing the reader to confront the sacrifices women are asked to make for social approval. A conventional opening ("We sat across the table") is juxtaposed with a critical male voice asking a woman to cut off body parts to gain acceptance, and she passively accepts. His demands are much longer and more negative than her responses, which become poignant, if not pathetic: "Yes" (the affirmative contrast to his negative voice — twice), and "I love you." His only response to her love is self-centered: "that's nice . . . I like to be loved." He offers no love in return, asking only if she's cut off her hands yet — and his question remains as the chilling parting line of this painful, powerful poem. In Piercy's collection *Hard Loving*, this poem appears in a section titled "The death of the small commune," which includes several poems about dissolving relationships and lack of communication, particularly between men and women. Dorothy Parker's "General Review of the Sex Situation" offers another view of the differences between what men and women want.

ROBERT PINSKY

If You Could Write One Great Poem, What Would You Want It to Be About?

The title and epigraph are essential to an understanding of, and are nearly as long as, the poem itself. The first three topics that students choose — Fire, Music, and Romantic Love — could be the choices of any students at any school. The fourth choice, Sign, is one that these particular students, precisely because they are deaf or hearing impaired, would understand in a unique way. Here *sign* does not refer just to sign language but to all language. The poem is therefore a mediation on the material from which poetry is made. You might begin discussion by asking the students which of these four answers the poet prefers and why.

SYLVIA PLATH

Metaphors

"I'm a riddle in nine syllables" cleverly invites the reader to guess the answer. The nine lines, each with nine syllables, parallel the nine months of pregnancy. Thus, the speaker compares being pregnant to feeling like a large elephant, house, melon, and so on. Playfully suggesting the baby inside her are these additional images: a rising loaf of bread (the slang expression for pregnancy — "a bun in the oven" — comes to mind), a fat purse, and the saying that eating green apples causes stomach aches. Plath shows how metaphors create playful language as well as express the mysterious riddle of giving birth. A comparison with the view of motherhood in Plath's "Morning Song" should generate discussion, and contrasting the tone in each of these with that in "Daddy" illustrates her different voices.

SYLVIA PLATH

Mirror

Personification endows inanimate objects or abstract ideas with life or with human characteristics. In this poem's first stanza, the speaker is a mirror that reflects exactly what comes before it, without human emotions such as love, dislike, or cruelty. In the second stanza, the lake serves a similar role in faithfully reflecting the image of a woman. Students will have varying interpretations of the last two lines — perhaps taking it literally that the woman has drowned a child or — more figuratively — has seen the loss of youth and now must face the self-reflection of an old woman.

EZRA POUND

The River-Merchant's Wife: A Letter

Pound's translation of Li Po's "Two Letters from Chang-Kan" characterizes the speaker as deeply in love with her husband. To intensify the feelings of loss and loneliness that consume her during her husband's absence, she recounts the history of their relationship — growing up together as playful children, marrying when she was fourteen, falling in love with him when she was fifteen. Now, at sixteen, having been separated from him for five months, the speaker describes her sorrow with images of near death in nature, such as the falling leaves in autumn.

HENRY REED

Naming of Parts

The speaker cleverly juxtaposes the life force of nature (flowers and bees) with the death force of human nature (rifle parts). The result is startlingly ironic with double entendres that students should be encouraged to catch. For instance, "easing the Spring" has a double meaning — the bees pollinate the flowers to bring on the early springtime, and the individual moves the bolt back and forth to open the breech. Thus, the speaker seems to be saying that using rifles — for example, to kill people in war — is contrary to nature's scheme of things.

EDWIN ARLINGTON ROBINSON

Miniver Cheevy

The past is superior to the present, thinks Miniver Cheevy, who dreams of heroic adventures from the days of Thebes, Camelot, and the Medici. Even his first name denotes a fur that trimmed ceremonial medieval robes. Consumed with the past, Cheevy feels cheated and curses his mundane existence. Refusing to take control of his own destiny, he thinks only about the past and continues drinking. Students' opinions of Cheevy will vary, though most will probably concur with the speaker in seeing the sadness and futility of a life wasted. Ironically, the exact rhyme scheme, which is indicative of a kind of conformity, works against Cheevy's nonconformity with his society.

EDWIN ARLINGTON ROBINSON

Richard Cory

DO YOUR STUDENTS KNOW . . .

The fictional Richard Cory may have committed suicide, but he does not rest in peace. The image created by Edwin Arlington Robinson has been resurrected twice in song. In 1965, Paul Simon wrote the song popularized by the duo, Simon and Garfunkel, with an updated take on the riches and despair of the Cory character. More than ten years later, in 1976, Paul McCartney and his band, Wings, recorded another song about Cory. Robinson, though, drew his inspiration from the real-life newspaper account of the death of a Frank Avery.

Richard Cory's appearance of wealth suggests to others that he must be happy. "Richard" connotes not only "rich" but also royal. His regal stature is reinforced by the words "crown" and "imperially"; in fact, the speaker states that Richard is even "richer than a king" (l. 8), suggesting King Richard. From the speaker's perspective of an ordinary working person, Cory has everything in the world. However, he commits suicide. The speaker is shocked at the incongruity of a glittering appearance masking such despair. Compare Simon and Garfunkel's musical version with this poem.

KAY RYAN

That Will to Divest

Ryan's poem appears so slight on the page that students may not at first realize that it is about anything more than a too-energetic cleaning spree. In fact, the poem is about the human need to simplify life and to be alone. If you go through the poem line by line with students, they will likely begin to realize this when the speaker mentions the urge "to dismiss / rooms." You might ask your class whether they agree that simplicity and solitude are both human needs.

CARL SANDBURG

Fog

In six short, quiet lines without rhyme, the speaker compares the fog to a cat. In the stealthlike way a cat moves, the fog slowly and silently creeps over the water and landscape. After observing the setting from its high vantage point, it passes on. Although this is not a narrative poem with much action other than the fog moving over a city, it presents an excellent opportunity to discuss the essence of lyric poetry's condensed form as it expresses the speaker's feelings, thoughts, and mood. Students who have known cats will have no trouble understanding Sandburg's visual analogy.

SONIA SANCHEZ

right on: white america

There is a great deal to talk about in this poem, both in terms of its message and its technique. Americans are typically proud of the country's pioneer past, but the speaker asserts that this past is not something of which they should be proud. In her view, America has always been a violent place, this violence directed primarily at African-Americans and Native Americans. The technique of the poem is as subversive as its message: capitalization is dispensed with, the slash (/) is used in unusual ways, and the grammar is nonstandard. Consider having students read the poem out loud so that they can hear the effects Sanchez intended.

WILLIAM SHAKESPEARE

Let me not to the marriage of true minds

This famous sonnet celebrates the permanence and constancy of true love. As the speaker's figures of speech suggest, love is like a compass or star that guides ships that wander from their course. Students will have different opinions about the immutability of love, based on their own experiences and what they have observed about their society (in which half of all marriages end in divorce). The concluding couplet, the signature of a Shakespearean sonnet, reiterates hyperbolically the speaker's heartfelt assumption that true love lasts forever.

WILLIAM SHAKESPEARE

Not marble, nor the gilded monuments

The speaker compares this poem to marble, golden monuments of princes, and stone — all objects of hard material that would seemingly last forever. Ironically, none will outlive "this powerful rhyme." Seen as a seduction poem, then, the sonnet attempts to assure the woman that his love for her will outlast other apparently ever-lasting testaments. You could pair this poem with Andrew Marvell's "To His Coy Mistress" with its equally extravagant metaphysical conceits.

PERCY BYSSHE SHELLEY

Ode to the West Wind

In the first three stanzas, the speaker reflects on various aspects of nature touched by spring's west wind — dead autumn leaves, swift clouds that bring rain, and the Mediterranean Sea. Then, in part four, the speaker imagines being a leaf, a cloud, a wave but is humbled by the power of the West Wind. We might imagine the speaker as a writer, the poet Shelley, who addresses the West Wind because he sees his "dead thoughts" on leaves (sheets of paper), like the dead autumn leaves, and implores the wind to scatter these words everywhere.

CHARLES SIMIC

Spring

As simple as the language in this poem is, students may find it baffling. Why, they may ask, is the scene that the speaker witnessed important, aside from the fact that it's charming? It may be best to begin the discussion by focusing on the connection between the title and the poem itself. The title might simply indicate the season in which the scene occurred, but why would that matter? The neighbor is both carefree and modest, uncovered and covered, and she laughs even as she is being buffeted by the wind. It is likely, then, that she is intended to be a kind of embodiment of spring.

LOUIS SIMPSON

A Shearling Coat

This poem is the deceptively simple tale of a botched robbery and murder. On second or third look, however, one sees that it is not at all clear whether the two men got away with the coat. The mystery deepens in the last two lines. Who is speaking here, and what is it he or she wants "to be rid of"? The coat? But it would be a relatively simple matter to dispose of the coat. The most likely answer is that the speaker wants to be rid of the knowledge of "this thing" that has happened to Ortiz and Gozalves. The tragedy and injustice of the situation are obvious enough, but they gain added poignancy when one remembers that a shearling coat is often made from the skin of a year-old lamb. A number of religious symbols are evoked in this way that add resonance to the poem.

STEVIE SMITH

Not Waving but Drowning

The speaker in this poem reports on the drowning of a man whose friends apparently thought he was waving, when actually he was signaling for help. His death becomes a metaphor for his life: his friends thought he "loved larking" (being playful, having a good time), when in fact he was always "too far out," always asking for help. The extent of his friends' misunderstanding is reinforced by the word "cold." They think the water was too cold for him, when, in fact, the world was. Contrast this poem with the drowning metaphor in Atwood's "This Is a Photograph of Me."

CATHY SONG

Lost Sister

DO YOUR STUDENTS KNOW. . .

Jade is worn in China as jewelry, for adornment, and to bring good luck and health to the wearer. But the well-being of female babies in China today is in jeopardy — the World Health Organization estimates that 50 million women are "missing" in China. Female infanticide, which was practiced for many generations and fallen out of practice in the 1950s, has been resurgent since the Chinese government instituted its "one child per family measure" in 1979.

The two parts contrast two women — one remained in China, like the traditional women who never leave home; the other traveled to America and accepted the ways of her new home. Closely related, both parts offer advantages and disadvantages of the women's choices. For example, one culture has its "demons" (l. 24); the other has its "giant snake" (l. 46, referring to the elevated train). Chinese women had fewer freedoms than American women, but both women identify with their heritage. This poem can be taught with Walker's "Everyday Use" or Tan's "Two Kinds."

GARY SOTO

Black Hair

Soto pays homage to Mexican-Americans, brown people with black hair. This autobiographical poem recounts a time when he was eight, weighed only 50 pounds, and did not excel as an athlete. But he saw himself as a brilliant spectator, waving his hands and stomping his feet. As a child, he sat in the bleachers and worshiped baseball player Hector Moreno. Hector (who shares the name of the Trojan hero in Homer's *Iliad*) is a strong role model in a society with few Hispanic heroes. The child (whose father has died) acquires more self-esteem by identifying with Moreno's accomplishments — along with his black hair and brown skin. The child experiences his hero's home run as if it were his own —"we were coming home" (l. 29). You might ask students about their childhood heroes and also about how important they believe it is to have role models within their own ethnic group.

WOLE SOYINKA

Hamlet

After his dramatic works, Shakespeare is best known for his sonnets. It is appropriate, then, that Soyinka uses the sonnet form for this meditation on Hamlet, although it is important to note that this poem is not a Shakespearean sonnet. The resulting poem is so dense with ideas that you will need to take students through it very slowly. It would be best to teach this poem with the play, since students will be unable to judge the fitness of the speaker's various observations without knowing the play fairly well. Looking at these two works together will illuminate both of them.

BARRY SPACKS

Finding a Yiddish Paper on the Riverside Line

Although this poem focuses specifically on the experience of a second-generation American, its application is universal because all of us find ourselves in transition from the past to the future. The speaker is in transition from the ethnic Jewish world of his parents to more the mainstream, assimilationist culture of modern America and from lower to middle class. Note how the father cleaning up after a long day is contrasted with the speaker as a boy who idly "drew [his] name on misted glass." The concluding couplet, in particular, with its juxtaposition of "lap" with "headlines" and "strangers" with "living room" gets at the combination of familiarity and alienation the speaker feels.

WILLIAM STAFFORD

Traveling through the Dark

The speaker suggests that "swerving" is important if we are to avoid tragedy as we all travel along in the dark on life's journey, not knowing what lies ahead. If the dead pregnant doe remains in the road, other travelers might die, swerving to avoid the carcass. But the speaker hesitates in contemplating whether or not to save the unborn fawn. His thinking is "swerving" in the sense of considering another course of action. Still, he takes the obvious way out and tosses the doe over the canyon edge into the river.

WALLACE STEVENS

Anecdote of the Jar

As a structured, man-made shape, the round jar contrasts sharply with the untamed wilderness. Each changes the other; the wilderness grows up to the jar, "no longer wild" as it embraces the object's form, and the jar takes on the "gray and bare" likeness of the wilderness. Here, Stevens looks at the jar as an object itself without imbuing it with symbolic meaning, much as he exemplifies in his poem "Not Ideas about the Thing but the Thing Itself."

WALLACE STEVENS

The Emperor of Ice-Cream

Stevens uses sensuous, even gaudy language to express metaphysical concerns, such as life and death, reality and illusion, the world of the imagination and experience. "Emperor" implies regal splendor and power, whereas "ice-cream" suggests pleasure, sensuality ("concupiscent" or sexual desire), and transience. The poem has been compared to Donne's "Death Be Not Proud," with death defeated by the promise of immortality. Similarly, Stevens shows the ineffectual domain of death which cannot diminish the luxuriance of big cigars and sinfully rich ice cream.

MARK STRAND

Old Man Leaves Party

It is difficult to say why the old man was conscious of the fact that he "still had / A beautiful body" when he left the party. Perhaps people had commented on how fit he looked. The party the old man leaves may be quite literally a festive gathering, but the word *party* can also mean a political organization, or a group of hunters, or any group that has some common purpose. The man achieves a kind of unity with nature, which coincides with his removing his clothing. It is important to note, however, that this is not a simple back-to-nature poem. He would not have stopped to take his clothes off if the mirror, a human artifact, had not been there. By leaving the party and by taking off his clothes, the old man has stepped away from every artifice of civilization except for the one that encourages self-reflection. By the end of the poem, he determines to be an individual and to live "from moment to moment."

All of the above notwithstanding, it is important to note how the poem's slightly comic tone keeps the poem from becoming pretentious. The presence of the mirror is lightly surrealistic, and the man's conviction that all of nature has been waiting to see him strip is charming but comical.

VIRGIL SUÁREZ

Aguacero

Although this poem is an intimate personal portrait of a man and his aspirations for his family, consider beginning the discussion on a technical point: students may be surprised to find that the first sentence ends more than halfway through the poem and that the second sentence does not end until the poem's conclusion. Once this is pointed out, they will be able, perhaps with some assistance, to see how these long, rambling sentences are intended to mimic the downpour, which in turn is intended to serve as a symbol of unlimited possibility.

ALFRED, LORD TENNYSON

Ulysses

Most readers consider this a heroic poem, extolling the spirit of Homer's hero who chooses to go out in the proverbial cloud of glory. But Dante created this story of the doomed last voyage and placed Ulysses in a ring of the inferno as an evil counselor to his followers. Victorians might have felt ambivalent about the speaker in this dramatic monologue, who reveals to his mariners his boredom as king and his scorn for his "agèd" wife, dutiful son, and "savage" subjects. Though he has achieved much, his pompousness and refusal to accept social responsibility might alienate readers. Yet Ulysses is also a grand figure, who knows he is approaching death and prefers to go to meet his fate rather than stand idly waiting. Restless, proud, courageous, and bigger than life, Ulysses will sail beyond the sunset. (Note images of aging throughout.) Some readers will take Ulysses at his word and believe he respects his son and is grateful that Telemachus prefers duty to adventure.

JOHN UPDIKE

Rainbow

DO YOUR STUDENTS KNOW . . .

A rainbow occurs when light is reflected through the water drops of rain, so it is possible to have a lunar rainbow. Although infrequent, there are records of lunar rainbows as far back as Aristotle. A full Moon, which shines brightly, will cast enough light to reflect the various colors of the rainbow, although the colors are very faint.

Updike's poem is a kind of sonnet, although it does not rhyme and not all of its lines are in iambic pentameter. One of the more interesting features is that the description of the rainbow is given before, in the ninth line, the speaker announces, "it has appeared." Immediately after this statement, the rainbow "fades." This verbal trick makes the rainbow, which has just been described in some detail, seem at once concrete and evanescent. The sestet of the sonnet is typically a place where the poet comments on or rethinks what he or she has said in the first eight lines. Here, Updike uses the sestet to comment on a phenomenon that is less frequent than the rainbow and that he only observes "today." In a sense, then, the poem is about those things that recur eternally — the rainbow — and those things that are one-time or rare occurrences — the reflections of the "[l]obster-pot markers."

GINA VALDES

My Mother Sews Blouses

A Mexican-American who grew up on both sides of the California border, Valdes often uses a woman's voice to protest social conditions. The speaker in this poem — daughter of an exploited pieceworker — conveys her mother's pain and resilience. The black cloth, suggesting death as well as blindness, clouds her mother's vision as a veil might. Its lint must be scraped away from her mother's eyelids before she can see clearly. The conclusion suggests that her mother now "sees" the way out of her condition — through night school, which she will attend, ironically, in darkness. Compare with Adamé's "My Grandmother Would Rock Quietly and Hum," noting the significance of "eyes."

MARGARET WALKER

Lineage

The speaker's admiration for her grandmothers, made strong by hard work, is emphasized by her repetition of the line "My grandmothers were strong." Shifting to the present tense, the speaker says her grandmothers "are full of memories" and clean words. The implication is that the speaker is neither strong nor filled with memories and clean words; she is young and has perhaps not worked so hard. Or perhaps her grandmothers' hard work has made life easier for her. Is she rebellious? Adolescent? Does she use "unclean words"? Clearly she admires her grandmothers and wants to be like them some day.

EDMUND WALLER

Go, lovely rose

In the *carpe diem* tradition, Waller uses the rose's beauty and short life to warn a young woman not to hide her charms lest she die a virgin. Less direct than Herrick's "To the Virgins, to Make Much of Time" and less hyperbolic than Marvell's "To His Coy Mistress," Waller nonetheless combines flattery and threat as his speaker tries to seduce a young woman. Notice the surprisingly complex lyrical verse form — each stanza follows the same pattern: lines 1 and 3 rhyme and have four beats; lines 2, 4, and 5 rhyme and have eight beats. The first three stanzas begin on a stressed syllable; and all stanzas contain at least one command ("Go," "Tell," "Bid," "Die.") The final stanza begins on an unstressed syllable emphasizing the chilling stress on the final command to the rose to "die" as a warning to the woman.

JAMES WELCH

The Man from Washington

A Native American himself, Welch presents the end of the Native American way of life — and the end of many Native American lives — as an inevitable outcome of the encounter with white civilization. The man from Washington represents the government, whose promises the speaker seems to portray as lies — until the surprise word "inoculated." The reader expects the speaker and his people to be inoculated (medically protected) against illness. Instead, they will be inoculated against the white world, in which they do not fit comfortably; the implication may be that the government will keep them "safely" separated on reservations.

PHILLIS WHEATLEY

On Being Brought from Africa to America

This autobiographical poem expresses Wheatley's pride in her adopted religion of Christianity and her compassion for Africa's pagan religions. Her Boston master, John Wheatley, writes in her *Poems on Various Subjects, Religious and Moral* (published in London in 1773 when she was about nineteen) that Phillis, having been brought from Africa to America at the age of seven or eight, astonished everyone with her mastery of the most difficult sacred texts within sixteen months. This remarkable woman, educated in both English and Latin, advises whites that blacks (given the opportunity to accept Christianity) are equal to whites in the sight of God.

WALT WHITMAN

A Noiseless Patient Spider

The comparison between the human soul and the spider is obvious — the isolated soul's search for spiritual meaning and emotional connection with others is like the isolated spider's endless work of spinning threads out of itself to connect its web to something. Both the individual and the spider are tiny specks in a vast universe, yet both strive to "catch somewhere." The second stanza presents a fascinating mirror image of the first, so encourage students to circle words and phrases about the spider and then to find the equivalent words and phrases about the soul; for example, filament = gossamer thread; tirelessly = ceaselessly; isolated = detached.

WALT WHITMAN

from "Song of Myself"

The poem is both autobiographical — reflecting the personal feelings and thoughts of Whitman, and generic — reflecting the more general view of humanity. This excerpt exemplifies the speaker's intimate, perhaps even erotic, relationship with nature. By including the second-person "you" several times (ll. 30–37),

Whitman broadens the perspective to invite the reader to share his cosmic vision and to "get at the meaning of poems" from the inner self (ll. 32–37). Note Whitman's characteristic inclusiveness and expansiveness (ll. 3, 37); his use of repetition and questions; and his emphasis on health and energy (ll. 13, 29) and on nature as the source of everything (ll. 6, 34).

C. K. WILLIAMS

Tantrum

This is essentially a poem about the inability of language to express adequately the feelings of frustration and anger that all human beings share. We can of course try to express these feelings in words, but the speaker points out that these words "take up so much emotive time, / entail such muffling, qualifying, attenuation" that they do not help as they should. This observation applies not only to our-day-to day problems but also to the insoluble existential questions of the human race. Thus, for the speaker, it would be best to have a scream at the ready.

WILLIAM CARLOS WILLIAMS

The Dance

Williams's uneven meter, with its many unstressed syllables and awkward run-on lines, creates the clumsy, jerking motion of rollicking dancers. In Bruegel's painting, the peasants dancing at the kermess — an outdoor low-country fair, perhaps a church fund-raiser — go "round and round." And Williams begins and ends his poem with the same line, so it too is rounded out. Note also the auditory imagery ("the squeal and the blare and the tweedle of bagpipes") and visual imagery ("swinging their butts") connoting peasant life.

WILLIAM WORDSWORTH

Composed upon Westminster Bridge, September 3, 1802

Turning from his usual rural scene to the city (London), Wordsworth creates an equally beautiful and uplifting urban morning. As his speaker gazes on the skyline, he personifies the calm, sleeping city (wearing the morning's beauty like a garment, possessing a "mighty heart"). He recognizes that when the day's work begins and the chimneys belch smoke, the city will become noisy and dirty; but at sunrise it epitomizes clean, glittering beauty and deep calm. This is almost a Petrarchan love sonnet. You may want to compare this with Blake's "London."

WILLIAM WORDSWORTH

I wandered lonely as a cloud

The expansiveness of the opening line, with the speaker free as a cloud, turns "lonely" into a positive state. Alone, the speaker is free to respond to the sudden appearance of the personified daffodils, "a host" that seem to be happily tossing their heads and dancing. He compares them to the stars ("continuous" and "never-ending"), and the waves (which they outsparkle). Students will need to know that the poet's gayness is joy (not sexual orientation) for this moment, and also for later, when the memory of the daffodils once again can bring him joy. This is a common Wordsworth theme: nature bringing inner joy now, and again when "recollected in tranquility."

WILLIAM WORDSWORTH

My heart leaps up when I behold

In the 1804 "Ode on Intimations of Immortality from Recollections of Early Childhood," Wordsworth suggests that as we age we lose our sense of joy at natural wonders such as the rainbow ("The Rainbow comes and goes, / and lovely is the Rose . . . But yet I know, where'er I go, / That there hath past away a glory from the earth.") Here, in contrast, he suggests that "natural piety"— a piety inspired by nature, and perhaps innate — remains equally strong throughout life. Readers may interpret "The Child is father of the Man" in various ways: we should learn from the natural spontaneity of children; "a little child shall lead them"; as we are shaped as children, so we shall be as adults; the Christ Child is father of humankind (not a likely interpretation at this point in Wordsworth's career).

WILLIAM WORDSWORTH

She dwelt among the untrodden ways

Using simple images and the rhythm and meter of the ballad, Wordsworth elicits strong emotions. As usual in Wordsworth, the speaker describes a single rural figure. This time she is a maid named Lucy, living in isolation and obscurity, like a violet half-hidden "by a mossy stone." She is also described as "fair" as a single star when no others are in the sky to outshine it.

WILLIAM WORDSWORTH

The Solitary Reaper

As usual, Wordsworth begins by setting the scene — an isolated figure against a rural landscape. Described as "single," "solitary," "by herself," and "alone," the Highland lass is singing as she works in the field, the prototype of the rustic figure closely allied to nature that Wordsworth admires. The passerby hears her "melancholy strain" and stops, deeply moved by the beauty of the music "overflowing" the vale in a language he does not know. As lovely and exotic as the music of nightingales in Araby or cuckoos in the Hebrides, the song seems timeless and eternal. Most important, besides present joy, the song promises future joy, as the speaker carries it with him in his heart. Compare this with "I Wandered Lonely as a Cloud."

WILLIAM BUTLER YEATS

Crazy Jane Talks with the Bishop

A man of God seems to be making inappropriate comments to a fallen woman, under the guise of giving her advice; and the woman (Crazy Jane) replies with bizarre comments, like the speeches of Shakespeare's fools. The bishop states that she should give up her sordid life and return to the church; but his references to her breasts suggest he has known them intimately. Linking foul and fair, she contrasts her own earthly love with the "Love" offered by the church and says the church's mansion has been pitched like a lowly tent in "the place of excrement." Jane's not-so-crazy wise words and clever puns (sole: alone — but also soul; whole: complete — but also a crude sexual allusion [hole]) reinforce the image of the bishop's pride and hypocrisy.

WILLIAM BUTLER YEATS

The Lake Isle of Innisfree

DO YOUR STUDENTS KNOW. . .

When Yeats died in 1939, he was far from the Irish countryside he so loved. The outbreak of World War II prevented arrangements for his final return. He wished to be buried in Country Sligo, the setting of many of his poems and the location of the Lake of Innisfree. Yeats was buried in France where he died, and his body was not returned to Ireland for burial until after the war in 1948. He was then buried, as he had instructed, at the small parish church in Drumcliffe.

The lyrical opening, simple old-fashioned diction, and pastoral images recall Wordsworth, as the speaker rejects city life for a return to the peaceful beauty of the island. Honeybees, linnets, crickets, lake water lapping — these are what he longs for as he stands on "pavements grey." The contrast between this poem's diction and theme and those in "Crazy Jane Talks with the Bishop" demonstrates Yeats's amazing range.

WILLIAM BUTLER YEATS

Sailing to Byzantium

The central contrasts of the poem link Ireland to the young, sensual, mortal, and pastoral. Yeats's speaker, probably an old man himself, rejects these and sails for Byzantium (now Istanbul), the ancient city of high culture (spirituality, intellect, art, the wisdom of ages) where East meets West in modern Turkey. He seeks release from his human, bodily form and transcendence into the world of "holy fire," "singing-masters of the soul," and "golden bough."

WILLIAM BUTLER YEATS

The Second Coming

The speaker suggests that like the falcon, the human spirit is breaking away from the rational restraints of civilization. Here and elsewhere, Yeats prophesies the dissolution of Western society and the emergence of another cycle of history. Thus, the Second Coming is envisioned as a sphinxlike beast with a lion's body and man's head to symbolize this evil spirit, a stark contrast with Christ as the messiah. Students may recall that the sphinx asked passersby a riddle and killed them when they could not answer correctly (Oedipus gave the right answer — man). The irony is that the modern world faces this beast, not Christ, on the Day of Judgment.

D R A M A

CHAPTER 28

UNDERSTANDING DRAMA

WRITING ACTIVITIES

1. Ask students to write about a dramatic performance they have attended. What did they enjoy about live theater?
2. Ask students to write about a play they read in high school. How do they think reading a play is different from seeing a play performed?
3. Ask students to write about a favorite film or television program or series. How do they think watching a drama on film or television is different from seeing a play performed on stage?

GROUP ACTIVITIES

Divide students into groups and ask them to decide which plays they would like to perform. Ask each group to select a director, a set manager, or a costume designer. Ask the group to agree on which member of their group should play each part. Then ask them to discuss or write about their choices. Be prepared to give a brief overview of each play the groups might be considering.

AUGUST STRINDBERG

The Stronger

WRITING ACTIVITIES

1. Have students write about what they believe Mrs. X's life will be like with Mr. X after she returns home.
2. Ask students to write about whether Miss Y has had an affair with Mr. X or not, giving reasons to support their conclusions.

GROUP ACTIVITY

Ask each group of students to construct a monologue for either Mr. X or Miss Y, in which they speak directly to Mrs. X (without her responding). Each group should create a monologue for a different purpose. For example, Miss Y might be trying to deny having an affair with Mr. X, might try to explain what happened with her engagement to cause her to break it off, or might even attempt to persuade Mrs. X to divorce her own husband. Mr. X might be comforting Mrs. X or ordering her to mind her own business. Let the class decide which monologues might work most effectively if expanded into a play like *The Stronger*.

DO YOUR STUDENTS KNOW . . .

According to *Language of Flowers*, a 1819 French book that codified the use of flowers to symbolize love, Strindberg's tulips, mentioned throughout the play, are a symbol of love and passion. Specifically, red tulips symbolize undying love, and yellow tulips are a sign of hopeless love.

DISCUSSION

The title is very important to the power struggle occurring in this play, and it may help to begin with what it means to these two women to be "stronger." In what arenas do Mrs. X and Miss Y compete, and what would make one of them stronger than the other? At several points in the one-act play, Mrs. X mentions acting, marriage, and children. How do we know the conversation, even on the first few pages, is more competitive than friendly? You might examine Mrs. X's use of props, showing off her gifts for her children and husband, reminding Miss Y that she has neither. Why are marriage and children so important to Mrs. X's identity in this play? Are both of these women strong, or is neither one strong?

Discussion of the play's structure should add to student understanding of the unusual dialogue of this play. Strindberg has designed the play so that only Mrs. X speaks. What does the format do to our understanding of the events? Miss Y only responds nonverbally, with certain expressions or with laughter. Mrs. X finally suggests that Miss Y is "always silent" (12), but students may find it helpful to discuss why Mrs. X feels the need to speak so much. Why does she continue to speak when Miss Y says nothing in return? This will lead into a discussion about nonverbal communication, both by Miss Y and Mrs. X. At key points, Miss Y's expressions move the monologue along. Her fear as Mrs. X points and shoots the toy pistol at her inspires Mrs. X's question, "Were you scared?" (5), but her question leads to a discussion of why Miss Y might want to shoot Mrs. X, because of their competition at the Grand Theatre.

The laughter may also reveal clues to the relationship between these two women, for Miss Y may be laughing at Mrs. X's antics with the slipper, but she might also be laughing because she has seen Mr. X in his slippers. Moreover, she may recognize his moods as intimately as Mrs. X does herself. Her laughter may suggest her close relationship to Mr. X and would lead naturally to Mrs. X's revelations near the end of the play.

Other elements work in the way the gun and the slippers do, and details that seem unimportant at first become clues when they are all put together. Mrs. X puts all of the pieces together in the final monologue and begins to answer the questions she has been asking Miss Y throughout the play. Suddenly, the tulips, which she admits she "loathes," stem from Miss Y's influence over her husband's taste. Her vacations, her son's name, even the hot chocolate she is drinking on stage have been introduced because of Miss Y's relationship to Mr. X. At least, that is the conclusion Mrs. X makes about these various details. In her final monologue, she moves dramatically from the revelation to an emotional burst of rage — attacking Miss Y and comparing her to a "worm," a "snake," a "crab"—before finally shifting to an attitude of acceptance and confidence. Mrs. X expresses pity for Miss Y because she has no husband and no children and because Miss Y's influence over Mr. X's tastes has had no effect on Mrs. X's position as his wife.

A discussion of Mrs. X and the truth of her accusations and claims may help students put the pieces together. You may want to discuss with the students what they believe really happened. Does Miss Y have a relationship with Mr. X? Do the tulips and chocolate reflect their affair? Is she a predator, waiting for Mrs. X to fail so that she can take her place? Right before the final monologue, Miss Y "makes a motion, as if about to speak." What would she say? Why does Mrs. X not let Miss Y speak now that she wants to?

The students can discuss what we cannot know for certain because Miss Y never speaks: we get all the details, all the suspicions, all the assumptions from Mrs. X, but we are never told by Miss Y whether they are true or false. Students can discuss how credible they believe Mrs. X's observations and claims to be. If Mrs. X is correct about all the events, why would she reveal her understanding and admit Miss Y's influence over her family to Miss Y? If her conclusions are wrong, why would she come to this particular interpretation? Mrs. X is fascinating on several levels, and her character and self-expression should be good topics for class discussion.

You may want to teach this text with other texts showing how characters deal with their unusual interpretation of events around them, including "The Yellow Wallpaper," "The Rocking-Horse Winner," and *Death of a Salesman*.

FURTHER READING

Martin, Jaqueline. "Strindberg in Performance." *Theatre Research International* 18 (1993): 1–2.

JANE MARTIN

Beauty

WRITING ACTIVITIES

1. Ask students to write an essay in which they explain what three things they would wish for and why.
2. Have students write an essay in which they demonstrate which of the two women is likelier to be happy with the switch and why.
3. Ask students to write an essay in which they speculate on how the play might have been different if it had involved two men instead of two women.

GROUP ACTIVITY

Is Carla as dumb as she claims, or is she simply trying to make Bethany feel better? Break the class into small groups and have them find evidence for both sides of the argument.

DO YOUR STUDENTS KNOW . . .

Related to the notion that angels represent perfection, the *halo effect* is a term psychologists use to describe the belief that physically attractive people are smarter, more popular, and mentally healthier. Research suggests that attractive people have more success and rewards in both their professional and personal lives, although a higher self-confidence may be responsible for their success.

DISCUSSION

A sense of humor and the willing suspension of disbelief are prerequisites for anyone trying to approach this play. Not only does Martin introduce an element of the supernatural, but she also introduces the genie. This figure will be familiar to students from the film *Aladdin* and from reruns of *I Dream of Jeannie*. Martin wisely chooses to have most of the supernatural events — the appearance of the genie, and the miraculous recovery of Bethany's uncle — occur offstage.

At heart, the play is a comic meditation on the old adage, "The grass is always greener on the other side." In conducting class discussion, you might raise the question of why Martin chose to introduce the supernatural at all. Why couldn't Carla and Bethany simply have a heart-to-heart conversation while having dinner or lying on the beach? One possibility is that such a conversation would not really lead to the sort of change that occurs in the play. The women might come to understand each other better, and each might come to be more satisfied with her own lot, but this would result in the type of personal growth that Martin does *not* want her characters to experience.

Another important question is why "Beauty" is so brief. There is obvious comic potential in seeing the two friends adjust to their new lives. This is a scenario that has been recycled many times. By keeping the play short, however, Martin focuses on the transformation itself — and on Bethany's reason for wanting it. Carla is really the wiser of the two because she prefers being the person she already is.

Consider teaching this play with *True West*, "The Littoral Zone," and *A Midsummer Night's Dream*. The first two selections are far more serious than *Beauty*, but each addresses some of the same issues. In *True West*, two brothers compete in destructive ways; in "The Littoral Zone," a couple begins an affair that promises things their marriages do not, only to find, after they marry each other, that their passion has cooled. *A Midsummer Night's Dream*, as a comedy that involves magic and transformations, has some similarities with *Beauty*.

CHAPTER 29

READING AND WRITING ABOUT DRAMA

WRITING ACTIVITIES

1. Briefly discuss how the excerpt from *Trifles* by Susan Glaspell is highlighted and annotated in the text. Then choose another dramatic excerpt to highlight and annotate as a class.
2. Ask students to plan an essay that could be written about the second excerpt that has been discussed. You might want students to write the essay, or you might want them to concentrate on planning at this point.
3. Ask students to write about what they have learned about reading and preparing to write about drama. How does writing about drama differ from writing about fiction or poetry?

GROUP ACTIVITY

You might ask students to highlight and annotate a text and plan an essay in groups (as in Writing Activities 1 and 2) and then ask them to work individually to write that essay. Or after the group-planning activity, you may want each student to plan and write his or her own essay about a topic that has not been discussed.

CHAPTER 30

PLOT

SUSAN GLASPELL

Trifles

WRITING ACTIVITIES

1. Have students reconstruct the events chronologically, beginning with events that took place before the action of the play and leading up to the end of the play itself.
2. Ask students if they think that Mrs. Wright had other options (besides murder).

GROUP ACTIVITY

Assign each group to examine one brief section of *Trifles* for contrast between what the men in the play and what Mrs. Hale and Mrs. Peters are doing.

DO YOUR STUDENTS KNOW . . .

Before becoming a playwright, Glaspell worked as a reporter for the *Des Moines Daily News*. She was inspired to write *Trifles* by an actual murder on which she reported, and she eventually quit her reporting job to become a full-time playwright and fiction writer.

DISCUSSION

Before you begin discussing this play, be sure students know what the word *trifles* means. Once the class has discussed this definition, they will be able to see how the quilt (Q 12), the messy kitchen, the bird, and so many other clues go unnoticed by the sheriff and his men, yet are vitally important to understanding the murder and why it occurred. The plot of *Trifles* gives the students ample opportunity to discuss such disparate topics as gender roles, the implications of withholding evidence, investigative techniques, and the attention to detail that the men seem to lack. In this neat one-act play, all the action occurs in the Wrights' kitchen. Although this static setting restricts "movement" and action, it demonstrates the importance of detail, whether it be the details onstage needed to solve a murder mystery or the details a careful audience must notice when watching or reading *any* play (Q 4).

The action follows two women, Mrs. Hale and Mrs. Peters, as they draw conclusions about Mrs. Wright's married life, her emotional state, and her murder of her husband, all from the state in which they find Mrs. Wright's kitchen (Q 2). Specifically, they discover a dirty kitchen towel, table, and sink (and this from a woman who does not feel complete in prison without her apron). Further details they note include the crazy stitches in the quilt, the empty bird cage, and finally, the strangled canary (Q 8). From these trifling details, plus Mrs. Hale's recollection of the unmarried Minnie Foster in a white dress with blue ribbons (134), the women are able to build a clear picture of Mrs. Wright's loneliness, her distress when her husband kills her only "pet"—a bird that sang as she used to do herself ("She used to sing. He killed that, too," 124)—and her confused state after she strangles her husband, when Mr. Hale discovers her in the rocking chair.

Ask students how reliable Mrs. Hale is as "historian"; much of what she recollects and concludes should suggest *her own* situation (and her own guilt about her failure to help Mrs. Wright) (Q 5). Ask students how Mrs. Wright's presence would change the play. Point out that, for one thing, the play could then seem to be Mrs. Wright's exclusively (Q 6). As it is, the lesson to be learned transcends one relationship (Mr. and Mrs. Wright's) and becomes more universally a lesson about how men and women perceive events and details differently. The men focus on the search for a motive and on traditional crime-scene details and characterize the "discoveries" the women might make as "trifles"; the women focus on emotions and relationships (Q 11). You might want to ask students if they believe men and women perceive events differently. You might also want to bring in the fact that several recent studies conclude that men and women actually express themselves differently—men use concrete language, whereas women use language that emphasizes the connotations of words. Ask students in what ways this information helps explain the outcome of the play.

The "box set" obliges the men to leave, looking for evidence that a *man* has committed the murder—signs of a break-in, extra pieces of rope, a disturbance in the barn (Q 8). Ask students to comment on what preconceptions cause the men to believe that a man must have committed the murder. The women can relax and see the evidence in front of them. The repeated interruptions by the county attorney—from his initial injunction to Mrs. Peters to "keep an eye out for anything that might be of use"—provide an ironic counterpoint to the careful process of detection in which the women are engaged. Humor results from his overhearing the conversation about the quilt, leading to his unconsciously punning question on knotting, while the enormity of the cover-up committed by the women is (again unconsciously) alluded to in his comment that Mrs. Peters is married to the law (Q 9). Mrs. Peters has moved from unconcerned observer to sympathetic accomplice in Mrs. Hale's decision to hide the evidence of murder (first apparent when she corrects the untidy stitching in the quilt); Mrs. Peters's decision to help is reached at line 131, when she recounts her understanding of a despair similar to Mrs. Wright's (Q 10). It is at this crucial point that Mrs. Peters turns her back on "men's law" and conspires with Mrs. Hale to hide the truth (Q 11). Ask students to try to justify the cover-up and to consider the possible results for all three women if Mrs. Hale and Mrs. Peters had revealed their findings (Q 13).

The fact that the murder takes place *before* the opening of the play (Q 1) does not detract from the atmosphere of despair built up as the women realize how miserable Mrs. Wright's life must have been (Q 7), married to such a hard man, "Like a raw wind that gets to the bone" (103). The plot centers not so much on physical events in chronologic order as on this reluctant realization and the women's tacit but moving resolve to impede the course of justice (Q 14). It also exposes the reason why the women can remove the evidence with little suspicion, for the men, assuming the killer is a man, ignore the "trifles" the women examine closely, even joking about them. They allow key evidence to elude them, even after they glance over the unfinished quilt and criticize Mrs. Wright's housekeeping.

You may want to ask students if the difficulty of Mrs. Wright's life in any way mitigates her crime. Remind them that until recently, battered wives who killed their husbands were found guilty of murder. Only in the last few years have they sometimes been acquitted by juries or granted clemency by governors who recognize that years of physical and emotional abuse might justify what in the past appeared to be premeditated murders.

Remind students that Glaspell's short story based on this play is called "A Jury of Her Peers" (Q 3). Whom do they see as Mrs. Wright's peers? Could she get a fair trial in her town, especially in 1916, when only men served on juries? What verdict would the men probably choose? What would the women's verdict be? (Self-defense? Insanity?) What might Mrs. Wright say if she took the stand? Do students think she should be punished for her crime?

You may want to compare this play to "A Rose for Emily," "The Yellow Wallpaper," "The Chrysanthemums," or *A Doll House*.

FURTHER READING

France, Rachel. "Susan Glaspell." *Twentieth-Century American Dramatists*. Ed. John MacNicholas. *Dictionary of Literary Biography*. Vol. 7, part 1. Detroit: Gale, 1981. 215–23.

SAM SHEPARD

True West

WRITING ACTIVITIES

1. Have students write a letter from Lee and Austin's mother to their father. How would she describe to him the conflict going on between the two brothers? What might she ask him to do?

2. The play ends suddenly in the middle of a fight between Lee and Austin. Ask students to write a three-page continuation of the play that brings it to a more traditional conclusion.

3. Ask students to write a short research essay on Sam Shepard's career as a playwright.

GROUP ACTIVITY

Divide the class into three groups. Ask each group to suggest one change they would like to see made in the play. Each group should list two reasons why their suggested change would represent an improvement and two reasons why it might detract from the pay as it currently stands.

DO YOUR STUDENTS KNOW . . .

The first television version of *True West* premiered in 1984 on *American Playhouse* and starred Gary Sinise as Austin and John Malkovich as Lee. This film was adapted from the original production of the Steppenwolf Theatre Company, a theatre company Sinise and Malkovich cofounded in 1974 in Chicago.

DISCUSSION

True West is the story of two brothers whose competition and tendency toward self-destruction threaten to destroy them both. Austin is an aspiring screenwriter, and his brother Lee is a drifter and small-time thief. When the play opens, Austin is staying at the house of their mother, who is on vacation in Alaska, and working on a play he hopes will provide him with his big break. Coincidentally, Lee has stopped by and decides to stay a while. Austin takes after their mother, who is settled and domestic, whereas Lee is a criminal who resembles their hard-drinking, impoverished father (Q 3). From the beginning, the tension between the two brothers is palpable. As the play develops, it becomes obvious how much they envy each other and how badly each wants to beat the other at his own game. The play is built around a series of oppositions, art/commerce and anarchy/order among them.

Austin would like to get Lee out of the house, but he is afraid that Lee will commit crimes that will place them both in jeopardy. Lee does in fact begin to burglarize houses, and at one point walks in with a stolen TV just as Austin is meeting with Saul Kimmer, a Hollywood producer, about his script. Although Austin tries to rush Saul out the door, Lee insists on talking with him and even attempts to interest Saul in an idea he has for a contemporary western. When he finds out the producer plays golf, he arranges a game with him for the next day. Lee then forces Austin to stay up all night working on a treatment of the story.

At this point, the play takes an unexpected turn. Although the audience never sees the golf game between Lee and Saul, Lee describes it to Austin afterwards. Not only has Lee beaten Saul at golf, but he has sold him on his story idea. Initially, it even seems that the producer is going to abandon Austin's script. The actual golf game is not included for a number of reasons. The play depends in part for its impact on the claustrophobic atmosphere achieved by Shepard's decision to confine the action to the small house. In addition, it is important that Lee be the one to tell Austin what has happened so that he has a chance to gloat. Finally, the omission helps create temporary uncertainty about whether Lee did in fact hurt or threaten Saul (Q 4). When Saul comes to the house again, he assures

Austin that their deal is still on, but that he wants Austin to be the screenwriter for Lee's movie.

This is too much for Austin, who feels he has a better sense of what the public wants than Lee does. He is both right and wrong about this. He may well be in touch with the everyday experience of the average theater goer, but that does not mean he knows "what people wanna see on the screen." In many cases, people want to see something very different from their daily lives (Q 8). When Austin refuses to help, Saul decides to drop his project and go with Lee's instead. This is the play's turning point. From now until the end of the play, each brother tries to supplant the other. Austin quickly descends into alcoholism and petty crime, and Lee tries desperately to become a writer, at first without Austin's help, then later with it. The two men soon realize that neither of them can achieve his goal without help from the other. Lee needs Austin to write the treatment of his film, and Austin, who has decided he wants to go into the desert, needs Lee to take him. Each feels that he needs the other's respect in order to be whole (Q 4). The screenplay, in which two men chase each other through a barren landscape, parallels the real-life competition between the two brothers. Lee is more right than he knows when he defends his plot by saying, "It's too much like real life."

The brothers' parents play a significant role in the play, although we never see the father and the mother only appears in the last scene. The parents represent, respectively, the opposite poles of wildness and domesticity. The father never appears, but Lee serves in a sense as his representative, and although the mother is away in Alaska for most of the play, she has left Austin to guard her home. By the time she returns, her sons have more or less destroyed the interior of the house. If Shepard had introduced her character earlier, she might have halted (or at least slowed) Austin's downward spiral. By bringing her in only when it is too late and having Austin refuse to listen to her, Shepard shows us how far even her once-responsible son is capable of falling (Q 10). The story Austin tells Lee about their father's teeth is important for two reasons: first, it allows Austin to demonstrate that he does in fact have a connection with their father; second, it allows him to tell a story about the West that he feels is more true to life than Lee's (Q 9).

Each of the props Shepard introduces contributes something significant to the play. The televisions Lee steals represent not only lawlessness but the intrusion of commercialized, dumbed-down entertainment. Austin's typewriter, though it would not have seemed as old-fashioned when the play was first performed in 1980, represents the type of art that requires imagination and personal engagement. The golf clubs Saul gives Lee are a testimony to Lee's ability to, both literally and figuratively, play the game. When Lee assaults the typewriter with one of the clubs, then, his action represents an assault on literature by the entertainment industry. The toasters that Austin steals, though he intends them to be symbols of his ability to compete with Lee, are such domestic items that their presence is comical. Austin is bound and determined to beat Lee at his own game, so money is not even an issue in his thefts (Q 7).

Although the action of the play is confined to one small house, a number of other places are invoked. Austin lives in Los Angeles; Lee and their father have been living in the desert; their mother has been vacationing in Alaska. Each of these places represents a vision of the West, and each of them is desolate in its own way (Q 11). In American mythology, the West has traditionally been seen as anarchic yet full of possibility. In the play, however, Austin and Lee throw away the possibility of successful careers and descend into purposeless violence. The barren, hostile emotional landscape the two men inhabit by play's end is the "True West" of the title (Q 2).

Consider teaching this play with "Cowboys Are My Weakness," "The Carnival Dog, the Buyer of Diamonds," "A Primer for the Punctuation of Heart Disease," or *Death of a Salesman*. The first selection deals with the ways that the myth of the Old West affects a woman's perceptions and expectations; the others examine difficult, sometimes volatile, family relationships.

FURTHER READING

Bigsby, C. W. E. "Blood and Bones Yet Dressed in Poetry: The Drama of Sam Shepard." *Contemporary Theatre Review* 8.3 (1998): 19–31.
Schvey, Henry I. "A Worm in the Wood: The Father–Son Relationship in the Plays of Sam Shepard." *Modern Drama* 36 (Mar. 1993): 12–27.

HENRIK IBSEN

A Doll House

WRITING ACTIVITIES

1. Ask students to write about whether they think *A Doll House* has a happy ending.
2. Have students write about the elements of the play that show Nora and Torvald live in a doll house.

GROUP ACTIVITY

Ask each group of students to collaborate on a letter from Nora to her children. Assign each group to write from a different perspective. For example, one might write an apology, one an attempt to justify her actions, and another an angry denunciation of Torvald Helmer. Have each group read its letter aloud and ask the class to decide which best fits Nora's character, motivation, and actions presented in the play.

DO YOUR STUDENTS KNOW . . .

Norway was one of the first countries to pass liberal divorce legislation, setting a tone of more equality for women in Norwegian society. In 1909, divorce by mutual consent was declared a legal and acceptable means of ending a marriage. The passage of this law reflects both a recognition of the equality of all citizens and a lessening of the authority and power of the church in regulating social behavior.

DISCUSSION

Before actually discussing the play, you should acquaint students with the status of women in nineteenth-century marriages. They may be surprised to hear that married women had almost no rights. Any possessions they brought into the marriage legally became the property of their husbands. If they left the marriage — as Nora does — their husbands got custody of their children. Married women of Nora's class almost never traveled alone and never worked outside the home. Indeed, without their husband's signature, they could not borrow money or enter into contracts. In this context, Nora's exit at the end of the play is not just an act of self-assertion; it is also an act of bravery — one that most women in Ibsen's contemporary audience would never contemplate, let alone carry out. Ask students whether this information suggests that the play is about Nora's struggle with Torvald (and her own sense of self) or about the needs of an individual — Nora, a woman — versus the preservation of a society. That is, ask students what it is that Ibsen seems to be criticizing (Q 11).

You might begin your discussion of the play by asking students to list key events that have occurred before the play begins, including Nora's forgery, Krogstad's crime, and Nora's friendship with Mrs. Linde (Q 2). The plot of this play is tight, emphasizing Ibsen's preoccupation at this time (1879) with realistic drama. You might want to point out to students that Ibsen was not preoccupied with realism throughout his entire career. His early plays — such as *Brand* (1866) and *The Master Builder* (1892) — and his last play, *When We Dead Awaken* (1900), are highly romantic. You may, for example, use *Peer Gynt* (1867), with its elves, trolls, and fantastic occurrences, to illustrate how realistic drama was one phase Ibsen passed through. A discussion of whether realism might best show the action in this play may be helpful, especially when the class considers the lack of reality in the lives of Nora and Torvald (Writing Activity 2).

All of the scenes of *A Doll House* lead to the denouement with inexorable logic. While Nora at first believes that her anxious preoccupation with the passing hours will lead to her suicide, the key final scene between Nora and Torvald shows the audience where the action has been leading all along: to Nora's slamming of the door as she leaves her doll house. All of the props are chosen with deliberate reference to the unfolding of the plot: the Christmas tree; the macaroons (and Nora's subterfuge in eating them that foreshadows the discovery of her forgery by demonstrating her willingness to reject her husband's ban on them, [Q 3]); the letter box in full view (Q 4); Nora's tarantella costume (Q 6). The different modes of dialogue (from references to squirrels and larks to the later serious discussion) reflect the plot and help reveal the theme. One factor that will affect student reaction to Nora is Torvald's pet names for her. Ask students (individually or in groups) to identify these, and then ask students to discuss their changing attitudes toward Nora as the play progresses (Q 1). The effect is indicative of Ibsen's "conviction that art should be a source of insights, a creator of discussion, a conveyor of ideas, something more than mere entertainment" (Brockett 550).

The central plot pits innocent intention against the reality of human need: Nora's forgery of her father's signature to save Torvald's health against the subsequent blackmail Krogstad feels forced to press on the wife of the man who has fired him from the only job that could help him recover his own lost reputation. Nora, hoping that Torvald will appreciate her attempts to save him, is led to believe that he is capable of both forgiving her crime and taking the blame himself (Q 5), the prevention of which could only be her final sacrifice for him, suicide. When this miracle is not forthcoming, she recognizes the hollowness of her marriage and her existence as a mere plaything for the benefit of first her father and now Torvald (3.1.285), making her departure the only possible course of action.

Krogstad is no melodramatic villain; he is as desperate and as helpless as Nora, until freed by Mrs. Linde's determination to help him recover his lost sense of worth and to devote herself to his future (Q 9). Torvald's comments in act 1 about Krogstad's children, "Every breath the children take in is filled with the germs of something degenerate," suggest Ibsen's constant preoccupation with heredity (Q 7). More importantly, however, Torvald's attitude urges Nora to realize she must leave her own children to avoid their being polluted by her crime (Q 8). This fear of the "sins of the father" being revisited on offspring is further reinforced by Torvald's views of Nora's father, a weak (although good-natured) man (Q 7).

The complexity of the action is attributable to the existence of several subplots (Q 8). Ibsen frequently introduces triangular relationships in his plays (see *Hedda Gabbler*, 1890); here Dr. Rank serves as mediator between husband and wife, friend to Nora, and representative of the physical effects of heredity: the announcement of his impending death is ominous in the context of act 3 (Q 8). Mrs. Linde, the steady working woman who knows hardship, sacrifice, and duty, at first would appear to be very different from her old friend Nora. However, her desire is to do for Krogstad what Nora has done for Torvald: sacrifice herself by working for his well-being (Q 9, 10). The main difference between her sacrifice and Nora's, however, is that she knows the choice she is making with Krogstad: she once chose to marry for the good of others, but now she is choosing to work toward her own well-being and happiness, not just Krogstad's. Her insistence that Krogstad not ask for the letter he sent to Torvald shows this. Both she and Krogstad are truthful with the other; each one knows the other's mistakes and weaknesses, and both agree to live with those mistakes, without criticism, deception, or recrimination. Mrs. Linde wants Nora to have the same level of trust in her marriage with Torvald, so she tells Krogstad to leave the letter in the mailbox. The real world that brings Krogstad and Mrs. Linde together is the same reality that shatters the make-believe world in which Nora and Torvald live.

Krogstad's recognition of Nora's panic and his comments on suicide ("down in the freezing, coal-black water? There, till you float up in the spring, ugly, unrecognizable, with your hair falling out —") (Q 7) also add to Nora's incipient hysteria while articulating her intention to kill herself. This leads to her wild interpretation of the tarantella, a visual demonstration of her inner torment, at the end of act 2 (Q 6). This moment —lost on Torvald, but not on the perceptive Dr. Rank — may be identified by students as the climax of the play (Q 6) although the decisive turning point of the action comes when Nora changes out of her party costume and talks to Torvald seriously in act 3. The upcoming costume party, always in the background, reminds the audience that Nora's time is running out. When it finally arrives, the party serves as a "play within a play" in that it parallels Nora's central predicament — she is wearing a mask and living a "party" (Q 6).

The party and the tarantella itself become markers for Nora of the end of existence as she knows it. After the party, Torvald reads the letter from Krogstad. His reaction will determine Nora's future; his selfishness, however, leads Nora to decide he is not worth killing herself for. By the time the second letter from Krogstad arrives, saving the day, Nora resolves that her duty to herself must outweigh her duty to her husband; she will never again be a "frightened little songbird" (Q 8). Nora and Mrs. Linde make opposite moves, but in some ways for the same reasons (Q 10).

The ending of the play has always generated much comment and controversy. Ask students to place themselves in the social situation of the nineteenth century and assess the appropriateness of Nora's decision (Q 12). Have students debate whether her actions are consistent with the changes in Nora's character exhibited throughout the play, or whether the decision to leave her children is too abrupt (or too impetuous) to be believable (Q 13).

You might want to teach this play with "Patterns," "The Yellow Wallpaper," or "A Rose for Emily."

FURTHER READING

Brockett, Oscar G. *The History of the Theater*. 5th ed. Boston: Allyn & Bacon, 1987.

Trudeau, Lawrence J., ed. *Drama Criticism*. Vol. 2. Detroit: Gale, 1992. 266–356.

CHAPTER 31

CHARACTER

ANTON CHEKHOV

The Brute

WRITING ACTIVITIES

1. Ask students to write about why Mrs. Popov and Mr. Smirnov are both so stubborn in their attitudes toward the opposite sex.
2. Do students think the outcome of this farce is to be expected? Why or why not?

GROUP ACTIVITY

Have different groups of two students act out brief scenes from the play, preferably scenes that involve high levels of emotional dialogue between the characters. Do they see the emotions or words expressed by the characters as plausible? Does it matter?

DO YOUR STUDENTS KNOW . . .

Chekhov is widely known for his serious plays, which commented on the social upheaval in Russia at the turn of the century. The Russian monarchy so feared the power of the theater that members of the secret police were often positioned as ushers in the theater of the Moscow Arts Theater, which produced Chekhov's plays.

DISCUSSION

It is a good idea to begin by explaining to students that a farce is a comedy in which stereotypical characters engage in horseplay and slapstick humor. You can get students to think about the issues examined in *The Brute* by asking them if they think that opposites really do attract. Can two people with different backgrounds and beliefs fall in love? Does Chekhov turn an old stereotype on its head or merely reinforce it?

Critic Harvey Pilcher also calls Chekhov's farce a "comedy of situation." Have students compare this "comedy of situation" to any popular television situation comedy. Focus particularly on predictability of plot and on the comedy created by characters using extraordinary methods to deal with ordinary situations. For example, Joey on the sitcom *Friends* needs a job, and there is an opening at his friend Chandler's company. Because he is afraid of problems that might arise from working with his friend, Joey decides to create an alter-ego personality and take on the role of "Richard" at work (Q 15).

In *The Brute*, Chekhov uses the age-old trick of dynamically reversing opposing characters' feelings toward one another. By centering on two characters who are determined to act in specific professed ways, Chekhov gives them both (or the audience, at any rate) the means to realize that their worldviews are, finally, inappropriate. Ask students to point, first, to the original attitudes of Mrs. Popov and Mr. Smirnov; then have them find the point at which each character's attitude begins to change. Mrs. Popov is committed to forcing the strictures of widowhood on herself and remaining faithful to the memory of a philandering late husband; Smirnov is committed to feelings of anger that she represents the oppressive upper classes who are out to cheat him and that all women are untrustworthy. Both, of course, reluctantly change their attitudes toward the other. These are round, dynamic characters (Q 1). Mrs. Popov seems to have the upper hand in the relationship with Mr. Smirnov because he needs her money to keep his creditors at bay. But in the end, it is his new emotion — love — that wins out over her anger (Q 2). Ask students whose side they would take, Mrs. Popov's or Mr. Smirnov's (Q 14). You will probably find students split in their preferences, and it is interesting to note whether their decisions cross gender lines (Q 5).

The audience sees that Mrs. Popov is using her late husband's memory as an excuse to feel exaggeratedly tragic: "Never more shall I see the light of day, never strip from my body this . . . raiment of death!" (4). This broad, melodramatic language is essential to the farce; it is undercut by Luka's familiarity with his mistress and his friendly advice to her that she go out and have fun. Luka is a flat character who serves as foil to Mrs. Popov. Their relationship, seen through their speech, makes clear both Mrs. Popov's exaggeration and Luka's attempts to "bring her back" to reality (Q 6, 10).

Mrs. Popov's tone changes as she becomes more honest and more graphic about her husband's unfaithfulness and general loose living (Q 9). Indeed, *he* is perhaps the real "brute" of the piece, and thus he is a formidable third character. It is he who "defines" his wife, who stubbornly clings to mourning in an effort to "beat" him, and it is he who creates the situation that puts Smirnov into an uncontrollable rage (Q 3).

Smirnov realizes that the qualities that he hates in Mrs. Popov are the strengths that cause him to love her. For example, even as he is challenging her to a duel, he capitulates — "Just as a matter of principle I'll bring her down like a duck. But what a woman! . . . Her cheeks were flushed, her eyes were gleaming!" (123). This is also the point at which Smirnov starts using more elaborate language, in keeping with what he obviously considers to be a high-flown emotion — love (Q 11). Ask students to point out additional uses of Smirnov's figurative language to support this idea that it reflects his emotion.

It is characteristic of comedy that emotions are so exaggerated and reactions so open to change at a moment's notice. However, Chekhov manages to include an exploration, no matter how cursory, of popular late nineteenth-century values and perceptions of gender roles. Both Mrs. Popov and Smirnov distrust the opposite sex. From Mrs. Popov's accounts of her marriage, it would seem that she has justification for her feelings; Smirnov, too, recounts how he has been taken in by appearances and betrayed by women in the past, so he now considers them all to be liars and play actors (73) (Q 4, 5). It is characteristic of farce that exaggerated actions accompany these emotions; Mrs. Popov stamps her foot, leaves the room, and tries to outshout Smirnov, while he jumps up wildly, gripping the backs of chairs so hard that they snap. In addition, Mrs. Popov's shredding of her handkerchief — a symbol of her mourning — reflects her changing attitude (153) (Q 7). Luka adds to the general mayhem by having a heart attack when threatened by Smirnov, from which he recovers enough to round up an axe, the gardener with a rake, the coachman with a pitchfork, and hired men with sticks, only to discover Smirnov and Popov engaged in that long kiss.

Smirnov's asides seem to create dramatic irony by letting the audience in on his thoughts, as when he examines the dueling pistols but remarks to the audience, "My God, what eyes she has! They're setting me on fire!" (130) (Q 13). This is not the first sign of his growing admiration for her, however, for he remarks at line 123: "But what a woman! . . . Her cheeks were flushed, her eyes were gleaming!" Such language, which ushers in Smirnov's changing attitude toward Mrs. Popov, emphasizes his emotion again (Q 11). Verbal irony is apparent when Smirnov, realizing his love, refuses to duel. Challenged by Mrs. Popov ("What's the matter? Scared?"), he replies, "That's right. I'm scared" (138) (Q 12).

Challenge students to see how each character's dialogue reveals much about the emotion each feels. Mrs. Popov's ambivalence toward her dead husband, for example, is obvious early on, especially in her revealing speeches about unfaithfulness (Q 8). The play's final line is hers, emphasizing the diminished role the dead man will play in her life from now on: Toby, her husband's favorite horse, "is *not* to have any oats today."

Try teaching this "battle-of-the-sexes" farce with the poems "A Passionate Shepherd to His Love" and "The Nymph's Reply to the Shepherd" for entertaining examples. Another poem that might add to a discussion of irony is "My Last Duchess."

FURTHER READING

Magarshack, David. *Chekhov the Dramatist*. New York: Hill & Wang, 1960.
Senelick, Laurence. "Stuffed Seagulls: Parody and the Reception of Chekhov's Plays." *Poetics Today* 8.2 (1987): 285–98.

PADDY CHAYEFSKY

Marty

WRITING ACTIVITIES

1. Have students imagine what happens to Marty and Clara after this play ends.
2. Ask students to explain why Marty acts the way he does. What do the other characters do to cause him to make certain decisions or actions in response?

GROUP ACTIVITIES

Assign each group a character for analysis and have the groups answer the following questions: How does this character feel about Marty and his bachelor lifestyle? What in the character's own experiences may affect his or her opinion? How does each character express his or her opinion to Marty himself? What is Marty's reaction to each character's advice?

DO YOUR STUDENTS KNOW . . .

Rod Steiger, a film actor known for his tough-guy roles, originated the role of Marty on television. He was so moved by the story that he cried often during rehearsals so much so that the director's last instructions to him before airtime were to "hold back the tears." He later lost the role to Ernest Borgnine in the film version when producer Burt Lancaster wanted a gentler actor for the role.

DISCUSSION

Before discussing the characters and plot of this play, bring up the format of *Marty*, discussing how this teleplay might allow for shifts in scene and time that would not occur so easily in a play. Most of all, point out how similar this play is to plays written for live theatrical performances: sets are still detailed as they would be on a traditional stage set, the play includes realistic characters in a realistic setting, and action occurs without any dramatic visual effects that could not occur onstage. The play is an intimate one because the audience, through the camera's eye, can watch key scenes that are observed by no one else. We are allowed to listen to conversations that even Marty's other relatives and friends — even those in the same room — cannot hear, and this access to certain events and exchanges helps us understand the tension in Marty's life and sympathize with him. Such intimacies would be less realistic and more awkward if the play were adapted for the stage.

Marty, the title character, is an unmarried man caught in conflict. On the one hand, every elderly or married woman, as well as his friend Angie, is urging him impatiently to marry. On the other hand, the young women who are looking for a husband do not find him appealing. While all of his relatives have moved into married relationships, the thirty-six-year-old Marty is stuck in his teenage years, going to dances reluctantly, asking women out while fearing rejection, and being rejected often. These rejections, along with the motherly regard of his clients at the butcher shop and his own mother, keep Marty acting the role of a man younger than himself (Q 2). Neither society nor his private life will allow him to mature until he marries, and that event does not seem likely until he finds Clara Davis. He is caught between friends and relatives' obvious expectations and his own bleak prospects.

His attempts to find female companionship have made little headway, as both the play's events and Marty's own words suggest. Marty discusses his frustration with his friend Angie as they sit in the restaurant in act 1, and he further opens up to Clara when they talk privately about how each has been ignored or insulted by the opposite sex (Q 4). These revelations, combined with our firsthand view of rejections on the phone and at the dance hall, may cause students to feel both uncomfortable for him and highly sympathetic to his situation, especially when these experiences give him the compassion to assist another less-than-beautiful human being. Students should discuss why Marty feels compelled to "rescue" Clara at the dance and also should examine conversations when Marty expresses doubts about his own physical attractiveness. Marty's discussion of dating with Clara when they speak privately in his mother's house may be especially illuminating. In effect, Marty rescues Clara that evening as he wishes he might have been saved during all these years of searching for someone who would not judge him by his appearance and reject him (Q 6).

It is Marty's compassionate rescue that pulls him out of his rut, for he and Clara have their humiliated lives in common, and each understands the pain and tears of the other as no one else in the play does (Q 7). "Dog," the title so many men give to Clara, has little effect on Marty. He ignores the epithet when her date so callously offers to pay him $5 to take her home so he can go off with another girl. In fact, it may be this very word, repeated so often by Angie and the other men at the bar in the last scene, that causes Marty to decide to call Clara and ask her out again. Ironically, just as Marty has found a woman who is both willing to date him and who understands his feelings — in other words, just as Marty has found his match — his friends and relatives switch sides and oppose his involvement with Clara, and Marty seems doomed to struggle against everyone else's opinions for the remainder of his life.

His mother's change of heart is most interesting, for it is sparked by a realization that Marty's bachelor status has allowed her to remain in her wifely role, cleaning house and cooking for her son now that her husband is gone. No one understands this more than Aunt Catherine, the mother's rather belligerent sister, caught in a world where her children — all that she has to live for — have married and moved away from her emotionally. She, like Marty, is confused by conflicting expectations. She has always been the mother to her son, but now her daughter-in-law resents any attempt she makes at cleaning or cooking, even though that is all she knows. Just as Marty is treated like a boy by all his customers and relatives, who incessantly advise him to get married, Aunt Catherine is being treated like an unruly child, passed from her son's house to her sister's (Q 1). What separates them is that Marty is in the enemy's camp: not married yet, but bound to do precisely what Aunt Catherine's sons have done.

Students may wish to speculate on whether Marty will fulfill Aunt Catherine's expectations if he marries, searching to find an apartment, taking his mother's place out from under her, and making her feel as lost as Aunt Catherine has been (Writing Activity 1). Marty's key lines in act 3, suggesting they move into an apartment and stating his interest in Clara, repeat Aunt Catherine's warning signs so beautifully that the audience may very well wonder whether she is not right about the situation. Marty's relationship with his mother is not typical by most standards, for he still lives at home with her, and the two deal with each other in much the same way they would deal with a spouse. She cooks him dinner and cleans the house, while he works in his butcher shop to pay the bills. Although his mother may repeat every day that he should marry, she serves as his wife in a new wife's absence, as he serves as her replacement for her deceased husband. This arrangement does not seem, by the end of the play, to be permanent, and Marty may very well find little room in his life for his mother once he has married. What the play does not reveal is whether Marty *will* marry. The final scene suggests that he is calling Clara, and the audience is left to decide the ending. Students may disagree, based on the play's evidence, about whether Marty will marry Clara. Help them discuss Marty's relationship to his mother when they consider this question.

This play may work well in context with other works concerned with family expectations and relationships, such as "Everyday Use," *The Cuban Swimmer*, and *Fences*.

FURTHER READING

Frank, Sam. "Paddy Chayefsky." *Dictionary of Literary Biography Documentary Series*. Vol. 44. Detroit: Gale, 1984. 83–91.

DAVID AUBURN

Proof

WRITING ACTIVITIES

1. Have students write a scene in which Claire comes back and confronts Catherine and Hal.
2. Assume that Catherine decides to go back to school. Ask the students in your class to write her application essay.
3. There is no indication in the stage directions that *Proof* is intended to have a soundtrack. Ask students to imagine, though, that someone is making a film version and wants to have music by popular artists playing softly in the background at several points. What three songs would students choose? At what points would they be played, and why?

GROUP ACTIVITIES

Break the class into groups of three and have each group rehearse the scene in which Catherine tells Hal and Claire that she wrote the proof. As part of this process, each group should write out detailed stage directions. (If the number of students in the class is not divisible by three, some students can play the parts of both Catherine and Claire.)

Divide the class into small groups and ask each group to decide which theme in the play they think is most important. The groups should be prepared to give reasons for their choice.

DO YOUR STUDENTS KNOW . . .

Pierre de Fermat, a seventeenth-century mathematician, wrote a theorem showing $x^n + y^n = z^n$, known as Fermat's last theorem. In 1630, Fermat, who never published his mathematical findings, wrote this theorem as a marginal note in Diophantus's *Arithmetica*, noting that "I have discovered a truly remarkable proof which this margin is too small to contain" and leaving no proof for this theorem. It was only in 1993 that Andrew Wiles, a British mathematician, finally completed the proof of Fermat's last theorem.

DISCUSSION

Although he is dead by the time the play begins, Robert is very much an essential character. It is only through his conversations with Catherine that we get a full sense of their relationship and learn why she is both attracted to and repulsed by mathematics (Q 15). We know from the first scene that Robert hoped Catherine would carry on his work, and we know that Catherine felt she could not live up to her father's expectations (Q 3). Of course, Auburn could have simply had the other characters, but particularly Catherine, fill in the audience on what sort of a man Robert was and his relationship with his daughter. By having Robert appear on stage, however, Auburn makes him a more powerful presence than he would otherwise have been. The fact that he appears to Catherine after his death also encourages the audience to question her mental stability.

One of the chief themes of the play is the close relationship between genius and insanity. It is true that Robert was wrong when he thought "aliens were sending him messages." It is also true that his description of those messages as "[b]eautiful mathematics. The most elegant proofs, perfect proofs, proofs like music" suggests there is some similarity between his delusions and his earlier flashes of genius. In scene 4, Robert believes that he is back in touch with the source of his inspiration, but Catherine realizes on looking at his notebook that he has lapsed back into madness.

Catherine is desperately afraid that she will also go insane. After all, the only genius she has personally known — aside from herself — is her father. And the play gives us no ensurance that Catherine will escape her father's fate. One assumes, though, that Sophie Germain, the other mathematical genius in whose life Catherine has taken an interest, did *not* suffer from mental illness or Catherine would have mentioned it. It is also important to note that, although some types of mental illness are genetically determined, this is by no means true in every case. Catherine is certainly behaving erratically, but this is more than understandable given the strain she is under (Q 1, 4).

Claire's chief function is to move the plot along: someone needs to throw a party and invite Hal and his friends, to raise questions about whether Catherine wrote the proof, and to sell the house. Given all of the above, it is hard to imagine that the play could work without her. It is also true, though, that she is the least developed and least sympathetic of the play's four characters (Q 9). She may be within her rights to sell the house, but she is certainly callous to do it so quickly, and her decision to give Hal the notebook is inexcusable (Q 14).

The play makes a point of flouting the popular stereotypes of mathematicians. Those who assume that mathematicians are staid, stable people will be surprised to find that in this play they are either party animals or mentally unstable. This is not to say that the stereotypes are without basis in fact, however, or that the characters are unaware of them. When Claire firsts asks Catherine if she and Rob are sleeping together, Catherine refers to Rob as a "math geek." While Rob and his friends may not, as members of a band, be typical mathematicians, he admits that they are "raging geeks," albeit "geeks who . . . can dress themselves" (Q 11). The mathematicians we meet in *Proof* are driven, energetic people who are addicted to the intellectual stimulation their work provides and desperately afraid that their sources of inspiration will run dry.

The question remains, though, about why Auburn chose to make his characters mathematicians as opposed to, say, historians or biologists. No doubt the challenge of portraying mathematicians as something other than passionless geeks was one that the playwright relished. Another, more important reason may be that "pure mathematics" is often thought to be just that, pure. In fact, the type of mathematics in which Robert, Catherine, and Hal are interested is so lofty that it may seem utterly irrelevant to most people. In many ways, then, it is an activity undertaken for its own sake. It should also, ideally, be free from the prejudices that can inhibit work in other fields (Q 2).

Unfortunately, the discipline of mathematics is not free of gender prejudice. When Catherine presses him, Hal admits that most of the prominent mathematicians are men, and this is likely one of the reasons that he later doubts she has written the proof (Q 8). The story Catherine tells of Sophie Germain serves to provide historical background on this situation. The story also provides the audience with an example of a woman who made a major contribution to the field, thereby inclining them to the view that Catherine may in fact be a mathematical genius. Although the audience will want to believe that this is the case, it should be noted that we are never given definitive proof.

What is the proof mentioned in the title? Obviously the title refers to Catherine's proof, but there is more to it than that. Catherine will have to prove that it was she, and not her father, who wrote it, and she will have to prove to herself and to everyone else that she is stronger than her father. The end of the play is positive in that it seems Catherine may get the chance to do what her father never could — carry out groundbreaking work without losing her grip on reality (Q 17).

Consider teaching this play with "The Littoral Zone," *Tender Offer*, "My Son, My Executioner," or "B. Wordsworth." "The Littoral Zone" and *Tender Offer* both rely on the language of particular occupations, with the former work focusing on a romantic relationship and the latter on the relationship between a father and daughter. "My Son, My Executioner" explores a father's awareness that his son will one day supplant him, and "B. Wordsworth" is a story about an unusual apprenticeship.

ARTHUR MILLER

Death of a Salesman

WRITING ACTIVITIES

1. Have students address in writing the question of who or what is at fault for Willy Loman's situation, and for his death.
2. Ask students to characterize Willy's version of the American Dream. Where does he go wrong?

GROUP ACTIVITY

Willy Loman commits suicide in a car accident at the end of this play. Assign a different character to each group, asking the groups to write a note from Willy to the assigned character. How would Willy explain his final action to this character? What message would he wish to leave with each one? Share the letters as a class, discussing Willy's hope for those around him and the effect these hopes have on his actions.

DO YOUR STUDENTS KNOW . . .

'Inside His Head' was the original name of Miller's Death of a Salesman. Miller also wanted the play staged on a set that was shaped like a head. Instead, the play uses techniques of memory, hallucination, and dialogue to convey Willie's breakdown.

DISCUSSION

You could begin consideration of Death of a Salesman with a writing activity that focuses on Willy or on any other character in the play. You might, for example, ask students if the play has a hero or villain; or ask with which character they most closely identify (Q 1, 5). This activity will provide a nice approach to detailed discussions of character. Asking students to characterize Willy will lead students to consider his philosophy of business (Q 8), the effects of The Woman (Q 3), the flashbacks and how they explain Willy's motivations (Q 10), his attitudes toward his sons (Q 4), and whether Willy is a sympathetic character (Q 2). Focusing on Linda will address questions about her sincerity (Q 9) and whether she is simply a stereotype (Q 11). Asking students to characterize Biff and Happy will illuminate differences between them (Q 7), and characterizing Bernard will highlight his function as foil to Willy, Biff, and Happy (Q 13). And, of course, all these discussions will help students understand the Requiem (Q 14). In addition, you should ask students to discuss the idea of the American Dream, the setting (especially the house surrounded by apartment buildings), and the role of the automobile and the kinds of freedom it represents to Willy.

Since Miller does not use a narrator in the play, stage directions indicate devices (including speech, movement, habits) that provide exposition to orient readers. For example, in the opening exchange between Willy and Linda, stage directions illustrate their relationship as Linda "calls with some trepidation," pauses and proceeds "very carefully, delicately," continues her speech "helpfully," then is "resigned," but always maintains "infinite patience." Willy speaks "with casual irritation," is "a little numb," continues "with wonder," is alternately "encouraged," "interested," and "worried and angered." In addition, Miller's introductory description of Willy provides necessary exposition: "He is past sixty years of age, dressed quietly. . . . [h]is exhaustion is apparent" (Q 6).

These stage directions also begin Willy's characterization. Ask students to comment on Willy's philosophy of business and lead them to see that Willy's ideas of what it takes to succeed are simplistic and misguided. To Willy, all it takes to succeed is name recognition — to be known and well liked will carry a salesman through a career, ending as the eighty-four-year-old who checks into his hotel, puts on his slippers, and makes a few telephone calls. But Willy has little understanding of what it really takes to be successful — work, dedication, and integrity (Q 8). He also seems to have no idea that economic forces beyond his control — depressions, recessions, and business reversals — can determine his ultimate success or failure. The bitter irony is that Willy refuses to acknowledge reality, a difficulty he has throughout the play. For example, Willy says that he will one day be more successful than Charley, who is a success both as a father and as a businessman, "Because Charley is not — liked. He's liked, but he's not — well liked" (Act 1, line 232). Although Willy does occasionally seem to understand what it takes to succeed in business, as when he tells Biff how to approach Oliver (wear "a business suit, and talk as little as possible, and don't crack any jokes"), it is evident that he is incapable of practicing what he preaches. Miller emphasizes this point even with small details like Willy's warning to Biff not to say "Gee": "'Gee' is a boy's word. A man walking in for fifteen thousand dollars does not say 'Gee!'" (1.747). A short time later, Willy concludes act 1 with, "Gee, look at the moon moving between the buildings" (1.801).

The existence of The Woman, hidden until act 2, explains the "mystery" of Willy's relationship with Biff. That Willy "buys" her with boxes of new stockings while Linda mends her own allows — indeed, forces — the audience to judge Willy: he is the cheat and fraud that Biff says he is. Consequently, Willy loses the audience's sympathy. Still, the scenes with The Woman, especially in the confrontation with Biff in the Boston hotel room, and Willy's *need* to be liked by her suggest that he is to be pitied (Q 3, 2). Linda's constant efforts to understand Willy and her patience with him also shape the audience's response to him. Linda does not give up on Willy, and Miller indicates that the Loman house has "An air of the dream . . . a dream rising out of reality" (opening stage directions).

The flashbacks demonstrate Willy's loss of reality; they also show when and where Willy has "slipped" and what went wrong. That is, the flashbacks are effective in explaining what motivates Willy: he cannot escape the past and move into the present or the future. Asking students in what other ways they might present the background information should lead to the realization that what Miller gains by use of flashbacks is an onstage confusion that mirrors Willy's predicament. During the course of the play Willy more and more loses his ability to distinguish past from present. The chaos he feels is experienced by the audience (Q 10).

One approach to the flashbacks is asking students to identify what they learn through them. The background information includes the recognition that Ben, Willy, Biff, and Happy are all cheats and that much of Willy's problem stems from a father who runs away when Willy is very young. In many ways, the tragedy of Willy Loman is his inability to cope with loss: the loss of any guidance he might have gained from his father, the loss of his own power to control his sons' destinies, the loss of his own dream — perhaps best represented by Ben and the "faraway places" and opportunities that Ben represents (Q 12) — and the loss of Willy's own integrity, illustrated by his adultery. Willy is displaced, physically — in a house surrounded by apartments (representing the advance of capitalism that will eventually crush people like Willy) — and psychologically (Q 10).

Willy is confused and his attitudes toward his sons indicate that he is lost. For example, Willy speaks of Biff as "lazy": "Biff is a lazy bum!" (1.50). A moment later Willy says of Biff: "And such a hard worker. There's one thing about Biff — he's not lazy" (1.54). Still later, Willy remarks, "Greatest thing in the world for him was to bum around" (1.775). Additionally, Willy's attitude toward the house, and the idea that "there'll be nobody home" once it is paid for, indicates his confusion and disappointment. "If only Biff would take this house, and raise a family" Willy laments (2.41). But of course Biff will not, cannot. These ambivalent attitudes toward Biff, and those toward Happy, indicate Willy's sense of lost control in life (Q 4). Willy's suicide, especially when it becomes apparent that his death is worth $10,000 to the family, comes as no surprise. Indeed, part of Willy's tragedy is that in the modern world he is worth more dead than alive. However, students may question whether the family will get *any* money, if Willy's death is ruled a suicide. Conclude the discussion of Willy's character by having students debate how much Willy is responsible for his own misfortunes and how much he is a victim of his changing society (Q 15). If students see Willy as victim, they are also likely to view the play as "pathetic" by Miller's definition (Q 16). If, however, they believe Willy could have been successful — had he not made certain mistakes in the past or if he had accepted the reality of the present — they are more likely to classify the play as tragedy.

After a thorough discussion of Willy, students will find it easier to characterize the other principals in the play because they can contrast them with him. Bernard, for example, serves as foil to Biff, demonstrating how a son can be successful (Q 13). Biff and Happy can be contrasted with Bernard, and you will want to direct student attention to the differences between the Loman boys revealed in their conversation in act 1. Biff, who "knows" his father after the experience in Boston, is paralyzed and unable to participate in life. Happy, oblivious to the "real" Willy, is "like his brother, lost, but in a different way, for he has never allowed himself to turn his face toward defeat and thus is more confused and hardskinned, although seemingly more content" (opening stage directions). Their exchange emphasizes these differences (1.95–195) (Q 7).

Happy's concern is for himself and his own "success," not for his parents or his brother. Rather than take some responsibility upon himself to help his family,

Happy makes empty promises ("I'm gonna get married, Mom. I wanted to tell you" [1.789]) that no one pays attention to, much as no one paid attention when, as a child, Happy tried to get his father's attention ("I'm losing weight, you notice, Pop?" [1.214]). The effect of this neglect is expressed when Happy denies his father in Frank's Chop House: "No, that's not my father. He's just a guy. Come on, we'll catch Biff, and, honey, we're going to paint this town!" (2.672).

Biff, on the other hand, is concerned for his parents, but his anger at his father makes it impossible for him to act. Both sons kid themselves about their possibilities for the future, as evidenced in their plan for going into business with financial backing from Oliver. But the differences between the two of them emerge with Happy's need to make money, which keeps him from joining Biff out West:

> The only thing is — what can you make out there? . . . I gotta show some of those pompous, self-important executives over there that Hap Loman can make the grade. . . . Then I'll go with you, Biff. We'll be together yet, I swear. But take those two we had tonight. Now weren't they gorgeous creatures? (1.156, 160) (Q 7)

Linda is more than a stereotype of the long-suffering wife; her humanity — patience, understanding, love, and pain — distinguishes her as an individualized, multidimensional character. From her admonition "Biff, dear, if you don't have any feeling for him, then you can't have any feeling for me" (1.610) to her "trembling with sorrow and joy" at Biff's possibilities (2.67) and, finally, to her self-assertion in Willy's defense after the fiasco at Frank's Chop House when she orders her sons to leave and never return (2.780), Linda demonstrates the understanding and concern that elevate her from a mere stereotype (Q 11).

Linda's statement, "And the boys, Willy. Few men are idolized by their children the way you are" (1.333), is both to be taken literally and to be recognized as bitterly ironic (Q 9). Linda means and believes what she says, and it is, in fact the boys' unconscious idolization of their father that defines Biff and Happy.

Ask students what they make of the Requiem. Some will suggest that it is unnecessary; we do not really learn anything about the characters here that we do not already know. Others will suggest that Charley's speech, "No man only needs a little salary" (Req.11), emphasizes the key theme of the play: Willy's search to "be somebody." Furthermore, Linda's ending speech shows the degree to which she suffers. Hap continues to fool himself and voice false promises, Biff seems to have come to terms with himself, and Charley "explains" Willy and the modern dilemma of all Willys (Q 14).

Related works following the theme of the elusive nature of the American Dream are *The Glass Menagerie* and *Fences*.

FURTHER READING

Helterman, Jeffrey. "Arthur Miller." *Twentieth-Century American Dramatists*. Ed. John MacNicholas. *Dictionary of Literary Biography*. Vol. 7, part 2. Detroit: Gale, 1981. 86–111.

Trudeau, Lawrence J., ed. *Drama Criticism*. Vol. 1. Detroit: Gale, 1991.

CHAPTER 32

STAGING

MILCHA SANCHEZ-SCOTT

The Cuban Swimmer

WRITING ACTIVITIES

1. Ask students to describe how they would stage this play, with its helicopter, lighting effects, boat, and swimming actor.
2. Ask students to compare their own family to the Suárez family members, describing what relationships or characters they see as typical.

GROUP ACTIVITY

Ask students to read the discussions of allegory in the Fiction and Poetry chapters. Have each group of students assign allegorical equivalents to the characters and events in *The Cuban Swimmer*. As a class, discuss whether or not the play works as an allegory.

DO YOUR STUDENTS KNOW . . .

Following the Cuban Revolution, which brought Fidel Castro to power, a virtual open-door policy existed for Cuban immigrants. However, a recent agreement between the two countries now limits legal immigration to 20,000 visas per year, and the Coast Guard interdicts any boats or rafts attempting illegal entry into the United States. Many Cubans still try to reach Florida's shores; the U.S. Border Patrol estimates that 5 percent of Cuban landings in the United States are by raft.

DISCUSSION

Students can begin by discussing the obvious technical difficulties of a realistic staging of this play. Once students depart from a dependence on realistic staging (which can be aided by consideration of Sanchez-Scott's provocative suggestion that live conga drums be used to punctuate the action), the play can be seen as a challenge to the imagination rather than to the stage carpenter. Thus, the setting of the play — "The Pacific Ocean between San Pedro and Catalina Island" — need not pose serious problems if the students are willing to envision props representing boats rather than real cabin cruisers and a sea without waves on which Margarita can triumphantly walk. Of course, a raised area is needed for the father's boat, and some kind of contraption is necessary to support the swimmer (Q 9); however, this play provides a good opportunity for students to realize the importance and effectiveness of *suggesting* rather than presenting. You might ask students how they would stage the play (Q 10). (Max Ferra's 1984 New York production used merely a watery blue floor and lighting to suggest the sea.)

Lighting and sound are instrumental in furthering the action. For example, the presence of the helicopter is made known by the sound of the blades and the shadows cast on the water, and Margarita's fall to the bottom of the sea at the end of scene 5 is suggested by lighting changes and soft music. The blackouts at the end of each scene help show the passing of time. The melancholy sound of dolphins at the end of scene 6 adds poignancy to Simon's search for his sister. The live conga drums, if employed, give the play a Caribbean feel, provide echoes for the rhythm of Margarita's swimming, and can be used later for her heartbeat (Q 2).

Students can have fun defining the themes of the play. Some ideas readily accessible to students are that the Cuban immigrants feel "very much at sea" when faced with Americans' attitudes of superiority (denoted by the obnoxious voice of Mel, the racist and sexist sportscaster). Cubans face obstacles similar to those other immigrants and cultural minorities must face in the United States. Therefore, "it's easy to go under" and lose any footing in a strange world of people so unlike those of an immigrant's own culture, and miracles such as walking on the water are needed to ensure the acceptance of Cubans by Americans. Another theme that has been suggested is minorities' use of "athletic skills to propel themselves into the mainstream of middle-class life in this country." Ask students if focusing on this traditional theme provides a fair and complete interpretation of the play.

The voices of Mel and Mary Beth provide a sharp contrast to the plight of the Suarez family. Their "newscaster English" contrasts with the Spanish-American English of the family, and their condescension is a cliché for the trite perceptions many Americans have of Latinos ("the simple people we see below us on the ragtag *La Havana*, taking their long-shot chance to victory" [50]). This condescension in turn provokes violent retorts from the family on the boat. Illustrating the point that their condescension is wrong-headed is Mel and Mary Beth's misperception of Margarita's efforts in the water. They see Margarita and her family as pulling together in "a family effort," all of them having "turned out to cheer little Margarita on to victory," while the Suarez family is in fact divided, struggling for survival in the face of an Americanization they both want and fear (Q 4). Although the entire family is riding in the boat as it follows Margarita, the family members do not seem focused on Margarita's strenuous attempt to win the race. Their efforts are trivialized by Mel and Mary Beth as a Cinderella story of no consequence. The irony is that Margarita's supposed demise turns into a surreal fairy tale as she wins the race by walking on the water. This "miracle" combines the tradition of Christian belief with the jargon of sportscasting in an ironic denouement (Q 6).

The use of Spanish in the play helps to show the degree of integration of the family into their new country: the grandmother speaks mostly Spanish, the parents some, Simon and Margarita little. Simon uses Spanish to make fun of stereotypes (as in his Ricky Ricardo impersonation). The grandmother's recitation of the Hail Mary in Spanish signals a return to family unity at the beginning of the last scene, after their conflict over Margarita's condition in the water when she encounters an oil slick and feels the effects of such a long swim (Q 3, 5). Additionally, other conflicts emerge, such as the continuing struggle between Eduardo and his son Simon, Eduardo and his wife Aida, and Eduardo and his mother Abuela, demonstrating the difficulty each generation has with the conflict between old and new worlds and their traditions (Q 5).

Margarita's struggle with the ocean can readily be seen as symbolic of the many conflicts faced by her family, and her victory as representative of their renewed hopes. This burden will probably cause students to sympathize with Margarita. Some may have felt similar pressures, even if not to the same degree or in so dramatic a form. Have students identify specific elements in the play that create empathy between themselves and Margarita (Q 11).

The female characters in the play demonstrate the degree to which the family has been subsumed into American culture. They also demonstrate the contrast between the plight of Cuban-Americans and the situation of WASPs such as Mary Beth White, literally in an elevated position over the floundering family. Ask students to characterize each woman, identifying both her role and how she is perceived by others in the play. Discuss the effects of the parental pressure on Margarita. How would they have viewed the parents if Margarita had drowned? What happens to the family members and their own difficulties or opinions when Margarita is lost? How do they view the expectations or demands they had for Margarita and each other? You may want to ask students what they think is gained and lost by becoming Americanized. Clearly, each succeeding generation of the Suarez family becomes more and more Americanized; consequently, Margarita, although still "dominated" by her father, is able to swim out from under his shadow. Mary Beth seems to be Mel's equal in the helicopter, demonstrating perhaps the improved status of women in America (Q 7).

You may also want to ask students what Sanchez-Scott could have added to the play and how any lengthening might affect an audience's response to it. It is interesting to see what students would like to see more of (perhaps cultural history, family background, characters' thoughts) (Q 1).

The Cuban Swimmer could be taught in a thematic unit focusing on assimilation and cultural identity along with Langston Hughes's poems in Chapter 26 or *Fences*, but you may not want to limit the students' view of this text by teaching it exclusively in this context. Other works that deal with the intimate dealings of family include *Death of a Salesman* and "My Papa's Waltz."

FURTHER READING

Mitgung, Herbert. "Dreamers." *New York Times* 10 May 1984: C32, 1.

SOPHOCLES

Oedipus the King

WRITING ACTIVITIES

1. Ask students to write about the characters who help Oedipus discover his history. Which ones try to hinder his search for truth? What is motivating their actions?
2. Ask students to compare the staging of *Oedipus the King* to a modern American mystery. How would events and facts be discovered differently? What would occur on stage, and how would other events and elements of the presentation change?

GROUP ACTIVITY

Using the Critical Perspective for *Oedipus the King*, assign each group a major character close to Oedipus, including characters we do not see in the play itself, such as Oedipus's father Laius or Oedipus's adoptive parents Polybus and Merope. Each group should write in this character's words his or her view of Oedipus's actions and decide the reasons behind his downfall. Share the results as a class, assessing each interpretation as probable or improbable.

DO YOUR STUDENTS KNOW . . .

Sophocles may have looked to contemporary events of his time to provide ideas for his play. Pericles and Ephialtes had been joint heads of state of Athens. When Ephialtes was murdered, Pericles was accused but is never found guilty of the crime. Pericles died soon after in the plague that killed many Athenian citizens. Like the play, Pericles' death may be seen as the justice of fate.

DISCUSSION

Students are often unable to visualize the action (such as it is) of Greek tragedies. There is no doubt that a large gulf exists between the staging of a physically distant ritual Greek drama and an intimate Shakespearean monologue where the actor speaks confidentially to an audience — often, as in the Globe theater, an audience within his reach. At the same time, the poetic form and formal language of Shakespeare's plays and *Oedipus the King* may also distance some students, especially when compared to the dialogue of *Proof* and other modern plays. Attempts to describe the visual spectacle of Greek drama must concentrate on the physical aspects of the productions: the costumes, the masks, and so on. Wearing copies of ancient Greek masks — as contemporary actors sometimes do — adds to the audience's ability to experience Greek drama as it was originally performed, but the effect can also be a distancing of the audience from the action (Q 3). The masks make the faces of the actors impossible to see, and the question of how students would react to an African American Oedipus or an Asian American Creon is moot if masks are used. The students may be able to visualize the more formal language if they imagine the dialogue being presented in the traditional manner, with large masks and large gestures and stage without scenery and props designed to depict the setting and events realistically.

The ritual chanting of the chorus is better understood when likened to religious chanting, in which the choral strophes and antistrophes have their roots. Thus, it may seem that the chorus's general function is to emphasize particular themes rather than to further the plot, although the suppliants on the steps of the city do establish the setting of the play as well as supply essential background information to the audience (Q 1). The absence of scenery forces the audience's attention onto the words being spoken by these larger-than-life yet distant figures, and in keeping with the decorum of the genre, all violence — including Oedipus's blinding himself — takes place off stage, thus avoiding sensationalism (Q 5). Comparing this idea that "less is more" to the American desire for graphic realism (especially in film) may help the students visualize the difference between ancient drama and theater today (see Writing Activity 2).

Oedipus's self-imposed ordeal requires that he discover his own identity in the process of seeking the cause of the public distress. This intense, almost courtroomlike examination of the past permits previous history to be discussed in memories and reported actions, thus allowing Sophocles to maintain the three unities of time, place, and action while incorporating mention of events in the far past (Q 6). Sophocles was aided in dealing with past events by the audience's familiarity with the events being portrayed on the stage (Q 7). Oedipus's tragedy is that he stays true to the task he has set himself, even when he realizes that he is the perpetrator of the crimes he is attempting to punish. He learns that the gods' will is implacable and that, even though he considers himself to be acting of his own free will, the gods have final control over his fate (Q 8).

Even if students have difficulty with the mechanics of Greek drama, they generally form strong opinions about the character of Oedipus. Have students discuss whether or not Oedipus deserves his fate. Is he a victim of the gods or a noble man accepting responsibility for his actions? Would the ancient Greek audience reach the same conclusion as modern readers (Q 10, 11)?

Everyone has difficulty staging the play in an accessible manner. To spark discussion among students about possible staging alternatives for the play (Q 2, 4), you may want to read to students Benedict Nightingale's description of the staging of Minos Volanakis's 1984 Greek National Theater production:

> [Volanakis] staged the action between jet-black curtains on a tilted O from which embryonic walls protruded, making us feel we were at an archeological dig at dead of night; and there he proceeded to give us a little bit of everything. We had moments of pomp and ceremony, with Oedipus's face covered with gold and everyone else in half-masks, and moments of intimacy, when king and subjects stripped to their vests, as if to admit they were only actors, and rather hot, sweaty actors at that. Meanwhile, the chorus of ghostly old men weaved and swirled about the stage, sometimes giving the honest impression that they were weak with hunger, exhaustion and dread, and sometimes that they were playing a sort of spectacular blind man's buff with each other. . . .

> Oedipus . . . emerged from the palace, blind and ruined . . . with what
> appeared to be a winding-cloth tied around his head, making him look as if
> he'd jumped off the table halfway through the process of being mummified. We
> didn't see his bleeding eyes, and we didn't feel his anguish. Instead of terror and
> pity, we ended by getting empty spectacle.

Have the students discuss this particular staging, deciding as a class when it
seems to reinforce the play, its themes, and its purpose and what parts of this example of staging might detract from the play's elements. You might teach this play
with "Young Goodman Brown," "Doe Season," "The Lamb," or "The Tyger"
(innocence/experience) or with "I Stand Here Ironing," "My Son, My Executioner," or "A Woman Mourned by Daughters" (parent/child relationships).

FURTHER READING

Nightingale, Benedict. Rev. of *Oedipus the King*, dir. Minos Volanakis. Greek
National Theater. *New York Times Theater Review* 5 August 1984: 3.
Trudeau, Lawrence J., ed. *Drama Criticism*. Vol. 1. Detroit: Gale, 1991. 412–71.

WILLIAM SHAKESPEARE

A Midsummer Night's Dream

WRITING ACTIVITIES

1. Have students describe how this play is inappropriate and/or appropriate for a wedding
   celebration.
2. Ask students to critique the play within a play, speculating on its purpose at the end of
   this play and comparing it to the events occurring in the larger play.

GROUP ACTIVITY

Place students in groups and assign each group a pair of lovers in the play: Oberon
and Titania, Helena and Demetrius, Lysander and Hermia, Theseus and Hip-
polyta, Pyramus and Thisbe. Include even those couples who are temporary, such
as Bottom and Titania or Lysander and Helena. Have each group analyze its assigned couple and decide the nature of love according to the couple's situation,
describing how that kind of love is dictated by the characters themselves and
their circumstances.

DO YOUR STUDENTS KNOW . . .

A Midsummer Night's Dream was not enthusiastically received and was not performed in its entirety for nearly two hundred years. Pieces of the play were adapted
and performed during the seventeenth and eighteenth centuries. The play was performed in its entirety with great success in England in 1840. Its revival was due in
large part to a fascination with fairies and the supernatural in England at that time.

DISCUSSION

This play may pose a challenge to many students, not because it is difficult to understand, but because students may be familiar only with Shakespeare's tragedies, and this play — probably intended for a wedding — draws out the weaknesses in human nature to chuckle at them, not to show their darker sides. The overwhelming theme is love and marriage, and each couple displays one or two aspects of love, whether flawed or pristine, although usually flawed (Q 11, Writing Activity 1). Lysander and Hermia seem to love each other, yet Lysander also seems proud of his conquest, gloating that he has been chosen over Demetrius, Hermia's other suitor in act 1. Helena's love for Demetrius seems misguided at best, and her fawning may disgust students, especially when she compares herself to Demetrius's dog (2.1). Titania and Oberon are in the midst of a battle over a boy, one that has kept them from speaking to each other for too long. Oberon's resentment of Titania's behavior is so strong that he plots his revenge by causing her to love a man with the head of an ass (Group Activity).

At no point is the audience told to take these characters seriously, and all these problems work out in the end. Although a reading may not reveal the humor, the play lends itself well to stage performance, and even an oral reading will help students see how lightly the action and characters are to be taken (Q 10). At every turn of the plot, although the lovers seem to be in rather desperate circumstances, we are given opportunities to laugh at their folly, at their seriousness, even at their pain. Discussing staging — costumes, lighting, sets — will help students understand how much this play is a sort of pageant, a mask, not a serious drama.

In a performance, the setting does a great deal to remind the audience of this play's dreamlike qualities. Past productions have ranged from open stages all in blue, with the fairies floating above the mortals' heads, to more down-to-earth productions in outdoor theaters. This play lends itself especially well to staging in an outdoor amphitheater, where actors may enter from trees behind the stage area and lie down to sleep in the grass. Discuss with students how they would like to stage this play and describe the limitations of the Elizabethan theater in this production. They could also discuss how this play would work as a movie and what role special effects would play.

Setting is very important in A *Midsummer Night's Dream*, however, for the play's action leaves the seemingly sane world of Athens and enters the eerie, magical world of the fairy forest. Here, the strict laws — which will soon force Hermia to choose marriage to Demetrius, death for refusing him, or celibacy in Diana's temple — all melt away. Lovers are swayed by a magic flower to reject former loves, a rustic actor is given the head of an ass, the fairy queen falls in love with him, and then the lovers wake at dawn, wondering whether their whole experience was merely a dream. The contrast between the two worlds is striking, but it is the magical world that causes happiness for the lovers when they return to their "real" world, for Oberon solves the lovers' difficulties when Athens cannot. Although the lovers must return to Athens, they return happily; the reason that made them leave no longer exists, for each couple now consists of two mutually loving partners (Q 1). A modern set lends itself well to a more vivid rendering of such a contrast, and electricity enables us to light the various scenes to reinforce the contrast not only between Athens and the fairy world but also between the rational world of day and the dreamlike quality of night (Q 9). Other special effects, in addition to a change in lighting, would reinforce this contrast.

Costuming also may show the contrast between worlds. Even when the lovers take to the woods, they are still in Athenian clothing, and that is how Puck and Oberon recognize them. Oberon, Puck, Titania, and the fairies may be costumed in various ways, as long as a contrast exists between their wardrobe and that of the mortals. Discuss with students how costumes might suggest these characters' other worldly origins and magical powers (Q 3). A third group, the rustics who are rehearsing for Theseus's wedding, should also be costumed to denote their status. Ask students how they might indicate the rustics' lower rank, even in a modern production, and how the head of an ass, placed on Bottom's head as part of Oberon's revenge on Titania, might be created for the best stage effect (Q 6). Oberon's flower is also open to interpretation, for it may be larger than life to catch the audience's attention, it may be made to look magical or strange, or it may be a simple silk flower, or a real one. Each choice in staging will affect the play's interpretation.

Staging the final play within a play brings all of the earlier comedy about unrequited love, role playing, and tragic consequences to a peak, for the lines are so terribly delivered that what was once a tragedy becomes arguably the most humorous part of the play. This play within a play is a more extreme form of the lampoon on love than is presented using the major characters, and now that their conflicts have ended, the characters can laugh at the rustic performers and the plot, just as the audience has laughed at them throughout the larger play's action.

Once the action of both plays has ended and Puck is alone on stage, his epilogue establishes a parallel between the lovers' journey through the forest and the audience's time spent at the play. This reminds us that the actors were "shadows," not real people. Puck even suggests that we pretend we "have but slumbered here / While these visions did appear" (5.1). We have become a part of the magic of theater. Suddenly, we realize we have been beguiled by the action, and we wake, pick up our programs, and leave for home.

This play may work well along with other texts about dreamlike worlds, including "The Rocking-Horse Winner." It might also lend itself to an exploration of marital or love themes when used with "The Yellow Wallpaper," "How Do I Love Thee?," "To His Coy Mistress," and "My mistress' eyes are nothing like the sun."

FURTHER READING

Dent, R. W. "Imagination in A Midsummer Night's Dream." Shakespeare Quarterly 15.2 (1964): 115–29.

Olson, Paul A. "A Midsummer Night's Dream and the Meaning of Court Marriage." English Literary History 24 (1957): 95–119.

CHAPTER 33

THEME

WENDY WASSERSTEIN

Tender Offer

WRITING ACTIVITIES

1. Have students write about why Paul and Lisa both, at some point, do not want to engage in any real conversation. What is holding each character back?
2. Ask students to describe how Paul and Lisa's relationship is both typical and unusual.

GROUP ACTIVITY

Give each group approximately one page of the play to work with and ask each group to examine the emotional pull between Lisa and Paul. When does each character express hurt, need, or emotion, and how does the other character react to that emotional line each time? As each group shares its findings with the class, compare different movements with the other one, looking for repetitive movements and differences between similar exchanges.

DO YOUR STUDENTS KNOW . . .

The June Taylor dancers, choreographed by June Taylor, were first seen on television in 1948 on Ed Sullivan's *Toast of the Town*. Later, they moved to the *Calvacade of Stars* where Jackie Gleason premiered his skit "The Honeymooners." The association between the troupe and Gleason lasted through his several television shows until 1970. When June Taylor ended her career in 1990, she had last been the choreographer for the Miami Dolphins cheerleaders.

DISCUSSION

You may want to begin by examining dance and music as they are used to support the action and theme of the play. At the beginning of the play, Lisa is dancing to "Nothing Could Be Finer Than to Be in Carolina," and her dance becomes one of the major focal points of the dialogue. Her reluctance to continue dancing as soon as she sees her father Paul enter shows us the tension between these two characters, and her description of her dancing as just "good," may cause us to wonder how much she is willing to share with Paul emotionally. Paul's lack of knowledge about leg warmers lets us know that he is not closely involved with Lisa or her interests; that becomes even clearer when we discover how little he knows about her dance practice and when Lisa expresses anger toward him because he missed her dance recital. In a way, each successive exchange of dialogue is part of a dance, where Paul and Lisa step around each other, avoid true communication, and react to each other's words with anger and mistrust.

The dance theme carries the characters through the entire play, and the play closes with the same song Lisa sang in the beginning, only with both characters joining in the song-and-dance number. The dance shows the resolution of the action more succinctly than an extended conversation would have done. Discuss as a class whether the resolution could have been depicted in other ways and still express the theme (Q 10).

Paul's world of business is also important to the theme of the play, to the title especially (Q 7). Just as Lisa is attuned to the world of dance, a world Paul neither understands nor seems to care about, Paul's attachment to making business deals, making money, and being financially successful takes up a great deal of his time. When Lisa finally asks him what he thinks about when he's "quiet," he admits "business, usually" (147). As he describes what else he ponders, he shows how much his thoughts bend toward Lisa. He is not really thinking about her commitment to dance, but he is certainly thinking about her future, but on his own terms, including graduate school and her future career (Q 2). Both his business terminology and her dance classes will cause students to see this family as privileged. Discuss with the class other ways fathers and daughters might grow apart from each other, regardless of social class (Q 6).

What causes the two characters to move toward each other, and away from their own pursuits, is the desire to communicate. At the beginning of the play, neither character is really communicating, and the dialogue each has with the other shows the stiffness and lack of understanding between them, the source of the play's conflict (Q 9). However, Lisa seems to want to talk to her father before they leave for home. She uses the lost leg warmers and Miss Judy, her ballet instructor, to delay leaving, annoying him with the delay. His comments show how distant he is from her, especially when he comments on how "sexy" her dance was, perhaps believing that would please her (Q 4). Her need to get his attention becomes more apparent as she uses her teacher to ask him why he was late and discusses several incidents on the radio and television that represent her idea of father/daughter relationships. Finally, she explodes and asks, "Why don't you want to talk to me?" (86). When she does not get the answer — or the conversation — she requests, she backs up, just as Paul realizes how little he does talk to Lisa (Q 3). This shift occurs quickly, and now Paul tries very hard to hold a conversation with Lisa about school, dance, and her friends.

His efforts do not pay off until he learns to join his business sense to her dancing and until both of them learn to communicate with each other using terms that each one introduces into the conversation. Words are very important in this play, for the words used at the beginning of the play — "sexy," "good," "procrastinating," and "maudlin" — are often misunderstood. There is play on words when Paul says that Daria "will probably grow up to be a homicidal maniac lesbian prostitute," and Lisa responds, "I know what the word prostitute is" (117–18). This word comes up again once Lisa rages at Paul, claiming, "Maybe I'll become a prostitute" (124). Once Paul realizes how upset Lisa is, he uses one final term: "tender offer." The double entendre of the word "tender" creates an interesting link between Paul's definition in the world of business, involving an exchange of money, and "tender" in its more general definition, signifying intimacy and caring. He explains what it means in the business world, just as he has defined words for Lisa earlier, but then he applies it to her, to their relationship, and its meaning changes to signify a more personal, emotional link between them. That is when the two characters really begin to move closer (Q 1, 8) and really talk to each other in a world both of them share.

Have your class use this final definition to examine the main theme of the play, concerning the communicative relationship between parents and children. Then, have them tie the other themes — dance and the business world — to this main purpose (Q 5). A good way of centering the discussion on family ties is to discuss with them whether the solution in the play resolves the tension completely. Many students will know, from their own experience, that any relationship needs continual communication and that the dance the two perform at the end of the play will be the beginning of more attempts Lisa and Paul make to move closer. Certainly, the class may find Lisa's mother an interesting character, although very little of her is revealed beyond her punctuality and close relationship with her daughter. How does this third character fit into the relationship Lisa and Paul are developing? How will these three characters now fit together as a family? How will each family member solve the "dilemma of living together" (Q 12)? Will they be able to set aside their instinctive misgivings or mistrust for the good of the family's communication?

Works dealing with father/daughter relationships might be helpful if taught with this text, including "A Rose for Emily."

FURTHER READING

Balakian, Jan. "Wendy Wasserstein." *Speaking on Stage: Interviews with Contemporary American Playwrights*. Ed. Philip C. Kolin and Colby H. Kullman. Tuscaloosa: U of Alabama P, 1996.

MARGARET EDSON

Wit

WRITING ACTIVITIES

1. Ask students to write a short research essay on the life of John Donne.
2. The play ends with Jason's exclamation, "Oh, God." Have students write an additional scene in which Jason tells Susie what he has learned from Vivian's death.
3. Have students write an essay in which they argue that Vivian is or is not a tragic hero.

GROUP ACTIVITIES

Break the class up into small groups and ask each group to decide which scene in the play they thought was most important for an understanding of Vivian's character.

DO YOUR STUDENTS KNOW . . .

In a 1999 interview, Edson admitted she never took any classes on John Donne in college because some classmates told her he was one of the most difficult poets to study. She studied up on Donne only for the play.

DISCUSSION

This play will be easier for students to grasp if you have already spent time on John Donne and possibly other metaphysical poets. *Wit* is currently thought of as the ability to make a funny or biting joke or retort. It is important that students understand that Donne and the other metaphysical poets regarded wit as something far more profound. For them, wit was a means of using paradox, wordplay, and extended metaphor not to avoid reality but to look more deeply at it. *Wit* was, for all its intellectuality, a passionate thing. It is precisely this combination of intellect and passion that Vivian Bearing has failed to achieve (Q 6). Donne's poetry was never intended merely as a test, "a chance," as Vivian puts it, "to see how good you really are." One of the most interesting critical questions about *Wit* is whether it should be seen as a critique of the metaphysical approach or simply of Vivian's misunderstanding of it.

The degeneration of Vivian's body goes on parallel with the growth of her character. Whereas at the beginning of the play Vivian was arrogant and condescending, by the end she is humble and grateful for any kindness she receives. This change occurs not because she wills it, but because she is no longer in control of her own life and the lives of others (Q 3). The less she is able to depend on her intellect, the more appealing she becomes as a character (Q 2).

One of the fundamental questions this change raises is, What is the proper place or proper use, of the intellect? There is a very real sense in which Vivian is better able to endure her experience because she is able to reflect on it and analyze it. As her illness takes its course, however, her intellect becomes less help to her, and she becomes more aware of her emotional needs (Q 4). It is this growing awareness that is responsible for her changed attitude toward Susie, her nurse (Q 7). Jason and Dr. Kelekian are more obviously intellectual than Susie, but they offer Vivian no emotional support. Susie, on the other hand, involves herself emotionally in Vivian's life and helps comfort her.

Vivian is a tragic figure in that her intellectual pride constitutes a tragic flaw. Tragic flaws typically lead to the character's downfall, however, and we cannot say that Vivian's pride led to her cancer. If Vivian has fallen, then she has done so before she even learns that she is sick. Her intellectual pride has isolated her from others and from a direct and genuine experience of her own life. The real tragedy of the play, then, is that Vivian only begins to live in the process of dying (Q 11).

The personal and medical details that Jason elicits from Vivian give us a further sense of the things that are missing from her life. We already know that there are no family members she needs to notify and that she is effectively alone in the world. By letting us know that Vivian is unmarried, premenopausal, and suffering from ovarian cancer, Edson makes a point of the fact that Vivian does not have and now never will have children (Q 9). Of course, as a teacher, she had countless chances to nurture people younger than herself, and there is no doubt that her brilliance inspired some of her more intellectually gifted students. There is little indication, however, that she did much to impress upon her students the true importance of Donne's work (Q 13).

The glimpses we are shown of Vivian's past life, and in particular of how she became a scholar, are essential to an understanding of her tragedy. Early in the play, we are shown a meeting Vivian had when she was a student with her mentor, E. M. Ashford. In this meeting, we see how Ashford's criticisms of Vivian's scholarship steered her in the wrong direction in her relation to texts and to life as a whole. Ashford informs her that she "must begin with a text . . . not a feeling." Although her professor is not arguing that emotion has no place in reading, let alone in life, Vivian comes to that conclusion and models her own scholarship accordingly (Q 10). Later, we are given a glimpse of what once was Vivian's childish but authentic delight in language when she discusses the meaning of the word *soporific* with her father.

Edson's critique of overintellectualization is not limited to the scholarly study of literature. Most of the action takes place in a hospital room, and this gives the playwright an opportunity to critique many of the tendencies in modern medical research. The doctors treating Vivian have little interest in her as a human being, a fact that she grows to resent. At play's end, when Jason refers to Vivian as "research," it is clear that he is willing to do anything in order to further scientific knowledge as well as his own career (Q 8).

Jason speaks the last line in the play: "Oh, God." This exclamation shows that he has been stripped of his arrogance and his ready answers (Q 12). The play, then, ends not with a glib remark from Vivian or Kelekian or Jason, but with a prayer, perhaps the shortest, least adorned prayer possible. Vivian reaches this stage earlier on when she responds to her pain and her nausea with the same exclamation, one that she had earlier characterized as "an unconvincing eruption of piety." She is an expert on Donne's "Holy Sonnets," and she understands, on an intellectual level, the theological issues with which they wrestle. It is only in dying, though, that she experiences in an inner way the conflicts that plagued Donne (Q 5). By the same token, Jason, who studied the sonnets with Vivian, only understands what they were really about as he watches her die.

Consider teaching this play with "Cathedral," "Do not go gentle into that good night," "In Memory of Donald A. Stauffer," "After great pain a formal feeling comes," "A Valediction: Forbidding Mourning," and "Death Be Not Proud." The first selection shows how an individual becomes more emotionally open through his participation in the creation of art, and the poems that follow all deal with the subject of death. The last two selections, both by John Donne, provide particularly interesting points of contact with *Wit*.

FURTHER READING

Eads, Martha Greene. "Margaret Edson." *Twentieth-Century American Dramatists, Fourth Series*. Ed. Christopher J. Wheatley. *Dictionary of Literary Biography*. Vol. 266. Detroit: Gale, 2002. 75–78.

SOPHOCLES

Antigone

WRITING ACTIVITIES

1. Have students write about what action has occurred before the play begins, as well as what bearing the previous events have upon the play's action.
2. Ask students to choose one character and examine how the individual follows his or her conscience and then faces the consequences of his or her choices and actions.

GROUP ACTIVITY

Separating the class into four groups, assign each group one of the four points below. Ask them to support their point with evidence from the text:

1. Antigone is the tragic figure of the play.
2. Creon is the tragic figure of the play.
3. Antigone is *not* the tragic figure.
4. Creon is *not* the tragic figure.

Have each group report to the class as a whole and then discuss as a class whether both Creon and Antigone are the tragic heroes or only one of them is.

DO YOUR STUDENTS KNOW . . .

Antigone predates *Oedipus the King* by nearly fifteen years, although this play is the story of Oedipus's children. Tragedies and comedies were produced for the Dionysia, a drama festival that lasted four to five days. The audience included free male citizens who could attend the festival with their family and slaves. All business came to a stop at this time, and prisoners were allowed out on bail to see the plays.

DISCUSSION

Before discussing the actual events in the play or the play's two main characters and their tragic tendencies (Group Activity), set up the events that preceded to the play's action. Students might benefit more from *Antigone* if they read *Oedipus the King*; Antigone's family has a history of ill fortune and tragic fate, and Greek audiences would not have been surprised when she succumbs to the family tendency to suffer. Also discuss with students the war that has just ended, for only if they understand the nature of the uprising against Thebes, will Creon's edict, the focal conflict of the play, be understandable. At the end of *Oedipus the King*, Oedipus blinds himself, kisses his daughters goodbye, and exiles himself. Once he has left Thebes, his sons, under Creon's guidance, share the throne of Thebes for a short time. Soon, however, the two brothers are not satisfied sharing, and Creon supports Eteocles as king. In angry retaliation for this new government, Polyneices and six other leaders, including Creon's own son Megareus, attack Thebes. Their attempt to overthrow the Theban government is unsuccessful, but it does result in Eteocles' death; he and his brother, the only two sons of Oedipus, continue the string of tragedy by killing each other on the battlefield. When we understand that Polyneices is a traitor to the Theban government, we can more easily understand Creon's edict to leave Polyneices' body unburied. Enemies rarely buried each other's corpses, so Creon's orders are not even unusual, but what is unusual is that Eteocles, although a traitor, is also a Theban, was once a ruler, and is the son of Oedipus. He is also survived by two sisters, Antigone and Ismene, who are torn between loyalty to Thebes and loyalty to him, despite his treason.

Creon's desire to quell any further rebellion by presenting a firm stance against treason is complicated by an equal, if not stronger, opposing of religious law, one to which families are bound. Even though enemies rarely care about the opposing force's dead, families of the deceased go to great lengths to retrieve the corpses and give them a proper burial for fear that their souls will not find rest in the underworld. Students should sympathize with both the need for order and the obligations to family (Q 4), although they might see both Antigone's and Creon's actions as rather extreme. Be sure to explain that both Antigone and Creon were following tradition in their own way. In Homer's epic poem *The Iliad*, Hector's father Priam, King of Troy, risks his life by sneaking into the Greek camp to gain his dead son's body, pleading at the knees of his son's killer Achilles. Antigone, angry that one of her brothers has been buried but the other left to be ravaged, begins the play by asking Ismene to help her bury her brother. Antigone at first seems most concerned with making sure her brother receives a burial of some kind — she sprinkles dust on his corpse, the only burial she has the time or strength to perform — but her actions later indicate part of her purpose is to expose Creon's harsh government, to publicly protest laws that go against religious law, and to make Creon feel the same misery she and her family have felt (Q 5).

Both Creon and Antigone embody the major theme of this play — the struggle between one's personal life and one's public duty — but the two characters clash because they see each other's actions differently (Q 1). Although Creon is determined to keep order and chooses to do so even when it means executing his future daughter-in-law, Antigone is just as determined to obey the religious laws of the time, even if she must die as a result (Q 3). The two characters are vastly different, however, in their development throughout the play. Whereas Antigone begins the play committed to her ideals and knowledgeable of the consequences, Creon at first does not understand the effects of his firm stance. Antigone is arrested and imprisoned in a dark cell, not executed as was at first intended, but she causes her own death rather than remain confined. She dies believing exactly what she did in her very first scene — in other words, she remains a static character throughout, no matter what is said. Perhaps her inability to change is her tragic flaw (Q 6, 7).

Creon, unlike Antigone, changes significantly over the course of the play. He lessens Antigone's punishment, at least in the eyes of a modern audience — life imprisonment instead of execution — but he remains firm about his condemnation of those who disobey the law, even when they are his own relatives. The chorus understands the verdict against Antigone is lawful, but they sympathize with her situation because she was burying her brother — her family ties were stronger than the law — and they see her crime as caused by love, not rebelliousness (Q 2). For Creon, the law must be stronger than his family ties, but he does not realize that adherence to the law could actually destroy his family. Creon realizes his mistakes too late. The result of Creon's stubbornness is the deaths of Antigone, his son, and his wife. All these deaths are placed upon Creon's head, but be sure to discuss with students who actually commits the acts. Whereas Oedipus unwittingly kills his father and marries his mother, Creon does not actually kill anyone — he only insists upon circumstances that cause those he loves to take their own lives. Creon does not actually wish any of these characters to die, and his sorrow is brought on both by their deaths and by his realization that he was the cause of their misery. While Antigone dies unchanged, Creon is a crushed man, and he goes into exile to punish himself for his misjudgment (Q 7).

Discuss with students what Creon has learned by the end of the play. Is he just grieving over a lost family? Does he truly realize how much his hubris has caused others' suffering? Does he see how his unbending loyalty to his position has destroyed all that he has ever loved? Also have students discuss how this play completes the cycle of plays from *Oedipus the King*, especially as it relates to Oedipus's family. Ismene is the only surviving family member, but she does not seem bound by the same fate as the others. Have students discuss her role in the play and her relationship to her sister and brothers.

This play will work well in a thematic discussion of the conflict between duty to one's self and duty to society if taught with *A Doll House*.

FURTHER READING

Trudeau, Lawrence J., ed. *Drama Criticism*. Vol. 1. Detroit: Gale, 1991. 412–71.

AUGUST WILSON

Fences

WRITING ACTIVITIES

1. Ask students to compare and contrast Lyons with Cory. In what ways are they similar? How are they different?
2. Have students examine the relationship between Troy and Rose. Which character do they empathize with or understand more? Why?

GROUP ACTIVITY

Assign a character to each group and have each group create a description of Troy from this character's point of view. Discuss as a class which characters see Troy most accurately and what causes each character to view him the way he or she does.

DO YOUR STUDENTS KNOW . . .

James Earl Jones won his second Tony Award for his performance as Troy Maxson on Broadway in 1987. Jones also appeared in *Field of Dreams*, a film that used baseball as a metaphor and focused on the complexities of a father/son relationship. In this film, Jones played Terrence Mann, a 1960s writer and radical who joins the search for the field of dreams.

DISCUSSION

It may be useful to begin discussion with some background on the social and political climate in America during the 1950s. It is important to note that each of Wilson's plays reflects the political, social, and cultural context of the decade in which the play is set. Students need to understand, for instance, that the 1950s were a time of change and progress for blacks in America. In particular, 1957 was the year that the first Civil Rights Act since the Reconstruction era was enacted, affirming African Americans' right to protest discrimination. Although legally blacks had been free for almost one hundred years, during this time they were still victims of overt discrimination and had little or no access to the benefits whites took for granted, especially in the areas of education and employment. All these issues are present in *Fences*.

Before the play begins, Wilson provides an historical context entitled "The Play," in which he draws a distinction between European emigrants and descendants of African slaves and the dreams both brought with them to America. He demonstrates how with hard work and hope the aspirations of European emigrants were realized and "won true." In contrast, he argues that "the descendants of African slaves were offered no such welcome or participation." Although they too came to America "strong" and "eager" with a capacity for hard work, "they cleaned houses and washed clothes, they shined shoes, and in quiet desperation and vengeful pride, they stole, and lived in pursuit of their own dream." So, from the beginning, Wilson introduces us to struggle and discrimination as the African American experience and prepares the reader for the events that follow in *Fences* (Q 3).

Wilson deals with many issues that are not specific to race and in fact are universal in their subject matter. However, because of the strong social and historical context, readers can't simply disregard Wilson's realistic depiction of the African American experience or substitute another ethnic group for blacks (Q 11).

The first scene of the play opens with the spirit of protest, as Troy Maxson, currently a garbage collector, informs his friend and coworker, Bono, that he has protested the unfairness of his working conditions. He is angry that only white men are allowed to drive the trucks, while the black men are limited to slinging trash all day. Troy Maxson is an ex-baseball player who was too old to join a white team when the major leagues began integrating. As a result, he will not let his son Cory go to college on a football scholarship, because he feels that Cory, too, will not have a future in sports. Troy's biggest flaw seems to be his inability to accept that social conditions are changing and that, with an education, Cory will have a better chance of realizing his ambitions than his father did (Q 6). Troy's criticisms are limited only to his own past experience, and as a result, they are absolute and unreasonable (Q 4).

Wilson creates in *Fences* a cyclic structure in which the sins of the fathers are visited upon the sons. Cory desperately wants to make his father proud and follow in his footsteps. He has an excellent chance at success because, unlike his father, he has been offered a college scholarship to play football. Cory's hopes seem reasonable, and the opportunities that are open to Cory because of his football scholarship are lost because Troy has already been shaped by his own past. Like his father, Troy is trapped in a life of hard labor and never realizes his dreams. Living such a life of struggle and drudgery, Troy is bitter and hopeless. It is this past from which Troy tries to save his son, but, unavoidably, he dominates his son in the same way his own father dominated him. Ironically, by trying to protect his son, he ruins Cory's chances. Students should identify strongly with Cory's loss of his college opportunity, and this should lead into a discussion of the differences between generations (Q 2).

In many ways, Troy's conflict with his son reflects contemporary African-American struggles. Haunted by a past of oppression and discrimination, blacks in America find life a constant battle to better conditions for future generations. The only way to ensure this situation is for young black men and women to understand the past and to make it a part of their future. Thus, a past of oppression becomes a tool for future empowerment in contemporary American society (Q 8).

Troy's character was shaped by his contact with the white world. At a young age, Troy learned the agony of separation and the struggle of African Americans to integrate into mainstream America. For blacks, the entrance into adulthood was particularly difficult. Troy's mother left home when he was a young boy, and he was forced to do the same when his father found him with a young girl and beat him severely. Troy discovered, however, that leaving home was just the beginning of an uphill battle. He wound up in prison when he was forced to steal to survive and killed a man in the process. It was here that he found his niche — baseball. It provided him with a new direction and an opportunity to prove that he could do something well. In fact, we learn that at his peak "was hitting .432 with thirty-seven home runs!" (1.1.76). He was even more talented than Selkirk, who was "batting .269 and playing right field for the Yankees!" (1.1.76). Unfortunately, during his prime, blacks were not yet playing in the major leagues. Now Troy is too old to be considered and hence never realizes his dream (Q 5).

Fences, clearly a central metaphor of the play, symbolize the theme of separation. Unfortunately, separation seems to be a prerequisite for establishing freedom for blacks in America. Throughout most of the play, Troy is building a fence around his yard. He constantly procrastinates, however, as his wife continually reminds him of his task. Bono, a lifelong friend and coworker, is correct in his interpretation of the fence. He knows that "some people build fences to keep people in. Rose wants to hold on to you all. She loves you" (2.1.26). In a sense, the fence serves as a protector of her family, as we see in her songs: "Jesus, be a fence all around me every day / Jesus, I want you to protect me as I travel on my way" (1.2.1). A fence can also serve as a barrier to the outside world, and Troy makes this distinction when he tells his son Cory as he is leaving home that he will find his things "on the other side of the fence" (2.4.274) (Q 1).

Wilson creates in this play various stereotypes that seem to serve a didactic purpose. In Rose Maxson, we see the passive mother who must forgo her own personal needs to provide a center for her family. We also see in Troy Maxson the hardened father incapable of affection because he must imbue his son with a strong sense of survival. And finally, we see in Cory the rebellious son who must rise up against the father to assert his autonomy and forge his own way in the world. One might argue that Wilson creates such stereotypes as honest depictions of people, to show a general trend in history and to enlighten future generations that attempt to shield their children from the indignities they suffered. The portrayal of such stereotypes can function as a catalyst to effect a change in the future (Q 7).

Wilson seems to evoke sympathy in the reader with most of his characters. We sympathize with Troy because we realize that although he often acts in an unsympathetic way, he is a victim of his past, and his intentions are well meaning. We sympathize with Cory because despite a desperate attempt to survive, he too becomes a victim of history and all its power to destroy. We also sadly realize at the end of the play that Cory will never actualize his dreams. Similarly, we feel sympathy for Lyons, the older son from a previous marriage, who fights his way past a hostile system by refusing to get a job that will put him in a vulnerable position. Lyons retreats to the unsuccessful, easygoing lifestyle of a musician because he asserts, "I need something that gonna help me get out of the bed in the morning. Make me feel like I belong in the world. I don't bother nobody. I just stay with my music cause that's the only way I can find to live in the world. Otherwise there ain't no telling what I might do" (1.1.149). Rose, too, evokes sympathy. When Troy confesses his affair to her, Rose's world crumbles. Everything she has worked toward is in danger of collapse. She has ignored her own personal needs and put her own dreams on hold in order to build a home and create a stable and loving environment for her family. Thus, by giving all of herself to her family, she is left with nothing when her world falls apart. She says, "I didn't know that to keep up his strength I had to give up little pieces of mine. I did that. I took on his life as mine and mixed up the pieces so that you couldn't hardly tell which was which anymore" (2.5.353) (Q 9).

In *Fences*, everyone is a victim, yet while Wilson's play is a tragic one, its primary message is optimistic. For in the end, although Troy dies before reconciling with his family, there is hope in his death. Troy's actions within the play propel his family toward progress and ultimately empower them. They realize that they must see his actions as a consequence of his struggle to save both himself and his family. Each is now imbued with a sense of purpose. Ironically, Troy's legacy to his family is his flaws, and because of these flaws, his family is stronger and has a surer sense of purpose (Q 10). To view Troy solely as a victim of racism is to oversimplify Wilson's aim and message. Although Wilson clearly regards racism as a major contributor to the development of his character, it should be considered along with many other factors, both cultural and historical, that go into making his protagonist such a complex character (Q 12).

Fences is a natural centerpiece for a unit that examines the struggles of African-Americans in twentieth-century society. Other works that might be read alongside *Fences* include "Big Black Good Man," "Emmett Till," "The White City," "We Wear the Mask," and "Harlem."

FURTHER READING

Nadel, Alan, Ed. *May All Your Fences Have Gates: Essays on the Drama of August Wilson.* Iowa City: U of Iowa P, 1994.

Pereira, Kim. *August Wilson and the African-American Odyssey.* Urbana: U of Illinois P, 1995.

CHAPTER 34

TENNESSEE WILLIAMS' *THE GLASS MENAGERIE:* A CASEBOOK FOR READING, RESEARCH, & WRITING

USING THE CASEBOOK

As with the other casebooks in the text, the drama casebook offers a wide variety of possibilities for teaching students how to use critical sources to write about drama. You may limit students' research to the seven sources reprinted in the text or have them locate additional source material on their own. In either case, reviewing the thirteen Reading and Reacting questions can help students develop paper topics for their research project. You can also assign the student paper and use it as a model for how to synthesize, cite, and document sources.

An autobiographical approach is particularly appropriate for this play. The sources included here offer insights from both Williams and his family, and students may locate other interviews or read a biography of Williams for more information. Highlighting those elements in the play that do *not* correspond to Williams's life and considering why he added them to the play would be a more productive course than merely looking for correspondences.

Students might also analyze the play from a psychological perspective. The play suggests a variety of topics relevant for such a study: relationships between specific family members, effects on the family when one member has a physical disability, and the legacy of an absent father. Gender issues can also be considered: the limited options for women and the mandatory (but neglected) provider role of the men.

READING AND REACTING

1. Outline the plot or action of the play. Which events constitute present-day activities and which occurred in the past?
2. What information is presented in stage directions that would not be available to audiences seeing the play? Give several examples. Is the absence of this information likely to put audiences at a disadvantage? Explain.
3. How do you think Laura's character might be different if she did not have a physical disability? To what degree is her inability to interact with society caused by her physical condition?
4. Do any of the characters change significantly during the play? If so, which characters and how do they change?

5. We know from Tom's final speech what happens to him; what do you think happens to Amanda and Laura after Tom leaves?

WRITING ACTIVITIES

1. Ask students to write about elements of the play that seem unusual — whether in the structure, set, or technical devices — as described in the text.
2. Have students identify and explain the images of glass and broken glass used in the play.

GROUP ACTIVITY

Ask, "Who is the play really about — Tom, Laura, or Amanda?" (Q 1). Divide the class into groups and ask each group to defend one character as the play's primary focus. As a class, examine each group's argument and discuss ways Williams makes all three characters empathetic, complex, and crucial to the play's movement.

DISCUSSION

The plot is simple: Tom tells about the events leading up to his escape from his own personal hell; as the story unfolds, he develops the characters of Laura and Amanda. Therefore, to a certain extent, all the play's action occurs in the past. Yet the specific events on which Tom focuses are presented to the audience as they happen (present tense) — Amanda's confrontation of Laura about attending business school and finding a husband, repeated arguments between Amanda and Tom, the arrival and departure of Laura's gentleman caller. However, other experiences — events that occur in the distant past and are revealed to the audience in past tense — have as significant an impact on the action of the play as those presented as "now." For example, Tom and Laura's father left the family many years before, yet the impact of that desertion is felt every day by each character (Q 2). Amanda's gentlemen callers have not been received for over twenty years, but their presence is a constant in the current Wingfield household. Given Williams's intention to write a "memory play," it is appropriate that the exact time an event occurs in is of less importance than the impression left by that event (Q 7).

A great deal of information is given in the stage directions that would be unavailable to audiences seeing the play performed:

- Tom, looking "like a voyager" in scene 6 as he leans over the fire escape rail to announce "I'm planning to change" (line 110).
- Laura, sitting on the couch while the floor lamp "gives a soft, becoming light to her face, bringing out the fragile, unearthly prettiness which usually escapes attention" (beginning of scene 7).
- Instructions to stress "that while the incident is apparently unimportant, it is to Laura the climax of her secret life" (scene 7, between lines 38 and 39).

- "Jim lights a cigarette and leans indolently back on his elbows smiling at Laura with a warmth and charm which light her inwardly with the altar candles" (scene 7, between lines 175 and 176).
- "The holy candles in the altar of Laura's face have been snuffed out!" (scene 7, after line 268).

Students should identify other examples. The information seems to be directed either at actors who would interpret these directions on stage or at readers, as though Williams expected the play to be read in addition to being performed. Some students may say that the viewing audience is at a disadvantage because they do not have these clues from the playwright. Others, however, may argue that the play is intended to be acted and that the actors will convey these nuances and much more — that the combination of live action, scenery, music, and lighting can offer the audience a far more engrossing experience than reading dialogue and stage directions, no matter how beautifully written (Q 2 in Reading and Reacting).

Laura's character is presented by narrator Tom as extremely fragile, incapable of coping with the outside world, restricted to replaying old phonograph records and watching over her glass menagerie. The physical disability, a limp, has been with her since childhood and has obviously contributed to what Jim identifies as her inferiority complex. But even without the physical problem, Laura would still have to contend with the psychological effects of her father's desertion, her mother's fixation on the past, her brother's rebellion, and the economic difficulties of the family. Students might wish to speculate on how Laura might have coped with the situation had she not been limited by her physical handicap. She is pretty; would she have desired attention from men to replace the love she had lost from her father and as a result have become sexually promiscuous? Might she have rebelled and run away as Tom does? Would she have become the caretaker of the family, especially of her mother (Q 3 in Reading and Reacting)?

Another approach to Laura's character is to examine whether or not she changes during the course of the play. Is meeting Jim and having him "break her heart" in person worse than imagining Jim married for six years to Emily Meisenbach? Our last glimpse of Laura is at once quite tragic — her blowing out the candles — and at the same time much like the Laura we see at the beginning of the play — smiling after being comforted by her mother (Q 10).

Ask students if the other characters change during the play. Tom's circumstances have changed, but students may question whether there are significant differences in his outlook and personality. He has escaped the physical barriers of the play's beginning, but he carries with him the same emotional and psychological burdens. Is our perception of growth (or lack of growth) in his character affected by the fact that Tom is the one telling the story? Through his description of Amanda in the final scene, Williams gives us a strong indication that she may have been altered somehow through the events of the play. Tom is downstage addressing the audience while upstage, without sound, Amanda is seen comforting Laura after Jim has left. The stage directions offer the following description of Amanda: "her silliness is gone and she has dignity and tragic beauty. . . . Amanda's gestures are slow and graceful, almost dancelike, as she comforts her daughter" (321).

Use the conclusions students reach about growth or change in the characters to move into a discussion of what happens to Amanda and Laura after Tom leaves (Q 5 Reading and Reacting). Since Tom serves as the narrator of this play and he leaves, we cannot know what happens, but Tom seems somewhat hopeful that the women will survive without him. Laura's blowing out the candle at the end suggests that the two women have now become a memory to Tom, as part of this "memory play," but this action does not suggest they no longer exist (Q 10).

Discuss Tom's motivations for leaving, and what steps lead up to his abandoning his mother and sister. Some foreshadowing, especially in Tom's comparison of himself with his father, suggests that he will leave, and his fights with Amanda and frequent nights out drinking or watching films also suggest his desire to be free from his family (Q 9). By contrast, Jim may help the students see into Tom's character. Although Tom seems to be involved in the world at large, he has few friends, and Jim's easy nature and laugh make Tom seem as reclusive as Laura (Q 3).

Tom is also interesting because he plays so many different roles (Q 5). He is a part of the action, yet he is also playing an uncomfortable role within his family structure, a role he finally abandons. He is also the play's narrator, and all the events that we see are products of his imagination. The play's screen projections, music, and unrealistic lighting suggest that each scene is one memory within Tom's mind, and these technical elements remind the audience how unreal the action is.

Be prepared for some confusion, especially when the students are dealing with technical notes, for reading them breaks the action within several scenes, and students may become frustrated. Discuss the effects of these technical elements, showing them the visual and auditory effect of this staging on the scenes (Q 6).

Another text that might add to your discussion of staging is *Death of a Salesman*. A more psychological approach dealing with dreams and memories, or unrealized expectations might include "Young Goodman Brown," "Patterns," and "La Belle Dame Sans Merci."

FURTHER READING

Van Antwerp, Margaret A., and Sally Johns, eds. "Tennessee Williams." *Dictionary of Literary Biography Documentary Series*. Vol. 4. Detroit: Gale, 1984.

CHAPTER 35

WILLIAM SHAKESPEARE'S *HAMLET:* A CASEBOOK FOR READING, RESEARCH, AND WRITING

USING THE CASEBOOK

This casebook contains the material students will need to write a research essay on *Hamlet*. In addition to several accessible critical articles, it includes a sample student essay incorporating two of these articles. Because students will not have a personal investment in this essay, they will be able to be more objective than they would if reviewing their own papers and more honest than they would if examining the work of their peers. In addition, the sample essay provides an additional opportunity to show students how to integrate quotations and cite sources using the MLA format. Even if the sample does not completely address the assignment you plan on giving, it may still serve the above purposes.

The sources included in this casebook express a range of critical viewpoints. "The Sublime or the Ridiculous," by Elizabeth Reitz Mullenix, examines Hamlet's place in American culture and may help change the minds of students who see the play as elitist "high art." Siyang Zhang's "Hamlet's Melancholy," an article translated from the Chinese, provides an analysis of what the author believes is the prince's distinguishing characteristic. Sandra K. Fisher presents a feminist reading of one aspect of the play in "Ophelia's Mad Speeches." Besides standing on their own merits, these and the other sources include bibliographies that will give students further research leads.

Students may initially be intimidated by the prospect of analyzing a work that has attracted as many critics over as long a period of time as has *Hamlet*. One of the chief advantages of the casebook, then, is that it makes the writing process more student friendly. You can of course require students to use other sources than those included here.

READING AND REACTING

1. What is the outstanding characteristic of Hamlet's personality? Look in particular at his soliloquies in determining the answer to this question.
2. Why are so many of the insults Hamlet directs at Ophelia in 3.1 of a sexual nature? Why would Hamlet suddenly become suspicious and insulting?
3. What part does Polonius play in the events of the tragedy?

4. Was there anything Ophelia could have done to change the course of events? Would it have helped matters at all if she had disobeyed her father's instructions to not see Hamlet?

WRITING ACTIVITIES

1. Have students pretend that they are psychiatrists called on by Claudius to examine either Hamlet or Ophelia. Then, have students write a psychological profile on the character they have chosen.
2. The approach that Hamlet takes to resolving his situation is obviously a colossal failure. Ask students to write up an alternative plan of action. This plan should be written to convince the prince that the action it recommends is preferable.
3. If you have read *Oedipus the King* with the class, you could ask students to write an essay in which they compare and contrast the characters of Hamlet and Oedipus.

GROUP ACTIVITY

Suppose Hamlet has survived his duel with Laertes and is on trial for the murder of Claudius and Laertes. His attorneys maintain that he is not guilty by reason of insanity. Divide the class into a prosecution team, a defense team, and a jury. Neither the prosecution nor the defense may present evidence from Hamlet's soliloquies or asides, although they may refer to statements by Polonius, Laertes, Ophelia, Gertrude, and Claudius, who are all dead when the trial begins. This activity will help students focus on how Hamlet appears to the other characters in the play.

DISCUSSION

Students are reluctant to fully engage Shakespearean plays for a variety of reasons. First, the language, although it grows clearer with repeated readings or listenings, is a real obstacle even for diligent students. Second, students may be unprepared to admit that characters from the remote past have anything in common with them. Finally, and most important, there is the fact that *Hamlet* is, by all estimations, "a classic" and therefore, in the minds of most students, deadly dull. The best way of addressing these issues is to show one or more of the film versions in class. Although it is approximately four hours long and you would probably only be able to show portions of it, Kenneth Branagh's version has some obvious advantages, not the least of which is an all-star cast that includes actors with whom your students may be familiar.

Hamlet is the hero of the play, and how the students react to the work as a whole will depend in large part on how they regard its central character. Although most students will sympathize with Hamlet's situation, some will grow impatient with his delaying tactics as the play progresses (Q 3). Rather than presenting a difficulty, however, these feelings of frustration may be an ideal place to begin a discussion of the character and why he behaves as he does. Hamlet is melancholy, obsessive, and full of self-doubt, yet as far as Gertrude is concerned, this is a recent development and a complete change in her son (Q 1, 5).

Hamlet's six soliloquies are crucial in what they reveal about the inner workings of his mind. The first (1.2.130–60) focuses on his distress at his mother's remarriage and on his own longing for death. The second (2.2.482–540) is an expression of his self-disgust at his own inaction. The third (3.1.63–97) is concerned almost exclusively with his suicidal impulses. The fourth (3.2.340–53) shows his doubts about the bloody task he has sworn to carry out. In the fifth (3.3.77–99), he debates whether to kill Claudius while he is praying and ultimately decides against it. And in the sixth and final soliloquy, Hamlet once again reproaches himself for inaction (Q 2). (Q 1 in Reading and Reacting)

Why doesn't Hamlet kill Claudius as soon as he has the chance? Certainly we would expect, given how profoundly upset he is by all that has happened, that the prince's anger and desire for revenge would outweigh any objections his intellect might raise. A partial explanation is that Hamlet does not entirely trust what he has heard from the ghost. After all, he reasons, the specter of his father may be the devil trying to trick him into killing an innocent man. He wants "grounds / More relative than this" (2.2.538–39). For this reason, he orders the visiting actors to perform the play that he himself rewrites (Q 10, 11). In a very real sense, the ghost drives the action of the play because Hamlet would have little excuse for indecision if he himself uncovers tangible evidence of Claudius' guilt (Q 12).

Hamlet feigns insanity because of the tremendous latitude of action it gives him. Anything he says that is intended to provoke Claudius and uncover his guilt can be excused as the ravings of a man who has been driven mad by grief. Even if he does not succeed in forcing a direct confession from his uncle, Hamlet still has the satisfaction of causing him visible discomfort. Finally, it is possible that Hamlet's feigned madness is a defense against genuine insanity. We know that the prince is devastated by the loss of his father and the remarriage of his mother. At the same time, he is urged by his uncle and his mother to "throw to earth / This unprevailing woe" (Q 11). Perhaps pretending to be insane enables him to vent emotions that he would otherwise have to keep bottled-up inside.

The court is well aware how much the prince cared for Ophelia. His violent rejection of her, then, is seen as further evidence of his madness. Hamlet has no intention of harming Ophelia, but her happiness has obviously become a secondary concern to him. At this point, the audience is likely to feel that a line has been crossed (Q 4). Ophelia, although she is completely innocent, is the person Hamlet hurts the most. Hamlet's rejection and humiliation of Ophelia is not based entirely on cold calculation, however. Most of the insults he directs at her are sexual in nature, and he questions in particular her faithfulness and her chastity. In his first soliloquy, he utters the famous line, "Frailty, thy name is woman!" The anger that he feels toward his mother is intense, yet Hamlet cannot give full expression to it. Instead, the full force of his rage at what he sees as the treachery and sexual immorality of his mother are directed at Ophelia (Q 2 in Reading and Reacting). He concludes his exchange with Ophelia with "To a nunnery, go." Although his dismissal and his anger would be better directed toward his mother (Q 13), Ophelia is a more convenient and accessible target.

The relationship between this only son and his mother has been the cause of some discussion, and a Freudian critic might well point to the play as an example of an Oedipal fantasy gone wrong. According to Freud, each son secretly wants to displace (even murder) his father and marry his mother. If one takes this view, then Hamlet may be frustrated on an unconscious level by the fact that Claudius has usurped the place that he himself wanted. This is of course a debatable point. Schluetter and Lusardi, in "The Camera in Gertrude's Closet," examine the ways in which modern productions have emphasized the sexual tensions within this relationship.

Although we are given the most insight into failures and misjudgments and although it is Hamlet who drives the action of the play, it would be a mistake to overlook the way in which the flaws of the other major characters influence the course of events. Things would have been considerably different, for example, if Claudius had not coveted both his brother's throne and his wife. It is his desire for power and his need to hold onto that power that set the events of the play in motion. Claudius is clearly the play's villain, but he does appear to feel genuine concern for Gertrude and attempts to stop her from drinking the poisoned cup (5.2.275). He also feels genuine remorse for the murder of his brother, although he is unwilling to give up the benefits that murder brought him (3.3.39–75) (Q 6).

Gertrude and Ophelia have often been described as passive, and there is much to be said for this point of view (Q 15). Gertrude could have displayed more strength of character and more loyalty to her recently deceased husband. Her quick remarriage is one of the things that weighs most heavily on Hamlet and which further impairs her judgment (Q 9). Ophelia, on her father's recommendation, refuses to see Hamlet at a point when he is emotionally vulnerable (Q 4 in Reading and Reacting). Although it is impossible to say what *might* have happened, it is possible that had Hamlet not been cut off from contact with Ophelia he might have confided in her (Q 9).

One could argue of course that Ophelia is simply being a dutiful daughter. It is Polonius, after all, who advises her not to see Hamlet. It is Polonius who arranges the disastrous meeting between Ophelia and Hamlet in 2.1. And it is Polonius who proposes that he hide behind the arras in Gertrude's room, where Hamlet subsequently kills him. It is this murder that drives the already bewildered Ophelia insane and that eventually leads to her death. It is when Laertes learns of these two deaths that he vows revenge and makes his pact with Claudius (Q 3 in Reading and Reacting). In each case, Polonius is too certain of his own wisdom and all too ready to give advice. If he possessed even a bit of Hamlet's indecisiveness, there might be fewer bodies on stage at play's end. Laertes has some of the same certainty as his father, and his advice to his sister does her little good (Q 9).

As the play moves toward its violent climax, Shakespeare introduces a scene (5.1) in which the men digging Ophelia's grave comment on her death and on the current situation. Their remarks help give both Hamlet and the audience a sense of the way in which death destroys human dignity and of its inevitability (Q 14). By the play's end, most of the people attending Ophelia's funeral are dead themselves, and Fortinbras has conquered Denmark. The main characters not only destroy themselves and each other but also leave their country unprotected in the process.

At the beginning of the play, we hear of the approach of Fortinbras, the son of Norway, whom the elder Hamlet defeated and killed. Fortinbras is certainly one of the flatter characters in the play — he appears complex and human only in the dignified treatment he accords Hamlet's body (Q 7). At the same time, he is an undeniably powerful presence. Vince Escanalar, in "Foils in *Hamlet*," argues that Fortinbras serves primarily as a foil to Hamlet and that his purposeful attack on and conquest of Denmark underscores Hamlet's ineffectuality (Q 8).

Consider teaching this play with *Oedipus the King*, *True West*, and "The Love Song of J. Alfred Prufrock." The first two selections are family tragedies that can easily be compared and contrasted with Hamlet, and the third is spoken by a character who in some ways is a modern Hamlet, albeit an even less decisive one.

FURTHER READING

Andrews, John F. "William Shakespeare." *Elizabethan Dramatists*. Ed. E. Fredson Bowers. *Dictionary of Literary Biography*. Vol. 62. Detroit: Gale, 1987. 267–353.

Roe, John. "Pleasing the Wiser Sort: Ethics and Genre in Lucrece and Hamlet." *Cambridge Quarterly* 23.2 (1994): 99–119. Reprinted in *Shakespearean Criticism*. Vol. 43.

Suhamy, Henri. "The Metaphorical Fallacy." *Cahiers Elizabethains* 24 (Oct. 1983): 27–31. Reprinted in *Shakespearean Criticism*. Vol. 35.

AUTHORS AND TITLES INDEX